CRITICAL CONCEPTS

An Introduction to Politics

Fifth Edition

Edited by

Janine Brodie
UNIVERSITY OF ALBERTA

Sandra Rein
UNIVERSITY OF ALBERTA

and Malinda Smith
UNIVERSITY OF ALBERTA

PEARSON

Toronto

Brief Contents

Contents

Preface

This introductory textbook is designed to address both the fundamentals of political science and many of the current challenges to governance in the twenty-first century, and to enhance the student's first encounter with political science. It examines the critical concepts that we believe students should master during their first encounter with political science. Each chapter introduces the student to a critical political concept, describes its importance in the study of politics, and outlines the debates that the concept has engendered in political life and for the discipline of political science. Each chapter also explores how the contemporary political environment challenges the meaning and relevance of these concepts. The text acquaints students with traditional debates in political science as well as those recently introduced to the discipline by critical scholars. Finally, each chapter provides discussion questions, suggested further readings, and weblinks for further research on the topic. Key terms are identified within the text and defined in a glossary at the end of the book.

This fifth edition of *Critical Concepts* speaks to a very different world than did the first edition, which appeared in 1999. The intervening decade and a half has been destabilized by the challenges of terrorism; wars in Iraq and Afghanistan; the birth of new nations such as South Sudan; the growing power and influence of China and India; struggles for memory, voice, and representation from the Arab Spring to Truth and Reconciliation Commissions in Chile and Canada; the vibrancy of civil society movements from the Indignados in Spain to the Occupy Wall Street movement in the United States and the student protest in Quebec; and a stubborn financial crisis that has spread from the United States to Europe and emerging economies. Contrary to the optimistic talk about the benefits and possibilities of globalization and global free markets at the dawn of the twenty-first century, we have inherited an uncertain world that is unsettled by multiple and overlapping crises—economic, political, social, and environmental. We also live in a world marked by anxiety and insecurity; we simply do not know how or when these multiple and overlapping crises will be resolved.

Our objective in this significantly revised fifth edition remains the same as in the first edition: to introduce students to the fundamentals of political science, to engage them with key and enduring debates, and to explore both conceptual continuities and shifts in a world marked by growing insecurity, political upheaval, and global tensions. Most important, the chapters in this text are designed to challenge students with the political issues and ethical dilemmas that they confront daily. Each chapter attempts to frame these issues as part of the disciplinary heritage of political science, and to make them accessible to students. The first section on politics and ideas traces traditions in political thought, competing ideas about democracy and radical politics, and adds a new chapter on neo-liberalism. The second section of this text explores institutional influences on political life, including chapters on the state, representation, administration, and the media. The third section examines diverse perspectives on contemporary politics: international relations, international organizations, global political economy, Indigenous peoples, and poverty. Each chapter provides students with the conceptual tools needed to better understand the major issues we face and how political science as a discipline helps us make sense of them.

These are both exciting and difficult times in which to study political science. They are exciting because, as the Arab Spring illustrates well, change is in the air. They are difficult because contemporary politics challenges many of our traditional approaches to the study of politics. In particular, national states appear to have diminished power with which to cope with political problems that are global in scope. The chapters in this fifth edition explore the key concepts arising from the Western tradition of political thought, the evolution of political regimes and institutions, civil society, and international and global systems. This edition has a number of changes and innovations. First, there are fewer chapters than in previous editions, making it more amenable to half-year courses, which are now the norm for introductory classes in Canada. Also, each section includes a chapter titled "What's Left Out?" These new chapters review the omissions in conventional political science as well as new developments in politics that challenge the ways we have traditionally thought about political life.

Introductory courses are often a challenge for political science instructors because of differing philosophies about how best to acquaint students with the complex world of politics. Some are convinced that an introductory course should concentrate on the foundations of political analysis, most notably the canons of Western political thought. These instructors emphasize the study of great thinkers. Others prefer a course that serves as an intensive institutional primer, reasoning that students require a working knowledge of the mechanics of political life before they can explore more advanced subject matter. These instructors focus on key political institutions, such as regimes, bureaucracies, and constitutions. Still others suggest that foundations and mechanics will come with time and that the primary goal of an introductory course should be to offer students a sampling of the many intriguing perspectives on the political world that political science offers. Each of these perspectives has merit when considering the multiple and complex dimensions of political life.

In political science there is no equivalent to the laws of supply and demand in economics or the laws of motion in physics. Neither is there a neutral doorway into the political world. Any entry to the study of politics is already saturated by, among other things, history, political ideas, institutional constraints, prejudices, and power inequalities among diverse political actors. Moreover, students come to their first course in political science already influenced by and engaged in the political world around them. Political science offers few road maps by which to move from the simple to the complex, in part because politics is always complex, and always contested. The early twenty-first century has witnessed the erosion of key assumptions and institutions that helped us "make sense" of the politics of the past century. Added to this, the planet itself is increasingly under threat, not from military or political forces, but, instead, from our everyday lifestyle decisions, from what we eat and wear to how we travel, all of which have micro and macro implications.

A Chinese proverb goes something like this: "May you live in interesting times." In many respects, students of politics have always lived in interesting times. The most enduring work in political science has taken up the challenges of "its time," both to make sense of political life and to change and improve it. Political scientists have studied the ravages of war, of industrialization, of colonialism, and of genocide. They also have advanced the causes of human rights, good governance, individual well-being, and peaceful co-existence within and among states. Perhaps more than ever before, however, citizens are asked to consider the implications of their everyday decisions, not only for the future of their neighbourhood and country, but also for the planet.

Supplements

No matter how comprehensive a textbook is, today's instructors and students require a complete teaching package. *Critical Concepts: An Introduction to Politics,* Fifth Edition, is accompanied by the following supplements. Instructor supplements are available for downloading from a password-protected section of Pearson Canada's online catalogue (www.pearson.ca/brodie). Navigate to your book's catalogue page to view a list of those supplements that are available. See your local sales representative for details and access.

Companion Website (www.pearsoncanada.ca/brodie) (ISBN 978-0-13-309275-2) An interactive website is available for instructors and students who use *Critical Concepts: An Introduction to Politics,* Fifth Edition. Visitors will find a range of interactive resources, including self-assessment quizzes, available in every chapter that can be emailed to instructors or teaching assistants.

Instructor's Resource Manual (ISBN 978-0-13-309272-1) *The Instructor's Resource Manual* features a variety of teaching resources, including chapter objectives, chapter summaries, and lecture suggestions.

PowerPoint Presentations (ISBN 987-0-13-308400-9) This supplement provides a comprehensive selection of slides highlighting key concepts featured in the text. The slides have been specifically developed for clear and easy communication of themes, ideas, and definitions.

Test Item File (ISBN 978-0-13-308398-9) This test bank, available in Word format, contains multiple-choice, true/false, and short answer/essay questions for every chapter.

MyTest (ISBN 978-0-13-308399-6) The MyTest from Pearson Education Canada is a powerful assessment generation program that helps instructors easily create and print quizzes, tests, exams, as well as homework or practice handouts. Questions and tests can all be authored online, allowing instructors ultimate flexibility and the ability to efficiently manage assessments at anytime, from anywhere.

peerScholar

Firmly grounded in published research, peerScholar is a powerful online pedagogical tool that helps develop students' critical and creative thinking skills through creation, evaluation, and reflection. Working in stages, students begin by submitting written assignments. peerScholar then circulates their work for others to review, a process that can be anonymous or not, depending on instructors' preferences. Students immediately receive peer feedback and evaluations, reinforcing their learning and driving development of higher-order thinking skills. Students can then re-submit revised work, again depending on instructors' preferences.

CourseSmart for Students (ISBN 978-0-13-309274-5)

CourseSmart goes beyond traditional expectations, providing instant, online access to the textbooks and course materials you need at an average savings of 60 percent. With instant access from any computer and the ability to search your text, you'll find the content you need quickly, no matter where you are. And with online tools like highlighting and note-taking, you can save time and study efficiently. See all the benefits at **www.coursesmart.com/students**.

CourseSmart for Instructors (ISBN 978-0-13-309274-5)

CourseSmart goes beyond traditional expectations, providing instant, online access to the textbooks and course materials you need at a lower cost for students. And even as students save money, you can save time and hassle with a digital eTextbook that allows you to search for the most relevant content at the very moment you need it. Whether it's evaluating textbooks or creating lecture notes to help students with difficult concepts, CourseSmart can make life a little easier. See how when you visit **www.coursesmart.com/instructors**.

Technology Specialists. Pearson's technology specialists work with faculty and campus course designers to ensure that Pearson technology products, assessment tools, and online course materials are tailored to meet your specific needs. This highly qualified team is dedicated to helping schools take full advantage of a wide range of educational resources, by assisting in the integration of a variety of instructional materials and media formats. Your local Pearson Canada sales representative can provide you with more details on this service program.

Acknowledgments

Many people deserve our thanks and appreciation for their contributions to this ongoing project. First, thanks must go to the reviewers who provided excellent feedback and helped shape the direction of this revised edition.

Allan E. Warnke — Vancouver Island University
Stewart Hyson — University of New Brunswick, Saint John
Sean Clark — Memorial University

xvi PREFACE

Brian Tanguay	Wilfrid Laurier University
Greg Pyrcz	Acadia University
J.P. Lewis	University of Guelph
Chris Erickson	University of British Columbia
Christopher G. Anderson	Wilfrid Laurier University
Barbara Arneil	University of British Columbia
Stephen McBride	McMaster University
Tracy Summerville	University of Northern British Columbia
Marc Hanvelt	Carleton University

Second, the authors wish to thank Deana Sigut and Rachel Stuckey at Pearson Canada, as well as Julie van Tol for her copyediting magic. Also, we extend our thanks to Brent Epperson for his outstanding research assistantship throughout the extensive reworking of this fifth edition. We also want to extend our thanks once again to Malcolm Mayes, editorial cartoonist at the *Edmonton Journal*, whose obvious talents, political insights, and, above all, sense of humour demonstrate that cartoons can deliver powerful political messages. Selecting which among Malcolm's many brilliant cartoons will accompany each chapter is one of the greatest pleasures of editing this book. A library of his work can be found at **www.artizans.com.** Last, but certainly not least, Sandra wishes to thank Sandeep for spending another year with *Critical Concepts* and providing his love and support.

Janine Brodie, Sandra Rein, and Malinda S. Smith
Edmonton, Fall 2012

About the Editors

Janine Brodie

Janine Brodie is a distinguished university professor and Canada Research Chair in Political Economy and Social Governance at the University of Alberta. Dr. Brodie was elected as a Fellow of the Royal Society of Canada in 2002 and awarded a Trudeau Fellowship in 2010. She has published widely in the areas of Canadian politics, gender and politics, and globalization and governance.

Sandra Rein

Sandra Rein is an associate professor of political studies and coordinator of the Augustana-in-Cuba study abroad program at the University of Alberta. Dr. Rein's current research investigates freedom as an important philosophical and political commitment in the works of Rosa Luxemburg, Raya Dunayevskaya, and Emma Goldman.

Malinda S. Smith

Malinda S. Smith is an associate professor and associate chair (Graduate Studies) in the Department of Political Science at the University of Alberta. Dr. Smith has published in the areas of African political economy; terrorism and the securitization of development; poverty and inequality; and race, equity, and social justice. Her current research investigates genealogies of race and equity in Canada.

About the Cartoonist

Malcolm Mayes

Malcolm Mayes was born in Edmonton, Alberta, in 1962. A love of cartooning and interest in newspapers steered him naturally toward political comment. He studied design art for two years at Grant MacEwan College in Edmonton and free-lanced for a dozen Alberta weeklies before accepting a full-time position at the *Edmonton Journal* in June 1986.

Mayes is one of Canada's most widely read political cartoonists; his work has been published in over 150 Canadian publications, including *Maclean's*, *The Toronto Star*, Montreal's *The Gazette*, and the *Ottawa Citizen*. He has been nominated three times for a National Newspaper Award and in 1996 he published a cartoon collection entitled *Political Asylum*.

Mayes is also the founder of Artizans.com, a comprehensive online service that delivers digital artwork to publications around the world.

About the Contributors

Rob Aitken is an associate professor in the Department of Political Science at the University of Alberta. His areas of research include international political economy, critical international relations and security studies, and governmentality and cultural economy.

Isabel Altamirano-Jiménez is an associate professor in the Department of Political Science and the Faculty of Native Studies at the University of Alberta. Her research focuses on Indigenous politics in Canada and Mexico, Indigenous land mapping, women, feminism and globalization, Indigenous women and water governance, and Indigenous nationalism.

Janine Brodie is a distinguished university professor, Canada Research Chair in Political Economy and Social Governance, and Trudeau Fellow in the Department of Political Science at the University of Alberta. Her current research interests include Canadian politics, political economy, social literacy, and social policy.

Siobhan Byrne is an assistant professor in the Department of Political Science, University of Alberta. Her primary areas of research include feminist anti-war activism and peace-building in societies in transition from conflict, with a particular focus on Northern Ireland and Israel/Palestine.

Alexa DeGagné is currently a Ph.D. candidate and SSHRC fellow in the Department of Political Science at the University of Alberta. Her research and dissertation focus on American lesbian, gay, and queer political organizations; social movements and activism; social conservative and neo-liberal political rationalities; and same-sex marriage debates and policies.

Roger Epp is a professor in the Department of Political Science at the University of Alberta. His research interests include politics of rural communities in the Prairie west, international relations theory, ethics and applied hermeneutics, and the critical side of the "English School."

Lois Harder is a professor of political science and associate dean (research and graduate) at the University of Alberta. Her research interests in gender and Canadian politics include social policy, political economy, social theory, and family policy in North America.

Tom Keating is a professor in the Political Science Department at the University of Alberta, teaching in the areas of international relations and Canadian foreign policy. His research focuses on Canadian foreign and defence policy and international organizations.

Catherine Kellogg is an associate professor in the Department of Political Science at the University of Alberta, specializing in political theory and gender and politics. Her research interests include psychoanalysis and deconstruction, and Marx and Hegel.

Sean F. McMahon is an assistant professor in the Department of Political Science at the American University in Cairo, Egypt. His teaching and research focuses on Palestinian–Israeli relations and Middle East politics.

Steve Patten is an associate professor in the Department of Political Science at the University of Alberta. His research and teaching interests focus on political parties, public policy, and the quality of democracy in Canada.

Sandra Rein is an associate professor of political studies and coordinator of the Augustana-in-Cuba study abroad program at the University of Alberta. Dr. Rein's current research investigates freedom as an important philosophical and political commitment in the works of Rosa Luxemburg, Raya Dunayevskaya, and Emma Goldman.

Falguni A. Sheth is an associate professor of philosophy and political theory at Hampshire College. Her teaching and research interests include continental philosophy, critical race theory and philosophy of race, Foucault's biopolitics in the context of legal subjectivity, and subaltern and gender studies.

Meenal Shrivastava is an associate professor of political economy and the Academic Coordinator for Political Economy and Global Studies at Athabasca University. Her research interests include the World Trade Organization, the politics of oil in Alberta, environmental politics and management, contemporary South Africa and India, and gender studies.

Malinda S. Smith is an associate professor and associate chair (graduate studies) in the Department of Political Science at the University of Alberta. She teaches international relations, comparative politics (global South) and the politics of race. Her research focuses on African political economy; terrorism and the securitization of development; poverty and inequality; and equity, diversity, and social justice.

Allan Tupper is a professor and head of the Department of Political Science, University of British Columbia. His major teaching and research interests are Canadian politics and government, public management, public policy, and western Canadian politics.

Ian Urquhart is an associate professor and associate chair (Undergraduate Studies) in the Department of Political Science at the University of Alberta, specializing in Canadian politics. His research interests include natural resources policy and environmental politics.

Shauna Wilton is an associate professor of political studies at the Augustana Campus of the University of Alberta. Her research and teaching focus on ethnicity and gender and their representation in political and popular texts, including the media.

Ideas and Politics

There is rarely a simple answer for why political events unfold as they do. Political outcomes are the combined product of many forces that often clash and pull in opposite directions. Some of these factors are immediate and observable, while others are more distant and concealed, lodged in historical legacies and political traditions. There is, however, one inescapable constant in political analyses. Everything political is embedded in ideas—in the way we understand the political world around us. All political and social interactions, both harmonious and conflict-ridden, are informed and directed by ideas. The six chapters in this section of the text provide an introduction to the key concepts and different streams of political thinking that have structured politics in the West for millennia. The chapters in this section link particular ideas about politics to historical contexts; however, they are organized around the critical and enduring concepts of power, sovereignty, authority, leadership, democracy, and radicalism. We will also discover that political science has not been immune to bias and exclusionary practices, and that we must always challenge the ideas and interpretations that are dominant In the discipline at any give time. What is clear from this section is that the questions of how we ought to live together and govern ourselves have always animated political thought and debate. We will also find that the issues of fairness, inclusion, freedom, and equality rest at the very heart of political choice and action. Political life, however constrained by historical and structural factors, is fundamentally about the choices that we make and about the consequences of those choices.

CHAPTER 1

POWER AND POLITICS

JANINE BRODIE

Learning Objectives

- Distinguishes between power and politics

- Provides examples of power to, power over

- Explains knowledge and power

- Defines sovereignty

- Discusses three kinds of authority

Introduction

Aristotle, contemplating political life over 2000 years ago, made an enduring observation regarding the human condition. "Man," he said, "is by nature a political animal." Aristotle quite literally meant *man*—indeed, only men of Ancient Greece's ruling class. Contemporary political theorists now understand Aristotle's man to be representative of all people and politics, as an ever-present force in all societies. Whenever two or more people come together, there is invariably some form of politics at play. Politics (whether we recognize it or not) informs how we think about ourselves, others, and the world. It flows through all social relationships. It is the glue that holds these relationships together. It also is the friction that erupts in disagreement and conflict, sometimes tearing apart friendships, neighbourhoods, nations, and the international community. Politics is all around us, not unlike the air we breathe. And, like air, it is often difficult to see, to capture, and to study. Politics, whether experienced at the level of the individual, community, country, or globe, is constantly shifting. The push and pull of conflict and consensus mean that political life is always moving in directions that we can never fully anticipate.

The study of politics helps us understand why political events unfold as they do and to see warning signs on the horizon, but it rarely enables us to predict the future with any certainty or precision. We know, for example, that political power, sustained solely through fear and force, has a short shelf life. But we could not have predicted that the suicide of Mohamed Bouazizi, a distressed Tunisian street merchant, in December 2010, would spark an unprecedented wave of civil unrest across the Middle East in 2011. The so-called "Arab Spring" effectively ended the repressive regimes of Hosni Mubarak in Egypt and Muammar Gaddafi in Libya, and has forced others to begin a process of democratic reform.

Many of the most politically transformative events of the early twenty-first century caught experts and political leaders by surprise, but they have had enduring consequences. The terrorist attacks on the United States on September 11, 2001, in particular, set in motion a war in Afghanistan, the ill-planned occupation of Iraq by a "coalition of the willing," and an ongoing war on terror. Wars normally are fought between states. The war on terror, however, has mobilized the vast military and surveillance capacities of the most powerful states in the world, not against other states, but instead, against small and scattered groups of non-state actors who deploy a particular form of political violence; notably, sporadic and violent attacks on civilian populations. This unique war has, nonetheless, transformed international travel, authorized extraordinary surveillance measures, and, indeed, changed common perceptions of who and what to fear. In the twenty-first century, security has become the overarching priority of governments around the world, and it accounts for ever-larger proportions of government spending. Yet, paradoxically, we feel less secure, not because of impending terrorist attacks, but, instead, because global financial uncertainty threatens both our economic security and the social programs that were designed to protect the vulnerable in hard times.

Unpredictability and uncertainty were for Karl Mannheim, writing over 80 years ago, at the very heart of the definition of politics. He drew a fundamental distinction between administration and politics. The administration of our daily lives was routinized, rule based, and predictable—what he called the "routine affairs of the state." The enforcement of criminal law, taxation, and implementation of social programs are some governmental activities that fall into Mannheim's "administration" category. In contrast, Mannheim insisted that politics involved the play of irrational forces, social competition, and struggle. Racism, sexism, the constant manoeuvring of partisan forces, and civil unrest are a few examples of politics whose outcomes cannot be known in advance. Mannheim identified two main sources of unpredictability and uncertainty fuelling political struggles: uncontrolled competition and domination by force. Both conditions, he argued, "constitute the realm of social life which is still unorganized and where politics becomes necessary" (1936, 115–16).

Politics is an inescapable human activity that revolves around the always-contentious process of deciding how to best manage our common affairs, whether at local, national, or global levels. How, then, are we to understand, let alone study, something that is so fundamental to our daily lives and yet so fluid and so unpredictable? The discipline of political science starts from the premise that politics does have a number of defining characteristics that make it amenable to study. While there is considerable debate about what these characteristics are, political scientists agree on at least one point of departure: politics revolves around the exercise of power. Political science, thus, is devoted to the study of power's various distributions, uses, and outcomes. Who has political power, and why? How does it flow through institutions and societies, and to what end? Can it be used ethically to build a better society?

Politics and Power

UNDERSTANDING THE FUNDAMENTAL LINKS BETWEEN ETHICS, POLITICS, and power has been a perennial issue for students of politics. Niccolò Machiavelli (1469–1527) is sometimes called the first modern political scientist because he distinguished between the "is" and the "ought" of politics. While religious and ethical codes may prescribe what action we, ideally, ought to take, the grim realities of politics are more often concerned with what is possible, if not always fair or desirable. Some 500 years ago, Machiavelli, in his famous book, *The Prince*, advised the ruling elite of Italy to give up any notion of governing according to ethical ideals and, instead, to use the power of both force and persuasion to disarm opponents. He believed that ethical codes and the demands of political survival often conflicted, and that princes sometimes had to act unethically in order to hold on to political power. The end—staying in power—could justify unethical and often brutal means.

For Machiavelli, politics was an elite preoccupation, focused primarily on the effective exercise and consolidation of political power and position. Others, however, have cast their definitional net more broadly. The great Russian revolutionary, Vladimir Lenin, for example, defined politics as "who does what to whom" (quoted in Guy 1995, 5). Perhaps the most often quoted definition of politics comes from Harold Lasswell, a distinguished American political scientist writing in the 1930s. For him, the study of politics was about "who gets what, when, and how" (1936).

Power to and Power over

Most political scientists would say that politics is about the exercise of power, but this observation raises the obvious question—what is **power**? Political scientists have generally treated power in one of two ways: power to do something or power over something. **Power to** signals the capacity to realize personal or collective goals or, in today's parlance, "being empowered" (Kourvetaris 1997, 41). The popular notion that, in democratic systems, power ultimately rests in the hands of citizens conveys the idea of "power to" reach a political consensus and to realize collective goals through democratic institutions, such as fair elections and representative legislative assemblies. Through democratic practices, citizens are supposed to be able to decide how best to live together, hold their political leaders accountable for their actions, and, if need be, throw them out of office.

The idea of power to is deeply embedded in our assumptions about how democracy ought to work. It also informs various perspectives on the study of politics, especially the pluralist school. Pluralists argue that the best way to understand the question of "who gets what, when, and how" is to focus on the activities of groups that compete to see their policy preferences translated into public policy.

Pluralists argue that modern society is far too complex and too large to allow for the direct political participation of everyone in the political process. Instead, individuals join groups that promote their interests. Since modern citizens have many interests, they may hold memberships in many different kinds of groups, ranging from parent-teacher organizations to environmental groups, anti-racist coalitions, a gun collectors' club, or a lesbian and gay choir. Many of the groups to which citizens belong have a direct interface with the public sphere, but most do not.

According to pluralist theory, groups become politically active around political issues that affect the interests and values of their members. They make coalitions and compete with other groups for preferred policy outcomes. No one group is a permanent player in pluralist politics. Neither does one group always win. Different groups with different resources move in and out of the political sphere when their interests are affected. Politics, then, resides in the constant play of groups that both advance the interests of their respective memberships and check the power of other groups. Everyone gets to play, and there are no winners assumed at the onset of a political debate. As prominent pluralist theorist Robert Dahl explained, "all active and legitimate groups in the population can make themselves heard at some critical stage in the process of decision making" (1956, 137). For pluralists, in other words, the game of politics is not stacked for or against anyone, at least not systematically. Everyone has the power to influence political outcomes through group membership, mobilization, and competition.

Critics argue that the idea of power to is, at best, naive and, at worst, an outright sham. They contend that people are encouraged to believe they can change political outcomes or govern themselves democratically when, in fact, the political game is rigged in favour of particular interests; for example, the capitalist class, political elites, or the oil industry. No one disputes that political power is unevenly divided even in the most equalitarian societies or among the international community of national states. But the suggestion that we are powerless to shape the kind of society in which we want to live also does not square with history. One need only think of the droves of citizens who occupied Cairo's Tahrir Square until they forced a regime change; the success of campaigns to ban landmines or stop pipelines; or Rosa Parks, who refused to go to the back of the bus in a racist American South, to realize that people, collectively and individually, have the power to bring about political change. The fight for political change may be protracted and usually brings only partial victories. Political action also exacts a cost, whether it is a small investment of time to attend a political rally, a lifetime's commitment to a political cause, or the ultimate price of one's life. Pareto once mused that "history is the graveyard of elites" (1976, 249), but even larger graveyards are filled with those who opposed them.

At the same time, the idea of power to yields only a partial view of the complexities of politics. Political outcomes invariably involve the interplay of forces of empowerment and disempowerment. The notion of **power over** focuses our attention on inequalities in the distribution of resources, might, and knowledge, and on the institutions and processes that hold regimes of inequality in place. The idea of "power over" reminds us that there are forces outside our control that privilege some groups and constrain and silence others. Many accounts of politics are grounded in the idea of power over. Feminism, for example, begins with the premise that our private and public lives are organized in ways that privilege the social, economic, and political power of men. Critical race studies focus on the ways in which power creates and reproduces hierarchies of people, based largely on skin colour, and how social resources and life chances are unevenly distributed across these hierarchies. We will review two perspectives on power over—the elite and class approaches—that often inform other perspectives on power and politics.

Elite theory has a long tradition within political theory and in the evolution of political science. It is based on a very different view of society than the one advanced in the pluralist model. While pluralism emphasizes the capacities of individuals and groups to affect political change, elitism envisions a stark political divide between the few and the many. The few, the elite, occupy the most powerful positions in the central institutions of society—the military, religion, economy, politics, and culture. The few hold the power, while the many do not.

There is little debate about the fact that there are leaders and followers in all societies. The questions posed by elite theory are, first, is this a good or bad thing, and second, do elites threaten democracy? Plato thought that elite rule was a good thing. He advanced the idea that good governance was best achieved when "philosopher kings," endowed with wisdom, virtue, and prudence, were given the exclusive power to rule. At the turn of the twentieth century, Italian sociologists Vilfredo Pareto (1848–1923) and Gaetano Mosca (1858–1941) claimed that elite rule was an inevitable fact of human existence. For these elite theorists, all societies were characterized by a fundamental truth: people were "physically, morally, and intellectually different" (Pareto 1978, 247). Some were fit to rule while the vast majority were not.

"In all societies," as Mosca explained, "two classes of people appear—a class that rules and a class that is ruled." The first class performs "all political functions, monopolizes power, and enjoys the advantages that power brings" while controlling the second class, which partakes in none of these things (quoted in Knuttila 1987, 50).

Pareto and Mosca advanced the case that elite rule is a basic fact of human existence, and inevitable. A meaningful democratic politics, therefore, was neither possible nor desirable. It is perhaps for this reason that European fascists of the 1930s embraced the social Darwinism and anti-democratic impulses within elite theory. Students of contemporary politics do well to remember that it is a short leap from the repugnant claim that some people are naturally superior and destined to hold power over others to all kinds of political pathologies, ranging from discrimination and social exclusion to so-called "ethnic cleansing" and genocide.

Roberto Michels (1876–1936), perhaps the most often cited elite theorist, also argued that elite rule was inevitable, although not necessarily desirable. Michels was active in social-democratic politics and observed how elites captured the party organization, even though party ideology was committed to democracy. According to Michels, modern society was governed by what he called "the iron law of the **oligarchy**" (rule by a few) (1962). Modern societies require large and complex organizations that are characterized by specialization and division of labour. The latter creates a hierarchy in which a few, because of their organizational position and skills, gain experience, expertise, power, and control. As the elite's skill set grows, and its grasp on power grows more complete, it becomes increasingly distant from the rank-and-file side of the organization, which, in turn, grows apathetic and disempowered. It is through this process, according to Michels, that democracy inevitably leads to oligarchy, or elite rule (Knuttila 1987, 52–3). Michels' point was that elites gain their power because of their strategic position within modern organizations and not because of their innate superiority.

It is hard to imagine examples in politics where there are no leaders and followers, where a few appear to have power over the many. The starting point of elite theory— society is composed of two groups, the elite and the masses—seems obvious, and many people across the centuries have viewed political life through this lens. During periods of economic crisis, in particular, popular opinion and social movements often point an accusing finger at the rich and bankers for controlling the system for their own ends to the exclusion and at the expense of everyone else. During the Great Depression of the 1930s, for example, social movements condemned the "fifty big shots" (bankers and business leaders) for manipulating Canadian politics. Similar analyses have appeared in the wake of the 2008 global financial crisis. In the fall of 2011, for example, the Occupy Wall Street (OWS) movement swept across more than

900 cities in the United States and around the world. Its central message was that the few, the 1%, held all the power and reaped all the benefits at the expense of the rest, the 99% that were forced into unemployment, poverty, and homelessness. Some argue that these kinds of elite analyses, however compelling, tell only part of the story, because economic and political inequalities are nestled within the broader context of capitalism and class relations.

Class Analysis

Class analysis locates the sources of power and conflict in the historical organization of economies and in social class. Karl Marx, who offered an enduring critique of capitalism, argued that all societies were divided along class lines and that, moreover, classes were necessarily and always in conflict over the distribution of material resources in society. Consider, for example, the depiction of power over provided by Karl Marx and Friedrich Engels in the *Communist Manifesto*: "The history of all hitherto existing societies," they write, "is the history of class struggles. Freeman and slave, patrician and plebeian, lord and serf, guildmaster and journeyman, in a word, oppressor and oppressed, stood in opposition to one another" (Marx and Engels 1998, 34).

Marx provided an overarching explanation of politics grounded in the historical organization of production. He argued that relations of production invariably provide the foundation for society's legal structure and politics. Democratic government was the result of a political revolution of a new class—the commercial and industrial capitalists or, as Marx called them, the **bourgeoisie**. At the same time, the emergence of capitalism created another new class—the working class, or **proletariat**—who sold their labour to capitalists and were exploited by them. Marx's careful analysis of the logic of capitalist production led him to conclude that, in time, the middle class would be absorbed into the working class and the living conditions of the working class would become more and more desperate. The politics of capitalist societies would then revolve around a struggle between capitalists and workers. The working classes of the world, through revolution, could then establish a communist society. Capitalism, unlike previous systems, Marx concluded, had a distinctive, identifying feature. As he and Engels put it in the *Communist Manifesto*, capitalism "has simplified the class antagonisms. Society as a whole is more and more splitting up into two great hostile camps, into two great classes directly facing each other, bourgeoisie and proletariat" (1998, 34).

Marx's work has been criticized for its economic determinism; that is, for reducing the explanation of all social phenomena to a single factor, the organization of the economy. Class analysis also has been challenged by feminist, anti-racist, and post-colonial theorists, because it prioritizes inequalities arising from the principles of capitalism. At different times and in different places, however, to be born black, indigenous, female, gay, or a member of a religious or ethnic minority, to name a few examples, placed people in a position of being subjected to power over within the broader historical contexts of racism, sexism, homophobia, and colonialism. Moreover, these social hierarchies were enforced by the bourgeoisie and working class alike. All societies, past and present, in other words, are divided by multiple systems of advantage and disadvantage, which are produced and reproduced in political institutions, social organizations, and common value systems.

Social stratification studies, following from the work of Max Weber, hold that social ranking and the capacity to exercise power over occurs along many dimensions that are not reducible to one's position in the organization of capitalism. When Weber contemplated the ways that societies were stratified, he saw quite a different world than the one seen by Marx. The starkly oppressive conditions of emerging industrialization had been somewhat improved, the working class had organized into unions and socialist political parties, democracy had expanded, and, as Weber saw it, society was increasingly governed by large bureaucracies. He argued that social stratification could no longer be studied as a product of social class alone. For Weber, social class remained an important determinant of power, but it was not the only factor. Modern society was divided into many status groups whose positions on the social hierarchy also were determined by prestige and political power. Prestige could involve things as intangible as tastes and patterns of consumption that are socially valued, such as driving a Mercedes or being a celebrated athlete, a hip-hop artist, or a movie star. This kind of social power, while not entirely unrelated to social class, is not reducible to economic relations alone.

Weber's work on status groups encouraged political scientists and sociologists to explain social divisions in influence and power on the basis of a variety of factors, including patterns of consumption; the social prestige assigned to some professions, such as medicine or law; and such factors as ethnicity, gender, race, and religion. Weber's work, thus, encouraged social scientists to talk about class divisions in non-antagonistic ways. Social class was analyzed along a continuum—upper class, middle class, and lower class—without any notion of exploitation or conflict among these groups. Weber's work, nonetheless, underlined the many ways that power and influence are unequally distributed in society, sometimes on the basis of characteristics we are assigned at birth, such as gender and race, and sometimes on the basis of things we achieve, such as a professional degree or a discerning taste for fine wine.

Power and Knowledge

In the late twentieth century, many social scientists began to explore different ways of thinking about power and politics that do not conform to the power to–power over dichotomy. The work of Michel Foucault prompted many to abandon thinking about power as something outside us, to be gained, lost, or used to empower ourselves or to disempower others. For Foucault, the most important thing to understand about power is that it is productive. He argued that we never stand outside power but instead are created (produced) by it. Power runs through our bodies and all social relations, like capillaries. These capillaries of power can be so innocuous, even commonsensical, as to be undetectable. They, nonetheless, have a defining influence on the way we think and behave, not only in politics but in every waking moment.

Foucault argued that there were different kinds of power and that their relative importance has shifted across time. In earlier periods, monarchs exercised **sovereign power**, that is ultimate power over their subjects, as is suggested in the phrase "off with their heads!" Foucault contends that in modern societies, non-sovereign forms of power have become far more important than the non-negotiable and often brutal exercise of the power by a king. Non-sovereign power is embedded in language and in knowledge systems that tell us what exists, who we are, and what is true. He used the term *discourse* to convey his assertion that power and knowledge are inseparable. For Foucault, discourses embody "an accumulation of concepts, practices, statements and beliefs" that "necessarily extend beyond language" (2003, 40, xix). By advancing particular ways of thinking and acting as unchallenged realities—the truth—discourses produce societies and social relations in their own image.

Foucault coined the terms **disciplinary power, normalization,** and **dividing practices** to describe modern non-sovereign forms of power. Disciplinary power exacts appropriate behaviours from individuals, not through force, but by defining what is normal. Dividing practices stigmatize those who do not fit the mould by naming them, often with scientific justification, as being different or abnormal. People exercise productive power over themselves and others quite unconsciously. For example, when a scientific discourse defines what is normal, we both discipline ourselves to conform to this definition in order to avoid social rejection and reject those who, through dividing practices, do not conform. Long before we act, we have power inscribed on us through these disciplinary, normalization, and dividing practices. As Foucault explains, power and knowledge directly imply one another. This means that there can be no knowledge "out there" that is free of power relations, to be used for good or evil. Claims to knowledge are also claims to power. Fields of knowledge empower certain kinds of expertise, categorize people, and discipline them to conform to particular ways of behaving and living.

Foucault's work focused on the dividing and disciplinary practices that came out of the scientific naming of homosexuals, the mentally ill, and criminals. The recent history of gays and lesbians, in fact, provides an illustration of what Foucault meant by productive power. Beginning in the nineteenth century, psychiatry began to establish itself as a branch of scientific-medical knowledge. It was an expert discourse with the capacity to define the normal and the abnormal. Reproducing long-standing religious and cultural taboos, this field of expertise diagnosed homosexuality as a mental illness. Gays and lesbians were thus produced through this discourse as being abnormal. They were socially ostracized, forced "into the closet," and subjected to all manner of medical and legal interventions and prohibitions. Far too many simply ended their lives. In the mid-twentieth century, however, the gay liberation movement challenged this discourse of abnormality, and the psychiatric profession eventually removed homosexuality from its official inventory of mental diseases. We should note that the behaviour had not changed—only the discourses and politics surrounding it. This discursive shift then opened space for gays and lesbians to make claims to equality rights, protection from hate speech and violence, and inclusion in mainstream social institutions, such as marriage.

Foucault's depiction of the intimate and productive work of power has been criticized for being too all-encompassing and for effectively foreclosing the possibility of individual action, political contestation, and political change. If we are all produced through discourse, so the argument goes, then where is there room for individual free will and collective action? While Foucault argued that the very idea of individual free will was a discursive construction, he also rejected the idea that there is no room in his work for political action. He argued that disciplinary power always evokes some form of political resistance; discourses always generate their mirror opposite. Official pronouncements of abnormality are met with claims to normality, as the above example of the gay and lesbian movement illustrates. He also recognized, however, that there were situations where opportunities for political opposition were limited, but he described these as examples of domination rather than power. Foucault suggested that some states of domination can be so complete that there is no room for resistance. "Slavery," for example, "is not a power relationship when man is in chains" (quoted in Simons 1995, 82).

Sovereignty and Authority

THIS INTRODUCTION TO POWER AND POLITICS WOULD BE INCOMPLETE without discussing two forms of power that are core themes in political science—notably, sovereignty and authority. The idea of sovereignty is intimately bound to the birth of the modern state. **Sovereignty** means supreme power. In feudal societies, power and authority were dispersed and divisible, often shared and struggled for among the nobility, the monarch, and the Church. Gradually, from the fifteenth to the seventeenth centuries, coinciding with the demise of feudalism and the ascendancy of capitalism, political power began to consolidate both territorially and practically within the early predecessors of the modern state. These predecessors took on two dominant personalities—the "absolute" monarchies of France, Prussia, Austria, Spain, and Russia and the "constitutional" monarchies and republics, based on representative government, that were beginning to take form in England and Holland (Held 1996, 66).

Under absolute monarchies, the sovereignty of traditional hereditary monarchs, such as King Louis XIV of France who ruled from 1638 to 1715, was effectively imposed on the state through the person of the king. Louis XIV, for example, pronounced that "*l'état, c'est moi.*" Absolute monarchs maintained that their power was God-given, and, thus, to disobey the monarch was to disobey God, which was the greatest offence in these times. Absolute monarchies eventually crumbled in the face of democratization, class conflict, and the idea of popular sovereignty; that is, the notion that political power ultimately rested in the hands of all citizens instead of with leaders alone. Absolute monarchies, nonetheless, provided the institutional underpinnings of the modern state, especially the centralization of political, military, and administrative powers within defined territorial boundaries (Held 1996, 68).

During the past four centuries, the modern state has taken on a number of different forms, ranging from representative democracies to fascist dictatorships to communist regimes. Regardless of form, states share one defining characteristic—the non-negotiable claim to sovereignty. All modern states claim the supreme and indivisible power to rule over a national territory. This non-negotiable monopoly of state sovereignty was recognized formally in the Peace of Westphalia in 1648, which began the partitioning of the world into "sovereign states." These states controlled their own territories and could legitimately use force to repel threats to national security and sovereignty arising from either domestic politics or external threats (Held 1996, 69). This idea of the fusion of power, sovereignty, authority, and legitimacy, which continues to structure current thinking about politics, is clearly conveyed by Weber's often-cited definition of the **state**. He called it "a human community that successfully claims monopoly of the legitimate use of physical force within a given territory" (quoted in Gerth and Mills 1958, 78). In recent years, a number of countries, many in Saharan Africa, have been identified as "failed states." This term applies when states lose their monopoly over the legitimate use of violence within their territories, usually because state armies have been displaced by war lords, private militias, tribal leaders, and other non-state actors who exercise violence and control over domestic populations.

Authority and sovereignty are closely related but quite different conceptions of power. In cases of authority, governments secure obedience from the governed without resorting to violence or force, because the governed accept that it is legitimate for certain institutions and individuals in society to have more power than others. Consider the following two scenarios. In the first, you are driving down the street and a police officer demands that you stop your car. You are likely to comply. In the second scenario, a naked person demands that you stop your car. In this case, you are probably more likely to lock your doors and speed down the street. What is the difference? It is the authority vested in a police officer's uniform. Authority is "socially approved power" (Kourvetaris 1997, 51). Someone is accorded power and legitimacy less for who they are than for the institution that they represent, whether that be the police, judiciary, or elected office. This legitimacy is often backed by the threat of sanction or punishment. Most us of obey the law both because we believe in the rule of law—that is, that everyone should be subject to the same laws—and because we realize that failure to comply with the law might very well result in a fine or jail sentence.

Max Weber (1864–1920), one of the fathers of modern social science, argued that societies have been governed by three different kinds of authority: traditional, charismatic, and legal-rational. He identifies **traditional authority** as the social glue that held together pre-industrial societies. Power was vested in certain individuals because of custom or heredity. The tribal chief or the king was obeyed because that was how it was intended or how it had always been. While traditional authorities might take advice from others, including a god, their authority was personal and incontestable. **Charismatic authority** is similarly vested in individuals. It, however, is grounded in the personal qualities of the charismatic leader, rather than in tradition or in birth. Weber argued that charismatic leaders tend to gain authority during periods of profound crisis and social upheaval. Their authority, he argued, grows out of "a certain quality of an individual personality by virtue of which he is set apart from ordinary men and treated as endowed with supernatural, superhuman, or at least specifically exceptional powers and qualities" (quoted in Bendix 1960, 88). The social upheavals of the Great Depression in the 1930s, which saw the rise of fascist dictators such as Hitler in Germany and Mussolini in Italy, provide obvious examples of what Weber meant by charismatic authority.

Writing over a century ago, Weber saw both traditional and charismatic authority as waning in modern societies, which were increasingly governed by **legal-rational authority**. This kind of authority is based in the rule of law and in the bureaucratic and impersonal procedures of modern institutions, such as the courts, constitutions, bureaucracy, and legislatures. Legal-rational authority is accorded to leaders who hold positions in, administer, and abide by the rules of these institutions. They, in turn, are considered legitimate by the public only to the extent that they uphold established rules and procedures. In a legal-rational system, claims to authority, even by charismatic leaders, are unlikely to be considered legitimate unless they are framed within a system of legal rationality. To put the point more clearly, no matter how charismatic an individual or how royal a bloodline, a person could not make claims to political leadership and authority in a legal-rational culture unless accorded legitimacy through, for example, a democratic election. Similarly, those in positions of power lose their legitimacy if they fail to adhere to institutional norms and expectations. A policeman "on the take" or a political leader caught in an influence-peddling scheme would be examples.

Although these different kinds of authority tend to characterize different kinds of society, from the simple to the complex, all can be found in contemporary political cultures. A religious leader or one's parents or teachers make claims to traditional authority, although many traditionalists lament that these authority figures no longer command the obedience that they once did. Any day of the week, you can find someone on television linking the problems of the world to lax discipline in schools, a decline in religious deference, and the collapse of family values. Charisma is also a fading force in political life. The somewhat perplexing leader Kim Jong-Il, who ruled North Korea until his death in 2011, developed an elaborate cult of personality as did his father, the "Great Leader" Kim Il Sung. It remains to be seen whether his son, Kim Jong-Un, can continue to hold on to power through charismatic appeals. The selection of political leaders through democratic election, some obviously less corrupt than others, is the dominant international norm. Charismatic leaders are condemned as throwbacks to another time and as anomalies that stand as obstacles to good governance and economic development.

Conclusion

IN THIS CHAPTER, WE HAVE EXPLORED SUCH CORE CRITICAL CONCEPTS as politics, power, sovereignty, and authority. A concept is an idea and a representation of a class of things or practices. The adjective *critical* is meant to convey three meanings that are elaborated in the chapters that follow. The first is that the concepts we identify are critical to our understanding of political processes and outcomes. Such concepts as democracy, the state, and international relations, to name a few, have been the bread and butter of political science since its conception. Second, the adjective "critical" is meant to convey the idea that these concepts are contested. They are the focus of ongoing debate and struggle about their very meaning and practice. Finally, these concepts are critical because the stakes of politics generally hinge on how foundational political concepts are commonly understood and practised by political actors and political institutions.

In recent decades, the traditional approaches and concerns of the discipline of political science have been challenged by, among others, feminist, critical race, and post-colonial studies. These emerging perspectives on politics and power rightly contend that the conceptual arsenal of political science has ignored the experiences of the vast majority of people around the world. Political science and the practice of politics also is challenged by globalization, which has undermined the capacity of national states to deal with critical issues that reach beyond their borders, including terrorism, climate change, and financial crises. There is a cliché that says, "We cannot understand where we are going unless we understand where we have been." This cliché resonates in contemporary political affairs. As we debate today's political issues, it is important to realize that similar questions vexed other societies and that, through politics, they arrived at either reasonable or horrible solutions. The kinds of politics we will have in the twenty-first century, as well as the solutions we find to enable global co-existence, are still ours to create, although, as Marx would remind us, not necessarily under conditions of our own choosing. Globalization challenges old assumptions and creates new political problems. It does not, however, release us from the responsibility of constantly revisiting the fundamental political questions of what is and, more importantly, what ought to be.

Summary

The chapter:

- Provided an overview of the critical concepts of politics and power
- Discussed different ways of thinking about power, including power to, power over, and knowledge and power
- Examined how pluralist, elite, and class analyses understand power
- Explained the key concepts of sovereignty, authority, and legitimacy

Discussion Questions

1. Think about your day. How often did you encounter politics? What kind of politics did you encounter? Were there some encounters that entailed more power than others? Why? In what ways could you have resisted that power?

2. Compare and contrast the "power to" and "power over" perspectives on power. Which perspective do you think better captures the exercise of power in contemporary politics?
3. Reflect on the idea of disciplinary power. Discuss some examples of the ways in which normalization and dividing practices influence your daily conduct.
4. What ought our politics to look like in the twenty-first century? Why?

References

Bendix, Reinhard. 1960. *Max Weber: An Intellectual Portrait.* Garden City, NY: Doubleday.

Dahl, Robert. 1956. *Preface to Democratic Theory.* Chicago: University of Chicago Press.

————. 1961. *Who Governs.* New Haven, CT: Yale University Press.

Foucault, Michel. 1977. *Power/Knowledge.* New York: Pantheon.

Gerth, H.H. and C.W. Mills, eds. 1958. *From Max Weber: Essays in Sociology.* New York: Oxford University Press.

Guy, James John. 1995. *People, Politics, Government: Political Science: A Canadian Perspective.* Scarborough, ON: Prentice Hall.

Held, David. 1996. "The Development of the Modern State." In *Modernity: An Introduction to the Modern Social Sciences,* edited by Stuart Hall, David Held, Don Hubert, and Kenneth Thompson. London: Blackwell.

Knuttila, Murray. 1987. *State Theories.* Toronto: Garamond.

Kourvetaris, George. 1997. *Political Sociology: Structure and Process.* Boston: Allyn and Bacon.

Lasswell, Harold. 1936. *Politics: Who Gets What, When, How.* New York: McGraw-Hill.

Mannheim, Karl. 1936. *Ideology and Utopia.* New York: Harvest Books.

Marx, Karl and Friedrich Engels. 1998. *The Communist Manifesto: A Modern Edition.* London: Verso.

Michels, Roberto. 1962. *Political Parties.* New York: The Free Press.

Pareto, Vilfredo. 1978. *Sociological Writings.* Oxford: Basil Blackwell.

Philip, Mark. 1985. "Power." In *The Social Science Encyclopedia,* edited by Adam Kuper and Jessica Kuper. New York: Routledge.

Simons, Jon. 1995. *Foucault and the Political.* New York: Routledge.

Further Readings

Bellamy, Richard and Andrew Mason. 2003. *Political Concepts.* Manchester: Manchester University Press.

Bottomore, Tom. 1979. *Political Sociology.* London: Harper and Row Publishers.

Foucault, Michel. 1977. *Power/Knowledge.* New York: Pantheon.

Hall, Stuart, David Held, Don Hubert, and Kenneth Thompson, eds. 1996. *Modernity: An Introduction to the Social Sciences.* London: Blackwell.

Weblinks

Janine Brodie. "Social Literacy and Social Justice in Uncertain Times." Big Thinking Lectures Series. Canadian Federation of the Humanities and Social Sciences, 2012, Congress, University of Waterloo.
www.youtube.com/watch?v=uxJw9nTNseo

American Political Science Association
www.apsanet.org

Canadian Political Science Association
www.sfu.ca/igs/CPSA.html

Department of Political Science, University of Alberta
www.ualberta.ca/~polisci/index.html

CHAPTER 2

BIG IDEAS

ROGER EPP

Learning Objectives

- Introduces political philosophy as a distinct kind of inquiry

- Demonstrates that political philosophy involves long standing, great conversations about ideas that matter

- Introduces some of the historical participants in these conversations

- Identifies some basic strands of these conversations as a way of showing their character, vocabulary, and everyday importance

Introduction

Political philosophy is thinking about the nature and **public** requirements of the good life. It is both systematic and creative. It is the realm of fundamental concepts such as freedom, justice, equality, rights, order, and authority. However, there is no single uncontested meaning attributed to these terms, and no agreement as to their limits, sources, or possibilities. What propels ideas about the good life in any given era or place? Is it God, nature, force, reason, the logic of history, or none of these? Is there a universal and timeless *human* nature? If so, must it be harnessed since, left to ourselves, like the characters of *Lord of the Flies*, we are self-destructively self-interested and fearful of others? Or must it be unleashed with the right social and political arrangements to find its potential, since we are a creative and capable species? Are cultural differences politically important? How can people who are not alike—whether in culture and ethnicity, physical characteristics, wealth, or basic beliefs—live peacefully together in a single polity? What purposes should government serve and not serve? Is there one form of government that is best for all political communities? What qualities are required of those who lead?

Introduced with big questions like this, political philosophy can seem intimidating. Or else, it can seem irrelevant to the "action" that draws most students to the study of politics: elections, policy-making, street demonstrations, international diplomacy, and war. Political philosophy does not offer the clarity or certainty of right answers. That does not mean that political philosophy, however, is merely an intellectual exercise. For one thing, the words that people use to participate in politics, the claims they make, and the assumptions embedded in them, are precisely the stuff of political philosophy. Such inquiry teaches us to pay attention to language and ideas where we find them. Not coincidentally, we have inherited from the ancient Greeks not just the word "politics"—the root, *polis*, refers to a city state and the active life among citizens in that place—but also the first systematic political texts by such thinkers as Plato (c. 427–347 B.C.E.) and Aristotle (384–322 B.C.E.).

The fact that texts as old as these continue to be read suggests that political philosophy represents a different kind of thinking than is found, say, in the sciences. While students in physics might be introduced to the history of human attempts to make sense of the universe—from Aristotle to Newton to Einstein—the subject is taught as a succession of wrong ideas. In keeping with the scientific method, discovery corrects and ultimately displaces older theories with new ones. Students in political philosophy, in contrast, are introduced to a "canon" of texts representing various times and genres. Most are formal treatises, while others take the form of dialogues, plays, letters, or manifestos issued in the heat of the moment. The selection of texts in that canon is itself a matter of debate; it is not fixed. Old works are rediscovered and newer ones are added. No doubt North American students will soon read ancient Chinese texts on statecraft alongside the Greek (Wang 2009; Yan 2011), and not just for historical interest but for perspective on our times. The point is that texts and thinkers endure. They are not necessarily dispatched to the museum by the arrival of a new mode of thinking. Instead, new editions are promoted side by side with new ideas in publishers' catalogues; old texts find new advocates, interpreters, and critics, and continue to shed light on political practice.

In this sense, political philosophy should be understood as an *extended conversation* involving different voices, traditions, and texts, as well as shifting subjects of interest. This conversation is more than a shouting match. Its participants, past and present, tend to change their own positions over lifetimes, in response to events and ideas around them, and cannot control the different ways in which others may have heard them. In any case, their positions are seldom reducible to simple study notes or short-hand labels. They are best read as whole texts, slowly, and with some knowledge of the historical context in which they were written.

The Ancient Beginnings of Western Political Philosophy

IMAGINE A WORLD IN WHICH THE LEADING DEMOCRACY OF THE DAY, sure of its strength and political appeal, has been drawn into war at the head of an alliance that resembled an empire. The democracy in the story is the ancient Greek city state of Athens. After the first year of the war, its leader, Pericles, asked citizens who gathered for a public funeral to look beyond the deaths and hardships they had experienced, to again "fall in love" with their city, to summon the courage and make the sacrifices necessary to ensure the greatness of their city. For theirs, he said, was an enviable form of government that put power in the hands of the people. Theirs was an open society that provided personal freedom and an abundance of consumer goods from around the world. By the next year, however, it was obvious that the war would be more difficult and destructive than first imagined. Pericles was forced to use the range of his rhetorical talents to quell the backlash. Athens, the city of freedom, had no choice but to continue the war and hang onto its empire; and its citizens, he said, needed to remain united just to save themselves. After a serious debate, Pericles was reprimanded, then re-elected, for it was said that he possessed intelligence, integrity, and a grasp of the state's character so that he could tell people what they needed to hear. But he soon died. His successors were more ambitious and less skilful, though one dissenter later asked how he could be praised when, like a bad animal trainer, he left the city fiercer than he found it.

In a generation of warfare that followed, the treasury was depleted, a rich culture died, and this society, like others drawn into the conflict, was deeply divided, often along class lines and sometimes within families. Brutality substituted for persuasion. Atrocities required revenge: "any idea of moderation was just an attempt to disguise one's unmanly character; ability to understand a question from all sides meant that one was totally unfitted for action. Fanatical enthusiasm was the mark of a real man"

(Thucydides 1972, 242). At one point, the democracy sent soldiers to a small island whose people declared they would rather stay neutral than give up 700 years of liberty. But there was no middle ground. The islanders were besieged, then killed or enslaved, on the argument that "the strong do what they have the power to do and the weak accept what they have to accept" (Thucydides 1972, 402). Justice was reduced to might. Judgment was replaced by appeals to natural instinct. The end finally came far from home with the failure of a massive and costly military expedition. It had been approved by citizen majority, swayed by the patriotic pitch of an Olympic champion–turned-politician. Most of the soldiers never returned. Back home, news of defeat was met, in turn, with disbelief, panic, and violence. The democracy was dissolved in a brutal *coup d'état*, then restored just in time to rally citizens to the defence of their homeland.

This is the kind of world—not some utopian oasis, not a classroom—in which political philosophy took shape. What did this experience teach? How radically did the polis need to be reimagined? While elements of the story might sound familiar, and perhaps prophetic, its claim on our attention does not rest on simple assumptions that history repeats itself or that politics is the same everywhere. But ideas do have long, powerful histories, and ancient Greece has had a particularly formative influence on Western culture. The Athenian polis, for example, has continued to inspire yearnings for a more robust democracy—despite its exclusion of women.

Ancient Political Thought

IF POLITICAL PHILOSOPHY IS AN EXTENDED CONVERSATION, TO PICK up the metaphor, we might say that it sometimes scatters into separate rooms—one group in the kitchen, another on the deck, with each occasionally in hearing distance of the other when one gets loud or the other quiet. The most common divide in political philosophy is between ancients and moderns, between the classical tradition starting with the Greeks and the thought that emerges with the "sovereign" state and market economy. This divide makes intuitive sense. The ancient Mediterranean world is distant in time and space. The ancient Greek texts will seem alien to those immersed from birth in liberal ideas about the primacy of individuals, constitutions, gender equality, representative democracy, and the rule of law. For that reason, to study them is to rethink the "common sense" of our own times.

In Athenian political culture, the polis outranked one's family in importance. Freedom was understood as an attribute of public life. It meant acting together with one's equals. Glory—a place in the stories told by future generations—was valued above one's safety. The philosophers, somewhat differently, emphasized that politics was a moral activity. It was about enabling the good life and the common good. The philosophers asked who should rule (one, a few, or the many), and what wisdom or character was required to do so. They assumed a close fit between the virtue of citizens and the quality of their regime, so that it would have been almost unthinkable to live well in a corrupt city. Immanuel Kant (1724–1804), by contrast, took a decidedly modern position when he wrote that a constitutional state could be established by "even a nation of devils," who could agree on an arrangement that would allow them to pursue their self-interests with minimal interference (Kant 1970, 112–13). For Kant and other modern thinkers, it mattered little if individuals were good or bad.

The classical texts, as noted, did not come from an era of quiet contemplation. They emerged from the rough politics of the assembly and the prolonged war that caused the collapse of the Athenian empire after a restless, foolish attempt to conquer inhospitable Sicily. Plato, we know, had resisted an invitation to join the brutal oligarchy that briefly seized power after the war. But it was the fragile post-war democracy that put Plato's teacher, Socrates, to death for impiety and corrupting the young. No wonder the question of whether truth and political power could be reconciled, whether the person who cared for truth should shun public life, was ever present in his writing. It animated his best-known work, *The Republic.* This meandering dialogue began with a late-night argument about whether justice was merely the advantage of the stronger—one, few, or many—and whether it was honest to admit that those who succeeded at injustice on a grand scale, conquering cities, were most admirable. The character Socrates proposed that people of good character would rule neither for honour nor money, but unwillingly, only out of fear of being ruled by someone worse (Plato 1974, 347b). He was dismissed as naive. He responded with an analogy. In the well-ordered soul, the parts of appetite and spirit were subjected to reason, and each part was directed to its particular "excellence": moderation, courage, and wisdom (the ability to see beyond the surface of things). In the well-ordered city, he said, there would be a similar division of labour. Those who loved money and things would provide for it materially, those who loved honour would protect it, and those few who loved and were capable of wisdom—philosophers—would rule it. Elsewhere, he likened these three types of people to sheep, watchdogs, and shepherds (416a). This picture of a city ruled by wisdom, not appetite, certainly reflected a fear of further discord and imperial ambition. It also assumed that most people were not fit to govern, since they could not even govern themselves.

In *The Republic,* Socrates' friends debated the practicalities of this city: How would it be established? Would the slate have to be wiped clean first? How would the philosopher-rulers be identified, trained, and persuaded to rule, and then reproduced? Who would watch the watchdogs? In the end Socrates grew pessimistic. Even if the city could be founded, it could not last forever against a predictable cycle of decay whose last stages would be unbridled liberty, the rise of a people's champion, and tyranny. Socrates had a compelling answer, however, for those who first proposed that the ruler who could act with impunity was most admirable. Such a tyrant, he said, was actually unhappiest of all. Lacking moderation, he was enslaved to his own appetites and to satisfy them kept taking things from others. He lived with flatterers but not friends. He could not abandon his position without worrying that he would face the punishment he had inflicted on others. He and his city were imprisoned by fear. He could not move about freely or travel abroad. Plato's psychological portrait recalls the experience of modern tyrants such as Iraq's Saddam Hussein (Al-Khalil 1990) and, in his last decade, Chile's Augusto Pinochet (Dorfman 2002).

Was it really possible, however, to establish a politics beyond decay and opinion? Plato was equivocal. *The Republic's* best-known story began with the philosopher's arduous climb out of the cave toward the sun. Having left behind those who lived by appearances—shadow images cast on a wall—and having grown accustomed to the light, he needed to be convinced to return to the cave, to occupy himself with human affairs, knowing he could not explain the reality that others could not see. By the other-worldly end of the long dialogue, Socrates seemed to have convinced himself that philosophy alone was powerless to bring his city into being. Short of "divine luck," the city should be regarded as "a model laid up in heaven," to which the "man of sense" will look in establishing order in his soul. Meanwhile, he would avoid politics (592 a/b). So Plato is a paradoxical first political philosopher: paradoxical because he was deeply ambivalent about politics, and first because the democratic era that preceded him produced no theorists or texts of the same stature.

Aristotle was Plato's student but, unlike his teacher, he did not denigrate politics or trade in out-of-reach ideal constitutions. He worked from observation, not abstract logic. He assumed that political arrangements varied according to the character of particular cities. At the same time, Aristotle began with the premise that the polis was the highest form of human association. It gave citizens a setting in which to pursue the good life. Through debating and deciding in the assembly, it also enabled them, as "political animals" equipped with language, to develop their full human capacity for reasoned speech. Remember that Aristotle wrote in the twilight of Athens' democracy. Indeed, he was tutor to the young Alexander the Great, who radically reconfigured the Mediterranean political landscape. But in his *Politics*, Aristotle defended the virtues of citizens: know how to rule and be ruled, hold office, defend the city, make laws, and respect them. Office holding was a matter of obligation to the polis and their friends. What Aristotle's citizens required, above all, was **phronesis**, or practical judgment, which they could gain only by experience and emulation of those who demonstrated it. He was, accordingly, suspicious of the young, who lacked experience and were prone to impetuous action (Aristotle 1980; 1985).

Aristotle was no modern egalitarian. Consistent with his culture, he accepted two assumptions that unsettle us. One was that slaves did the work of the household, which, in turn, freed citizens to participate in the assembly. The other was that women lacked the rational capacity or at least the opportunity, as recent commentators tend to argue, to develop *phronesis*. (Socrates in *The Republic* had scandalized his listeners with the idea that women could have a philosophic nature.) All that said, when Aristotle considered who should rule, his qualified answer was, the many. A wise king might be best, but what about succession? In most cases, the collective wisdom was more reliable. Aristotle compared it to the advantages of a potluck meal over a single delicious dish. The collective wisdom drew on diverse perspectives whereas a king had only one pair of eyes and ears—no equal, so no true friends or sense of mutual obligation. The many, Aristotle reasoned, were also less corruptible or temperamental. But they still needed virtue and good judgment because, he believed, they were as capable of losing sight of the common good as one or a few.

While Aristotle shared Plato's bias in favour of contemplative thought, he did not follow his teacher in imagining an eternal standard of goodness outside of human affairs. His ethics retained a down-to-earth quality, and still represent an influential alternative for ethicists. For Aristotle, ethics were about good character more than right decisions. Ethics involved knowing who we wanted to be, cultivating virtue by doing virtuous acts until they became engrained, finding a balance between extremes, and emulating good persons. This way of thinking mixed new and old elements. Thucydides' history of the war was also filled with reminders of what happened when balance was lost; for example, when Athens could act with impunity because rival Sparta was weakened, or when the young, wanting their own glory, disregarded their elders.

Thucydides' history, in turn, reflected another Greek ethical perspective, the **tragic**. It derived from dramatists such as Sophocles, whose classic *Antigone* is still performed and transposed to contemporary political settings. The story of a young woman who defied the edict of her uncle, the ruler, and buried her brother though he was declared a traitor, the play is now often read as a defence of individual conscience against arbitrary state power. This theme certainly speaks to modern preoccupations. Greek audiences, however, would have watched it as a real conflict between the claims of family and city. The play is tragic not because sad things happened, but because people single-mindedly pursued one good thing to the exclusion of others, past a point of no return, and as a result lost something that mattered deeply to them. The worst of human afflictions, it was said, was "lack of judgment" (Sophocles c. 442 B.C.E. 123).

And then there is the story of Socrates' trial and death, which is inscribed deeply in the Western imagination. It was written by Plato early in his career and, unlike the later dialogues, is considered a fairly close representation of something like the historical Socrates. It portrayed a self-confessed gadfly whose divine purpose was to trouble people with questions and prod them to care for virtue. While Socrates did not convince the large jury of his innocence, his story was not quite a tragedy. He did not beg for acquittal. He declared that the "unexamined life is not worth living." He refused his friends' offer of escape and exile. Instead, he proposed that "the most important thing is not life, but the good life," that it was better to suffer wrong than to do it, and that a good man could not, in fact, be harmed. Finally, he challenged himself in the name of the city that brought him to birth: "You must either persuade it or obey its orders, and endure in silence whatever it instructs you to endure" (Plato 1975, 38a, 45d, 48b, 51b). This capacity for self-interrogation was what the twentieth-century political theorist Hannah Arendt called *thinking*. She found it strikingly absent in the Nazi functionaries like Adolf Eichmann—not "monsters" but respectable, career-minded members of society—who could plan the transport of millions of Jews to concentration camps and gas chambers and then claim they were only following orders. While Arendt could be sharply critical of Plato's anti-political "tyranny of truth" (2005, 5–39), she upheld his Socrates as a model of inner ethical dialogue. Conscience often failed, but the need to answer to oneself, to be at peace with oneself, *to think*, she said, was crucial for people who found themselves in dark times (2003).

Early Modern Political Thought

A LEAP FROM ANTIQUITY TO EARLY MODERN EUROPE IS COMMON IN surveys of political philosophy, though it glosses over important historical developments: the rise of Christianity, the decline of the Roman Empire into agrarian feudalism, the struggles of popes and princes for pre-eminence, and the complex relationship with the Islamic world that once stretched to Spain. But if not for Islamic scholarship and the great library at Alexandria, Egypt, most Greek texts would not have been preserved to be read in Europe. Medieval philosophy absorbed at least some of Aristotle, including his stress on character; but it lacked anything like a polis in which the idea of citizenship and an active public life could even make sense. In the work of writers like Christine de Pizan (c. 1364–1431), the *body politic* was conceived as an organic whole in which people were joined in mutual dependence, the ruler being the head, others the hands, feet, and stomach. Rulers in particular became the subject of a new genre of writing, "mirror of princes," that advised them how to govern virtuously: keep promises, punish without cruelty, protect the weak, and so on. The political spectrum ranged on a single axis from good kings to tyrants.

This medieval world was crumbling when it was dealt a double intellectual blow early in the sixteenth century. First, Protestant reformer Martin Luther (1483–1546), among others, challenged the Catholic Church's authority. His position gave a limited legitimacy to the rising territorial princes. They were "hangmen" not "shepherds"— divinely ordained to keep public order but not to make people good or fit them for eternal salvation. Second, Niccolò Machiavelli (1469–1527), a civic official and diplomat in the Italian city state of Florence, exiled to the countryside by a regime change, wrote a controversial treatise called *The Prince*. The book's purpose has been debated ever since: was it satire, a job application, a call to unify Italy against foreign domination, or simply a counsel of evil? Machiavelli pulled no punches. His intention, he said, was to draw up "an original set of rules" based on political reality rather than on the naivety of the mirror-of-princes authors: "The fact is that a man who wants to act virtuously in every way necessarily comes to grief among so many who are not virtuous. Therefore if a prince wants to maintain his rule he must learn how not to be virtuous, and to make use of this or not according to need" (1981, ch. XV, 91).

Machiavelli was a transitional thinker. He accepted the classical interest in the character of rule while turning the old virtues upside down. He advised the prince to learn from history, imitate great rulers, and never be timid. In seizing a state, for example, he must "determine all the injuries that he will need to inflict" and "inflict them once for all" (ch. VIII, 66). Machiavelli did not advise that the prince be a thug, but rather that he should use violence sparingly to maximum effect. The prince's real *virtu*—the root of virtuosity, a word for skilful solo musicians—was his ability to anticipate change and act accordingly. It helped to appear compassionate, truthful, and pious, and to be those things, but it also helped to "know how to do evil" if necessary. Machiavelli's maxims remind us that politics is part theatre. They seem ready-made for the spin doctors of the television age: "everyone is in a position to watch . . . few experience what you really are. . . . The common people are always impressed by appearances and results" (ch. XVIII, 101).

The ideas that emerged to dominate the modern era, however, were liberal ones. The vocabulary was that of right, consent, and authority. The intent of leading liberal philosophers such as Thomas Hobbes (1588–1679) and John Locke (1632–1704) was, respectively, to pacify politics after a time of civil war and to fence in arbitrary power.

Hobbes' *Leviathan* (1651) painted in powerful words a **state of nature**: a world stripped of institutions and reduced to bare elements, *individuals* who were *fearful* of their own survival but capable of calculating their best advantage. There was no higher wisdom. In his famous phrase, life in this state would be "solitary, poor, nasty, brutish, and short" (1994, ch. 13, 76). If people thought about it, though, such a state of nature would seem so intolerable that they would surrender their **natural right** to do what they wished and constitute a government strong enough to protect them. Hobbes' radical, rationalist turn was to locate political authority in the **consent** of the governed, rather than, say, in divine revelation, nature, kinship relations, or even force. Hobbes did not write primarily for rulers. The governed were the ones who needed to reckon every day that it was better to obey the sovereign, *any sovereign*, than risk sliding back toward disorder. That kind of rational calculation was in reach of almost everyone. It might, in fact, not seem so extreme in places like post-Saddam Iraq. Or it might describe the bargain in contemporary China—as does a recent novel, citing Hobbes (Chan 2011)—between the single-party state, social order, and rising levels of prosperity for most people.

John Locke, too, built his case for authority by consent from the state of nature, but with much less emphasis on order. Why would free people establish a government over themselves? Why give it the power to punish? The only good reason was the "mutual preservation of their lives, liberties, and estates" (1980, ch. 9, §124), which required law, impartial judges, and a capacity to enforce justice, for people could not be judges and executioners in their own case. Locke's target was arbitrary rule by kings who legitimized their authority by divine right or fatherly analogies. Authority, he wrote, came only from the conditional consent of the governed. A ruler who broke trust put himself above the law and declared war on his society; rebellion was then a matter of duty. Locke was no democratic theorist, but, then, there was no real citizen politics on offer in his day. The main political role of the governed was vigilance. Politics was a necessary evil to protect the freedom people exercised in the marketplace, the printing press, or the church.

Jean-Jacques Rousseau (1712–1778) made a more provocative attempt to reconcile state authority with individual freedom in *The Social Contract*. Starting with the state-of-nature motif, but aware of inequalities that had grown once the first fence posts were put in the ground, he imagined a republic that would restore legitimacy to a world in which people were "born free," yet "everywhere in chains" (Book I.1, 49). In that republic, founded by covenant, people would be free because they were bound only by those laws they had imposed on themselves. But such a republic, Rousseau conceded, would have to be small. Its citizens would have to be fairly independent, equal, and culturally alike. And then there was the problem of how to establish it. How could the same people Rousseau saw in the streets suddenly learn to think in terms of a "general will"? Perhaps an exceptionally wise and powerful legislator was needed at the start.

For all its contradictions, Rousseau's essay was part of the ideological battering ram that swept aside France's *ancien régime* in 1789 in the name of "the rights of men and citizens." The nation was sovereign, not the king. "Men" were born free and equal. The only purpose of political association was to preserve their rights to liberty, property, and security, and to resist oppression—and to make laws only through their duly chosen representatives. Those were the same liberal principles affirmed in the American Revolution, though in each case they proved less universal in practice than on parchment paper. In the United States, for example, the declaration of liberty and equality coexisted with slavery. Mary Wollstonecraft (1759–1797) respond to inequality with her *Vindication of the Rights of Women*, asking, among other things, why a society would deny itself the talents of half its population.

The problem of how to realize freedom and equality took on greater urgency as the Industrial Revolution drew more people into growing cities and factory work. The small, propertied political class fretted about the masses. Leading liberal thinkers argued that the rising tide of equality was unstoppable, but they also worried it would mean the triumph of mediocrity and threats to freedom as much from society as from the state. John Stuart Mill (1806–1873) in his essay *On Liberty* made the case for individual autonomy, short of harm to others. He based his argument not on natural right but on usefulness: the societal benefits of open debate and different ways of living. Mill proposed obligations on the state to support those, especially children, who would otherwise be disadvantaged by their upbringing. He championed the vote for women. Where the ancient Greeks and the early liberals demarcated household and polity as different associations, with different purposes and modes of authority, Mill's political philosophy was about the family as much as about parliament.

Alexis de Tocqueville (1805–1859) is arguably the more interesting thinker among those of the early modern period. His *Democracy in America*, which Mill read with great interest, described for Europeans the future he had seen in his travels: a new political project, a robust, literate pioneer society without an aristocracy to overcome, founded on practices of local democracy and not a centralized state. In America, he wrote, even religion was not the reactionary force it was in France. Rather, it functioned as one of several counterweights to the exercise of power, which democracy needed more than any other kind of regime.

Tocqueville's study, however, had a less cheery undertone. For there were new and subtle dangers inherent in the democratic society he had experienced. One was the spectre of a **tyranny of the majority**. Already in America, he said, there was more conformity in ideas than existed even in the conservative monarchies of Europe (vol. 1, 273). More troubling were the signs of what he called "soft despotism." People withdrew from public life into the privacy of their homes and personal pleasures, as their desire for security, equality, and happiness would be satisfied by the state—an "immense and tutelary power," albeit a gentle one. It would do things for people. But the effect would be to crowd out citizen initiatives and reduce democracy to voting in periodic elections (vol. 2, 334–48): "By this system the people shake off their state of dependence just long enough to select their master and then relapse into it again." They imagined themselves free, but were like "a flock of timid and industrious animals, of which the government is the shepherd" (vol. 2, 337). Tocqueville's warning about soft despotism should not be confused with the current chatter about downsizing government and cutting taxes. He was informed by a much older, richer tradition reaching back as far as ancient Greece. As one commentator has written, he was "perhaps the last influential theorist who can be said to have truly cared about political life" (Wolin 2001, 5).

Conclusion

THIS CHAPTER SKATES LIGHTLY OVER A FEW COMPLEX TEXTS AND A long political history. It says nothing about non-Western traditions. It leaves more radical ideas for Chapter 4. It is also unapologetic, however, about the importance of political philosophy as a form of inquiry. It offers a story and an interpretation of texts that are themselves part of the conversation and, as such, open to challenge. It is not the last word.

This chapter focused on ancient Greek and modern liberal clusters of that conversation. There are real differences between the two. Unlike the ancients, modern thinkers have tended not to start with questions of which regime is best, or to assume that politics was an ethical activity concerned with the good life and cultivation of virtues. Liberal thinkers in increasingly pluralistic societies have been reluctant to say what is good for everyone. They began with individuals, abstracted from communities in ways that would have made no sense to the Greeks. They endowed them with rights and reason, and regarded government as a created servant of the governed for limited purposes. They raised the status of property. They created room for religious minorities against church-state establishments. They assumed a more private definition of freedom as autonomy and non-interference. Ethically, they thought in terms of rights, civility, or else utility—the greatest good of the greatest number—but not about what made people virtuous.

That said, there is reason to treat political philosophy as one conversation. Modern thinkers, liberal and radical, have often been influenced by ancient texts; sometimes, in thinking about their own world, they have turned them upside down. On both sides, one of the puzzles observed here is that the conversation has been dominated by thinkers wary of politics and more likely to regard it as a necessary evil, a means to some other end, and not a good thing in itself. That may partly be a reflection of the kinds of dangerous circumstances that have evoked some of the most imaginative political thinking.

As this chapter was written, demonstrators had again packed the main square in Cairo—a reminder that politics is a serious endeavour with uncertain outcomes. It is an endeavour undertaken with words: rights, order, duty, faithfulness, democracy, justice, vengeance. What new meanings do those words graft across cultures? What aspirations and fears do they express? Who is inside and who is not? On what authority is a new regime to be founded? To what end? Who will stand far enough outside the fray to warn against excesses, new tyrannies, and tragic points of no return? These are not just tactical questions. You will recognize them as political philosophy.

Summary

The chapter:

- Introduced questions pursued by political philosophers over time
- Highlighted political philosophy's lack of "right" or easy answers, and an approach to the study as a conversation
- Presented a history of ideas, ancient and modern, in the Western tradition
- Encouraged continued reading of both ancient and modern thinkers

Discussion Questions

1. The chapter says that political philosophy has tended to distinguish the polity from the family as a different kind of association, with a different purpose and mode of authority. Is this defensible? Isn't a family just a small polity?

2. Have we arrived at the "soft despotism" that worried Tocqueville in the nineteenth century? What evidence would you cite? And what is the problem with it anyway?

3. Rank the following in order of importance: order, equality, democracy, justice, and freedom. Which two concepts in this list are most in tension?

4. Is it a fair measure of a political leader to ask whether she/he has left a polity better than she/he found it? What would "better" mean?

References

Al-Khalil, Samir. 1990. *The Republic of Fear: Inside Saddam's Iraq.* New York: Pantheon.

Arendt, Hannah. 2003. *The Promise of Politics.* Edited by Jerome Kohn. New York: Schocken.

———. 2005. *Responsibility and Judgment.* Edited by Jerome Kohn. New York: Schocken.

Aristotle. 1980. *The Politics*. Translated by T.A. Sinclair. Harmondsworth, U.K.: Penguin.

———. 1985. *Nichomachean Ethics*. Translated by Terence Irwin. Indianapolis, IN: Hackett.

Chan, Koonchung. 2011. *The Fat Years*. London: Random House.

Dorfman, Ariel. 2002. *Exorcising Terror*. New York: Seven Stories Press.

Hobbes, Thomas. 1994 [1651]. *Leviathan*. Edited by Edwin Curley. Indianapolis, IN: Hackett.

Kant, Immanuel. 1970 [1795]. "Perpetual Peace." In *Kant's Political Writing*, edited by Hans Reiss and H.B. Nisbet. Cambridge, U.K.: Cambridge University Press.

Locke, John. 1980 [1690]. *Second Treatise of Government*. Indianapolis, IN: Hackett.

Luther, Martin. 1974. *Selected Political Writings*. Edited by J.M. Porter. Philadelphia: Fortress Press.

Machiavelli, Niccolo. 1981 [c. 1514]. *The Prince*. Translated by George Bull. London: Penguin.

Mill, John Stuart. 1991. *On Liberty and Other Essays*. Oxford: Oxford University Press.

Pizan, Christine de. 1994 [c. 1407]. *The Body of the Body Politic*. Edited by Kate Langdon Forhan. Cambridge, U.K.: Cambridge University Press.

Plato. 1974. *The Republic*. Translated by G.M.A. Grube. Indianapolis, IN: Hackett.

———. 1975. *The Trial and Death of Socrates*. Translated by G.M.A. Grube. Indianapolis, IN: Hackett.

Rousseau, Jean-Jacques. 1968 [1762]. *The Social Contract*. Translated by Maurice Cranston. Harmondsworth, U.K.: Penguin.

Sophocles. 1984. *The Three Theban Plays*. Translated by Robert Fagles. Harmondsworth, U.K.: Penguin.

Thucydides. 1972. *The Peloponnesian War*. Translated by Rex Warner. Harmondsworth, U.K.: Penguin.

Tocqueville, Alexis de. 1945 [1835, 1840]. *Democracy in America*, 2 vols. Translated by Bradley Phillips. New York: Alfred A. Knopf.

Wang Hui. 2009. *The End of the Revolution: China and the Limits of Modernity*. London: Verso.

Wolin, Sheldon. 2003. *Tocqueville between Two Worlds: The Making of a Political and Theoretical Life*. Princeton, NJ: Princeton University Press.

Wollstonecraft, Mary. 2004 [1792]. *A Vindication of the Rights of Women*. Harmondsworth, U.K.: Penguin.

Yan Xuetong. 2011. *Ancient Chinese Thought, Modern Chinese Power*. Edited by Daniel Bell and Sun Zhe. Princeton, NJ: Princeton University Press.

Further Readings

Plato. 1974. *The Republic*. Translated by G.M.A. Grube. Indianapolis: Hackett.

Rousseau, Jean-Jacques. 1968 [1762]. *The Social Contract*. Translated by Maurice Cranston. Harmondsworth, U.K.: Penguin.

————. 1997 [1754]. *The Discourses and Other Early Political Writings.* Edited by Victor Gourevitch. Cambridge, U.K.: Cambridge University Press.

Tocqueville, Alexis de. 1945 [1835, 1840]. *Democracy in America,* 2 vols. Translated by Bradley Phillips. New York: Alfred A. Knopf.

Weblinks

Stanford Encyclopaedia of Philosophy: Liberalism
http://plato.stanford.edu/entries/liberalism

Stanford Encyclopaedia of Philosophy: John Locke
http://plato.stanford.edu/entries/locke

Stanford Encyclopaedia of Philosophy: Communitarianism
http://plato.stanford.edu/entries/communitarianism/

Stanford Encyclopaedia of Philosophy: Jean-Jacques Rousseau
http://plato.stanford.edu/entries/rousseau

"THEY SAID WE CAN OCCUPY THIS SPACE FOR AS LONG AS WE WANT..."

CHAPTER 3

DEMOCRATIC IDEAS

CATHERINE KELLOGG

Learning Objectives

- Places the ideas of democracy in historical context

- Defines democracy, public and private, freedom and citizenship

- Examines the crisis of modern democracy

- Speculates about democracy's future in the context of new uprisings and citizen demands

Introduction

It is safe to say that the idea of **democracy** is one of the most important concepts in modern politics. The word "democracy" has been with us a very long time, dating back to ancient Greece; however, the roots of modern ideas of liberal democracy, as practised by many countries today, lie in the Enlightenment of eighteenth-century Europe and the rise of capitalism. Given the apparent success of liberal democracies, like those found in the United States and Canada, some may be inclined to say that the story of democracy has already been told. Yet the sudden rise of new movements like Occupy Wall Street (OWS), the "retail riots" in the United Kingdom, and the demands for political reform and freedom across North Africa and the Middle East all suggest that the meaning of democracy and the types of politics that are practised in its name remain a subject for debate. In fact, key assumptions about governing, such as the nature of the capitalist market and its relationship with the state, are now being revisited and reformulated. Some would go so far as to suggest that liberal democratic forms of governance are in a period of profound crisis.

The word "democracy" comes from the Greek *demos* (people) and *kratos* (rule). Thus, democracy means the "rule of the many," which during ancient times was contrasted with the "rule of the few" (aristocracy) or the "rule of one" (monarchy). More recently, however, democracy has been used in reference to its literal meaning, the rule of the people. Simply put, democracy is any form of government in which the rules of society are decided by the people who will be bound by them. This is how the concept of democracy implicates the public; it suggests that public affairs, the rules of society, should be decided by the public itself. At the root of the practice of democracy lies a faith in the capacity of people to decide key issues of governance for themselves.

In this chapter, we review the history of democratic thought, focusing on key eras in its development, including Ancient Greece, the Middle Ages, and the Liberal revolution of the Enlightenment. The chapter next turns to key issues in contemporary democratic politics. Although there are many challenges to democratic governance in the contemporary era, we will focus on the public–private divide and the Arab Spring of 2010–11.

A Brief History of Democratic Theory

BEFORE EXAMINING THE HISTORY OF DEMOCRATIC THEORY, IT IS important to understand that we organize and make our lives meaningful through the process of constructing theories. Even, for instance, while performing mundane tasks, we do so within a set of assumptions that render that activity meaningful in some way. In this sense, all social life is based on theory—a compilation of ideas that tell a coherent story about a given human practice. Theorizing is an activity that goes on all the time, even if we are unaware of it.

Like every other kind of human activity, politics has its own set of theories. Political theories are interpretations—coherent stories that order and make sense of the world and politics. But at certain moments, the theories giving meaning to our political lives no longer seem to fit our experience or make sense. These are times of crisis. In fact, the history of political thought can be understood as the history of waves of *crises* that have forced human beings to reflect upon practices of human governance—democratic and otherwise. One of the most interesting things about the current state of democratic theory is that it is now at a point of crisis. This crisis stems from a variety of factors, including a general lack of confidence among citizens that they are being fully represented by democratic institutions, and growing social and economic inequality across the globe. In order to gain a sense of how democratic theories have developed over time and how the current crisis of democracy shapes our current politics, it is useful to trace its historical development.

Ancient Greek Democracy

The development of democracy in Athens during its "golden age," which lasted for about 50 years in the fifth century B.C.E., has been the source of inspiration for much modern democratic political thought. For instance, the modern ideals of equality before the law, liberty, and respect are often traced to the ancient Greek polis. This small, self-contained institutional model nurtured intense communal life. The polis informed the ethical concerns of subsequent thinkers as diverse as Thomas Hobbes, John Locke, Alexis de Tocqueville, Jean-Jacques Rousseau, and G.W.F. Hegel.

The Greek word "polis" is the root for a range of English words, including politics, politician, political, and police. While there is no exact English equivalent, polis is commonly translated as both "state" and "city" because it possesses the attributes of both. Central to the Athenian polis was smallness of scale. Although scholars do not agree on precise figures, it is estimated that some 300 000 people lived in Athens at its height. Only 40 000, however, were citizens. The rest of the population—women, children, foreign residents, and slaves—were excluded from the rank of citizen and from formal participation in political life. The "public" realm, then, was actually made up of a very small percentage of the inhabitants of the Greek city state. The small size of the polis allowed citizens to partake in a distinctive, communal way of life. Spheres of life we now consider non-political, such as religion, art, sport, and commerce, were all considered within the purview of politics. They were, therefore, subject to democratic deliberation. The small size of the polis also provided its citizens with a sense of active involvement in public affairs that has not been duplicated since then. Greek direct democracy was probably the most *participatory* form of politics that Western civilization has ever seen.

After flourishing for approximately 50 years, ancient Athens and its allies entered into a conflict with oligarchies that sided with Sparta. This conflict, known as the Peloponnesian Wars, ended with the complete defeat and occupation of democratic Athens. Precisely because the Greek city state, or polis, was in crisis, Plato and Aristotle were compelled to think about politics in a new way and to write their important works. For instance, the trial and execution of Socrates inspired Plato to question the validity of rule by those who were ignorant of the most pressing questions of the purpose of life. Perhaps, he suggested, Greek citizens were not truly able to rule themselves but required the leadership of those specifically trained in the art of state and soul craft. Despite the democratic nature of the ancient Greek state then, the political thinkers we most associate with ancient Greece—Plato, Aristotle, and Thucydides—were uniformly hostile to the direct democracy represented by the Greek polis.

Notwithstanding their hostility to democracy, both Plato and Aristotle were profoundly influenced by the participatory nature of the Greek city state. Significantly, Aristotle argued, "Man is a political animal." By this, he meant that human beings could attain their full potential only by living in political association with each other. It is only through active involvement in the life of their political community that citizens can know what is truly important. Thus, we can see that for the ancient Greeks, a good citizen was someone actively involved in day-to-day government.

The Middle Ages and Italian Republicanism

A strange silence in the history of democratic thought begins shortly after the demise of Athenian democracy and ends with the early Renaissance of fourteenth-century Europe. This period of silence overlaps significantly with what we call the medieval period, or the Middle Ages, which are meant to mark the "middle" period between the collapse of the Roman Empire in the fifth century and the beginning of the Renaissance in the fourteenth. This silence in the history of political thought is a complex matter to explain, but, in its simplest terms, the ascendancy of the Christian faith in the Western world and the rise of feudal forms of social organization meant that the "good" citizen of the Ancient Greek polis was replaced by the "true believer." The Greek world view, which suggested that political good could be found in active participation in public affairs, was replaced by political fatalism and the idea that everyone's fate was predetermined by God. The idea that humans could organize a common future democratically was supplanted by the belief that the "highest good" was to be found in afterlife, in the next world.

By the middle part of the medieval period, European social life was also dominated by **feudalism**. This form of social and economic organization was characterized by a strict hierarchal relationship between the property-owning aristocracy and the landless peasants, a structure that emphasized the deeply held belief that people were fundamentally unequal and that those who held power did so because they were essentially "better" than those whom they ruled. Feudalism itself existed against the backdrop of the Holy Roman Empire, with its governing structure of a complex web of kings and rulers who were understood to rule by "divine right"; that is, their authority came directly from God. In short, throughout the Middle Ages, European politics was determined by three great supra-national institutions: the Church, the Holy Roman Empire, and feudalism.

By the beginning of the sixteenth century, a number of political communities had established some form of popular control, especially in northern Italy. What eventually became the new "city states" or city republics were run by elected councillors. Councillors were ultimately accountable to male householders with taxable property. This notion of accountability represented an important challenge to the prevailing understanding that authority was God-given. This emerging social order was a return to the ideas of **civic republicanism** first articulated by Aristotle: active involvement in the state as a mark of good citizenship and of a good life. Recall that Aristotle regarded human beings as essentially political and able to flourish only when involved in making the important decisions of public life. Central to this concept is the notion of a political community with a shared history and a shared destiny. Thus, the **Renaissance** (literally, *rebirth*) was so named because it recalled many of the ideas of ancient Greek democracy.

Capitalism and the Liberal Revolution

The beliefs informing the Middle Ages were gradually but progressively disrupted by the revival of many of the ideals of Greek democracy (the Renaissance), a revolution against the traditional church, the Reformation of the sixteenth century, and the **Enlightenment** of the seventeenth century. The Enlightenment was a revolution against traditional philosophy and science. It was a social movement that sought to understand the world and humanity on a new basis. This period was accompanied by the growing belief that all people were equal because, no matter what their social position, each possessed the capacity for reason. The presumption of equality was revolutionary, because it led people to challenge the validity of political institutions that distributed power and wealth unequally among citizens. Legitimate political power was seen to emanate from the people themselves; people were the source of ultimate political and legal authority.

The Reformation and the Enlightenment were accompanied (and in some senses precipitated) by the end of feudal way of life and the rise of capitalism and market economies. While feudal society did have market activity—there were individual transactions of labour goods and services—it was not a market economy. Within feudalism, most economic activity was for the purposes of immediate consumption, rather than exclusively for resale. What was distinctive about capitalism was the newly emerging notion of private property and the accompanying right of an individual (or corporate entity) to exclude others from the use or benefit of it. Human labour also became a commodity that could be bought and traded on the market. The transformation from feudal forms of social organization—characterized by the predominance of the Church, absolutist sovereigns, and a landless peasantry—to a market of "free" producers and buyers was a complex one that had profound social, political, and cultural consequences. In short, the Reformation, the Enlightenment, and the emergence of capitalism were not separate events but, rather, events that reinforced each other.

These mutually reinforcing events are together known as the *liberal revolution,* a crisis in governing that marks the passing from feudal society to what we now recognize as capitalist modernity. An organic, hierarchical, traditional society was rapidly being replaced by an individualistic, fluid, and pluralist society in which reason replaced custom as a standard by which to judge policy and institutions. Perhaps the most graphic representations of this liberal revolution were the American Revolution of 1776 and the French Revolution of 1789. Both were dramatic uprisings against traditional, hierarchical forms of rule, and both were infused with the energy and enthusiasm of the liberal slogan, *liberty, equality, and solidarity.*

Early Liberal Democratic Theory

The dramatic changes in political rule in Europe and North America brought with them the most important variant of democratic thought: *liberal democratic theory.* This view was first articulated by such theorists as Thomas Hobbes, John Locke, and John Stuart Mill. The most important aspect of liberal democratic theory, and what distinguishes it from the models of democratic thought reviewed so far, was the belief in the importance of political, moral, and economic liberty. This variant of democratic theory clearly distinguished the public—understood as the institutions of the state—from the private. This was significantly different from the civic republicanism and the Greek *ethos* of the polis that preceded it. For both of the previous models, the *public* included some dimensions of human life that were consigned to the private sphere in the modern model.

The notion of freedom was very important to these liberal thinkers, but it was a very specific kind of freedom. As C.B. MacPherson explains, liberal democrats believed passionately in the freedom to pursue private property. Moreover, liberal democrats, no less than the democratic theorists who preceded them, had a distinct view of what constitutes human nature and a distinct view of the whole society in which the democratic political system operates.

According to liberal democrats, individuals are rational maximizers of self-interest. That is to say, for most liberal democrats, individuals will rationally choose what is in their own best interests, even when those interests are not necessarily those that grant them the most immediate satisfaction. For example, individuals will choose to live under a government that restricts some of their destructive activities because it will also restrict the destructive activities of others. Thus, they will rationally choose to outlaw theft and be policed because they will weigh their own desires to rob against the possibility of being robbed by others.

One of the most passionate defenders of this perspective was Thomas Hobbes. While he was no advocate of democracy in principle, his justification of government was that state authority, rather than monarchs or God, was created by individuals acting out of self-interest. People created the authority of the state to protect themselves from each other. Hobbes believed that individuals ought willingly to surrender their rights of self-government to a powerful single authority. Democracy, in this view, was the mechanism by which citizens could check the powers of the state against arbitrarily punishing its citizens.

John Locke revised Hobbes' argument with the view that "government" should be conceived as an instrument for the defence of "life, liberty and estate" (Locke 1965). One important difference between Hobbes and Locke is that whereas Hobbes emphasized democracy as a mechanism for protecting *individuals* from the state, Locke understood democracy as a mechanism for protecting the *market* from the state. And here is the second important assumption shared by classical liberal democrats: the society in which the democratic political system operates is understood to be a capitalist one. This is why, in Locke's view, the state should leave the "private" economic transactions of individuals entirely unregulated.

In the nineteenth century, John Stuart Mill developed his important objection to the purely formal dimensions of the position laid down by earlier liberal democrats. Mill went far beyond previous liberal democrats with respect to *moral* freedom. Mill formulated his theory with a view to protecting iconoclasts or "free thinkers" from the imposition of conventional or traditional morality. In this sense, Mill was passionately dedicated to the protection of minorities within a majoritarian system. Classical liberal democrats, then, constructed a relatively coherent theory of democracy. In it, the major institutions of modern governance—in particular, the various institutions of the state—were understood to be public and, therefore, subject to collective control. The modern distinction between the public realm of the state and the private, unregulated, and apolitical realms of the family and the economy was vital to this theoretical framework.

Under Pressure: Democratic Ideas Today

Public and Private: Democracy and the Public Sphere

When we think about the difference between public and private, there are a number of things that come to mind. We might think about public discourse versus private conscience, public services versus private property, or maybe even public work life versus private family life. When we think of what is most private, we are often thinking about what seems to lie most inward—what seems to be most intensely bound up with our "personal" lives, and what should, therefore, be of no interest to public or political life. But, of course, we also know that religious or moral beliefs, sexual feelings or identities, even private property and the so-called private family, are the objects of intense political debate and scrutiny. This last point is amply demonstrated by debates about gay marriage or the "it gets better" campaign designed to highlight problems of gender-variant students being bullied or debates about women wearing the veil when they take citizenship oaths. Things that are called "private" in each of these situations are, in fact, social and historical artifacts, which is to say that they are all objects of public debate and, in many cases, intense legal and state intervention.

For instance, private property means that an individual or a corporation has the exclusive right to the use of what belongs to them. On first glance, it might appear as though there has always been such a thing as this form of private property, and that life is unthinkable without it. However, the present form of private property is a political and social institution, protected by law, and guarded by the institutions of the state, including the judiciary, the police, and standing armies. More than half of those incarcerated in Canadian prisons are there for crimes against private property. What does it mean when banks and private institutions are making super-profits or when ordinary working people are becoming increasingly poor? How private is private property?

Another important way of thinking about what is private is in terms of what gets called "private life" or what can also be understood as one's personal, emotional, sexual, or conjugal life. This often also includes religious or moral beliefs. While it might seem that religious or moral beliefs are beyond the public, the political, or the social, some have suggested that these are in fact a response to what is most intensely political, social, and public; the response of those who have little power over their lives. As Marx said in the nineteenth century, "religious belief is the heart of a heartless world as it is the spirit of spiritless conditions" (Marx 1989, 28). As he put it, because the poor, the disenfranchised, or the most wretched of the earth feel that they have no control over their present lives, they dream of an afterlife, when they might finally find happiness. In so doing, they misrecognize the very human power to change the world and create it as a power that is superhuman.

And finally, of course, while it seems as though there is nothing more private than one's sexual and intimate life, debates about reproductive rights, the "age of consent," homosexuality, and gay marriage or debates about what can be taught in schools about sexual minorities indicate that there is an enormous machinery of state involvement, legislation, and public debate about these seemingly most private areas of our lives. In short, the line between what is understood as being private and as being public is always in question when one looks at this line from the perspective of the rule of the people.

Freedom and Democracy: Arab Spring

The freedom that is so often associated with the term *democracy* is not just freedom of religion, assembly, conscience, or free elections. It is also, perhaps more interestingly, the freedom of democracy's *form*, to put it in philosophical terms. Democracy's form is *free*, or without determinate content, insofar as its promise is always to include those not yet included. Democracy, at its heart, is a process that is always promising to include more and more under the umbrella of what is deemed "the people." We saw this idea at work most vividly in the widespread wave of protests and occupations that swept North Africa and the Middle East during the winter and spring of 2010–11. The hundreds of thousands who gathered in Tahrir Square in Cairo demanding the resignation of President Hosni Mubarak insisted that their voices be heard. With them, we saw the demand to make good on the claim that "the people" and not their rulers, have the ultimate power and authority for the governing of society. Those who demonstrated in Cairo found their legitimacy and global solidarity precisely in the idea of "the people." Some argue that these protests were not about democracy at all but about freedom from state repression. Whether a democracy or some other form of rule would emerge is another question.

What has become known as the "Arab Spring" was first sparked by the protests in Tunisia on December 18, 2010, when a 26-year-old fruit vendor named Mohamed Bouazizi set himself on fire to protest police violence. His family recounted that the police had harassed Bouazizi, fining him and making him jump through endless bureaucratic hoops. On December 17, 2010, when he was harassed yet again, he walked to the provincial capital building to complain and got no response. At the gate, he drenched himself in paint thinner and lit a match. This act, caught on cellphone cameras and spread through various social media, led to a widespread demand for democracy, first in Tunisia and then in Egypt.

In Egypt, Khaled Said's death at the hands of the Egyptian internal security service led to the creation of a Facebook group called "We are all Khaled Said" by bloggers interested in the unfolding events. The name soon became a rallying cry for a popular movement intent on bringing those responsible, be they security forces or political leaders, to justice. And in Sidi Bouzid and Tunis, in Alexandria and Cairo, in cities and towns across the 6000 miles from the Persian Gulf, and across Europe in Madrid, Athens, and London, uncontainable anger erupted toward governments and the networks of corrupt officials controlling the wealth, access to wealth, and running of these countries.

During this period of regional unrest, not only did Egyptian President Hosni Mubarak eventually step down, but several other leaders announced their intentions to step down at the end of their current terms as well. The president of Sudan, Omar al-Bashir, announced that he would not seek re-election in 2015, as did Nouri al-Maliki, the prime minister of Iraq whose term ends in 2014. President Ali Abdullah Saleh of Yemen announced on April 23, 2012, that he would step down within 30 days in exchange for immunity, a deal the Yemeni opposition informally accepted on April 26, 2012. Saleh then reneged on the deal, prolonging the Yemeni uprising. These protests have drawn global attention, and Yemen's Tawakel Karmen, a prominent leader in the Arab Spring, was one of the three laureates awarded the 2011 Nobel Peace Prize.

Many factors led to these uprisings, including human rights violations, government corruption, torture and violence, lack of transparency, economic decline, unemployment, extreme poverty, and unemployment among youth. The concentration of wealth in the hands of those who have been in power for decades, food prices, and the question of food security were fundamental. Many important critics have attempted to outline the reasons for this uprising. However, a video of a young girl explaining the uprisings in Egypt puts the situation in very simple and clear terms. As she said, "The president has a lot of money and the normal people, the no-money people, just have to work and no money" (www.huffingtonpost.com/2011/02/08/nina-explains-egypt_n_820371.html).

The freedom associated with democracy, then, is much more than freedom from oppression or freedom to vote or freedom of expression. It is also a kind of freedom that can express itself only under conditions where the people themselves become animated by a call *for* freedom, which sometimes involves rejecting received forms of politics.

Equality and Democracy: Occupy Wall Street Movement

In large part inspired by the Arab Spring, beginning in December 2012, a small group of dissidents in New York decided to refuse to recognize the legitimacy of the existing political authorities. They occupied a public space without asking for permission, declaring non-violently that the entire system was corrupt and they, therefore, rejected it. Willing to stand firm against the state's inevitable response, hundreds of thousands of Americans, Canadians, and Europeans, from Portland to Toronto, from Edmonton to Tuscaloosa, began rallying in support. The movement's early slogan, "we are the 99%," quickly went viral. Political analyst Jodi Dean suggests that the success of this simple slogan lies in the fact that it marks a sea change, in the situation of America in particular, capturing the fact that "people no longer believed the myths that greed is good and inequality benefits everyone" (Dean 2011). As Dean points out, the phrase "we are the 99%" highlights a division and a gap. It identifies the gap between the wealth of the top 1% and the rest of us. At the same time, as she notes, "the slogan asserts a collectivity." And it does not "unify this collectivity under a substantial identity—race, ethnicity, religion, nationality," but rather it asserts it as the "we" of a people divided between those who have obscene wealth and those who often struggle to make ends meet.

One of the most interesting dimensions of the Occupy movement, like the Arab Spring, was its use of various social media. On the one hand, the occupiers were very good at using social media such as Facebook and Twitter to let their supporters know what was happening and to communicate with one another. But on the other hand— inspired by the Zapatistas in Mexico who had no microphones and, therefore, had to improvise when trying to pass important messages across large groups of people—the human microphone became a moving and powerful way for those with a message to get their point across, as the speaker's message is passed from those closest, who repeat it, phrase by phrase, so that it travels across the space.

The Occupy movement is not the first movement based on direct action, direct democracy, and a rejection of existing political institutions. Nor is it the first movement that attempts to create alternative forms of power and alternative institutions. The civil rights movement, the women's movement, the environmental movement, and the global justice movement all took similar directions. Rarely, however, has any movement named the inequality between the very rich and the rest of us as its central concern, and none has grown so startlingly quickly and had such widespread popular support.

It may be too soon to say exactly what this movement is about. But one thing seems clear. The Occupy movement flourished amid widespread frustration among citizens who feel that something is terribly wrong with their country: that its key institutions are controlled by an arrogant elite, that these wealthy elite are somehow untouchable, and that radical change of some kind is long since overdue. The formal political equality promised by democracy is a paltry offering given the division in well-being and life chances between the 99% and the 1%.

Solidarity and Democracy: Friendship

Since Aristotle, democratic citizenship has been understood as a concept analogous to that of friendship; analogous to the Greek proverb that friendship is the "sharing of things in common." Democratic forms of solidarity have always been understood in terms of what we have in common—what we share. What we find in Aristotle, though, is in fact two versions of the friend: one who is just like me, a mirror or another self; and one who is very different from me, a stranger. As Aristotle first articulated it, democracy may be a community of friends who are "equals," but by that he meant a community of those who are *equally excellent or superior.* In a slave owning society like ancient Athens, this could only have referred to property-owning men.

However, we no longer live in a slave-owning society. Indeed, one of the things that such phenomena as the Occupy movement and the Arab Spring have insisted on is that *the equality of those who are all equally superior* is inadequate to contemporary forms of democracy.

How is democracy thought of as friendship re-oriented if I embrace the possibility that the friend is very different from me—a stranger who cannot be known in advance? This kind of stranger is no longer recognizable just in terms of nationality or ethnicity. Indeed, many people are excited about the kinds of solidarities that have emerged out of innovative use of new media and other technologies in the recent events we have just discussed. These include things like the image of Mohamed Bouazizi captured on cellphones and sent around the globe, the Facebook group "We are all Khaled Said" that mobilized people throughout the world, the use of new social media to organize spontaneous occupations and demonstrations, or low-tech alternatives like the human microphone. Clearly an equalizing instrument, democracy privileges solidarity over ego. Charisma, celebrity, and status all matter less over the human microphone.

What does it mean to think of solidarity not in terms of those with whom we share much, but in terms of those with whom we share the experience of being part of the 99%? What does it mean to think of solidarity no longer in terms of those with whom you share your nationality, your ethnicity, or even your state, but in terms of those with whom you share the mere fact of being human?

Conclusion

THIS CHAPTER HAS SURVEYED THE WAY IN WHICH DEMOCRATIC PRACTICES and theories have consistently raised the question of the relationship between what is "public" and what is "private." The fundamental premise of democracy is the importance of individual, political, moral, and economic *freedom.* But looked at from the perspective of the "rule of the people," the line between the public and the private is blurred. Specifically, the family and the market are carved off from what was understood as "public" and placed in the category of "private." They are, thus, outside the purview of those issues that traditionally concerned democratic politics.

But does democracy require *economic* or simply *political* equality? Does democracy imply the end of social discrimination? In the shift in emphasis from freedom to equality, many contemporary democratic theorists are challenging the validity of the claim that the market or the family is private and, therefore, outside the bounds of democratic deliberation. We investigated the major critical concepts associated with democracy— freedom, equality, and solidarity—using the contemporary examples of the Arab Spring, the Occupy movement, and new forms of social networking, to place these ideas in a context. We conclude that despite the apparent success of democracy as the dominant ideal and practice of governing worldwide, it remains an unfinished project.

Summary

The chapter:

- Told a history of the ideas of democracy from the ancient times to the present
- Defined democracy, public and private freedom, equality, and solidarity
- Examined the crisis of modern democracy
- Speculated about democracy's future in the context of new uprisings and citizen demands

Discussion Questions

1. Comment on the idea put forward here that democracy understood as "the rule of the people" implies a promise that more and more will be included in that category.

2. Do you think that democracy should imply economic as well as political equality in the way that those involved in the Occupy movement are suggesting?

3. Comment on the Occupy movement's claim that there is a fundamental division in our society between the 99% and the 1%.

4. Do you think that the new solidarities enabled by innovative uses of media are transformative? Or do you think that our allegiances to our nation or our religion are stronger than these new solidarities allow for?

References

Aristotle. 1948. *Politics.* Translated by Ernest Barker. Oxford: Oxford University Press.

Bernal, Martin. 1987. *Black Athena: The Afroasiatic Roots of Classical Civilization.* New Brunswick, NJ: Rutgers University Press.

Connolly, William. 1991. *Identity/Difference: Democratic Negotiation of Political Paradox.* Ithaca, NY: Cornell University Press.

Dahl, Robert. 1989. *Democracy and Its Critics.* New Haven, CT: Yale University Press.

Dean, Jodi. 2011. "Claiming Division: Righting a Wrong." *Theory and Event* 14(4), DOI:10.1353/tae.2011.0069.

Dworkin, Ronald. 1977. *Taking Rights Seriously.* Cambridge, MA: Harvard University Press.

Held, David. 1987. *Models of Democracy.* Cambridge, U.K.: Polity Press.

Hobbes, Thomas. 1977. *Leviathan.* Hammondsworth, U.K.: Penguin.

Keenan, Alan. 2003. *Democracy in Question: Democratic Openness in a Time of Political Closure.* Stanford, CA: Stanford University Press.

Kymlicha, Will. 1995. *Multicultural Citizenship.* Oxford: Oxford University Press.

Laclau, Ernesto. 1996. "Deconstruction, Pragmatism, Hegemony." In *Deconstruction and Pragmatism,* edited by Chantal Mouffe. New York: Routledge.

Locke, John. 1965. *Second Treatise on Government.* New York: Mentor Press.

MacPherson, C.B. 1965. *The Real World of Democracy.* Toronto: CBC Publications.

———. 1977. *The Life and Times of Liberal Democracy.* Oxford: Oxford University Press.

Marx, Karl and Friedrich Engels. 1968. "The Communist Manifesto." In *Selected Works.* London: Lawrence and Wishart.

———. 1969. "Towards a Critique of Hegel's Philosophy of Right." In *Selected Works.* London: Lawrence and Wishart.

McIntryre, Alasdaire. 1981. *After Virtue.* Notre Dame, IN: University of Notre Dame Press.

Mouffe, Chantal. 1994. *The Return to the Political.* London: Verso.

Philips, Anne. 1991. *Engendering Democracy.* Cambridge, U.K.: Polity Press.

Rawls, John. 1971. *A Theory of Justice.* Cambridge, MA: Harvard University Press.

Rousseau, Jean-Jacques. 1964. *A Discourse on the Origins of Inequality.* New York: St. Martin's Press.

Sandel, Michael. 1984. *Liberalism and Its Critics.* Oxford: Clarendon Press.

Taylor, Charles. 1992. *Multiculturalism and the Politics of Recognition.* Princeton, NJ: Princeton University Press.

Trend, David, ed. 1996. *Radical Democracy: Identity, Citizenship and the State.* London: Routledge.

Wolin, Sheldon. 1996. "Norm and Form: The Constitutionalization of Democracy." In *Athenian Political Thought and the Reconstruction of American Democracy.* Princeton, NJ: Princeton University Press.

Further Readings

Aristotle. 1948. *Politics*. Translated by Ernest Barker. Oxford: Oxford University Press.

Brown, Wendy. 2006. "Subjects of Tolerance: "Why We Are Civilized and They Are Barbarians." In *Political Theologies: Public Relations in a Post-Secular World*, edited by H. de Vries and L.E. Sullivan. New York: Fordham University Press.

Held, David. 1987. *Models of Democracy*. Cambridge, U.K.: Polity Press.

———. 1995. *Democracy and the Global Order*. Oxford: Polity Press.

MacPherson, C.B. 1973. *Democratic Theory: Essays in Retrieval*. Oxford: Oxford University Press.

Tocqueville, Alexis de. 1946. *Democracy in America*. New York: Knopf.

Wolin, Sheldon. "Fugitive Democracy." In *Democracy and Difference: Contesting the Boundaries of the Political*, edited by Seyla Benhabib. Princeton, NJ: Princeton University Press.

Wood, Ellen Meiksins. 1995. *Democracy Against Capitalism*. Cambridge, U.K.: Cambridge University Press.

Weblinks

Amnesty International
www.amnesty.org/ailib/intcam/femgen/fgm1.htm

Canadians for Direct Democracy
www.npsnet.com/cdd

Canadian Centre for Policy Alternatives
www.policyalternatives.ca

Democracy Watch
www.dwatch.ca

CHAPTER 4

RADICAL IDEAS

SANDRA REIN

Learning Objectives

- Defines radical ideas and their subsequent ideologies as key concepts for understanding modern politics

- Examines modern political ideologies that have been particularly influential

- Traces the lineage of these ideologies in contemporary politics

Introduction

What do Islamic Jihad, Al-Qaeda, Occupy Wall Street, the International Socialists, the World Social Forum, the Tea Party, the Nationalist Socialist Movement, and the Arab Spring all have in common? All are political movements founded on critiques of the root causes of various social problems, as defined by the movement itself. Each movement has identified and proscribed very different solutions to what they regarded as society's ills, but these solutions are all based on radical ideas. On the political spectrum, these movements can be identified as on the far Right to on the far Left. Their prescriptions for society often display no commonality at all, some rooted in religious fundamentalism and others in exclusive secularism. But all are radical.

In this chapter, we will explore radical ideas and their congealment into political ideologies. Over time, it is often the case that ideas that were once very radical become accepted as dominant social ideas. A powerful example of such a transformation is liberal democracy. At one time in history, only a few political reformers argued that all individuals had a right to participate in politics as free and equal citizens. However, today in most parts of the world, it is hardly viewed as radical to think that suffrage should be universally shared among citizens, and that women should be able to cast a vote just as men do. In other words, ideas that are radical are also ideas that have a very specific history, context, and meaning. Attaching the label "radical" to an idea does not indicate that it is desirable or undesirable, but only that it challenges other dominant ideas. Decisions on desirability are a matter of timing, political judgment, and ethics.

Saying What We Mean

In order to discuss the relationship between ideas and political practice, it is essential that we clearly define what we mean when we invoke such words as **"radical"** and "ideas." When one hears the word "radical," undoubtedly images of armed insurgents come to mind, or, if one is more generously disposed, perhaps images of 1970s-styled hippies, or "granolas." However, underlying both images is a pejorative assessment of radicalism—that these are people with ideas designed to overthrow the world as we know it. Yet, if we take time to really examine radicalism, we find a more nuanced meaning that does not simply invoke senseless extremism. Rather than beginning our analysis by pre-judging radical thought, we are better served by seeing it as critical social theory. The Latin origin of radical is *radic*, meaning root. Radical ideas propose to go to the root of a problem, and to critique society by addressing its root problems. The definition of the "root problem," as we will see in our discussion of different radical ideas, varies greatly, depending on the social theory of the radicals engaged in the critique. Regardless of the ideas being engaged, all radical projects are based on a critique of status quo political arrangements and distributions of political power. The determination of the desirability of radical ideas and projects revolves around one's political judgment and popular assessments of the fit between radical ideas and lived experience.

Before turning to the definition of ideas, a word should be said about the notions of "Left" and "Right" in politics. As suggested above, radical ideas and political projects aim to uproot existing society. However, you have likely heard politics characterized as "left wing" or "right wing." Often, when considering radical projects, we will also characterize these as the "radical left" or the "radical right." This particular geography of the political spectrum originated in the French Revolution. As Steger recounts, the French National Assembly in 1789 faced the question of the royal veto over legislation. Those who opposed the royal veto on the basis of popular sovereignty aligned themselves on the left of the Assembly and those who supported the royal veto aligned themselves on the right of the chamber. For those who supported a conditional veto, space was reserved in the centre (Steger 2008, 22). In very general terms, when we invoke terms like Left or left wing today, we are indicating radical political projects that embrace revolutionary change in the name of oppressed groups (for example, workers or colonized peoples). Right or right-wing labels are assigned to projects that may still be radical in the sense of changing the status quo, but they are often undertaken in the name of very conservative values and sometimes closely linked to religious movements (such as the Christian Right in the United States). For our purposes in this chapter, we will examine radical movements from both the Left and the Right.

The study of ideas has a long and contested history in the social sciences. Generally, when studying ideas, we refer to the merged constellation of concepts, theories, and political projects as **ideologies**. Much like the word "radical," the word "ideology" also raises negative connotations in the minds of most people. As renowned social theorist Terry Eagleton once quipped, "ideology, like halitosis, is in this sense, what the other person has" (Eagleton 1991, 2). However, in the social sciences, ideology has served as an analytical concept that has embedded within it much more textured and nuanced meanings. The systematic study and organization of ideas and concepts can be traced back to Aristotle, but the modern usage of the term *ideology* arises from the French Revolution. First put into print by Antoine Louis Claude Destutt, Comte de Tracy, ideology was generally understood to mean the study of ideas. At the turn of the nineteenth century, a group known as the *Ideologues* committed themselves to understanding how ideas come to be formed and transmitted in society. Tracy and the Ideologues were scholars who were also interested in relating the concepts of the French Revolution to the building of a French Republic; linking ideas and practice was seen as paramount to realizing the successful triumph of the Revolution (Steger 2008, 1). Although the trajectory of the French Revolution is beyond our scope here, it is interesting to note that while the Ideologues were attempting the rational study of ideas and their social importance, their work was quickly demonized by the rising political star, Napoleon Bonaparte. As Manfred Steger recounts, it was the "wily Emperor" who won out "for it was [Napoleon's] pejorative connotation that stuck in the public mind" (Steger 2008, 2). Napoleon's chief argument against ideology was that it meddled in state affairs; the scientific study of ideas was also attempting to articulate a political vision for the French Republic that did not coincide with Napoleon's ambitions (Steger 2008, 34).

Ideology as a Negative Concept

The negative connotation of ideology as the promotion of misleading ideas was further developed by the work of Karl Marx and Friedrich Engels. Marx and Engels argued that bourgeois ideology acted as a *camera obscura*, inverting the real-life experiences of human beings to conform to ideas supporting capitalism. In particular, they argued that the alienation of workers and their class struggle with the owners of the means of production (the bourgeoisie) was obscured by ideas of liberal individualism and laissez-faire economics (Marx and Engels 1976, 36). Ideology, to Marx and Engels, distorted the reality of workers' lives and social organization in favour of the ruling interests of society. For subsequent theorists in the Marxist tradition, ideology came to be equated with the notion of *false consciousness*, which promoted bourgeois ideas that obscured the real causes of working-class oppression.

Marx and Engels were not alone in identifying ideology as a set of ideas that serves to distort reality. Several key political philosophers and sociologists also apply a negative conception of ideology to all forms of political radicalism. However, these authors also argue that ideology, even as it distorts reality, often provides a positive goal around which people can contest the political status quo and bring about social change. Georges Sorel (1847–1922), for example, used the word "myth" rather than ideology when referring to the narratives developed by social groups, particularly political movements, to generate solidarity among members (Sargent 1996, 9).

Another example from the Marxist tradition can be found in the work of Italian communist Antonio Gramsci (1891–1937). Gramsci, who was imprisoned by the Italian Fascists in the 1930s, wrote extensively about the political importance of ideology. His idea of hegemony is particularly relevant to this discussion. Gramsci argued that the success of modern rulers and ruling classes was only assured by their ability to establish a hegemonic position in society. By this he meant that the ruling class must enjoy widespread popular support for its ideas. However, Gramsci also insisted that no hegemonic project is complete. There is always critical space for groups with different ideas to challenge the values and consensus being promoted by the ruling class. Gramsci called these counter-hegemonic movements. While Gramsci's analysis maintained Marx and Engel's original insight about the distorting nature of dominant ideologies—that is, that they serve the interests of the ruling class—the strength of his analysis lies in drawing attention to groups and ideas that constantly arise to challenge that hegemony.

Ideology as a Neutral Concept

As mentioned above, the original intent of Tracy's approach to ideology was to create a scientific study of ideas and how they relate to society. This neutral approach to the study of ideas was effectively reinvigorated in the twentieth century by the work of Karl Mannheim (1893–1947). Although Mannheim agreed with Marx and others that ideology serves the interest of the ruling class, he wanted to understand how different ideas come to be held by specific segments of society. Through his study, Mannheim differentiated between *particular* and *total* conceptions of ideology. While the particular conception concerned the beliefs and values held by individuals, the total conception of ideology allowed Mannheim to investigate how historical groups are formed as a result of commonly held beliefs and values. The result of his analysis was the creation of five ideological ideal types, which he termed "historical political parties." From his development of ideological ideal types, Mannheim was able to demonstrate the value of tracing ideas through various social formations. Building on this work, anthropologist and social theorist Clifford Geertz (1926–2006) argued that ideologies only emerge when there is significant social disruption and political dislocation. For Geertz, ideologies play an important role by filling in when reality is no longer clear. Ultimately, ideology plays an important social role by providing people and groups with a necessary point of reference for making sense of the world around them.

Ideology Today

The role of ideology fuels an ongoing debate among political scientists. In 1990, scholar Terry Eagleton undertook a study of the legion of definitions surrounding the term *ideology*. Eagleton found that there are more than 16 different uses commonly invoked by scholars. For Eagleton, and for our purposes here, it is useful to find a definition that allows us to recognize the importance of ideology in shaping politics without falling victim to overly negative connotations (Eagleton 1991). Drawing on Eagleton's analysis, we need to think about ideology as key sets of those beliefs and values that serve to legitimize a certain social order and those values and beliefs that may be said to oppose or challenge the dominant social order. Steger succinctly defines ideology as ". . . comprehensive belief systems composed of patterned ideas and claims to truth" (Steger 2008, 5). This straddling of the neutral and negative conceptions allows us to study the relationship of politics and ideas without losing sight of the fact that there is a great deal at stake for individuals, groups, and societies when certain ideas prevail over others.

What Do We Get When We Combine Radical and Ideology?

IDEOLOGIES AS SETS OF BELIEFS AND VALUES ARE AN ESSENTIAL part of the armoury that political movements use to challenge and undermine, and sometime displace, status quo political orders. As mentioned before, liberal ideas taken up by large groups of people provided fuel for the American and French Revolutions. Although there are many ideologies in circulation at any given time, in modern times, arguably only a handful have had a lasting effect on the distribution of political power and social structures. Here, we examine three key ideologies: **socialism**,

communism, and **fascism**. In the subsequent section, we will examine other ideologies that have emerged either out of these key historical ideologies or as a challenge to them. Of course, there are other ways to categorize the ideas driving political processes today, but these three draw together the most radical critiques of modern society and provide the foundation for various movements, projects, and political contests around the globe. It is important to remember that these are not definitive lists of radical political ideologies, but samples that provide us with the foundations for making political judgments.

Socialism

Contemporary references to socialism are usually framed as pejoratives, especially in the North American context. However, it is not possible to think of socialism as a single idea; in fact, there are many socialisms. The intellectual heritage of the key ideas of socialism are generally traced to Rousseau's critique of the differences in property ownership, the concept of organic society, and the belief that individuals can aspire to the greater good, which are laid out in his two most famous works: *Discourse on the Origin and Foundations of Inequality Among Men* (1754) and *The Social Contract* (1762) (Baradat 1988, 170). Another important early socialist was Francis Babeuf (1760–1797). He advanced an extreme socialism that called for revolutionary transformation and the existence of an elite corps to lead the masses to revolution. Generally, socialism offers a critique of the way that society offers access to property and social goods (such as education and health care), privileging social elites. Historically, socialists advocated the revolutionary, rather than evolutionary, restructuring of all social relations. Typically, socialism can be delineated as having utopian, scientific, and democratic strains. Each is briefly discussed below.

Utopian Socialism

Utopian socialists tended to depart from the notion of revolutionary change and, instead, advocated for the public ownership of the means of production (industry), for democratic social organizations, and for the eradication of all want in society. It should be acknowledged, however, that utopian socialists did not themselves adopt the term *utopian*; it was applied to their thinking by other socialists as a means of discrediting the ideas. Robert Owen (1771–1858) is identified as the "father" of utopian socialism. Ironically, Owen was a successful industrial capitalist who embarked on realizing his utopian vision after retiring from business. He was convinced that his factories had been productive because he treated his employees ethically. To prove his point, Owen participated in setting up communes on the principles of economic self-sufficiency and democratic decision making. The New Harmony commune, established in 1825 in Indiana, is recognized as one of Owen's most successful attempts at communal living. New Harmony ultimately failed, however, because of an inability to be economically independent and to sustain democratic group decision making.

Scientific Socialism

When people invoke the term *socialism* today, they are usually gesturing at scientific socialism and the theoretical work of Karl Marx and Friedrich Engels. In fact, it is nearly impossible to discuss socialism without drawing from the thought of Marx and others who carried on the Marxist tradition (for example, Rosa Luxemburg, Leon Trotsky, and Vladimir Lenin). However, it is useful to distinguish between Marxism and scientific socialism, because Marxism is about a method of analysis and scientific socialism (while sharing the method) is attached to organizations such as the 1st and 2nd Communist Internationals.

Marxist political thought is first and foremost distinguished by its method, which is a dialectical method known as the materialist conception of history or **historical materialism**. At the risk of oversimplification, this approach led Marx to examine society by looking at how things are produced. He called this the *mode of production*. The elements that are actually producing things he called the *means of production*. Although Marx engaged in historical analysis, he primarily wanted to understand how capitalism organized production, and to assess the key class antagonism that developed between the owners of the means of production (the bourgeoisie) and the means of production (the proletariat). In his very in-depth and detailed studies of capitalist society, which was emerging during the Industrial Revolution, Marx found that human beings were forced into wage labour in order to sustain their lives and families. In so doing, they created **surplus value** for capitalists. This meant that workers produced more value for the industrialists than that for which they were compensated. This wage-capital relationship, as Marx termed it, was a new social relationship that turned human beings into commodities and created conditions for ever-increasing levels of exploitation by the industrial owners in an attempt to realize more surplus value from each worker in each hour of employment. Today, we are very familiar with the ideas of off-shore production, flexible labour contracts, and corporations chasing ever-cheaper sources of labour around the globe. In Marx's time, however, this was an entirely new phenomenon and its social and political implications were not apparent.

Marx speculated that workers would face diminishing working conditions and ultimately revolt against the production conditions to which they were subjected. Moreover, Marx discovered that over time there is a tendency for the rate of profit to fall (across all industry), leading to general capitalist crises. Marx's analysis culminated in what we know today as the three volumes of *Capital* (although only Volume I was published while Marx was alive) and provides the foundation for many Left radical political projects across the globe. The core of Marx's analysis and its application to modern conditions of global capitalism is hotly debated among political activists and scholars alike. The type of socialism advocated by Marx and subsequent Marxists was known as scientific socialism, both to distinguish it from utopian forms and to highlight its links to Enlightenment notions of rationality and science. Scientific socialism, in most cases, drew on Marx's analysis to provide the theoretical basis for a political program that demanded the overthrow of capitalism.

Democratic Socialism or Social Democracy

Where scientific socialism retained a commitment to overturning capitalism through revolution, socialist thinking favoured evolutionary change through political parties that advanced notions of mixed public-private enterprise, more robust social welfare provisions than typically found in liberal democracies, and more grassroots, democratic decision making within states as well as more democratic decision making in international institutions. Social democracy retains some of the Marxist critiques of capitalism and is a strong advocate of workers' rights and labour organizations. In a contemporary context, social democracy remains a cornerstone of many Western European political parties. In 2012, for example, France elected a socialist president and a socialist-controlled legislative assembly. In Canada, the socialist-leaning Co-operative Commonwealth Federation (CCF), founded in the depths of the Great Depression of the 1930s, formed the government in Saskatchewan in the 1940s, and introduced the first universal health care program in Canada.

Communism

In many ways, communism is the most difficult ideology to define of those we are discussing in this chapter. This is due to the fact that many revolutions in the twentieth century called themselves communist; for example, the former Soviet Union, China, Cuba, North Korea, and the former Yugoslavia. With the demise of many of these communist regimes, we are left with the sense that communism is a failed experiment, a political ideology that was "good in theory" but did not work in practice. This is far too simplistic a dismissal of communism. Many traditional Marxists were highly critical of the Soviet and Chinese experiments in particular. As with all ideologies, there is often a large gap between political ideas and their concrete expression in political actions and institutions.

In theory, communism was seen as a final stage of human emancipation following the overthrow of capitalism and a temporary "socialist" moment through which the state would "wither away." Communist society would involve the social ownership of the means of production (factories and so on), absolute social equality (a classless society), and the end of the national state as we know it. For Marx and many others espousing communism, its ethic is embedded in the famous statement "from each according to his abilities, to each according to his needs" (Marx 1989, 87). Much of communist ideology is derived from the work of Marx, although he actually wrote very little about the shape and scope of a post-revolutionary society. Other Marxists began to develop a more defined picture of communism. Most notable among them is V.I. Lenin (1870–1924). Lenin's project was to translate Marx's theory into political action. He was uniquely positioned to do so because he was one of the key leaders of the Russian Revolution. Lenin was consumed by two interests: to understand how capitalism worked internationally and to understand how to organize a successful revolution. With regard to the latter concern, Lenin developed the notion of the vanguard party. Lenin argued that to successfully organize a revolution, it would be necessary to have a well-trained cadre of dedicated revolutionaries who would work tirelessly for the success of the revolution. Following the revolution, this vanguard would ensure the nationalization of all heavy industry and the "dictatorship of the proletariat."

Following Lenin's death in 1924, Joseph Stalin came to power in the Soviet Union. Stalin consolidated his personal authority through bloody purges and political intrigue and challenged one of the fundamental precepts of Marx's thought. Marx argued that socialism had to be an international project. Stalin, in contrast, contended that "socialism in one country" was not only possible (as proven by the USSR) but also desirable. To this end, Stalin implemented intense industrialization and centralized planning, which have become the hallmark of communist ideology although neither was theorized by Marx.

Like Stalin, Mao Tse-tung (1893–1976), who led the Chinese revolution, also significantly revised Marx's theory, particularly in relation to the revolutionary role of the peasants. Mao's communist reforms focused on collectivization of farming, as opposed to the Soviet model of rapid industrialization. Although China today is an industrial powerhouse producing a substantial portion of global consumer goods, it would be very difficult to argue that it is a communist state as one would envision from the notions of a classless society, social ownership of production, or the redistribution from ability to need.

While the twentieth-century experiments in communist government appear to have failed, there remains lively and engaged political debate about finding alternatives to capitalism and the grotesque social inequalities that it generates, especially in the contemporary era.

Fascism

Socialism and communism are associated with Left thinking. They propose a massive redistribution of wealth, resources, and power from elites and governing classes to workers and oppressed peoples. At their best, they propose real, democratic decision making that goes beyond the liberal democratic notion of representative democracy with regular elections. All socialist and communist thought calls for democracy to penetrate beyond legislatures to the very core of society, including the production of goods and necessities. Fascism, however, is a radial project that is best understood as emerging from the Right.

If communist ideology is difficult to pin down because of the divergence between theory and practice, fascism presents an equally difficult exercise in definition because it could be said to have existed more in practice than theory. Political scientists approach fascism in a historically contingent fashion. They tend to study it in the context of the fascist parties of pre-World War II, in particular those that "won" popular support in Germany (National Socialism or Nazism) and Italy (the Nationalist Fascist Party). In Germany, the party was headed by Adolf Hitler and in Italy, it was headed by Benito Mussolini. Although there are significant differences between the German and Italian experiences, some similarities are also apparent. Most importantly, fascist thought has been ultra-nationalist in its orientation. Citizens are called upon as a collective to make sacrifice for the nation above all else. Sacrifice and indoctrination are handled through national youth organizations, for example, and groups that are seen as resistant (for example, members of communist parties, minority ethnic and religious groups, social non-conformists) are to be excluded from the nation. In the case of Nazism, ultra-nationalism was also attached to the belief in "Aryan superiority," which laid the groundwork for the mass expulsion and execution of Jews, Romanies, Slavic peoples, the mentally ill or disabled, lesbians and gays, and other racialized minority groups. The fascist states of Germany and Italy also were characterized by charismatic leadership and the accommodation of business interests and free enterprise, rather than the nationalization of industry. Finally, both Germany and Italy manifested a desire for expansion throughout Europe and abroad, enacted in part through strong national militaries and the promotion of militarism throughout society. It is also important to note that the way in which the fascists came to power in both Italy and Germany was enacted not through the revolutionary overthrow of government, but by popular election. Moreover, once in power, the fascists continued to utilize the notion of the "rule of law" to create constitutional and legislative frameworks for fascist policies. The use of rule of law was most developed in Germany, where the Nuremburg laws were enacted to disenfranchise German Jews from civic life and to establish the guidelines to legally protect "German blood and honour."

While one aspect of the academic study of fascism is directed at defining what constitutes the ideology, another aspect that has gripped many social scientists since the end of World War II is finding an explanation for the rise of fascism and, in particular, its genocidal compulsion as demonstrated by the Nazi regime. This second aspect of scholarship is particularly important to those who want to ensure that such regimes never again gather popular support or carry out such devastating loss of life. In the post-World War II environment, attempts have been made to create international agreements, frameworks, and laws to protect the human rights of all peoples and to be able to respond to instances of genocide. However, as the 1994 Rwanda genocide so graphically demonstrated, the desire for "never again" has yet to be met with workable measures in international politics. Moreover, scholars working in this area remind us that many of the xenophobic and ultra-national ideals of fascism continue to make their presence felt in a variety of ultra–Right wing, anti-immigration parties across Europe and the "white pride" movement, which has a significant presence in North America and Western Europe. In fact, in 2012, the Golden Dawn, a modern-day fascist party, won 21 seats in Greece's elected assembly. If we think back to Geertz's suggestion that ideologies emerge in instances of significant social disruption—as was certainly the case in the late 1920s and 1930s when these ideas attracted masses of followers— then we need to be particularly attentive to the nature of the ideologies emerging in this time of social dislocation and economic hardship.

'Isms for Today?

SOCIALISM, COMMUNISM, AND FASCISM HAVE HAD SIGNIFICANT impacts on various states since their emergence onto the historical stage. Before turning to the "progeny" of these ideologies, it is worthwhile to add one more historical "ism" to the list; that is, **anarchism**. Anarchism is not included in the "key" historical ideologies because (and the obvious reasons will become apparent in discussing its tenets) anarchism has not had the same widespread impact as the three ideologies we have already covered. Nonetheless, it shares a general historical lineage with these three and has a tendency to be taken up by youth activists in particular. Self-proclaimed anarchists, for example, have been a visible and loud component of recent anti-globalization rallies and the Occupy Wall Street protests.

Anarchism

Defined most simply, anarchism is the rejection of hierarchical forms of governance. Yet this definition fails to capture the rich history of anarchist thought. Anarchism as a political ideology became popular in the early nineteenth century in response to the Industrial Revolution. Since that time, subscribers to anarchist thought have organized in most industrialized countries. Generally, anarchist thinking can be divided into two distinct categories: social or collectivist versus individualist anarchism. We will examine each in turn.

Social Anarchism

Pierre-Joseph Proudhon (1809–1865) was the first political thinker to call himself an anarchist. Proudhon is best remembered for his answer to the question, "What is property?" He replied, "Property is theft." Proudhon outlined the key elements of anarchism that would see the eradication of the state and the free and harmonious association of individuals. Specifically, Proudhon advocated the organization of workers into syndicates that would collectively make all decisions about production and collectively share ownership. Proudhon's form of anarchism is often referred to as anarcho-syndicalism. Anarchist syndicate experiments did enjoy some short-lived success in Spain between 1936 and 1939. However, these syndicates obtained worker control through violent means, in contrast to Proudhon's non-violent prescription.

One of the best-known anarchists, Mikhail Bakunin (1814–1876), believed that violence was necessary to achieve an anarchist society. Closely associated with social (or communist) anarchism, Bakunin argued that revolution would be achieved by arming the most undesirable elements of the population. Clearly, one of the most radical anarchists, Bakunin left a legacy of his strong belief in the necessary role of violence in effecting social change. Another well-known anarchist who subscribed to Bakunin's radicalism is Emma Goldman (1869–1940), who carried her anarchist message throughout the United States, the Soviet Union, and Canada. A tireless radical, Goldman was also outspoken on issues concerning women's rights and was particularly active in working for the legalization of contraception for women.

In her later years, however, Goldman became less committed to violent overthrow, largely because of the influence of Peter Kropotkin (1842–1921). Kropotkin argued that society was more likely to progress through cooperation than aggression. Also a communist anarchist, Kropotkin believed that the modern state was "the personification of injustice, oppression, and monopoly" (Kropotkin 1926, 29). Kropotkin's vision of anarchist society was one of harmony and cooperation. He rejected the idea that revolutions were the best way to change social organization. He also believed that industrial progress and technology would eventually eradicate human want. Once this level of technological advancement had occurred, Kropotkin believed, society would evolve to communism.

Noam Chomsky is likely the best-known, self-professing anarchist today. A linguist by training, Chomsky has made it his life's work to "speak truth to power" and reveal a myriad of foreign policy failures and outright lies on the part of the U.S. government. As Chomsky eloquently writes,

> Anarchism, in my view, is an expression of the idea that the burden of proof is always on those who argue that authority and domination are necessary. They have to demonstrate, with powerful argument, that that conclusion is correct. If they cannot, then the institutions they defend should be considered illegitimate. How one should react to illegitimate authority depends on circumstances and conditions: there are no formulas. (Chomsky 1996, www.chomsky.info/interviews/19961223.htm)

Individualist Anarchism

Individualist anarchist thought is historically associated with Max Stirner (1806–1856), who nicely summarized his political ideology with the slogan "The people are dead. Up with me!" Stirner represents individualist anarchism at its most extreme. A softer variant of Stirner's philosophy is found in libertarianism, which continues to have a significant impact on contemporary politics, especially in the United States. Libertarianism is closely associated with the work of Robert Nozick, who asserts the "pre-eminent right" of private property.

Libertarians reject government intervention in areas of social life and economic markets, although they concede the need for a very limited government. Threads of libertarian thought run through the rhetoric of political movements and political parties that promise to "downsize government" and to liberate the "free market." In the lead up to the 2012 Republican Convention in the United States, candidate Ron Paul offered a libertarian vision to Americans that promised a return to personal responsibility and freedom from government intervention. Although Paul did not secure the Republican nomination, his campaign caught the attention of many younger voters and demonstrated the attractiveness of libertarian thought to many people who feel frustrated by the ineffectiveness of modern government.

From the "People of '68" to "Occupy" to the "Maple Spring"

In May 1968, students in Paris organized a sustained revolt, supported by industrial workers, which spread across the country; some would say around the world. Although there are many interpretations of the events and the conditions that fostered them, what is clear is that the student protestors were drawing on critiques of capitalist society and calling for revolutionary change. These protests were not exclusive to France and, in fact, took place worldwide. In the United States, opposition to the Vietnam War was a major catalyst for organizing protest groups, which engaged in critiquing American society and challenging American imperialism around the globe. To sustain their radical commentary, these varied movements drew on Marx's critique of capitalist society and the anarchist tendency toward open, non-hierarchical forms of social organization. The commune movement within "hippie culture" was itself an attempt to practise a form of communist social organization. In short, the radical politics of the nineteenth century was adapted to the critical practices of the mid-twentieth century.

The radicalism of the 1960s also gave form and substance to the U.S. Civil Rights Movement that overturned racial segregation in the United States, and a global women's movement that demanded meaningful equality. Outside of Western Europe and North America, the ideas that mobilized student protests and an anti-war movement also inspired liberation movements in Africa and ignited socialist projects in places such as India and Chile. And, not coincidentally, the last "proto-fascist" rulers in Spain and Portugal also fell to popular uprisings (sometime aided by the military) in the early 1970s. Even in the context of Cold War propaganda, the ideas of Marx, Lenin, and various anarchists and the attainment of a communist ideal still held sway with large numbers of workers, students, women, youth, people of colour, and other activists. In other words, even when the historical political project that first arose from a political ideology seems to have reached a point of termination, the ideas themselves continue to be present and can reappear in more or less desirable forms. Such appears to be the case in recent years.

If one just contemplates politics since the start of the 2008 financial crisis, a number of political projects have appeared with links to historical ideologies. For example, in 2011, masses of people across Northern Africa and the Middle East began to make demands for democratic change. However, the opening of that space has not simply resulted in "U.S. styled" politics but has been much more complicated, leaving us witness to Syria's descent into civil war and the election of a Muslim Brotherhood candidate to Egypt's presidency. Fed up with the appearance of an indifferent Wall Street, "Main Street" literally took to the streets and "occupied" Wall Street and some 900 other cities across the globe. As of yet, there is not a clear ideology driving the Occupy movement, but that does not diminish its importance as a marker of deep political dissatisfaction. Likewise, the rise of politically active, neo-conservative, religiously based movements (one can think of the Tea Party in the United States as a recent example) also signals a critique of capitalist society and the attendant loss of identities and cultures in the face of an overwhelming compulsion on the part of capitalism to "commodify" all social relationships. Finally, if we look closer to home, we find Quebec students resisting legislative authority in the form of walkouts, strikes, and public demonstrations. While the Quebec student strike was prompted by the decision of the provincial government to raise tuition fees, the protest quickly evolved into a more broadly framed social justice movement that gathered support from trade unions, environmentalists, and anti-racist groups. The so-called "Maple Spring," the Occupy movement, and the various political uprisings around the globe all call upon people to embrace different ideas and different forms of political engagement.

Conclusion

THIS CHAPTER HAS COVERED CONSIDERABLE GROUND—FROM DEFINING
what we mean when we say "radical," to the importance of ideology to the study and
practice of politics. The chapter also offered an overview of three of the key ideologies that have helped shape political orders (and responses to those orders) since the
nineteenth century. With the fall of the Soviet Union in 1989, many political scientists
announced the "end of ideology"; however, to make such a statement is to ignore the
ongoing importance of ideas or the manner in which people mobilize ideas through
organizations, movements, or political parties. Returning to Eagleton for a moment,
ideology's role of making sense of our lived experiences and helping us envision new
forms of social organization is going to be a consistent feature of our social existence.
To argue that ideology is no longer a relevant concept and that radical politics is
dead is to deny our ability as human beings to contest current social conditions and
to create alternative ways of living. In fact, the study of ideologies and the politics they
inspire demonstrate the creative capacity of human beings "to think" and "to act"
different futures. As is obvious from the ideologies studied here, not all are desirable,
but many do demonstrate an ongoing resistance to various forms of domination and
a strong, lasting commitment to realizing social justice for all people.

Summary

The chapter:

- Defined radical ideas and their subsequent ideologies as key concepts for understanding modern politics
- Examined the modern political ideologies of socialism, communism, fascism, and
  anarchism
- Reviewed the linkages of major ideologies to the rise of contemporary social justice
  and protest movements

Discussion Questions

1. Do you think you subscribe to an ideology? If so, why and how would you describe
   it? If not, why not?
2. What would be the basis for your exercise of political judgment for the key ideologies
   considered in this chapter? In other words, how do you assess the desirability of
   political orders influenced by these ideologies?

3. What do you think is the future of radical ideologies? What movements do you think will have the most significant impact on our future politics?

4. Have you participated in a political group/project/party that draws from the ideologies discussed in this chapter? What was the relationship between the ideas and the practices carried out by the organization/movement/political party?

References

Baradat, Leon. 1988. *Political Ideologies: Their Origins and Impact.* Scarborough, ON: Prentice Hall.

Eagleton, Terry. 1991. *Ideology: An Introduction.* New York: Verso.

Kropotkin, Peter. 1926. *The Conquest of Bread.* New York: Vanguard Press.

Marx, Karl. 1989. "Critique of the Gotha Programme." In *Collected Works: Volume 24.* New York: International Publishers.

Marx, Karl and Frederick Engels. 1976. "The German Ideology." In *Collected Works: Volume 5.* New York: International Publishers.

Sargent, Lyman Tower. 1996. *Contemporary Political Ideologies: A Comparative Analysis.* New York: ITP.

Steger, Manfred B. 2008. *The Rise of the Global Imaginary: Political Ideologies from the French Revolution to the Global War on Terror.* Oxford: Oxford University Press.

Further Readings

Dunayevskaya, Raya. 1991. *Women's Liberation, and Marx's Philosophy of Revolution,* 2nd edition. Chicago: University of Illinois Press.

Goldman, Emma. 1969. *Anarchism and Other Essays.* New York: Dover Publications.

Woodley, Daniel. 2010. *Fascism and Political Theory: Critical Perspectives on Fascist Ideology.* New York: Routledge.

Weblinks

The Socialist International
www.socialistinternational.org

Institute for Anarchist Studies
www.anarchist-studies.org

World Socialist Web Site
www.wsws.org

The Communist Party of Canada
www.communist-party.ca

Marxists.org Internet Archive
www.marxists.org

CHAPTER 5

NEO-LIBERALISM

JANINE BRODIE AND ALEXA DeGAGNÉ

Learning Objectives

- Explains the terms the Great Depression and the Great Recession

- Explains the origins and key assumptions of the post-war social settlement and social liberalism

- Draws distinctions between neo-liberalism, classical liberalism, neo-conservatism, and social conservatism

- Outlines the policies, political interests, and world view informing the neo-liberal experiment in governance

- Formulates an opinion on neo-liberal thinking and its impact on contemporary politics

Introduction

Political commentators refer to the 2008 financial crisis and its lingering consequences as the Great Recession. After five years of global upheaval, the Great Recession has earned the dubious distinction of being the longest and deepest economic crisis since the Great Depression of the 1930s. The Great Recession began in an American housing market bubble, which had been inflated by financial speculation, questionable mortgage deals, greed, and outright fraud. As the Great Recession drags on, a growing number of economists believe that it has taken on many of the distinguishing markers of the Great Depression of the 1930s. Then, governments were slow to respond to the economic crisis, not the least because they did not know how to turn the economy around. They held on to old governing assumptions and practices—the economic orthodoxy of the day—hoping that past practices would also work in the future. They did not. As the Depression persisted, trade unions, social movements, and academic critics alike began to mobilize around new ways of thinking about how to organize and regulate capitalist economies to better redistribute the benefits of economic growth to the lower and middle classes, and to prevent future crises. It took almost two decades of mass unemployment, violent clashes in the streets, fascist genocide, and a world war, however, before advanced democracies settled on a new governing formula. It is usually referred to as "the post-war settlement," "social liberalism," or "the Keynesian welfare state."

Similar to the 1930s, many regard the Great Recession as evidence that the neo liberal governing formula, which has prevailed over international and national settings since the 1980s, has outlived its usefulness. In fact, it never lived up to its promises. The neo-liberal era has been marked by a series of financial crises, sharp recessions, and meagre growth gains. At the outset of the 2008 crisis, many demanded that governments take immediate and firm action to regulate the banks and hedge-fund managers to prevent future financial meltdowns. International policy networks also asserted the need for a new global financial regime that would help contain the spread of a financial crisis. This new regime, however, never materialized. Similar to the thinking of the early years of the Great Depression, key decision makers argued that the system itself was not at fault, only so-called "rogue elements" within it; with a few adjustments here and there the economy could be set back on course. G20 leaders agreed to coordinate and implement a series of restoration strategies to breathe life back into broken economies and get on with business as usual (Clarke 2012, 44–5). But even after massive public bailouts of global financial institutions, hefty public borrowing to stimulate economic activity, more tax cuts for the rich and corporations, and historically low interest rates, business has been far from usual.

The Great Recession's depth, duration, and spread have progressively undermined the assumptions embedded in neo-liberal thinking and governing outcomes. Yet even after dominating policy-making for three decades, opinion is still divided about the key features of neo-liberalism, its origins, and its relationship with other strands of contemporary political thinking. This chapter discusses the intellectual origins and central threads of neo-liberal ideas. It describes neo-liberalism as a set of policies, as a political project, and as a world view. Finally, the chapter focuses on the issue of income inequality, and reflects on the arguments of social movements and policy networks that have come to identify it as the defining failure of neo-liberal governance.

The Road to Neo-Liberalism

NEO-LIBERALISM IS A CONTESTED CONCEPT THAT SOCIAL SCIENTISTS use, sometimes reluctantly, to describe the many and different policies and practices introduced in the past three decades, which first eroded and then displaced the post-war consensus and the Keynesian welfare state. In place of these, proponents of neo-liberalism envisioned a new approach to political affairs that would liberate capitalist markets from political interference and create new markets. The turn to neo-liberalism, beginning in the 1970s, was a radical experiment in market governance, just as the post-war compromise was an untried experiment in government intervention and social protection. All political change finds its roots in the failures of existing governing regimes. In this sense, then, we cannot fully grasp the significance of the neo-liberal turn without first reviewing the key governing assumptions embedded in the post-war social settlement.

Across the industrialized world, the Great Depression of the 1930s prompted a widespread repudiation of capitalism and the prevailing governing orthodoxy, laissez-faire liberalism. It had effectively prescribed that government intervention in the market and in the private lives of individuals and families should always be held to a minimum. This governing formula, however, proved unable to cope with the mass unemployment, poverty, and social unrest generated by the Depression. The labour movement, religious congregations, parties of the left, and other social movements mobilized against sitting governments, demanding that the state provide citizens with some economic security and protection against shared social risks, such as unemployment, disability, illness, and old age.

During the 1930s and 1940s, a number of alternatives to laissez-faire, including fascism, social democracy, and communism, vied for public support, but, after World War II, **social liberalism** gained ascendancy in most advanced democracies, and the pillars of the post-war Keynesian welfare state were set in place (Brodie 2008). The terms of the post-war social settlement differed across national boundaries, ranging from the modest social welfare policies of Anglo-American democracies to the encompassing and generous social policy regimes of Northern Europe. Yet despite pronounced differences in the social protection offered by post-war welfare states, all were informed by three foundational governing assumptions. First, it was widely accepted that capitalist markets were inherently unstable and that governments had to intervene to stabilize business cycles and provide social programs to citizens and families to help them cope in hard economic times, create opportunities for the disadvantaged, and provide for the elderly and infirmed. Second, it was widely accepted that anyone could fall on hard times through no fault of their own and that the broader community should provide a social safety net to all citizens through government programs and progressive taxation. Finally, it was widely accepted that citizens could make claims to social rights in addition to civil and political rights. This meant that all citizens could expect from government a bare minimum of economic and social support as well as other measures, such as affordable education and health care, which helped equalize life chances for everyone.

These foundational orientations of social liberalism would later become primary targets for neo-liberal critics of the post-war settlement. Neo-liberalism, like Keynesianism, was born in the imagination of economic theorists. And similar to all theories, neo-liberal theory privileged certain kinds of government interventions, particular political interests, and a specific world view. The early advocates of neo-liberalism promised to end what they condemned as the social engineering of the post-war social state, to free entrepreneurs from the constraints of regulation and taxation and to contain the alleged excesses of democratic politics with the discipline of market logics. During its relatively short lifespan, this experiment in market governance has been called many things, among them restructuring, the Washington Consensus, globalization, globalism, neo-conservatism (primarily in the United States), and, most recently, neo-liberalism. This latter term is used so often that one would assume that it has always been part of our vocabulary. But the term has only gained widespread usage in the twenty-first century (Peck et al. 2009, 96).

Not everyone is satisfied with the accuracy or utility of the term *neo-liberalism*. Some argue that neo-liberalism is misnamed because it bears only a faint resemblance to the rich tradition of classical liberalism, which assigns to the state responsibility for advancing the political, civil, and economic freedoms of individuals (Brown 2005, 39). Classical liberalism traces its lineage back to the dying days of European feudalism. Revolting against the privileged status of the landed aristocracy in both political and economic life, liberals advanced the ideas of individual freedom, political equality, and democratic accountability. Both the American and French Revolutions find their origins in this vein of early liberal thinking. Critics of neo-liberalism argue that it is only partially liberal, because it focuses almost exclusively on property rights and the rights of individuals to consume and accumulate wealth without government interference. While classical liberalism envisioned separate but interdependent roles for the state and the market, neo-liberalism envisions a social order comprising self-serving individuals and a state dwarfed and disciplined by free markets.

Libertarianism is the most extreme expression of this position. It holds that liberty, understood as the right of "each individual to be left alone by others and by government," is the ultimate value of open societies. Accordingly, libertarians believe that there is "no legitimate role for government" beyond the bare minimum of maintaining law and order through the military, police, and justice system. Libertarians resist taxation and the idea of collective action and collective responsibility. Instead, they believe that the free market best provides for everyone, and, just as important, acts as a barrier to the inherent despotism of governments (Sachs 2011, 36–8). This world view insists that individuals should be free to make their own choices, without state interference, and live with the consequences, good and bad, of their choices. This world view has been an important undercurrent in American politics, most recently informing the demands of the Tea Party movement. Many American libertarians, including 2012 Republican vice-presidential candidate Paul Ryan, are devotees of the writing and philosophy of Ayn Rand. An exile from Soviet Russia, her widely read novels, particularly *The Fountainhead* (1943), reject collectivism and statism and extol the virtues of self-interested individualism.

These anti-statist and market-oriented commitments are not new: their intellectual lineage reaches back to Europe in the 1920s. Then, the Austrian School of economics, led by Ludwig von Mises and his student, Friedrich von Hayek, celebrated private property as a mark of civilization and railed against all forms of state intervention. They argued that human freedom and progress depended on strict adherence to the alleged virtues of a self-regulating market. Hayek, in particular, was a zealous opponent of **Keynesian** ideas about government management of business cycles through taxation and social spending. Hayek argued that booms and busts were natural parts of capitalism. Government intervention to smooth out wide fluctuations in investment and employment was a dangerous and futile enterprise that only made matters worse. Hayek was recruited to the London School of Economics in the 1930s to counter the growing influence of Keynesianism in British universities and policy circles, but, at the time, his work ignited the imaginations of only a few devout followers. His celebrations of the free market were drowned out by fresh memories of the Great Depression, which had revealed in bold relief the economic and social costs of unregulated markets. The idea of a self-regulating market also was rejected by the framers of the post-war compromise.

The post-war formula, however, also had its detractors, not the least being a small group of American academic economists bent on reviving market fundamentalism. In particular, Milton Friedman, an economist at the University of Chicago, condemned Keynesian economics because it disrupted what he described as the "natural" rate of unemployment. Government intervention impaired and distorted the market's inherent capacity to correct itself. As a result, he argued, Keynesianism would ultimately generate rampant inflation and economic stagnation. Echoing the Austrian School, Friedman's 1962 book *Capitalism and Freedom* celebrated capitalism as a necessary precondition of political freedom, and recommended numerous policy changes, such as vouchers and a flat tax, which promised to unleash the freedom of individual choice and enhance the efficiencies of the free market. In the early 1960s, however, such odes to capitalist markets found only small and largely academic audiences. As political economist Susan George reflected, the ideas that were to form the foundations of contemporary neo-liberalism, such as unregulated markets, a minimalist state, and corporate freedom were "utterly foreign to the spirit of the time" (quoted in Giroux, xxii).

The post-war welfare state also was resisted by a small but increasingly influential group of American intellectuals who wanted a strong state, not to protect citizens from economic insecurity, but, instead, to advance the American project of liberal democracy around the world. **Neo-conservatism** was the intellectual project of formerly left-wing American intellectuals who, affronted by the relentless atrocities of Stalinist Russia, became disillusioned with the politics of the Left. Unlike the nascent neo-liberal movement that celebrated the individual and the market as the cornerstones of freedom and democracy, neo-conservatives prioritized the idea of community, the primary role of government in protecting community values and advancing the American model of liberal democracy around the world. Neo-conservatives believed that there were forces inside (materialism, welfarism) and outside (communism) of the United States that threatened the American way of life. They also were wary of mass democracy, believing that social change had to be managed, nurtured, and supervised by elites who knew what should be valued in American society and how best to protect and advance these values (Thompson 2010, 168). Neo-conservatives were strongly influenced by the political philosophy of Leo Strauss, who, following the teachings of Plato, firmly believed that like-minded philosophers had a critical role in preserving American values in government. In recent decades, American neo-conservatives have forged strategic alliances with social conservatives. The two movements share the belief that the state should engage in the social engineering of citizens' personal lives, and that the community is more important than the individual. Unlike neo-conservatives, social conservatives cling to tradition, religion, and the family as the basic building blocks of society and community. Neo-conservatives would prefer that citizens' primary allegiances be to the nation and state. For social conservatives, the family, in particular, is foundational to the creation of a proper society because it instills tradition, religious devotion, morality, responsibility, and appropriate gender roles. **Social conservatives** associate social policies, such as income support for single mothers, and some political equality rights, such as gay marriage, as threats to the necessity and authority of the traditional nuclear family.

Despite these pockets of opposition, the post-war consensus informed the prevailing "common sense" about the goals and responsibilities of advanced democracies, until this consensus began to unravel in the 1970s. This decade was challenged by a large American trade deficit with the rest of the world, two sudden and substantial increases in the price of oil, mounting inflation, escalating wage settlements, and stagflation. A combination of economic stagnation and inflation, named stagflation, confounded mainstream economists and the finance ministries of the day. According to textbook Keynesian economics, national governments could manipulate interest rates, taxation, and government spending either to contain inflation—understood as a product of an overheated economy—or to stimulate growth and employment during economic slowdowns. Keynesian theory did not anticipate a scenario where high levels of inflation and recessionary conditions could co-exist, but this was precisely the policy challenge of the mid-1970s. Stagflation proved largely unresponsive to familiar Keynesian approaches and, thus, governments began to look for other solutions. It was apparent to policy-makers that there was an unanticipated flaw in Keynesian logic. While Keynesianism was able to control fluctuations in the business cycle within national economics, it was unable to cope with economic shocks that came from outside of national borders. The 1973 oil embargo imposed by OAPEC (Organization of Arab Petroleum Exporting Countries) and the 1979 oil shortage prompted by the Iranian Revolution demonstrated that external shocks could both ignite inflation and depress the economy at the same time.

For long-time opponents of the post-war compromise, however, the appearance that government had lost control of the economy provided a window of opportunity to advance their alternative world view. From the outset, the very wealthy had been fiercely opposed to Keynesianism, not least because it redistributed income down the economic ladder (Krugman 2012, 92). The nascent neo-liberal movement argued that stagflation was a verification of their long-held critiques of government intervention, Keynesianism, and the social state writ large. In fact, however, the American debt had ballooned due to the incredible costs of the Vietnam War and not because of social spending. The work of Milton Friedman and other neo-liberal economists, nonetheless, was soon embraced by conservative parties in the United Kingdom (U.K.) and the United States. In 1979, Margaret Thatcher was elected as prime minister of the U.K. on the promise that she would free enterprise from what she depicted as the suffocating grasp of the nanny state. Thatcher was a committed market fundamentalist with discernible libertarian leanings. She once famously pronounced that "There is no such thing as society. There are [only] individual men and women and there are families . . . people must look after themselves first" (quoted in Carroll and Little 2001, 48). Thatcherism restructured government through deregulation, especially of the financial sector, labour market reforms that were designed to create more flexible labour markets and reduce the power of trade unions, and the widespread privatization of state-owned companies and public housing.

A year later, Ronald Reagan was elected as president of the United States. Like Thatcher, Reagan was fond of blaming government for almost everything that was wrong with the American economy and society, but he also appealed to the aspirations of American neo-conservatives to revive the stature of the United States in international affairs. He launched a program comprising of deregulation, tax reduction for corporations and top income earners, cuts to social programs, and massive infusions of cash into military budgets. Although Reagan repeatedly condemned the very idea of government, he substantially increased the American debt during his two terms in office. Many other countries, including Canada, also elected governments that campaigned on some combination of these themes. By the mid-1980s, the neo-liberal revolution had successfully displaced Keynesianism in the economics departments of prestigious universities, in key international policy networks and institutions, and in the halls of government. No longer a distant academic project, neo-liberalism was fast becoming the new economic orthodoxy (Brenner et al. 2010, 182).

Neo-Liberalism: Policies, Interests, and World View

THATCHERISM AND REAGANOMICS WERE INITIAL EXAMPLES OF THE neo-liberal turn among advanced democracies. The experience of the past three decades, however, suggests that neo-liberalism is less a singular governing template than a highly experimental and evolving governing project. The application of neo-liberal principles has varied substantially across different national and international settings and across time. It has been stressed by a series of financial crises, significant shifts in the axes of economic power from advanced democracies to BRIC (Brazil, Russia, India, and China) countries, and growing political opposition. It has been a crisis-ridden governing formula that has been progressively reformulated, often in ways that contradict its foundational commitments, to cope with problems often of its own making (Peck et al. 2009). The massive public bailouts of banks and the automotive industries in the wake of the 2008 financial crisis, for example, contradict neo-liberalism's foundational commitments to self-regulating markets and minimal government. Political parties also cloud the mix by combining strands of neo-liberalism, neo-conservatism, and libertarianism in their electoral platforms. Political philosophies and economic theory never translate perfectly into everyday politics, but neo-liberalism has been particularly promiscuous, allying with different world views to appeal to voters, and chameleon-like, changing its colours as situations demand (Bremer et al. 2010, 184). Despite this variation, neo-liberalism can be distinguished from previous governing formulae on three dimensions: preferred policies, political interests, and world view (Larner 2000). Although these three dimensions are analytically distinct, they reinforce one another in political practice.

Preferred Policies

The neo-liberal revolution marked a radical departure from the post-war consensus first and foremost in terms of the policy package that it advanced. The three pillars in this package—privatization, liberalization, and deregulation—were designed to eliminate barriers to the free flow of business around the world and to create new global markets for goods and services. Globalization and neo-liberalism, thus, are intimately related but should not be confused with one another. In the second half of the twentieth century, the development of new communications technologies and air travel crafted the globe as emerging and increasingly important social and political space. This unique development in modern social and political life is called globalization, or globality. Neo-liberalism, in contrast, is a political claim about how this transnational space should be governed (Scholte 2005, 8). The privatization principle was nestled within the claim that markets were more efficient than governments in the provision of goods and services, and that public goods crowded out and distorted market activity. Thus, neo-liberalism demanded that governments sell off publicly owned companies and contract out government services to the private sector. The liberalization principle asserted that governments should remove all barriers to the free movement of goods, services, and investment across national boundaries by eliminating tariffs and measures to protect national industries and culture, and by signing binding international trade agreements, which, among other things, required governments to treat foreign and domestic companies in the same way. Finally, the deregulation principle required governments to scale back on all measures that allegedly impeded market forces, including corporate taxes, environmental regulations, bureaucratic oversight (red tape), and business fees and subsidies (Scholte 2005, 8–11).

These principles were initially consolidated under the so-called "Washington Consensus." In the early 1980s, international financial institutions such as the International Monetary Fund (IMF) and the World Bank (WB) imposed this package of policies on debtor countries in the developing world through Structural Adjustment Policies (SAPs) as a condition for financial aid. These countries were obliged to redirect their production, primarily in agricultural commodities, from domestic to international markets and to open key sectors of their economies to foreign investment. But few of these countries reaped the promised miracles of free markets. International commodity markets were flooded, driving down prices, while domestic populations experienced food shortages. At the same time, the profits from exports were used to pay back loans to international banks and financial institutions rather than to develop domestic infrastructures and improve domestic living conditions. Eventually, this one-size-fits-all approach to developing countries was judged to be too harsh and too insensitive to local particularities. SAPs were replaced with Poverty Reduction Strategies (PRSP), which purportedly paid greater attention to individual country conditions, the social consequences of marketization, and good governance. The PRSP approach, however, remained resolutely committed to the principles of privatization, liberalization, and deregulation (Scholte 2005, 15).

The governments of advanced economics variously adopted the core principles of neo-liberalism through the election of like-minded political parties, the obligations of membership in international institutions such as the World Trade Organization, and bilateral and multilateral free trade agreements. The application of the principles of privatization, liberalization, and deregulation among advanced democracies was by no means uniform, as various countries were differently constrained by political and institutional factors. In Canada, for example, the Conservative government of Brian Mulroney, first elected in 1984, selectively privatized Crown (public) corporations in the energy and transportation sectors, partially deregulated other industries, and progressively shifted the tax burden from the wealthy and the corporate sector to consumers. Mulroney's agenda, however, was constrained by ongoing public support for social programs and by federalism. Nonetheless, Canada was increasingly implicated in accelerated liberalization through free trade agreements, first with the United States in 1989 (CUSFTA) and then with the United States and Mexico in 1995

(NAFTA). Beyond formal institutional agreements, however, it is commonly argued that the neo-liberal turn internationally effectively forced national governments to follow suit. Neo-liberal policies gave capital an unprecedented capacity to move around the world, thereby forcing national governments to adhere to neo-liberal fundamentals in order to maintain and attract investment. This is called "the race to the bottom"—the relentless process in which the implementation of a business-friendly regime in one country forces others to follow suit.

Political Interests

A second perspective, certainly complementary to the first, understands neo-liberalism as a political project aimed at advancing the material interests of the wealthy, global corporations, and the global North at the expense of the middle and lower classes and the global South. According to this view, the welfare state successfully redistributed income and life chances from the wealthy to the rest in the three decades following World War II. The wealthy and business interests had only reluctantly accepted the post-war compromise and, thus, enthusiastically supported neo-liberal alternatives once Keynesianism faltered in the 1970s. Thus, despite all of the neo-liberal rhetoric about individual freedom, democracy, and the free market, prominent social scientists such as David Harvey argue that, at its core, neo-liberalism sought to restore and, in the past three decades did effectively consolidate, class power. (Harvey 2009, 1). This argument was echoed by Nobel Laureate in economics and former World Bank official Joseph Stiglitz at the outset of the 2008 financial crisis. Thatcherism, Reaganomics, and the so-called Washington Consensus, he said, were "always a political doctrine serving certain interests" (quoted in Peck et al. 2009, 97). More pointedly, Doreen Massey argues that neo-liberalism was "a tool in the armoury . . . in the battle to restore profits from the social democratic settlement that gave the labour force substantial gains" (2012, 81).

While political motivations are difficult to distill from aggregate statistics, the neo-liberal era witnessed an unprecedented transfer of income and wealth to the few very rich from the rest. Globally, it is estimated that the richest 1 percent of adults controls 43 percent of the world's assets, and the wealthiest 10 percent control 83 percent, while the bottom 50 percent control only 2 percent (*The Economist* 2011a, 6). Gini coefficients, which calculate the extent to which the income distributions deviate from a perfectly equal distribution, have grown significantly and rapidly in the past three decades almost everywhere. Among advanced economies, pre-crisis OECD data show that, from the mid-1980s to the mid-2000s, real income growth among the top income earners was twice as large as that of the bottom in such diverse countries as Finland, Sweden, the U.K., Germany, and Italy (CBC 2011).

Statistics from the United States, where income inequality is severe, provide a more detailed picture of the experience of the past 30 years. Before the Great Depression of the 1930s, the top 1 percent of income earners took approximately 18 percent of total national income in the United States, but this percentage was more than cut in half in the 1950s and 1960s—years of unprecedented growth. Beginning in the 1980s, the growth of income inequality was rapid and deep, surpassing levels reached in the pre-depression years. In 1987, the top 1 percent of U.S. earners took home 12.3 percent of all pre-tax income, but by 2007 their share had almost doubled to 23.5 percent (CBC 2011). At the onset of the Great Recession, the richest 10 percent of U.S. income earners accounted for almost one-half of total national income (CBC 2011). More starkly, the 400 richest Americans have more wealth than the bottom half of income earners—some 150 million people. During these same years, however, the U.S. median wage stagnated and actually dropped after 2001. Adjusted for inflation, the average American worker makes about $300 more than he or she did 30 years ago (Reich 2012). Studies show that the middle class in the United States (and elsewhere) largely maintained its standard of living during these years first by becoming dual-earner households, as millions of women entered the workforce, and, then, by borrowing, often against the equity in their homes. Millions more Americans have fallen into poverty. According to the U.S. Census Bureau, 46 million Americans live in poverty in the United States, the highest number recorded since it began collecting poverty data over 50 years ago. One in seven Americans depends on food stamps, a benefit of, on average, $133 (USD) a month to put food on the table (*The Economist* 2011b).

The growth of income inequalities has been especially rapid in Canada. As in the United States, the richest have dramatically increased their share of total national income while the middle and poorest income groups have lost ground. A 2010 study by Armine Yalnizyan reports that between 1997 and 2007 the top 1 percent of Canadian income earners (246 000 people with incomes exceeding $405 000 CAD) took home almost one-third (32 percent) of all income growth compared to 8 percent in the 1950s and 1960s. Since the late 1970s, the richest 1 percent of Canadians saw their share of total income double, while the shares of the richest 0.01 percent tripled (Yalnizyan 2010, 3–4). More recent data show that between 1980 and 2009, market incomes increased by 38 percent for the top 20 percent of earners, remained stagnant for the middle 20 percent, and dropped by 11 percent for the bottom 20 percent (Grant 2011a). As is the situation in the United States, the stagnation of middle-class incomes has been accompanied by a dramatic increase in household debt. In late 2011, the ratio of debt to personal disposable income stood at $152.98 CAD (Grant 2011b).

Income inequalities also have been aggravated by public policies that give generous tax cuts to the rich and the corporate sector. In the United States, for example, the tax cuts introduced in 2001 and 2003 by then–President George W. Bush and extended for two years in 2011 by President Barack Obama saved the richest 1 percent of American taxpayers more money than the rest of America (approximately 150 million Americans) received in total income. Obama's two-year extension of the Bush tax regime will add $1.2 trillion to the American deficit (Reich 2012). In 2012, Prime Minister Stephen Harper's Conservative government began an austerity program that will close key government services, including the collection of data on poverty, Aboriginal Canadians, and the environment; reduce the federal public service by some 20 000 jobs; and erode such key social programs as employment insurance and Old Age Security. Between 2006 and 2013, however, Harper has reduced federal tax revenue by $218 billion CAD, a figure that dwarfs the Canadian federal deficit (Campbell 2012). After years of tax cuts to the wealthy and corporations, governments starved of revenue have eroded social programs, ignored crumbling public infrastructures, neglected research and development, and abandoned public education—the very factors that build jobs and global competitiveness.

World View

This chapter has touched upon key elements of the neo-liberal world view; among them, an abiding faith in the efficiencies of unfettered global markets, an abhorrence of government intervention in economic and social life, and a commitment to the primacy of the individual at the expense of society. This section briefly explores the ideas that promote vast disparities in wealth between the very rich and the rest. These gross inequalities in income and life chances were largely concealed and justified by the neo-liberal world view that has been incessantly promoted by neo-liberal governments and the mainstream media for more than a generation. Uncontested until very recently, these ideas were embedded in public opinion and common sense understandings of the way things work.

Neo-liberal orthodoxy actually expects and celebrates income inequality. Market fundamentalists assert that in a free society inequality stimulates entrepreneurship and economic growth. Markets rightly paid an entrepreneurial risk premium to those who invested and took risks. However, so the theory went, disproportionate rewards for innovation, creativity, and risk-taking ultimately benefited everyone. Neo-liberals, committed to the miracles of the self-regulating market, maintained that as the rich got richer, the benefits would trickle down to everyone else. The rising tide of economic activity, additionally fuelled by public policies such as deregulation and selected tax cuts for the wealthy, would raise all boats in the harbour. Moreover, tax cuts to the wealthy and corporations would be more than recovered in increased economic growth that would generate far more revenue for governments. It was a win-win scenario. It was and continues to be an article of neo-liberal faith that the unrestricted pursuit of profit and individual gain as well as disparities in wealth and income are a necessary part of generating jobs, innovation, and growth.

Neo-liberalism pronounced a new formula for economic growth that privileged the market, market actors, and market logics in the distribution of income and social goods. But, as Wendy Brown argues, neo-liberalism was "not only or even primarily focused on the economy" (2005, 39–40). It is a moral tale about good and bad that reshaped popular perceptions about government, citizenship, and us. In its simplest form, this discourse pronounced that the free market is good because it unleashes the entrepreneurial spirit and guarantees individual freedom, while government is inherently bad because it obstructs freedom and the natural order of things (Campbell 2011, 20).

Neo-liberalism also provided a new moral tale about us and others. The post-war consensus advanced the idea that all citizens were potentially vulnerable to market volatility and personal hardships, but that these shared fates could be alleviated through social insurance and social programs, which, in turn, were funded by corporate and income taxes. Neo-liberalism, however, interpreted success as always deserved, and lack of success as also deserved. It was evidence of defects in the individual moral character; among them, laziness, lack of initiative, and dependence on the state and social programs (Somers 2008, 3). Self-interested entrepreneurs, the so-called "job creators," were the model citizens of the neo-liberal social order. This representation left little room for explanations of inequality and poverty that focused on structural factors, such as the economy, class, gender, and racial inequalities, or on unequal access to education and other social goods. In the neo-liberal world view, individuals were individualized (Brodie 2008).

Neo-liberal individualization, as a governing strategy, demands that people be self-sufficient market actors, and, as such, bear full responsibility for themselves, their families, and their futures. The incessant rhetoric and policies of individualization demand that everyone find personal causes and personal responses, what Beck terms "biographic solutions" to what are, in effect, the shared social challenges of our era. The problem with this formulation is not that individuals and families do not work hard to find personal solutions, as all of us struggle with these expectations on a daily basis. Financing our education, finding employment, arranging child or elder care, or acquiring new skills to adapt to changing labour markets are obvious examples. Rather, the problem, as Bauman explains, is that the knowledge and resources that we bring to our life choices are "not themselves matters of choice" (2002, 69). In a highly unequal society, many people simply have more money, resources, and connections to find personal solutions to the contemporary social challenges of training for a knowledge-based economy, finding appropriate care for dependants, and adapting to rapidly shifting global conditions. The inescapable paradox of neo-liberal individualization is that it is a collective condition. Almost everyone is in the same boat, expected to chart their own course on uncertain waters without the necessary resources to do so successfully. But, somehow, we have accepted the neo-liberal moral tale that there is something wrong with us personally, rather than with the game, when we are dealt a losing hand from a stacked deck. This is especially true for the millennial generation that will be less likely than their parents' generation to earn to decent wage or to have a secure job or employment benefits or own a house. As it stands, the present global economic crisis denies the next generation the promise of social mobility, which is so critical to the implicit social contract of liberal democracies.

Rethinking Neo-Liberalism

FIVE YEARS INTO THE GREATEST ECONOMIC DOWNTURN SINCE THE 1930s, there are growing doubts about whether neo-liberalism is worth reviving yet another time. The Great Recession appears to have dispelled the elaborate myths that have been woven around this governing template in the past three decades. Protesters have hit the streets around the world because they are no longer willing to accept a system that does not work for the vast majority. Austerity programs, unemployment, and deep cuts to social programs are the price that many ordinary people are no longer willing to pay for the excesses of financial speculators or to keep a highly ineq-uitable system afloat until the next inevitable crisis erupts.

The growing wave of protest movements from the Indignants in Spain, to the Occupy Wall Street movement, to the Quebec student strike does not sing in unison. But each group has asserted a new collective identity that challenges the fundamen-tal tenets of neo-liberalism. The Occupy movement, which erupted in Zuccotti Park in New York in the fall of 2011 and then spread to over 900 cities around the world, for example, envisions an unequal and unfair world that comprises the very rich 1% and the 99% that is struggling to cope with unemployment, stagnating incomes, and economic insecurity. Others describe the neo-liberal social order as a world starkly divided between a *plutonomy*, a select few who enjoy the benefits of neo-liberal glo-balization, and a *precariat*, all the rest who are increasingly forced into a precarious and insecure existence (Chomsky 2012, 33–5). Across advanced democracies, public opinion polls consistently report that growing numbers of people no longer believe that the system and their governments are working for them.

Influential international institutions and policy networks that were once devotees of neo-liberal governing principles also appear to have lost faith. In late 2011, for example, the Organisation for Economic Co-operation and Development (OECD) published a scathing assessment of the dystopias of neo-liberal governance. In "Divided We Stand" (2011), the OECD argued that the winner-take-all culture cultivated by neo-liberalism has created "deeply rooted social imbalances" and pervasive fears of decline in the middle class. Inequality, the report explained, is now a "live" political issue that threatens both economic recovery and social cohesion. The OECD pronounced, in capital letters, that "the benefits of economic growth DO NOT trickle down automatically," and that "greater inequality DOES NOT foster social mobility." "Our policies," the OECD concluded, "have created a system that makes [inequalities] grow and it's time to change these policies." "Addressing the question of fairness," the report contended, "is the *sine qua non* for the necessary restoring of confidence today" (OECD 2011, emphasis in the original).

Conclusion

THIS CHAPTER HAS REVIEWED THE ORIGINS AND THE KEY DIMENSIONS of contemporary neo-liberalism. This governing framework took root in advanced democracies as the post-war consensus began to unravel in the 1970s. During the past 30 years, neo-liberalism has shifted trajectories to respond to slow and uneven growth, repeated fiscal crises, and several deep recessions. Although neo-liberalism was embraced with the expectation that it would generate unprecedented growth, it has been far less successful in doing so than was the post-war governing formula. Its greatest flaw and liability, however, has been the production of unacceptable dispari-ties in income and life chances between the very few and the rest.

In 2008, Nobel Laureate Joseph Stiglitz argued that neo-liberal governance was always based on a grab-bag of ideas that were never supported by economic theory or historical experience. He mused that "learning this lesson may be the silver lining in the cloud now hanging over the global economy" (quoted in Peck 2009, 97). Thirty years ago, voters were told that "there is no alternative" other than to bend public policies and the economic security of ordinary people to satisfy the demands of global market forces. Similar to our predecessors in the 1930s, we have come to understand that there must be an alternative. Our collective challenge is to build a new consensus around alternatives that are equitable and sustainable on a global scale.

Summary

The chapter:

- Explored the road to neo-liberalism in advanced democracies
- Discussed the rise and fall and key assumptions of the post-war settlement
- Summarized the intellectual origins and key policies, political interests, and world view of contemporary neo-liberalism
- Presented an overview of neo-liberalism's shortcomings, especially the production of unprecedented income inequalities
- Assessed the continuing viability of the neo-liberal experiment

Discussion Questions

1. Are the key commitments of social liberalism still relevant in contemporary politics? What are the obstacles to reforming government in ways that would enhance the economic security of the average citizen?
2. Distinguish between globalization and neo-liberalism. Are there other ways to imagine how the planet should be governed? What should be prioritized in a new governing formula?
3. Think about the challenges of your daily life. Do you feel the pressures of individualization? In what ways? How could these pressures be reduced through collective action and public policy?
4. What do you think about the Occupy movement's depiction of the 1% and the 99%? Do you think that the contemporary social order is best described with the terms *plutonomy* and *precariat*? Why or why not?

References

Bauman, Zygmunt. 2002. *Society under Siege*. London: Polity Press.

Brenner, Neil, Jamie Peck, and Nik Theodore. 2010. "Variegated Neoliberalization: Geographies, Modalities, Pathways." *Global Networks* 10(2): 182–222.

Brodie, Janine. 2008. "Rethinking the Social in Social Citizenship." In *Rethinking the Social in Citizenship*, edited by E. Isin, 22–50. Toronto: University of Toronto Press.

Brown, Wendy. 2005. *Edgework: Critical Essays in Knowledge and Politics.* Princeton, NJ: Princeton University Press.

Campbell, Bruce. 2011. "Harper's Policies Reflect Hard-Right Conservative Values." *CCPA Monitor* 18(5): 20–2.

———. 2012. "Canada Has Become More Unequal as It Grows Less Democratic." *CCPA Monitor* 18(7): 1, 6–7.

Carroll, William and William Little. 2004. "Neoliberal Transformation and Antiglobalization Politics in Canada." *International Journal of Political Economy* 31(3): 33–66.

CBC (Conference Board of Canada). 2011. "Hot Topics: Canadian Inequality." www.conference board.ca/hcp/hot-topics/can/inequality.aspx.

Chomsky, Noam. 2012. Occupy. *Occupied Media Pamphlet Series.* Brooklyn, NY: Zuccotti Park Press.

Clarke, John. 2012. "What Crisis Is This?" In *Soundings on the Neoliberal Crisis*, edited by Jonathan Rutherford and Sally Davison, 44–54. London: Soundings.

The Economist. 2011a. "A Special Report on Global Leaders." January 22: 6–11.

———. 2011b. "The Struggle to Eat." July 16: 29.

Giroux, Henry. 2004. *The Terror of Neoliberalism: Authoritarianism and the Eclipse of Democracy.* Boulder, CO: Paradigm Publishers.

The Globe and Mail. 2011. "OECD Calls Time on Trickle Down Theory." www.theglobeandmail/report-on-business/economy/oecd-calls-time-on-trickle-down-theory/article226065.

Grant, Tavia. 2011a "Income Inequality Rising Quickly in Canada." *The Globe and Mail*, September 13.

———. 2011b. "Household Debt in Canada Triggers Alarm." *The Globe and Mail*, December 13. www.theglobeandmail.com/globe-investor/personal-finance/household-debt-in-Canada-triggers-alarm/article2269210/.

Hall, Stuart. 2012. "The Neoliberal Crisis." In *Soundings on the Neoliberal Crisis*, edited by Jonathan Rutherford and Sally Davison, 8–26. London: Soundings.

Harvey, David. 2009. "Is This Really the END of Neoliberalism?" www.counterpunch.org/harvey03132009.html.

Krugman, Paul. 2012. *End This Depression Now.* New York: W.W. Norton Company.

Larner, Wendy. 2000. "Neo-liberalism, Policy, Ideology, Governmentality." *Studies in Political Economy* 63: 3–25.

Massey, Doreen. 2012. "The Struggle Ahead." In *Soundings on the Neoliberal Crisis*, edited by Jonathan Rutherford and Sally Davison, 70–83. London: Soundings.

OECD. 2011. "Divided We Stand: Why Inequality Keeps Rising," Remarks by Angel Gurria, OECD Secretary General. Paris: 5 December. www.oecd.org.document/22/0,3746,en_21571361_44315118_49185046_1_1_1_1,00.html.

Peck, James, Nick Theodore, and Neil Brenner. 2009. "Post-neoliberalism and its Malcontents." *Antipode* 41(1): 94–116.

Rand, Ayn. 1943. *The Fountainhead.* New York: Bobbs-Merrill Company.

Reich, Robert. 2012. *Beyond Outrage: What Has Gone Wrong with Our Economy and Our Democracy and How to Fix It.* New York: Alfred A. Knopf.

Sachs, Jeffrey. 2011. *The Price of Civilization: Economics and Ethics After the Fall.* Toronto: Random House Canada.

Scholte, Jan Aart. 2005. *The Sources of Neoliberal Globalization.* New York: United Nations Research Institute for Social Development.

Somers, Margaret. 2008. *Genealogies of Citizenship: Markets, Statelessness, and the Right to Have Rights.* New York: Cambridge University Press.

Stiglitz, Joseph. 2008. "The End of Neo-liberalism?" www.project-syndicate.org/commentary/the-end-of-neo-liberalism-.

Thompson, Bradley. 2010. *Neoconservatism: An Obituary for an Idea.* London: Paradigm Publishers.

Yalnizyan, Armine. 2010. "The Rise of Canada's Richest 1%." Ottawa: Canadian Centre for Policy Alternatives, December.

Further Readings

George, Susan. 1999. "A Short History of Neo-liberalism: Twenty Years of Elite Economics and Emerging Opportunities for Structural Change." www.globalexchange.org/campaigns/econ101/neoliberalism.html.pf.

Lansley, Stewart. 2012. "Inequality, the Crash and the Crisis: Part 1 Defining the Issue of Our Times." www.oecdinsights.org/category/insights/2012/06/11/inequality-the-crash-and-the-crisis-part-1-the-defining-issue-of-our-times/.

———. 2012. "Inequality, the Crash and the Crisis: Part 2 A Model of Capitalism That Fails to Share the Fruits of Growth." www.oecdinsights.org/category/insights/2012/06/11/inequality-the-crash-and-the-crisis-part-2-a-model-of-capitalism-that-fails-to-share-the-fruits-of-growth/.

———. 2012. "Inequality, the Crash and the Crisis. Part 3: The Limit to Inequality." www.oecdinsights.org/2012/06/15/inequality-the-crash-and-the-crisis-part-3-the-limit-to-inequality/.

Weblinks

Janine Brodie. 2012. "Social Literacy and Social Justice in Times of Crisis." Big Thinking Lecture Series. Trudeau Foundation/Congress of the Humanities and Social Sciences, Wilfrid Laurier University, 30 May.
www.youtube.com/watch?v=uxJw9nTNseo

Harvey, David. 2011. "Crisis of Capitalism."
www.youtube.com/watch?v=qOP2V_np2c0

Rutherford, Jonathan and Sally Davison. *Soundings on the Neoliberal Crisis.* London: Soundings.
www.lwbooks.co.uk/ebooks/NeoliberalCrisis.html.

OECD. 2011. "Divided We Stand: Why Inequality Keeps Rising." Remarks by Angel Gurria, OECD Secretary General. Paris: 5 December.
www.oecd.org.document/22/0,3746,en_21571361_44315118_49185046_1_1_1_1,00.html.

CHAPTER 6

WHAT'S LEFT OUT? DISSENT, RACE, AND THE SOCIAL CONTRACT

FALGUNI A. SHETH

Learning Objectives

- Explores the gap between the promise of justice and equal protection for everyone

- Discusses the ways in which the social contract functions differently for individuals of different race and culture

- Illustrates some of the founding mythologies of liberal political theories, such as the social contract and the labour theory of property

- Explores the differential consequences of dissent and protest, especially as these pertain to minorities or populations of colour

Introduction

Modern liberal political philosophy is predicated on two important ideas. The first is that the purpose of political societies is to work toward, if not to ensure, justice. Political justice, from a liberal perspective, includes protection of rights and property, as well as personal and political freedoms of the individual; fair adjudication of wrongdoing (this includes due process for the accused and the equal application of the law); and political representation of the members of society by the sovereign. Historically, rights were restricted to adult, property-owning men, with the understanding that they would protect others under their care and authority, such as female relatives and minors, and indentured servants and slaves. Gradually, struggles over rights have ensured the extension of them to white women, men and women of colour, indigenous people, and also, in qualified contexts, minors. However, these inclusions have been fairly recent in liberalism's long history. Women and men of colour, especially those of African descent or indigenous origins, were not recognized by Western liberal states as independent members of society, with equal political rights, until the late nineteenth and early twentieth centuries. By extension, political justice would include the observance of procedures and norms by which representative bodies are selected or elected, and checks against the excesses of sovereign power.

The second important idea of modern political philosophy is that rights and duties are extended to every member of society, and that these rights and duties are reciprocal. In other words, my rights and duties can only be upheld and guaranteed if I observe your rights and duties, and vice versa. If our reciprocal rights and duties are observed, then you and I will both be protected, and we will be safe and free to pursue our interests and ideas to our own satisfaction. We recognize the latter right, broadly, as the right to freedom. The limit to the right to freedom is that we must refrain from harming others while in pursuit of our own happiness. These freedoms are understood, respectively, as positive and negative liberty. Positive liberty is that freedom that allows individuals to pursue their own interests and goals. Your ability to pursue your own "happiness" can only be achieved by limiting the interference of the state and other individuals upon your actions—except to the extent that your actions are self-destructive. Those limits are understood as negative liberty. Negative and positive liberty are intrinsically intertwined, although, as political philosopher Isaiah Berlin points out, the line between your ability to do as you wish and the state's rightful claim to stop you is a difficult one to draw and can border on excessive interference.

We see these principles reflected in any number of frameworks of political theory. For example, philosopher John Locke, whose *Second Treatise of Government* (1688) is a template for a modern liberal polity, writes about rights and freedoms as belonging to men in the state of nature. According to Locke, we know that we have God-given rights, because God also gave us reason by which to discern these rights (Locke Ch. 2, para. 6). Among those rights are the rights of retribution (to make up for the theft of my property by taking in kind from the thief), the right to punish, and the right to dispose of my possessions as I wish (which is also part of the right to property) (Locke

Ch. 2, para. 8; para. 4). While Locke believed that men lived peacefully in a state of nature, there are moments when that peace is ruptured by an excess of retribution or ill will. These ruptures and the discontents behind them make it necessary to turn to political society, at which point those rights that we had in nature are confirmed and established as existing for each of us, to be observed reciprocally by all of us. Hence, we arrive at Locke's idea of the **social contract**: all men consent to enter into a mutual agreement (the social contract) in which they observe each other's rights and responsibilities, elect an impartial magistrate to adjudicate disputes, and give up their right to punish to the magistrate (Locke Ch. 7, para. 88).

The social contract framework sets a common foundation upon which men need depend only on the labour of their own bodies and their reason to cultivate the earth that God gave "to mankind in common" (Locke Ch. 5, para. 25). By mixing their labour with the earth, men can sustain themselves and acquire property. Locke's narrative is a beautiful picture of the ideal modern political framework: harmonious, equal, fair, and with plenty of room for political and personal freedom and for personal wealth. There are critical omissions in Locke's story, however. The most immediate shortcoming is his assumption that the earth was uncultivated until rational individuals mixed their labour with the land to make it their own property. This reading excludes altogether the existence of indigenous peoples and their cultivation of the earth for sustenance long before European settlers arrived in the Caribbean and the Americas. As Carole Pateman explains, the European idea of *Terra nullius*, or empty land, simply justified the wholesale appropriation of the land inhabited by indigenous people. As Pateman further argues, Locke's contention that the earth was uncultivated unless and until (European) labour was added, valourized the conquest of North America, marginalized indigenous peoples, and, later, criminalized both the poor and those who resisted this vision of economic and political development. For Locke, criminality was an example of men living "by another law than reason" (Locke, Ch. 2, para. 8). He understood slavery, moreover, to be the result of a state of war, where the original attackers have lost and are given a chance to save their lives by giving up their freedom to another (Locke, Ch. 4). In Locke's imagination, even women seem to have the equal opportunity to own property, parent their children, and govern society, if they are of royal lineage (Locke, Ch. 6 & 7).

And yet, even as one reads the idyllic picture drawn by Locke, certain questions keep rushing to mind. For example, his version of slavery is a particularly peculiar one. Locke justifies slavery as the gracious granting of life by the victor of a war, and as an act that is initiated by an opponent. In his debt, the opponent is enslaved to the victor. This Lockean story of slavery varies greatly from the historical accounts that contemporary readers have come to know, such as the stories of the transatlantic slave trade and of the brutish conditions of plantation slavery. Millions of enslaved Africans, who were transplanted in the Caribbean and the Americas, had not gone to war with either slave traders or slave owners.

From actual historical and experiential accounts, we are aware that slavery was an exploitative economic and cultural system initiated by European colonial powers—such as the British, French, and Spanish—to provide inexpensive labour to their North

American and Caribbean colonies (Williams 1944). The European colonial powers were engaged in an extensive trade that shipped West Africans to North America and the Caribbean. Moreover, Locke's account of rights is at variance with the treatment that various minorities in North America have received in the several hundred years since the colonization. From historical accounts, we know that the United States and Canadian governments dealt with the uncomfortable presence of indigenous populations by sequestering them in delineated territories; that is, in small parcels of land where they were effectively quarantined, both isolated from and governed by European settlers. The colonizing authorities often forced indigenous populations to relocate to reserved lands that might be hundreds of kilometres from their original communities, often at the ends of rifles and in extreme weather without adequate protection, shelter, food, and water. Moreover, as highlighted by the stories collected by Canada's Truth and Reconciliation Commission (TRC)—the first TRC dedicated to children—indigenous children living on these reserves were sent to government residential schools, required to speak in English and learn English customs, and "acculturated" to loathe and surrender their traditions, languages, and customs.

The historical record of treatment received by indigenous populations often is divorced from the modern understanding of liberalism and rights, which are thought to extend to everyone living within the borders of these modern states. The language of equal rights is considered ahistorical, applying to everyone equally. Ignoring the historical realities of different peoples, whether descended from indigenous populations or African slaves, effectively obscures how the descendants of European settlers benefited from their labour as well as the economic and cultural exploitation of indigenous and slave populations. Until these histories are taken into account in political and social debates, we misunderstand history and inadequately comprehend arguments in favour of social justice policies, such as equity, affirmative action, reconciliation, and reparations.

How do we reconcile historical events of inequality and exploitation with the promises of justice, preservation of rights, and protection under the law that modern political philosophy, especially liberal theory, claims to offers us? Liberal political philosophy leaves out three important premises that are overlooked in the general promise of protection of individual liberty and rights inherent in liberalism.

Criminality versus Dissent: Breaking the Social Contract

THE SOCIAL CONTRACT WAS ORIGINALLY CONCEIVED OF AS AN AGREEment between men to abide by a set of mutually agreed-upon principles and rules. It addressed the problem of disagreements and acts of aggression that individuals may direct toward each other, and afforded a set of equal protections for each member who has agreed to live by this mutually constituted agreement. Political philosophers such as Thomas Hobbes (1588–1679), John Locke (1632–1704), and Jean-Jacques Rousseau (1712–1778) advanced different versions of the social contract in response to the injustices, aggressions, and violence that individuals may be subjected to "in the state of nature," that is to say, in the absence of a social contract. The social contract is considered to differentiate a civilized society from the state of nature, and it is considered to be central to the founding of a modern liberal society.

Is the social contract a real agreement, or is it, as David Hume argued in "Of Civil Liberty" (1742), a fiction? The social contract may be thought of as a heuristic rather than as an actual historical moment in any society. Put differently, the social contract is a theoretical device often used to identify the foundational commitments of the modern state. In the United States, for example, the Declaration of Independence and the Constitution are considered to be social contracts. In Canada, the *British North America Act* and the *Charter of Rights and Freedoms* may be considered foundational to an evolving notion of a social contract.

The social contract, according to Hobbes, Locke, or Rousseau, is based on a tenuous understanding of consent. Although each philosopher speaks generally of the moment at which men join together in the social contract, it is difficult to identify the moment of consent, affecting all who are born in its shadow. The descendants of the "founders" of a society, those "born" into it, have not consented, but perhaps by staying in that society they can be seen as agreeing to live by its laws. By extension, dissent can be exhibited through a visible rejection of the polity that one inhabits; that is, by a decision to give up protection by the state through moving (or in contemporary times, applying to move) to another society.

The history of modern political philosophy often minimizes or erases profound political disagreement, dissent, or disobedience. Disagreement, in minor and particular ways, can be construed as one's particular will and interest, as Jean-Jacques Rousseau, an eighteenth-century Swiss-French political philosopher mentions in his 1762 work, *Social Contract*. Political dissent might also be understood as the right to live by a different social contract; that is, leaving the society with whose laws you disagree. We see this possibility in Thomas Hobbes' *Leviathan*, written in 1651, and John Locke's *Second Treatise*, written in 1690. According to Hobbes, one gives up the right to disagree with the **Leviathan** (the sovereign authority) once one enters a **covenant** with him. A covenant is an agreement based on trust in which each party promises to carry out certain actions in the future (Hobbes, Ch. 14). For Hobbes, men make that agreement with the Leviathan, the sovereign authority chosen by the members of society, to protect themselves against the antagonistic intentions of others. The Leviathan promises to protect men who enter into such a covenant, and men transfer their decision-making authority (that is, their will) and the right to retribution and punishment to the Leviathan. In turn, the Leviathan now represents the will of those men and acts on their behalf for their protection. As such, the Leviathan becomes both the "Actor" and the "Author" of men's wills (Hobbes, Ch. 16). In Hobbes' view, if a subject believes him- or herself (and Hobbes *did* include women in his writing), then he or she can find someone stronger for protection. Everyone also has the right to "secede," as it were, from the present ruler (Hobbes, Ch. 20). For Locke, as well, there is no right to dissent unless one chooses to secede from the social contract altogether and move to another society.

The notion of dissent does not receive full treatment in these philosophical frameworks, not least because dissent is a difficult concept to accommodate in a theory describing what a successful society ought to look like. But we can find dissent hidden between the lines in John Locke's framework. For example, dissent is ascribed to those who refuse to join the social contract, such as the so-called savages and Indians who live "naturally in [the] state [of nature] and remain so until by their own consent they make themselves members of some politic society" (Locke, Ch. 3). Slaves, namely those who "attacked" and lost, are also considered to be dissenters: "The state of war is a state of enmity and destruction, and therefore, by declaring by word or action . . . a sedate, settled design upon another man's life, puts him in a state of war with him against whom he has declared such an intention and so has exposed his life to the other's power to be taken away by him" (Locke, Ch. 3). Taking possessions without permission is also an act of dissent, and by this act thieves declare themselves to live by another law than that of reason: "In transgressing the law of nature, the offender declares himself to live by another rule than that of reason and common equity, which is that measure God has set to the actions of men for their mutual security; and so he becomes dangerous to mankind, the tie which is to secure them from injury and violence being slighted and broken by him" (Locke, Ch. 2, para. 8). Locke considers a thief to be someone who has robbed another of his or her freedom. There is little way to rebut this claim by suggesting that property was taken unjustly from those who inhabited North America prior to European settlers.

In contrast, contemporary political theorist Carole Pateman has shown in her article "The Settler Contract" (2007) that the founding assumptions of liberal political theory are in fact founding mythologies. These early liberal mythologies, however, all contain hints of dissent, ready to be teased out, managed, and reconfigured as threats to the state, whether performed by a thief, a criminal, an indigenous person, or a slave. While liberal political theory has found it very difficult to accommodate dissent or political protest, activists and intellectuals have shown that these can be a core part of the practice of liberalism. For example, Dr. Martin Luther King Jr. and other civil rights leaders in the United States used peaceful protest and claims to citizenship successfully (although they often met with violence and anger from the state) to champion civil rights for African Americans and other minority populations.

Slavery and Poverty

IN THE FAMOUS "BOOK V, ON PROPERTY," LOCKE POINTS TO THE EARTH as given to all men in common (by God) to cultivate and improve. The **labour theory of property,** as this is commonly known, is conceived of as a responsibility for all men (sic) to undertake. According to Locke, men have the moral, existential obligation to cultivate the land that God has given them in order to sustain themselves and their families (Locke, *Second Treatise*, Chapter V, para. 26). Through the mixing of one's labour with the earth, one acquires property. Thus, farming the land makes it a man's own, and it becomes the basis by which men can make their subsistence. And how do men know about the obligation to cultivate the land for sustenance? Simply put, it is because they have been imbued by God with reason, which guides "rational beings" in how to live. Notice that the labour theory of property refers to rational men, while Locke also makes reference to the indigenous population as the "wild Indian," who for sustenance can also obtain fruit and venison (Locke, Chapter 5, para. 26), both of which are his property even though he "knows no enclosure"; that is to say, he acknowledges no fences nor the ownership of land by individuals. They are either stupid (without reason) or lazy (immoral) because they have not undertaken their rational obligations. By extension of this theory then, those who do not own land or possessions and those who are poor must be stupid, lazy, or crazy; the labour theory of property cannot account for poverty without, in effect, blaming the victim.

Unlike Locke, Rousseau does account for structural poverty in his famous discussion in the second part of the *Discourse on the Origins of Inequality*. Here he declares that the first person to put a fence around a piece of land was "the true founder of civil society!" (Rousseau, *Discourse on the Origins*, Part II, para. 1). Rousseau here recognizes what Locke fails to account for: greed, avarice, and **structural theft**. Structural theft refers to events such as the conquest or usurpation of land that was previously being used by others, such as indigenous peoples, and excluding or restricting them in the use of that land. This was the case for Native Americans when British, French, and Spanish colonists settled on North American land, but also again in the mid-nineteenth century when, in 1848, the United States government appropriated most of California, Colorado, New Mexico, Arizona, and Texas from the Spanish government through the *Treaty of Guadeloupe Hidalgo*. Even though Mexican rancheros owned much of that land, they were gradually dispossessed of it through Supreme Court decisions. This dispossession, or structural theft, coincided with the forced labour of enslaved Africans and indigenous people, for the profit of Mexican and American plantation owners.

Locke also felt that those who did not own property were dangerous. For a modern-day example of the basis of his reasoning, today African Americans, many of whom are descendants of slaves, are on average much poorer than white Americans or certain migrant populations. And 33 percent of men of African-American descent between the ages of 18 and 35 are likely to be incarcerated during their lifetime (Lyons and Pettit 2011). Angela Davis (2003, 2005), a philosopher who advocates for prison abolition, argues that these two facts—poverty and incarceration rates—cannot be seen as coincidental but are, in fact, coextensive with post-slavery poverty and the continuation of slavery through other political and economic systems.

Persons versus Sub-persons (Race)

THE ABOVE DISCUSSION OF LIBERAL THEORY GIVES US AN OPENING BY which to understand why racial or cultural difference may be seen as threatening. This stream of thinking suggests that if others were rational like "us," they would be able to infer the same guidance from the law of nature that "we" do. They would understand what it means to live by the law of nature, since they would live as we do, and they would value many of the same things we do (private property, the ownership of land, market exchange, capital, etc.). What happens when someone lives differently—in fact, does not recognize the same values we hold, such as property or land ownership? We can only infer that this individual either has not understood what it means to live according to the law of nature or has rejected it. In either case, that someone is a threat to be feared because he or she does not participate in the social contract, or does not own private property.

We see some evidence of this in a curious passage in which Locke responds to the question of whether there is any place in the world where men exist outside of a social contract: he points to various indigenous populations who have not participated in the social contract. Another narrative might account for this phenomenon using terms such as *conquest, genocide,* or *Imperialism.* As we know, the indigenous population that inhabited North America was summarily attacked, their lands overtaken, and war declared upon them, ultimately, for not cooperating with English, French, and Dutch settlers. Many indigenous peoples were not respected as potential partners in the social contract, nor was there an interest among settlers and the colonial state in including indigenous populations in it.

Lapses like these in the writings of Locke are seen in the work of more contemporary political philosophers such as Robert Nozick, who wrote *Anarchy, State and Utopia* (1974), a theory of libertarian political justice, and John Rawls, who wrote *A Theory of Justice* (1971). While both point to a state of nature as the starting point for their models of political philosophy, neither of them accounts for slavery except as a momentary aberration in their respective theories of justice. Such an omission is confronted head on by other contemporary political philosophers such as Charles W. Mills. Mills points to the social contract, with its various historical omissions and racial blindness, as revealing the true nature of the social contract to be the **racial contract**. As Mills discusses in his book *The Racial Contract* (1997), there is some question about to whom the social contract applies. Does it apply to everyone, or only to those who are considered "persons"? Does it extend to those who are characterized as "sub-persons" as well?

As Mills suggests, the social contract extended to "persons," but those who might qualify as "a person" were subject to certain powerful opinions. Persons are those who are understood as being reasonable and rational and, although not explicitly stated, the term is most often understood to mean those who are white and male (Mills 1997, Ch. 2). Historically speaking, this interpretation thus extends to those who are not only in charge of creating the social contract (in the instance of Locke, these are the colonists in North America in the seventeenth century), but also in charge of the colonizing project of expropriating land, resources, services, and people as property for the purposes of creating a profit for the metropole. For example, the British Plymouth Colony consisted of English settlers whose mission was to create an economy that would eventually thrive. They did so by extracting the resources of various regional lands. It will come as no surprise to you that John Locke was an adviser to Anthony Ashley-Cooper, the First Earl of Shaftesbury and one of the primary proprietors of the Colony of Carolina (1669). Locke was responsible for writing the Fundamental Constitutions of Carolina, portions of which became the basis for the United States Constitution.

There were settlers other than English males in North America during the seventeenth century. There were Danes, Dutch, and French settlers also, as well as African slaves, white women, and indigenous populations (Kanstroom 2007). The social contract was not "agreed to" by all of them. In fact, this diversity reinforces the notion that the social contract is a historical fiction, the implications of which are very important in the quest to discover what gets left out of the history of political philosophy and the history of liberalism. Depending upon the version of the social contract, it becomes easy to see how the world is divided into those who hold power disproportionately and those who are subject to power disproportionately. For Thomas Hobbes, whose *Leviathan* was written 50 years prior to John Locke's *Treatise of Government*, the social contract was with the Leviathan who agreed to protect you from the nasty and brutish state of nature, and from your neighbour's unchecked greed and avarice. In turn, the Leviathan would become both the author and the actor representing the will of his constituents, and he was owed unconditional obedience, unless a stronger ruler could be found to protect you. In a notable departure from other social contract theories, within Hobbes' contract, women had a similar kind of covenant with the Leviathan.

By contrast, for Locke, the "universalism" of the social contract is much more deceptive: despite the fact that all persons can be privy to the social contract in the abstract, as Charles Mills points out, these rights, if we try to map the social contract historically, are not extended to all persons. The indigenous peoples of North America, for example, were attacked, murdered, and expelled from their ancestral lands or sequestered on "reservations," and often were not considered to be members of sovereign nations. Mills takes his lead for the racial contract notion from Carole Pateman, a political philosopher and author of the *Sexual Contract*, who critiques Hobbes, Locke, and Mills for the sexual double standards embedded in the social contract. White women had their "peculiar" contract to what was theirs by right (Locke, Ch. 7, para. 82), but these rights were ultimately not recognized by the state except through their husbands. The same is true for children. What about the standing and status of racial minority populations in the social contract?

As Mills suggests, the relationship of minority populations to "persons," and to the social contract, is varied. They can be the invisible counterpart of the persons who are part of the contract. They can be part of the "racial contract," as a contract that underlies the social contract; that is to say, they can be classified as "the remaining subset of humans . . . 'nonwhite' and of a different and inferior moral status, subpersons, so that they have a subordinate civil standing in the white or white-ruled polities the whites either already inhabit or establish or in transactions as aliens with these polities" (Mills 1997, 11). Moreover, Mills states, "[T]he moral and juridical rules normally regulating the behavior of whites in their dealings with one another either do not apply at all in dealings with nonwhites or apply only in a qualified form" (1997, 11). And, as importantly, "[T]he general purpose of the Contract is always the differential privileging of the whites as a group with respect to the nonwhites as a group, the exploitation of their bodies, land, and resources, and the denial of equal socioeconomic opportunities to them." All whites, says Mills, "are beneficiaries of the Contract, though some whites are not signatories to it" (1997, 11).

The social contract, then, primarily applies to those who are assumed to be part of the polity, and it can be hesitantly, grudgingly, extended to others. But which others shall be granted access to the social contract? The explicit language of current political discourse suggests that it will be those who "apply legally" to enter the polity. But a careful examination of immigration through the last century in the United States tells us that mostly white, northern Europeans—Swedes, English, Scots, Germans, Irish—and, at various points, southern Europeans such as Italians and Greeks were allowed to enter and reside in the United States. However, South Asian and East Asian immigrants have been entering the United States since as early as 1820. In 1854, for example, 13 000 Chinese migrants entered the United States. Immigration figures for Chinese remained in the four- or five-digit numbers until 1882, when 39 000 Chinese migrants arrived, anticipating the imminent passing of the *Chinese Exclusion Act*. The number of Chinese immigrants then dropped to 8000 in 1883, and to less than 300 in 1884 (Barde, Carter, and Sutch 2006). The irony, of course, is that much of the United States was inhabited by numerous indigenous groups before the Spanish colonized it, and their colonization left the legacy of Mexican rancheros and working-class Mexicans. In contemporary discussions in the United States, the discourse about illegal immigration and illegal aliens implicitly points to Mexican and South American migration into the nation. These populations are not privy to the social contract on the grounds that they are not welcome into the polity because they have not applied. However, reading between the lines, we can infer that these populations are not welcome to join the social contract because they are racially, culturally, and linguistically distinct from "white Americans."

Samuel Huntington was a political scientist who wrote two books that have had a significant impact on how we think about and understand Latino and Arab migrants in the United States. His book *The Clash of Civilizations* describes a deep civilizational clash that would pit the "East" and "West" against each other. Huntington's book indicates an antagonism that the West had for the East, and it also was a harbinger of the unequal impact of the War on Terror on ordinary Muslim, Arab, and South Asian migrants after 19 men flew planes into the World Trade Center and Pentagon, leading to the deaths of approximately 3000 people. The War on Terror, and the racial profiling that ensued, continues to raise questions about unequal access to racial and religious justice, and the extent to which racial minorities and people of diverse faiths are understood as part of the social contract in modern liberal democracies. Take the highly publicized case of Maher Arar, a Canadian citizen of Syrian descent, who was detained at JFK International Airport in New York City on his way back to Canada from a family holiday and sent to Syria, as part of an "extraordinary rendition" plan designed by United States government officials, where he was tortured. Arar was sent first to Egypt and then to Syria, and was tortured and held in a six-foot by nine-foot jail cell for the next 11 months. After a concerted campaign by his spouse, Monia Mazigh, and civil liberties groups, he was finally released and returned to Canada. The Government of Canada's Commission of Inquiry into the Actions of Canadian Officials in Relation to Maher Arar led the Government of Canada to issue an apology and $12.5 million in compensation for abandoning its responsibility to protect Arar, a Canadian citizen, according to the liberal principles of the nation. The United States has never apologized to Arar and still prohibits him and his family from crossing its borders. This may be seen as an example of how racism violates notions of justice and the principles of due process and equal treatment before the law—principles that are thought to be the cornerstone of the social contract in liberal polities.

In the United States, similar actions have occurred, with the indefinite detention of young Muslim men without charges. Some of those men, such as Syed Fahad Hashmi and Tarek Mehanna, have finally had trials, only to be convicted and sentenced to decades in prison on weak evidence. The social contract has not been extended to the Muslim men, who became the targets of the War on Terror. Neither has it been extended to Latino men, women, and children who were subsequently deprived of any judicial review or due process before being deported. Since 2000, nearly 1.5 million Mexicans have been deported from the United States, with 1.2 million of those being deported in the years between 2008 and 2011 (Immigration and Citizenship Enforcement Removal Statistics, 2011). One can only surmise that Charles W. Mills' analysis of the racial contract, although written well before the events of September 11, 2001, have found their way into our current reality, and that racial conspicuousness, especially when articulated as a threat, has an important adverse effect on one's ability to join the social contract.

Dissent and Race: Conspicuousness as a Threat

THERE ARE SEVERAL WAYS IN WHICH RACE AND DISSENT WORK IN A parallel fashion. Racial distinctiveness, when seen against the backdrop of a set of culturally similar values, can be seen as threatening to the cohesiveness of a polity premised on homogeneity. Dominant members of the polity worry that racial conspicuousness, in forms such as diverse religions, cuisines, cultural practices, and even political opinions that are linked to cultural values, will lead to the divisiveness of the polity. For some inhabitants, newcomers are regarded negatively, as upsetting the general agreement of that tightly knit community.

For example, residents of Fort Wayne, an Indiana neighborhood that saw the creation of a Buddhist temple, were very worried about the presence of saffron-robed monks coming and going from the temple, and about parking on the lawns, which they argued violated the aesthetic values of neighbours in the town (Salter Rodriguez 2007). In Hérouxville, Quebec, the town passed a code of conduct outlawing the stoning, burning, or public beating of women; female genital circumcision; burning women; or wearing face veils "except on Halloween." This conduct was directed toward Muslim migrants, despite the fact that the there was not a single Muslim residing in the town (Adams 2007). Other towns worry that the presence of minorities who speak a language different from the official language of the nation will disrupt communities as well.

Dissent, especially political dissent, also is considered quite threatening to liberal polities, especially during times of political uncertainty, such as a war or a recession. Dissent, when formulated as criticism of ruling powers, is a long-standing principle of liberal polities. Nevertheless, considered a threat by state powers, dissent is often pre-empted through legislation. This has been seen in the United States periodically, from the time of the Japanese internment during World War II, during the McCarthy era of the 1950s, and over the last decade since the events of September 11, 2001. The U.S. government has passed the *USA PATRIOT Act*, the 2006 Authorization of Military Force, the 2006 *Military Commissions Act*, and the 2012 *National Defense Authorization Act*. In each of these Bills, there have been increasing restrictions on the kinds of speech deemed acceptable within the United States, on the grounds that certain kinds of speech are "terror"-inducing and must be regulated or investigated for potential security threats to the polity.

Conclusion

THE NARRATIVE OF MODERN LIBERALISM DEPENDS UPON SEVERAL fictions in order for it to hold. It requires an ascription to the social contract, a collective agreement between men that upholds the mutual rights and duties between those men. The original version of the social contract does not overtly distinguish between the actual signatories, who were white, male property owners, and those who were subject to the social contract, such as slaves, women, indigenous populations, and other minorities. However, as Carol Pateman notes in *Sexual Contract*, the social contract is a gendered contract, and as Charles W. Mills notes, it is in fact a racial contract, which depends upon the existence of sub-persons in order for the social contract to hold (see also Pateman and Mills 2007). The idea of the labour theory of property, which justifies the individual's appropriation of land by mixing his labour with it, ignores that the land had been inhabited, utilized, and cultivated by earlier, indigenous populations. Liberal political theory also has difficulties with accommodating political dissent or cultural difference. Those who are minorities or who criticize or dissent from the prevailing laws of the liberal polity are often constrained or punished for attempting to exercise their dissent or difference within the context of society.

Summary

The chapter:

- Explored the gap between the promise of a justice and equal protection for everyone
- Discussed the ways in which the social contract functions differently for individuals who are seen as being of a different culture or race
- Illustrated some of the founding mythologies of liberal political theories, such as the social contract and the labour theory of property
- Explored the differential consequences of dissent and protest, especially as these pertain to minorities or populations of colour

Discussion Questions

1. Is there an actual social contract or is it a fiction?
2. If the social contract has force, to whom does it apply? Does it apply to all individuals equally regardless of race or political opinion, or does it discriminate?
3. What are some ways in which dissent is or is not tolerated within the polity?
4. Can you name examples, outside of those discussed in this chapter, of groups who have been treated unfairly in North America?
5. Can you describe the difference between a person and a sub-person?

References

Adams, Michael. 2007. "Surprise, Canadian Pluralism is Working." *Toronto Star*, November 10.

Allen, Barbara. 2000. "Martin Luther King's Civil Disobedience and the American Covenant Tradition." *Publius* 30(4): 71–83.

Almaguer, Tomas. 1994. *Racial Faultlines: The Historical Origins of White Supremacy in California*. Berkeley and Los Angeles, CA: University of California Press.

Barde, Robert, Susan Carter, and Richard Sutch. 2006. Nonimmigrants Admitted, by Class of Admission: 1925–1996. Table Ad1014-1022. In *Historical Statistics of the United States, Earliest Times to the Present: Millennial Edition,* edited by S. Carter, S. Gartner, M. Haines, A. Olmstead, R. Sutch, and G. Wright. New York: Cambridge University Press. http://dx.doi.or.

Berlin, Isaiah. 1969. *Four Essays on Liberty.* London: Oxford University Press.

Davis, Angela Y. 2003. *Are Prisons Obsolete?* San Francisco: City Lights Open Media.

———. 2005. *Abolition Democracy: Beyond Empire, Prison and Torture.* New York: Seven Stories Press.

Government of Canada. 2006. *Report of the Events Relating to Maher Arar: Analysis and Recommendations.* Commission of Inquiry into the Actions of Canadian Officials in Relation to Maher Arar. Ottawa: Government of Canada.

Hobbes, Thomas. 1985. *Leviathan.* London: Penguin.

Huntington, Samuel. 1998. *The Clash of Civilizations and the Remaking of the World Order.* New York: Simon & Schuster.

———. 2004. *Who Are We? The Challenges to America's National Identity.* New York: Simon & Schuster.

Kanstroom, Daniel. 2007. *Deportation Nation: Outsiders in American History.* Cambridge, MA: Harvard.

Lai, Walton. 1993. *Indentured Labour, Caribbean Sugar: Chinese and Indian Migrants to the British West Indies, 1838–1918.* Baltimore: Johns Hopkins University Press.

Locke, John. 1947. *Two Treatises of Government.* New York: Hafner Press.

Lyons, Christopher and Becky Pettit. 2011. "Compound Disadvantage: Race, Incarceration, and Wage Growth." *Social Problems* 58(2): 257–80.

Mill, John Stuart. 1978. *On Liberty.* Indianapolis, IN: Hackett Press.

Mills, Charles. 1997. *The Racial Contract.* Ithaca, NY: Cornell University Press.

Pateman, Carole. 1988. *The Sexual Contract.* Stanford, CA: Stanford University Press.

Pateman, Carole and Charles Mills. 2007. *Contract and Domination.* Cambridge, U.K.: Polity Press.

Rousseau, Jean-Jacques. 1987. *Basic Political Writings.* Trans. Donald Cress. Indianapolis, IN: Hackett Press.

Salter Rodriguez, Rosa. 2007. "Friction Surprises Buddhist Leaders." *The Journal Gazette* (Fort Wayne, IN), April 29.

Shora, Kareem and Shoba Sivaprasad Wadhia. 2009. *NSEERS: The Consequences of America's Efforts to Secure Its Borders.* American-Arab Anti-Discrimination Committee/Dickinson Law School, Penn State University, March 31, www.adv.org/PDF/nseerspaper.pdf.

United States Immigration and Citizenship Enforcement (ICE). 2011. www.ice.gov/removal-statistics/

Williams, Eric. 1944. *Capitalism and Slavery.* Richmond, VA: University of North Carolina Press.

Further Readings

Adams, Michael. 2007. "Surprise, Canadian Pluralism is Working," *Toronto Star*, November 10.

Berlin, Isaiah. 1969. *Four Essays on Liberty*. London: Oxford University Press.

Pateman, Carole and Charles Mills. 2007. *Contract and Domination*. Cambridge, U.K.: Polity Press.

Rousseau, Jean-Jacques. 1987. *Basic Political Writings*. Trans. Donald Cress. Indianapolis, IN: Hackett Press.

Weblinks

2001 USA PATRIOT Act
http://thomas.loc.gov/cgi-bin/query/z?c107:H.R.3162.ENR:

2006 Authorization of Military Force
www.gpo.gov/fdsys/pkg/PLAW-107publ243/html/PLAW-107publ243.htm

2012 National Defense Authorization Act
http://thomas.loc.gov/cgi-bin/query/z?c112:S.1867

FAIR Media (For Accurate Indigenous Representations)
**www.facebook.com/#!/photo.php?fbid=460093534002792&set=
a.185902321421916.47434.129619997050149&type=1&theater**

Arenas of Politics

"Governance," simply defined, refers to the ways in which we organize our common affairs. Although the exercise of political power and authority is often informal, all modern societies are governed by formal rules and practices exercised through political institutions. In political science, institutions are defined as deliberate, formalized, and expected patterns of behaviour. Political institutions are the embodiment of a state's history of conflict and compromise, as well as sites of ongoing political struggles. In this section of the text, we will discover the origins of the modern state, examine how states constitute the rules of citizenship, review mechanisms of administration and its relationship to politics, and consider the important role of the media for the maintenance of strong democracies. The core institutions of the modern state contain and manage political conflict, make and enforce public policies, and realize political ideas and visions. The final chapter in this section, however, raises the critical issue of how we understand conflict and violence in the creation of the modern state and practice of contemporary politics.

CHAPTER 7

THE STATE

LOIS HARDER

Learning Objectives

- Describes the origin of the concept of the state and clarifies the distinction between state and government

- Summarizes the functions of the state (legislative, executive, administrative, and judicial), and describes some distinctions between legislative and executive functions in presidential and parliamentary systems

- Identifies three variations of the liberal-democratic state

- Outlines three challenges to the nation-state in the contemporary global era

Introduction

The state is the core concept in political science that identifies where the formal and institutional terrain of politics begins and ends. There have been many different kinds of states in recorded history, ranging from the early Greek city state to the modern liberal democratic state. All states, however, perform similar tasks, such as making and implementing political decisions and protecting communities from internal and external threats. This chapter explores the role of the modern state, which traces its origin to sixteenth-century Western Europe.

All societies, from the most simple to the most complex, have organized some way to govern. Some forms of governance have been efficient and enduring, while others have been decided disasters. The sheer number and variety of forms of governance, generally, and of states, in particular, make a simple definition of "the state" elusive. The famous political sociologist Max Weber described the state as a distinct entity that can "successfully claim the monopoly of the legitimate use of physical force within a given territory" (1947, 154). Others make the circular argument that the state is everything that civil society is not. The state is, thus, contrasted with those areas of social life—the domestic world, the economic sphere, and cultural activities—organized by private and voluntary arrangements, individuals, and groups (Held 1996, 57).

Sometimes, the terms *state* and *government* are used interchangeably, but it is important to draw a distinction between the two. One way to think about the difference between state and government is to imagine a car and its driver. The car is analogous to the state, while the driver is analogous to government. All cars have certain components that are required for them to run and distinguish them from other modes of transportation. These components may be organized in a variety of ways and may be more or less powerful depending on the car's design. Similarly, all states perform certain basic functions, such as maintaining the rules through which people interact, though some states may do this more actively than others. Obviously, a driver is essential if the car is to move, but there is no requirement that the driver always be the same. Different drivers may treat the car differently and may choose to steer the vehicle down different paths. They may be more active or passive, but there are limits as to what the machine itself will bear.

Consider the replacement of one political party by another within a modern liberal democracy. A **liberal democracy** is the system of government in which citizens elect representatives in periodic elections. When a new party is elected to form the government, voters have chosen to alter the leadership or policy orientation of the government by selecting a party that will drive the state differently. The offices of the state, however, remain largely the same. The positions of president or prime minister remain, as do general institutions and constitutions. In other words, the offices of the state persist despite the change in government, although the policies pursued by these departments may be altered.

Political scientists generally trace the origins of the modern state to the Treaty of Westphalia of 1648. The treaty brought an end to almost 150 years of religious and territorial conflicts and settled the Thirty Years' War, the first pan-European war. In one sense, the Treaty of Westphalia was simply an agreement to cease hostilities and impose specific terms of settlement. But it also laid the foundations for the modern state, as well as articulating the rules that govern interstate relations, even to the present day (Schmidt 2011).

Contributions of the Treaty of Westphalia to the modern state system include

- Recognition of the primacy of sovereignty—each state exercises absolute authority over the fixed geographic territory it governs, and the national state is recognized as the ultimate power in international relations
- Emergence of international law based on treaties between sovereign countries—all states are regarded as equal before the law (Held 1996, 70)
- Retention of war as a recognized instrument of international relations and the ultimate expression of sovereignty (Schmidt 2011)

What States Do

AFTER RECOGNIZING THE MODERN STATE'S TERRITORIALITY AND sovereignty, political scientists typically study the state in terms of what it does. The most important among the state's functions are its legislative, executive, administrative, and judicial ones. Legislative functions refer to the process of proposing and passing laws. The executive functions of a state refer to the offices that are responsible for implementing and upholding the law as passed by the legislative branch of government. Depending on the system of government, legislative and executive functions can be separate or fused, as discussed below. The administrative function of government refers specifically to the activities of the bureaucracy and involves the day-to-day implementation of laws and public policy. Finally, the judicial function of government concerns the adjudication and application of law, usually carried out by the courts. It is important to recognize that while all states perform these roles, the specific mechanisms or institutions that perform them vary from one country to another and across history. In liberal democratic systems, for example, institutional configurations vary most sharply between presidential and parliamentary systems.

Generally speaking, the legislative function of the state is concerned with making laws. Who makes the laws, what areas of social life are governed by law, and the process of law-making are all dimensions of the legislative function. The legislative function is undertaken by people formally elected as legislators, although the executive and the bureaucracy also play an influential role in law-making. For the purposes of this discussion, we are concerned with two broad approaches to the role of legislatures. In a congressional model of government, such as that of the United States, the power of the legislature (or Congress) is separated from that of the executive (the president and the Cabinet). In such a system, the legislature plays an active role in the legislative process. By contrast, in parliamentary systems of government, such as those of Canada, the United Kingdom, Australia, and New Zealand, there is a fusion of legislative and executive powers. Hence, the initiation and formulation of legislation is largely undertaken by the executive (the prime minister and the Cabinet), while the legislature serves an overseeing and approval function.

The active role of legislatures in congressional systems results from the strict separation of power that characterizes this system. The architects of the American Constitution—the originators of the congressional model—were particularly concerned with limiting the powers of the state generally and also ensuring that no single branch of the state would dominate the others. As a result, they implemented a system of checks and balances through which the legislature (the House of Representatives and the Senate) and the executive (the president) have the power to review each other's decisions, while also having unique responsibilities. For example, executive choices for judges to sit on the U.S. Supreme Court are subject to confirmation by the Senate. Bills passed by Congress must receive the assent of the president before they become law. In both situations, the opportunity exists to overturn the desired action of the president or Congress, respectively.

Fixed terms of office (the American president serves four years, members of the House of Representatives two years, and Senators six years) and separate electoral contests for these branches of government further reinforce the separation, tension, and distinct powers of the legislature and executive. Although citizens of parliamentary democracies sometimes envy the degree of legislative autonomy built into the congressional model, it does have its drawbacks. The legislative process can be very drawn out and unwieldy, with no guarantee that the platform of either the president or the majority party in either house of Congress will be realized. Indeed, if any legislative action is to occur, cooperation between the branches of government is essential.

In contrast to the **separation of powers** in the congressional system, parliamentary systems of government are characterized by the **fusion of power** between the legislative and executive branches. Rather than holding separate elections for these branches, a single electoral process is undertaken. The leader of the party that gains the most seats in that election is named prime minister (PM). The PM subsequently chooses the members of his or her Cabinet (also known as ministers of government departments), generally from among the elected members of the PM's party. The PM and Cabinet then constitute the executive, also known as the government. The remaining elected representatives serve as legislators.

Fixed terms of office are not characteristic of the parliamentary system, although there is a maximum time limit that a government can remain in office before an election must be called. As a result, the government must maintain the confidence of the legislature to remain in office—a feature of parliamentary systems known as responsible government. If the executive is unable to maintain this confidence (that is, majority support of the elected members), the government must resign and, usually, an election will ensue.

Because of this uncertain tenure, party discipline is a key feature of parliamentary governments. It is only through the reliable support of all government party members, be they members of the executive (Cabinet) or the legislature (backbenchers), that the government can be assured of its ongoing survival. Of course, this situation does not require that all members of the various opposition parties vote along party lines. Nonetheless, if they are to represent themselves as a potential alternative to the current government, a coherent voice of opposition is the logical stance to assume.

While legislatures form the heart of democratic representation and policy-making, the growing complexity of law-making has shifted the active process away from legislatures and toward the bureaucracy and the executive. The result has been a decline in the role and power of Parliament, with elected legislators serving an overseeing role and rubber-stamping initiatives taken elsewhere.

In both presidential and parliamentary systems, the formal role of a state's executive is to implement the laws passed by legislators. Presidents and prime ministers, assisted by members of the Cabinet, oversee the implementation process within specific areas of jurisdiction. They set the policy agenda, determining which issues will command the most attention.

Obviously, it is the head of government—that is, the president or prime minister—who is the most prominent member of the executive. But these positions are not synonymous, given the rather distinctive systems of government in which they operate. As we noted previously, for the president's agenda and decisions to be accepted, a high degree of cooperation with the legislature is required. As a result, a considerable portion of the president's staff and executive offices are engaged in this process of negotiation. The president does have a Cabinet, but its members are selected from the country at large, rather than from among the elected representatives. Cabinet members serve at the discretion of the president and are not responsible to either Congress or voters.

The prime minister, as both the leader of the largest party in Parliament and the head of the Cabinet, has a great deal more control over the policy agenda than his presidential counterpart. Nonetheless, the prime minister does not simply proclaim her wishes to Cabinet members and proceed to pass legislation through Parliament. Instead, the Cabinet members work together to formulate the general principles of the government's legislative program, and Cabinet members stand together to support this program.

An additional distinction that must be drawn between the roles of the chief executives in presidential and parliamentary systems is the designation "head of state." The term *head of state* refers to the symbolic representation of a country's identity both to its own citizens and to the world. In the United States, this symbolism is embodied in the person of the president, who also serves as the head of government. In Canada, the head of state is the Queen or, more practically, her representative, the Governor General, while the prime minister serves as the head of government. In functional terms, however, the president and the prime minister both serve as the highest-ranking decision maker for his or her country in international forums. Advocates of the separation of these executive functions observe that the reputation of the country remains untainted when it is represented by someone who is detached from the gritty world of politics. The example of the Watergate scandal that eventually forced

President Nixon from the White House is generally offered as evidence for the benefits of a split executive.

The high profile of heads of state and government aside, it is non-elected officials who undertake the majority of executive functions. In this regard, we might think of the offices and agencies we typically recognize as the bureaucracy. Unlike the elected politicians or political appointees who make up the Cabinet, the role of the bureaucracy is to provide the means by which that policy direction can be achieved (Denhardt and Denhardt 2011).

In simple terms, administering requires making distinct entities work toward a set of common goals. Coordination is central to successful administration. The governance of society is a highly complex administrative task, in terms of the relationships among the state, citizens, organizations, and corporate entities, and within the myriad offices of the state itself. It should not be surprising, then, that administration is a key function of the state. It is made more complex in a democratic society by the demand for accountability. As citizens, we want to know how decisions are made and why things are done as they are. This demand for knowledge requires that the trail of decision making be easily followed.

As modern democracies have attempted to reduce the size of the state in recent years, many governments have shifted some administrative functions to the private sphere. Community groups deliver some social services, private firms may administer the government's payroll, and private corporations run public utilities. As a result, the government's budget may be reduced but citizens have less capacity to ensure that these private entities work in the service of the public good. Further, the opportunity for governments to reward supporters through the granting of contracts can counter the cost-saving rationale of privatization and undermine the government's credibility. In Canada, the auditor general has regularly exposed breaches of accountability guidelines in government contracts to private corporations and inappropriate spending of public funds.

The fourth function integral to the state is the judicial function. Laws are not always precise, and hence there may be differing views as to whether and how they should be enforced. It is the state's role to undertake this process of determining whether actions fit within the purview of the law. The largest share of this function is undertaken by a country's court system, but judicial functions also may be undertaken in less formal settings with less punitive outcomes. The state is responsible for ensuring that the "rule of law" is upheld. Effectively, the rule of law refers to the conditions that must exist for a law to be justified. Certain procedures must be followed in the development of law for it to be considered valid: the punishment for breaking a law must be the same for all people, and laws must apply to everyone equally, regardless of their position within society.

So far, we have outlined the basic functions of the state. However, knowing that all states fulfill legislative, executive, administrative, and judicial functions does not tell us much about how power operates within states or about how the operation of power may be altered over time. To begin exploring these questions, we can examine some of the different forms assumed by the liberal democratic state.

Variations on the Liberal Democratic State

EARLIER IN THIS CHAPTER, WE EXPLORED THE ANALOGY BETWEEN CAR and state and between driver and government. Within the context of that discussion, it was asserted that drivers may change but the structure of the car remains more or less the same. Over time though, the vehicle's structure is subject to innovation and redesign in response to new demands, new technologies, and changed conditions in which it must operate. Similarly, the form of the state has also undergone transformations. Revolutions represent the most dramatic method of altering the form of the state, shifting dictatorships to democracies, as may be occurring in the phenomenon of the Arab Spring, and democracies to dictatorships, as occurred in Guatemala in 1956 and Chile in 1973. Less radically, modern liberal democratic states also evolve and transform. These changes in state form are significant because they reflect a reordering or rebalancing of power within society and, as such, indicate the parameters framing citizen participation in their own governance. For the purposes of this introduction we will examine three liberal democratic state forms that have been implemented in Western liberal democracies in the past two centuries. These include the night watchman or minimalist state, which saw its most profound incarnation in Britain's Industrial Revolution in the nineteenth and early twentieth centuries; the welfare state, which prevailed, in varying degrees, within all Western liberal democracies in the period between the 1930s and the early 1970s; and the neo-liberal state, which ascended in the 1980s but is currently under considerable stress due to mounting economic, social, and environmental crises.

The Night Watchman State

It is not surprising that Marx, writing in the mid-nineteenth century during Britain's Industrial Revolution, would assert that the state was nothing more than "an executive committee of the whole bourgeoisie." He was arguing that the state operated solely in the interests of capital. During this period, participation in elections and the holding of public office were limited to property owners, who had little compulsion to consider the interests of the majority of the population. Because of the unprecedented level of technological development that was occurring during this period, the production of goods increased at an astounding rate and industrialists were enriched accordingly. Agents of the state and elected representatives, most of whom were part-time politicians and full-time businessmen, saw their role as facilitating economic growth, primarily by allowing the market to function with as little regulation as possible, while upholding the laws of property, contract, weight and measurement, and the criminal code.

On the surface, the night watchman state, also termed the **laissez-faire** or minimalist state, appears passive, but its effects on the majority of people were profound. In the absence of any regulation of the conditions of work and the length of the working day, business owners required their employees to labour for long periods of time in dangerous environments. By refusing to play a role in regulating the workplace, the state appeared to be acting passively. However, for the majority of the population, this passivity had significant consequences in terms of their health and independence. While business owners enjoyed an impressive level of personal liberty, such was not the case for the workers who were the vast majority of the population.

This minimalist approach to the regulation of business—the distance between the rhetoric of equality, liberty, and solidarity that imbued the liberal democratic tradition and the real conditions of life for the majority of people—could not be maintained indefinitely. It became increasingly apparent that the long-term success of capitalism was not being well served through employment practices that regularly left workers debilitated and, hence, unable to provide for themselves. To persist with such practices would mean either that factories would run out of workers or that workers would become so disillusioned or angered by their ill-treatment that they would organize to overthrow their employers and perhaps the state as well. It would take the Great Depression of the 1930s, however, before sufficient support for a more interventionist role for the liberal democratic state was achieved.

The Welfare State

The economic crisis that gripped the world in the aftermath of the American stock market crash in October 1929 represented a dramatic challenge to the existing economic and political order. The breadth of the collapse cast so many workers into the ranks of the unemployed that it was no longer possible to blame individuals and their moral weaknesses for their inability to find work. It was clear that some action on the part of the state would have to be undertaken to prevent people from perishing and to salvage failing capitalist economies. It was during this period that social welfare and unemployment insurance programs began to be implemented and legislation expanding workplace organization by trade unions was put into place. It should be noted, however, that these initiatives, particularly in Canada and the United States, were rather tentative in their initial stages. In fact, it was only after World War II that most of the policies and programs of the welfare state were developed.

The war's devastating effect on the economies of Europe and Japan and the sacrifice of so many soldiers' and civilians' lives were powerful catalysts for a rethinking of the role of the state within society. It was clear that an active state would be necessary to rebuild war-torn countries. Further, the extension of voting rights to virtually the entire adult population of most Western countries meant that the interests of a broad range of the population would have to be incorporated within the decision-making process. It was under these conditions that the welfare state realized its fullest expression.

Wanting to prevent further economic dislocations of such magnitude, governments in Western industrialized countries attempted to regulate their economies through the taxing and spending, or fiscal, policies that were first advocated by the British economist John Maynard Keynes. Keynes and the governments that took up his ideas wanted to balance out the boom-and-bust cycles that are characteristic of capitalist economies. In times of economic downturn, governments would use their capacity to borrow as well as the revenues generated during times of growth to inject funds into the economy. Make-work projects, such as bridge and road construction and other public works initiatives, as well as unemployment insurance and social assistance payments, would ensure that people had money to purchase goods, maintain demand, and fuel production. To offset the deficits created during these periods of economic downturn, the state would extract surplus funds during periods of economic growth, thereby creating a balanced budget over the long term.

The **welfare state** also is associated with a variety of universal social programs, including public education, health care, child care, and wage replacement programs, such as unemployment insurance, old age pensions, maternity benefits, and social assistance. Of course, not every country offered the same range of services. Neither were services equally generous across national borders. In the Anglo-American democracies of Canada, Great Britain, the United States, and Australia, for example, many social programs were not universally available to all citizens. Those with adequate incomes might be required to purchase services through the market rather than rely on the state. Other services, particularly public education, would be available to all citizens regardless of income. With regard to services provided on an income, or means-tested, basis, citizens who could not afford to purchase services in the market were subject to the surveillance and regulations of state officials to prove their need and establish their worthiness. Moreover, because women were more likely to seek social assistance, they often were evaluated by social assistance workers with respect to their worthiness as "good women" or "good mothers." It is not surprising, then, that as the economic interventionism of the welfare state came into question, so too did the interventionism of state agents in the lives of citizens.

Perhaps the greatest promise of the welfare state lay in its presumption that all citizens should be able to maintain a minimum standard of living—that there should be some rough equality, if not in terms of outcome, then certainly in terms of opportunity. Initially, this equality was to be realized among members of the working class. White male industrial workers and their families, in particular, were the objects of these ambitions. Yet many other groups were also interested in taking advantage of the opportunities promised by the welfare state. Hence, the post-war period is marked by the struggles of various groups. The Civil Rights movement, Aboriginal peoples, women, the disabled, and youth demanded that the state include their concerns and perspectives within the policy-making process. These growing demands on state resources by groups previously marginalized by the economy and the political process were perceived as a threat by the established order, whose members had long benefited from those exclusionary practices. In addition to the economic crisis and the criticism of the welfare state's methods of service provision, then, the welfare state was subject to criticism from groups that viewed the broadening of the welfare state's constituency as an unwarranted drain on increasingly limited resources leading to demand overload and a crisis in governability. Others viewed these welfare-related controversies as a distraction from the more fundamental role of the state in ensuring the smooth functioning of the market.

As these criticisms intensified and various Western industrialized countries elected governments inclined to rethink the welfare state, it underwent a profound crisis. Although certain elements of the welfare state persist in the state form prevalent in liberal democracies today, a new arrangement between state and society has been consolidated. This new state form has been named the neo-liberal state.

The Neo-Liberal State

The central concern of the agencies of the **neo-liberal state** is to expand the terrain of the free market through cutbacks in social spending, the deregulation of industry, and the privatization of public services (Plant 2010). This objective is reminiscent of that of the night watchman state of nineteenth-century Britain. The current neo-liberal state, however, emerges amid the increased complexity of contemporary societies, the historical experience of the welfare state, and popular expectations regarding the accountability of democratically elected governments. The welfare state both made the promise of equality and incorporated an ever-broadening circle of legitimate claims-makers within the purview of policy-making. In the process, it created expectations of openness among those who wished to challenge the new state form. Nonetheless, the neo-liberal state's emphasis on the primacy of the market has closed many familiar avenues for groups to challenge its policy objectives. As a result, many citizens have become disillusioned with the state's lack of response to their demands and to the emphasis on individual responsibility. People are turning to new forms of political action, such as those used by the Occupy movement.

The emergence of the neo-liberal state form reflects the belief that the power of the state has extended too far, with deleterious consequences for the market and for individual freedom. Proponents of this view argue that power would be better organized on the basis of the informal networks of the family, community, and market, with the state limiting its role to ensuring suitable conditions for economic growth. Accordingly, state policies should support this indirect form of governance through the state's purposeful withdrawal. For example, neo-liberals assert that the national state should divest itself of those functions that impede the market's operation. There may be a limit to market freedom, however. The financial crisis and bank failures that began in 2008 were widely assessed as resulting from too little state regulation.

Another significant motivation behind the push for the neo-liberal state is the desire to accommodate the global mobility of capital. In the attempt to address the problem of over-production and declining profitability that contributed to the demise of the welfare state, large corporations increasingly moved their manufacturing operations and call centres beyond their home countries. Subsequently, a global marketplace has been created in which states compete with each other to attract and maintain increasingly mobile capital. To succeed in this process, many governments have chosen to re-orient the state structures they administer so as to create an appealing environment for investors. While such an environment may be created through a highly educated and skilled workforce, a healthy population, a safe physical environment, and an efficient and effective infrastructure, such an approach requires high levels of public expenditure. Rather than making these investments, many governments have chosen, instead, to promote a low-wage workforce, minimum levels of regulation, and low taxes, especially for the corporate sector. Not surprisingly, levels of public service provision have been reduced accordingly. The degree of citizen participation in governance has also dropped. International trade agreements, such as the *North American Free Trade Agreement*, the trade agreements of the World Trade Organization, and the European Union, limit the range of policies available to governments. Proposals that might be perceived as infringing on profitability or as protecting the domestic economy are open to challenge from other countries. The elevation of the economy and of trade liberalization as primary organizing principles in public policy, in turn, gives financial managers and business interests inordinate influence in the policy-making process. The capacity of citizens to influence their national governments has been reduced, both in terms of opportunities and avenues of appeal, and in terms of the social acceptability of organized dissent. Protests against the imposition of austerity measures in Greece, Italy, and the U.K. in the fall of 2011 demonstrate how frustrating this lack of citizenship engagement has become to many people directly affected by neo-liberal economic policies.

The State in a Globalizing Era

AS THE CONTEMPORARY PROCESS OF GLOBALIZATION HAS ADVANCED, scholars have engaged in lively debates concerning the ongoing relevance of the state. Reductions in barriers to the flow of goods, services, and finance capital and the promotion of production for global, rather than national, markets have created a situation in which economies no longer correspond to nation-states. In this context, it is asserted that the national state has become less significant. Power has moved to other levels or scales of governance—upward to international institutions, such as the WTO; outward to the market; and downward to sub-national levels of government, the family, and the individual (Jessop 2009).

But as the effects of globalization become increasingly apparent, the voices of moderation are becoming louder. Even the most fervent supporters of the global market, from the World Bank to the World Economic Forum (WEF), now concede the need for a reinvigorated state and a renewed focus on the need for social cohesion and political stability. As well, growing international concern surrounding the effects of climate change has intensified demands for increased state regulation of high-polluting industries and implementation of programs designed to reduce greenhouse gas emissions.

The reassertion of a role for the national state is also evident in responses to the increased security concerns that have emerged after September 11, 2001. A raft of legislation has been passed in liberal democracies, enabling national governments to infringe on democratic rights, including free speech, freedom of association, and the right to privacy. As these rights were enacted to protect citizens from the arbitrary use of state power, their diminishment is a clear representation of a perceived need for a strong state in the face of ambiguous but certain threats. The exercise of nation-state power in areas including security, disease, surveillance, immigration, and border controls aptly demonstrates that the nation-state continues to command considerable power.

Conclusion

THIS CHAPTER DEMONSTRATES THAT THE STATE IS BOTH CONSTANT IN its enforcement and reflection of the power dynamics at work within a given society and adaptable to the historical circumstances in which it is situated. Although the state is often perceived as monolithic and impenetrable, a long-term view reveals that the institutions and functions of the state change considerably over time.

This introduction to the state provides a sense of the breadth of this topic, an overview of the key functions of the state, a brief account of the various forms of the liberal democratic state, and some consideration of contemporary challenges facing the state. The state is not fixed in time but is reformed through political struggle and altered circumstances. The study of the state should be viewed as a rich field of inquiry and one that, in all its complexity, is an essential component of the study of politics.

Summary

The chapter:

- Traced the origin of the concept of the state and clarified the distinction between state and government
- Summarized the functions of the state (legislative, executive, administrative, and judicial), and described how legislative and executive functions differ in presidential and parliamentary systems
- Described the transformation of the liberal democratic state from night watchman through welfare to a neo-liberal form
- Outlined contemporary challenges to the nation-state in an era of globalization

Discussion Questions

1. What are the primary functions of the state, and how do they relate to each other?
2. Assess the strengths and weaknesses of the congressional and parliamentary models of government.
3. Is it fair to say that Canada's national state is undergoing a change in its form? What evidence can you produce to support your claim?
4. What is the likelihood that international institutions will replace nation-states as the primary mechanisms for governance?

References

Denhardt, Janet V. and Robert B. Denhardt. 2011. *The New Public Service: Serving, Not Steering*. Armonk, NY: M.E. Sharpe Inc.

Held, David. 1996. "The Development of the Modern State." In *Modernity*, edited by Stuart Hall, David Held, Don Hubert, and Kenneth Thompson. London: Blackwell.

Jessop, Bob. 2009. "From Governance to Governance Failure and from Multi-level Governance to Multi-scalar Meta-governance." *Environment and Policy* 49(2): 79–98.

Plant, Raymond. 2010. *The Neo-liberal State*. Oxford: Oxford University Press.

Schmidt, Sebastian. 2011. "To Order the Minds of Scholars: The Discourse of the Peace of Westphalia in International Relations Literature," *International Studies Quarterly* 55(3): 601–23.

Weber, Max. 1947. *The Theory of Social and Economic Organization*. New York: Free Press.

Further Readings

Held, David. 1989. *Political Theory and the Modern State: Essays on State, Power and Democracy*. Stanford, CA: Stanford University Press.

Klein, Naomi. 2007. *The Shock Doctrine: The Rise of Disaster Capitalism*. New York: Metropolitan Books.

Pierson, Christopher. 2004. *The Modern State*, 2nd edition. London: Routledge.

Scott, James C. 1998. *Seeing Like a State*. New Haven, CT: Yale University Press.

Weblinks

AgoraXchange—global politics game
www.agoraxchange.net

Centre for the Future State
www2.ids.ac.uk/gdr/cfs/

Government of Canada
www.gc.ca

United States Government
www.usa.gov

CHAPTER 8

CONSTITUTIONS AND INSTITUTIONS

IAN URQUHART

Learning Objectives

- Introduces the concept of rule of law

- Examines key formal political institutions of democratic governance

- Outlines the importance of constitutions for political participation

- Critically assesses key institutions of liberal democracies and their impact on citizen rights

Introduction

Over the ages, power is one constant in political life. How much power does the state have over citizens, over society? Is state power concentrated in one level of government or is it divided among several levels of government? Similarly, are key state functions, such as making laws or implementing legislation, the exclusive property of one branch of a government or are they shared between several?

This chapter addresses these questions by introducing you to the institutional characters of liberal-democratic political life. "Characters" alludes first to the executive, legislative, and judicial branches of government (e.g., the presidency, Parliament, and the Supreme Court). We also examine key relationships between these institutions and important differences in the institutional complexion of liberal democracies. These institutional relationships and differences, in turn, influence the possibility, nature, and quality of public participation in political life.

The chapter opens with a statement about the importance of the rule of law to governing in liberal democracies. It then considers some of the details of constitutions. Constitutions provide the blueprints for the operations of modern governments. They also suggest the suite of values that are important in their host polities, both now and in the past. It goes on to suggest that, while all liberal democracies are likely to declare their devotion to ideals, such as public participation, their institutional arrangements will affect the de facto strength of that devotion. We end by looking critically at how the institutions of liberal democracies protect citizen rights.

Rule of Law

SADDAM HUSSEIN WAS THE NOTORIOUS PRESIDENT OVERTHROWN BY the American-led invasion of Iraq in 2003. Representative Tom DeLay was the leader of the Republican-party majority that controlled the United States House of Representatives when American forces captured Baghdad. What, other than connections to the war in Iraq, could possibly link a brutal dictator with one of America's most powerful politicians?

The answer is the **rule of law**, a cornerstone of democratic political regimes. In its decision in *Reference re Manitoba Language Rights* (1985), the Court said the rule of law demanded at least two things. First, it required "that the law is supreme over officials of the government as well as private individuals, and thereby preclusive of the influence of arbitrary power." The abrupt end of Tom DeLay's hold on political power also illustrates this point well. DeLay resigned from the House in June 2006 amidst political corruption allegations. In January 2011, he was sentenced to three years in prison for money laundering—illegally funnelling corporate donations to Republicans running for the Texas legislature. The judge who sentenced DeLay emphasized that the politicians who write laws must "be bound by them." He appeared to accept a prosecutor's argument that DeLay should not be treated leniently just because of the status and political power he enjoyed. Leniency would violate a fundamental premise of the rule of law: all citizens, regardless of wealth, social status, or political position, are subordinate to the law.

Saddam Hussein's conviction for executing 148 Shia men and boys in Dujail in 1982 can be linked to the second condition articulated by the Supreme Court of Canada. Here, the rule of law "requires the creation and maintenance of an actual order of positive laws that preserves and embodies the more general principle of normative order. Law and order are indispensable elements of civilized life." Ensuring his fair trial was regarded as essential to the legitimacy of overthrowing Hussein, and to enhancing prospects for democratizing Iraq. The irregularities and chaos surrounding his trial led legal experts to conclude that Hussein was not given the essential right to present a full defence against the charges against him (three defence lawyers were murdered, judges were under intense political pressure from the Iraqi government to deliver a quick conviction, and more than two dozen witnesses were too intimidated to testify). International legal experts ultimately concluded that Hussein's trial was "reasonably fair"; however, in order for Iraq to realize its full democratic possibilities, the rule of law must be more robust than "reasonably fair."

Constitutions: Guides to Political Processes and Values

IF THE RULE OF LAW IS A CRUCIAL ELEMENT OF DEMOCRATIC POLITICS, then a **constitution** stands as the most important source of legal authority. Its overarching importance stems from the fact that constitutional provisions regulate the fundamental operations of a polity's institutions and the relationships between them. Constitutions offer us basic information about the rules of the political game, who may play, and who is likely to play starring and supporting roles.

Unwritten/Written Constitutions and Conventions

In the study of constitutions, a key distinction is made between *written* and *unwritten* constitutions. Written, sometimes called *codified*, constitutions generally refer to a single document that is the supreme law of the country. Among other things, a written constitution can specify founding values, citizenship rights, the distribution of political power within a country, and the respective roles of the executive, legislature, and courts. The Constitution of the United States, first adopted in 1787, is one of the best known and longest surviving written constitutions in the world. It has been amended 27 times, most recently in 1992. Perhaps the best known *unwritten* constitution is that of the United Kingdom. In the U.K., many of the most significant and well-accepted constitutional practices of the country are not contained in a constitution-like document but rather exist as *constitutional conventions*. Conventions may be regarded as extra-legal rules or practices that have been consistently

(Continued)

(Continued)

followed over a long historical period. Although in Canada many of the key components of the constitution are included in the Constitution Acts of 1867 and 1982, others exist merely as convention. For example, the office of prime minister is not mentioned in any written constitutional document; it exists by convention.

The American Constitution illustrates this point well. Its first three articles clearly delineate the separation of powers among the **legislature**, the **executive**, and the **judiciary** (see Box titled, Three Branches of Government, below). Article I of the Constitution locates legislative power in the House of Representatives and the Senate. It next outlines the structure and powers of these institutions, the qualifications needed to run for electoral office, and the timing of elections. What powers does the president have? Who can run for president? Such questions are answered in Article II's discussion of the executive powers of the presidency. Information about the responsibilities of the federal courts rests in Article III.

Three Branches of Government

When examining the governing structures of any country, it is possible to see government as divided among three functions or branches: the executive branch, the legislative branch, and the judiciary. Most easily understood, the executive is responsible for the execution of laws and for the bureaucratic arm of government. Generally, the executive also can propose laws for legislative review, while the legislature creates, debates, and enacts legislation. Although power in most political systems increasingly rests in the executive, the legislature has authority because it is understood as representing the will of the people. The judiciary is generally independent from the executive and legislature and adjudicates disputes over the legality and application of various laws. The organization of the three branches of government varies from country to country. For example, Canada and the United States, both liberal democracies, have organized the three branches of government differently. The United States is a federal republic. The head of state and head of government is the president of the United States. The president and his Cabinet cannot sit simultaneously in Congress due to a constitutionally mandated **separation of powers**. The legislature in the U.S. is bicameral (meaning two houses), composed of the House of Representatives and the Senate. Both houses are elected. Finally, the judiciary is divided into municipal, state, and federal jurisdictions, and some jurisdictions elect judges in general elections. The Supreme Court of the United States is the highest court of appeal.

Canada is also a federal state, but it is organized in keeping with the British parliamentary tradition. In Canada, the head of state is the Queen, represented by the Governor General, and the head of government (by convention) is the prime minister of Canada. The executive is composed of the prime minister and his Cabinet. All are members of Parliament (MPs). This merger of the executive and the legislative branches produces a **fusion of powers**. Canada's national legislature is also bicameral, consisting of the House of Commons and the Senate. Only MPs of the House of Commons are elected, while members of the Senate are appointed. Canada's judiciary is organized on a provincial and national level. All judges are appointed and the Supreme Court of Canada is the highest judicial authority.

Not all written constitutions, however, offer good guidance about how a political system operates. In Zimbabwe, for example, government-orchestrated political assaults, murders, and intimidation of opposition party candidates and supporters characterized recent election campaigns despite the constitution's impressive written commitment to rights.

In well-established liberal democracies, too, political practice may stray—but far less severely and regularly—from constitutional expectations. Some will say that the case of Alex Hundert, a key figure in the protests held during the G20 meetings in Toronto in June 2010, illustrates how liberal democracies may stray from democratic ideals. Toronto police arrested Hundert in September 2010 for violating one of his bail conditions. What was his crime? He participated in a panel discussion about the G20 summit at Ryerson University. Authorities insisted this violated the condition that Hundert not participate in any public demonstration. Civil libertarians were outraged at the "generous" interpretation of what constituted a public demonstration; his bail agreement also forbade Hundert from speaking to the media. Anyone concerned about the rights to participate politically should be concerned when someone accused of a crime is forbidden to speak.

Constitutions as Barometers of Political Conflict

CONSTITUTIONS AND CONSTITUTIONAL POLITICS SHOULD BE STUDIED for reasons other than for what they tell us about how the political process operates. They bear examination for what they reveal about the nature of political conflict and the balance of political power in countries we study. The politics of constitutional change also tells us a great deal about societal conflicts and changes.

Amendments to the United States Constitution testify to how emerging political issues and conflicts modified the original political consensus forged in the 1787 Constitution. The American Bill of Rights of 1791—the first ten amendments to the Constitution— harkened back to the American Revolution's emphasis on individual liberty. It addressed the absence of an explicit commitment to protect individual freedoms in the original constitution; those who feared that a strengthened national government would be emboldened enough to try on the robes of the English king demanded the addition of this list of constitutionally guaranteed freedoms.

Conflicts over the meaning of political equality in the United States also may be seen through the lens of American constitutional politics. Three constitutional amendments, the Thirteenth to the Fifteenth, adopted in the aftermath of the Civil War promoted political equality for African Americans. Expanding the boundaries of political equality also inspired several twentieth-century amendments, the most significant being the Seventeenth (popular election of senators), the Nineteenth (extending the right to vote to women), and the Twenty-sixth (reducing the voting age to 18).

A similar story is told by the 1982 amendments to the Canadian constitution through which Canada's federal and provincial governments (over the objections of Quebec) accomplished two significant goals. First, they patriated Canada's original written constitution (the *British North America Act* now referred to as the *Constitution Act 1867*) from Britain. Second, through the *Constitution Act 1982* they added a *Charter of Rights and Freedoms*, Aboriginal rights, an amending formula, a commitment to promote equal opportunities and public services, and a natural resources amendment to the *Constitution Act 1867*. Governments incorporated the Charter into the constitution to protect individual rights and freedoms with respect to the actions of both federal and provincial governments. Many sections of the Charter highlight the political debates that were ongoing in Canada in the 1970s. For example, section 15 addressed concerns about discrimination against marginalized groups, section 23 established the linguistic educational rights for anglophones and francophones, and section 27 offered support to multiculturalism in Canada. Thirteen years after the entrenchment of the Charter, the Supreme Court ruled that sexual orientation also was a prohibited ground of discrimination because it was analogous to the other personal characteristics protected by section 15. Several non-Charter sections of the *Constitution Act 1982*—those pertaining to Aboriginal rights, the amending formulae, and natural resources—also address important political controversies of that era. The nature of today's politics illustrates well that addressing controversies in a constitution does not guarantee their resolution.

Constitutions alone cannot ensure that the political differences responsible for conflict will be accommodated successfully. Democratic constitutional government is based on will as well as words; it demands certain attitudinal commitments, such as to accommodation, tolerance, and a willingness to live together. Without these attitudes, constitutions may be written in ways that exclude and disadvantage some citizens while including and privileging others. Constitutional politics in post- Hussein Iraq illustrate this point. In 2005, Iraqis ratified a new constitution for their fledgling democracy. Two of Iraq's three main sectarian/ethnic groups, the Shiites and Kurds, strongly supported ratification. Sunnis, who had profited handsomely during Hussein's rule, generally opposed ratification but could not deliver the super-majorities needed to defeat the referendum. Their fear, shared with Sunni constitutional negotiators, was that the majority Shiite population and the Kurdish minority would use the new constitutional arrangements to punish the minority Sunnis for the largesse they enjoyed at the hands of Hussein. Ideally, constitutions safeguard minority rights, but this is not always the case, as the Zimbabwe case illustrates. The competition for power often trumps constitutional intentions and practice.

Unitary or Federal?

ONE OF THE MORE CONTENTIOUS ISSUES OF CONSTITUTIONAL development in Iraq revolved around how power should be divided between national and regional governments. Would Iraqis adopt a unitary or a federal system of government?

What do we mean when we say that a constitution is federal? A federal constitution divides sovereignty between a national government and sub-national governments (American states, Canadian provinces). In federal systems, the national government has exclusive jurisdiction over some constitutionally specified areas, while sub-national governments exercise exclusive jurisdiction over others. Some federal constitutions also specify areas of shared jurisdiction. For example, in Canada the national government has exclusive jurisdiction over defence and banking; provinces enjoy this authority over education and natural resources (except for their export); jurisdiction is shared over agriculture and immigration (but national laws are paramount over provincial ones when they conflict). How sovereignty is divided among national and sub-national governments varies widely from one country to another. Canadian provinces, for example, have greater powers than American states.

The concept of sovereignty offers a useful means to distinguish between federal and unitary constitutional systems. In a **unitary constitutional system**, as is found in the United Kingdom or France, sovereignty rests solely with the national government. Although unitary states may include regional or local governments, their responsibilities and powers are set by the national government and not by the constitution. This means that national governments can give power to sub-national governments, although legally they also can take this power back. For example, in 1998, after a 1997 referendum, the Parliament of the United Kingdom passed the *Scotland Act.* The Act reserved certain powers for the U.K. Parliament and devolved the remaining powers to a newly created Scottish Parliament. Elected in 1999, it was granted the power to legislate on matters such as education, health, and local government. It also may vary the income tax Scots pay by a very small amount—a so-called "Tartan Tax." But these powers were not entrenched in a constitutional document. To the dismay of Scottish nationalists then, the British Parliament retained the power to modify the Scots' basket of powers in any way it wishes. Thus, the Scottish Parliament has passed legislation to hold a referendum on Scottish independence in the fall of 2014.

Fusion or Separation of Powers? Legislative/Executive Relationships in Canada and the United States

WE NOTED EARLIER THAT THE AMERICAN CONSTITUTION OUTLINES the separation of powers between the legislative, executive, and judicial branches of government. To a significant extent, this choice underlined why Americans rejected the British system, which fuses executive and legislative power. Canada, in contrast, chose to emulate rather than reject the British model of parliamentary government. Consequently, Canada was constituted as a Westminster-styled parliamentary democracy that unifies the powers of the executive (the prime minister and Cabinet) with the legislature. Moreover, unlike the United States, all members of Cabinet must be either elected to the House of Commons or appointed to the Senate of Canada.

These historical constitutional choices have important consequences today for the power and responsibilities of their respective executives and legislatures. Ask yourself if you would rather be the American president or the Canadian prime minister. Or, if you could be either a Canadian member of Parliament or a member of the American House of Representatives or Senate, what choice would you make? If you are interested in seeing your vision prevail in laws and policies, you should want to be the Canadian prime minister, not the president of the most powerful country in the world today. Following this logic, your backup plan should be to become a member of the American Congress, not a Canadian MP. Why? The fusion of powers in Canada's parliamentary system enable the political executive (the prime minister and Cabinet) to dominate the legislature when the governing party holds the majority of seats in the House of Commons. Prime ministerial domination, enforced through strict **party discipline**, disempowers individual members of Parliament when it comes to making laws. The American president, generally (foreign policy may be an exception here), cannot dominate Congress in the same way. The president must negotiate with Congress on most matters. This process is most difficult when the president and the majority of the members of Congress come from different parties. As President Barack Obama's first term clearly demonstrates, partisan divisions between the two branches of government can lead to legislative inertia and stalemate. Members of the American House of Representatives and the Senate are far more powerful than Canadian legislators.

The difference between these two governing systems is clearly illustrated through the budgetary process. Trolling through the media waters for comments on President Obama's $3.8 trillion 2013 fiscal year budget, one is struck by the words used to describe it. *The New York Times* and *The Washington Post* both called it a "proposal," CNN called it a "request," and NBC Politics flatly answered "no" to a question asking if Congress was required to vote on the Obama budget. The Canadian media's descriptions of the Conservative government's March 29, 2012, budget couldn't be more different. With a majority in the House of Commons, reporters wrote as if there was no doubt that the budget would essentially be approved without any significant changes. Certainty about the budget's timely passage through Parliament also could be seen in the fact that, within a few days of the budget's release, the government started informing public servants that they would lose their jobs. There was no doubt, in other words, that the job cuts promised in the budget would be made. Although opposition MPs forced a series of votes on proposed amendments to the budget in June 2012, the Conservative majority voted each amendment down in a marathon session. That majority made parliamentary opposition to the budget largely symbolic.

These examples illustrate the sharp differences between the strengths of the executive and legislative branches in Canadian and American national politics. Congress's crucial legislative role gives its members real power to challenge and amend presidential spending priorities and plans. The public questioning of presidential spending priorities that Oval Office occupants regularly endure from Congressional members of their own parties is unheard of in Canadian politics. Although opposition parties can influence the government's agenda in minority parliaments, individual members of Parliament rarely shape legislation on their own. Moreover, members of the governing party risk their political careers if they publicly criticize the government's agenda, as the Prime Minister's Office determines committee assignments and promotion to Cabinet. The lengthy, often tortuous, path of legislation in American politics—a rarity in Canadian politics when a prime minister enjoys a parliamentary majority—suggests other notable aspects of executive/legislative relationships. They pertain to the efficacy, transparency, and accessibility of parliamentary and congressional politics in Canada and the United States. Efficacy, understood as quickly passing bills once they are introduced in the legislature, is a hallmark of Canadian parliamentary life during periods of majority government. This strength, though, often comes at the expense of transparency and accessibility. The reverse is typical of American politics.

Budgetary politics, again, may be used to illustrate this point. In Canada, the norm has been for the finance minister to deliver a budget speech sometime during the first three months of the calendar year. That speech outlines the government's general spending and revenue targets. It offers Canadians an economic forecast, and tells them whether the government expects to deliver a surplus or a deficit; it tells them what measures the governing party believes need to be implemented in order to reach those fiscal targets. A bill seeking to implement the measures announced in the budget will be tabled in the House of Commons at this time. This bill generally is passed quite expeditiously; for example, the *Budget Implementation Act of 2009* was introduced on January 29, 2009, and became law just six weeks later. This process was certainly efficacious. The *Budget Implementation Act of 2009*, at 552 pages, amended more than two dozen federal laws and authorized payments of nearly $6 billion for 17 infrastructure and housing programs. But, by amending so many pieces of legislation in such a short time frame, the governing Conservative party sacrificed the values of accessibility and transparency. In fact, the House of Commons Standing Committee on Finance was the only committee that considered the massive implementation bill and devoted a mere two days to considering all of the legislative amendments and measures it contained. Public scrutiny and public participation are not valued highly in such a process. In the United States, by contrast, the two Houses of Congress will deliberate for seven months or more on the budget. In February, the president sends his budget request to Congress. The request is reviewed by budget committees in both the House of Representatives and the Senate. These committees draft separate budget resolutions (a general blueprint for how much individual federal departments and agencies will spend). Any differences between these blueprints are reconciled through a joint House-Senate conference committee. Next, 12 appropriations sub-committees in each chamber meet to consider the discretionary budget amounts requested for the federal agencies the respective committees are responsible for. Hearings are held, witnesses are called, the 24 subcommittees pass their appropriations measures and submit them to the full appropriations committees for their approval. After this committee approval, the House and Senate then vote on the appropriations bills crafted by their respective subcommittees; differences between these bills, and there usually are differences, are then worked out through another joint conference. The House and Senate vote again on the reconciled appropriations bill, and this final product goes to the president.

Laborious, time-consuming, maddening—these are some of the words used to describe the American budget process. Efficacious is not likely to spring from the lips of many. But this process clearly is more transparent and more accessible than its Canadian counterpart.

Rights and Constitutions

JUST AS FEDERAL CONSTITUTIONS LIMIT THE LEGAL AUTHORITY OF governments vis-à-vis each other, constitutions also limit the legal authority governments exercise vis-à-vis their citizens. This function is both important and controversial. The Bill of Rights and other constitutional amendments limit American governmental power over their citizens. Canada's *Charter of Rights and Freedoms* plays the same role. Part of the drive to incorporate the Charter into Canada's constitution developed out of a major shortcoming of the *Canadian Bill of Rights* (1960), which was an ordinary piece of federal legislation that did not apply to provincial actions.

Viewers of American police dramas may be familiar with the Miranda warning American police officers must give to arrested suspects. The requirement to warn suspects that they have the right to remain silent and to consult a lawyer arose from the case of *Miranda v. Arizona*. In that case, the U.S. Supreme Court overturned the conviction of a confessed kidnapper and rapist because the police violated Miranda's Fifth Amendment right not to be compelled to make self-incriminating statements. This Fifth Amendment protection exemplifies **negative rights**—rights individuals have against being interfered with by other actors, such as government. In the relationship between government and citizens, negative rights protect people from government interference.

Written constitutions also may guarantee **positive rights**—rights requiring government intervention in order to be realized. The minority-language educational rights outlined in section 23 of the *Canadian Charter of Rights and Freedoms* illustrate this alternative form of rights guarantee. This section stipulates that, where the numbers of children warrant, Canadian citizens have the right to have minority language (English/French) education and educational facilities provided and paid for by the government.

Constitutional guarantees of rights are controversial for many reasons. The Miranda case raised one of the controversies associated with legal rights. Respecting individual rights, occasionally, may mean that the guilty escape punishment because their rights were violated. For some, constitutional rights are controversial, because interpreting constitutional meaning is turned over to the courts. Some critics of judicial review in Canada and the United States argue that judges have the power to change the constitution in ways never intended by its the framers. In Canada, these constitutional literalists also argue that the Charter is undemocratic because it gives power to unelected judges to overturn the decisions of elected legislatures.

Courts, Legislatures, and Rights

Important as these controversies are, it is prudent to warn against a mythology, particularly significant in Canada, about constitutional rights. The core of the mythology is that judges, through judicial review, further rights while politicians and public servants, through their laws and actions, restrict rights. This is a dangerous caricature. It exaggerates the rights-protecting nature of the judiciary and undervalues the extent to which legislatures also may champion the rights and well-being of citizens. There are several important fallacies in the conventional outlook on rights, courts, and legislatures. One fallacy lies in the message that the Charter simply protects the rights of individuals against the state. While this is sometimes true, it is also the case that the courts can interpret the Charter in ways that protect the rights of some individuals at the expense of another category of individuals. In other words, individuals or groups of similar individuals both gain and lose in some Charter decisions. Judicial review of the Charter may involve considerably more than upholding the rights of the individual against the government.

This general point that Charter cases may deal with inter-group conflict was illustrated dramatically in *R. v. Seaboyer*, a case that struck down Canada's rape-shield law. This federal law had abolished some old common-law rules that permitted evidence of a rape victim's sexual conduct to be heard by a jury, irrespective of whether the evidence was relevant to the case at hand. The judge in Seaboyer's trial followed the letter of the rape-shield law; he refused to let the defence question the complainant about her sexual history. Seaboyer's attorney argued this decision denied Seaboyer his section 11(d) Charter right to a fair trial. Justice Beverley McLachlin, writing for a majority of the Supreme Court in a 7–2 decision, agreed. She concluded the law created "the real risk that an innocent person may be convicted." At one level, the Seaboyer decision fits the individual versus the state framework well. Government law treated Seaboyer harshly; the Supreme Court vindicated his rights. However, at another level we can also see that the state's law existed to protect the rights or interests of the vulnerable, the victims of sexual assault. In this case, the decision protected the interests of one category of individuals (the accused) at the expense of the interests of others (the alleged victims). Court battles over whether laws violate the Charter may well be battles between classes of individuals and not simply battles between individuals and the state.

The Seaboyer case also allows us to argue that the core of the constitutional rights mythology, that courts protect rights and legislatures restrict rights, is fallacious. The example of Seaboyer shows the reality to be far more complicated. Government legislation actually may protect or further the rights or interests of particular, not necessarily majority, constituencies. Through legislation such as the rape-shield law, governments may improve the position in our society of vulnerable or disadvantaged groups. This possibility also casts a more favourable light on the often criticized **notwithstanding clause**. This clause, section 33 of the *Canadian Charter of Rights and Freedoms*, enables the federal and provincial governments to reinstate laws found to be unreasonable violations of the rights guaranteed under sections 2 (fundamental freedoms) and 7 to 15 (legal and equality rights). That government so seldom even considers using section 33 to sustain legislative protection of the vulnerable may testify well to the strong grip the constitutional rights mythology has on Canadian psyches. Regardless of what institution you believe best protects rights, it would be naive to let that view blind you to the possibility that other considerations may temper the judiciary's enthusiasm for playing this role. Courts may be rather meek defenders of rights claims if strongly upholding those claims may threaten their political legitimacy and relationship with other institutions, such as the political executive. The tragic example of Omar Khadr, the Canadian convicted by a U.S. Military Commission of murdering a U.S. soldier in Afghanistan, may illustrate well how such other considerations temper the judiciary's enthusiasm to uphold rights.

On July 27, 2002, the 15-year-old Khadr was taken prisoner by United States troops after a battle with Taliban and Al-Qaeda forces. Near the end of that battle Khadr allegedly threw a grenade that killed an American soldier. In October, Khadr was transferred to Guantanamo Bay where the juvenile, like other Guantanamo detainees, was enrolled in the "frequent flyer program"—a sleep deprivation technique designed to break one's resistance to interrogation. In 2003, Canadian officials interviewed Khadr to gather intelligence. They shared this information with American officials despite knowing about the interrogation tactics used to extract information from Khadr. The U.S. finally laid charges against Khadr more than two years later, an extraordinary length of time, after his capture. Then Khadr's lawyers demanded the disclosure of all documents relevant to those charges that the Canadian government possessed. Canada refused to disclose the Guantanamo interview records. In 2008, Canada's Supreme Court decided in *Canada (Justice) v. Khadr* that the government's refusal to disclose this material violated the young man's rights under section 7 of the *Charter of Rights and Freedoms*. A unanimous Court wrote, "The remedy of disclosure being granted to Mr. Khadr is for breach of a constitutional duty that arose when Canadian agents became participants in a process that violates Canada's international obligations." With this ruling, Khadr's lawyers obtained most of the information they sought in order to defend their client. To this point, the Supreme Court upheld Khadr's constitutional citizenship rights.

Khadr's lawyers were back in court making another constitutional argument less than three months after the May 2008 ruling. This second case, building on the first ruling's declaration that Khadr's section 7 rights had been violated, sought to bring Khadr back to Canada to stand trial. They argued that Khadr's right to liberty and security of the person had been violated by his treatment, and that the appropriate remedy would be to repatriate Khadr to Canada. A unanimous Supreme Court in *Canada (Prime Minister) v. Khadr* agreed again that Khadr's section 7 rights had been violated. It wrote, "The interrogation of a youth detained without access to counsel, to elicit statements about serious criminal charges while knowing that the youth had been subjected to sleep deprivation and while knowing that the fruits of the interrogations would be shared with the prosecutors, offends the most basic Canadian standards about the treatment of detained youth suspects." The Court also agreed that the remedy sought, that the Canadian government request his repatriation, was "sufficiently connected" to the government's violation of Khadr's rights. But the Court refused to order the executive to make such a request. Instead, its decision only provided a "declaratory remedy"—declaring that Khadr's rights were violated, without ordering that anything actually be done about the violation. Some interpreted the Court's timidity as reflecting the judiciary's desire to avoid a constitutional crisis. Such a crisis might have developed if the Prime Minister refused to accept an order to request repatriation. This could have happened, considering Prime Minister Harper's longstanding refusal to request Khadr's repatriation. Potential institutional conflict arguably trumped a clear violation of individual rights in this instance. Khadr was eventually repatriated to Canada in October 2012 to serve out the rest of his sentence in a Canadian prison, reportedly at the insistence of the American government.

Conclusion

IN THIS CHAPTER, WE HAVE TRIED TO GIVE YOU A BRIEF TASTE OF THE institutional character of liberal democracies. We sketched out several roles that constitutions play in liberal democracies, where they establish the essential rules of political competition. They define the relationships among a country's key political actors. In this respect, they may or may not divide sovereignty between different levels of government and stipulate the sorts of protections and duties citizens can expect from their governments. We have also argued that constitutions are focal points for political conflict. For centuries, political actors have regarded constitutional provisions as key political resources. We also introduced you to the idea that the relationships between the executive, legislative, and judicial branches may vary in important ways from one liberal democracy to the next. The character of those relationships has important implications for the relative prominence different political values will enjoy.

Summary

The chapter:

- Introduced the concept of rule of law
- Examined the key formal political institutions of democratic governance
- Outlined the importance of constitutions for political participation
- Assessed the relationship of constitutions to the judiciary in regard to citizenship rights
- Outlined the importance of constitutions

Discussion Questions

1. What do sections 21 to 23 (regarding the Senate); 93 (education); 55, 56, 57, and 90 (to reserve and disallow); and 92.10 of the *Constitution Act 1867* suggest about the nature of Canadian politics in the 1860s?

2. If you were writing a constitution, would you opt for a federal or unitary system and/or a parliamentary or congressional system? Explain the reasons for your choices. Would making the Canadian Parliament operate more like the United States Congress improve the Canadian system of government? What factors might complicate such a change?

3. "The notwithstanding clause is a valuable addition to Canada's constitution." Would you agree with this statement? Why?

4. What issues, if any, do you think require constitutional change in Canada or the United States? Why?

Further Readings

Docherty, David. 2004. *Legislatures*. Vancouver: University of British Columbia Press.

Russell, Peter H. 1991. "Standing Up for Notwithstanding." *Alberta Law Review* XXIX(2): 293–309.

Smith, Jennifer. 2004. *Federalism*. Vancouver: University of British Columbia Press.

White, Graham. 2005. *Cabinets and First Ministers*. Vancouver: University of British Columbia Press.

Whyte, John D. 1990. "On Not Standing for Notwithstanding." *Alberta Law Review* XXVIII(2): 347–57.

Weblinks

The Solon Law Archive
www.solon.org/index.html

Centre for Constitutional Studies
www.law.ualberta.ca/centres/ccs

Political Database of the Americas—Georgetown University
pdba.georgetown.edu/

Pondering the Patriation
www.cbc.ca/ideas/episodes/2012/06/21/pondering-the-patriation/

CHAPTER 9

REPRESENTATION

STEVE PATTEN

Learning Objectives

- Explains the difference between the instrumental and constitutive dimensions of representation

- Contrasts the assumptions about political representation that underpin the delegate and trustee models of political representation

- Compares and contrasts the various institutions and processes of political representation

- Formulates an opinion on what constitutes a democratic approach to political representation

Introduction

The study of modern democratic politics requires an understanding of the meaning and practices of political representation. This chapter explores different perspectives on political representation and examines the character and biases of several important institutions and processes of political representation—including electoral systems, legislatures, political parties, interest groups, social movement organizations, and mini-publics. The goal of the chapter is to encourage critical reflection. As such, the discussion pushes beyond providing basic definitions and descriptions of representational practices. Readers are challenged to consider the claim that political representation is an active and formative relationship that shapes political identities and interests and the character and content of politics. Questions also are raised about the complex relationship between representation and democracy.

The chapter begins with an introduction to the concept of political representation, and then examines competing models for understanding the proper roles and relationships between representatives and those who are represented. This is followed by a discussion of the ways in which the processes of representational politics constitute our political identities and shape our understandings of politics and political action. Attention then turns to an examination of the core institutions, mechanisms, and processes of political representation. Readers are encouraged to reflect on the unique purposes and biases of these various institutions and processes. The concluding section of the chapter offers some observations regarding the relationship between political representation and the quality of democracy.

The Concept of Political Representation

POLITICAL REPRESENTATION IS CENTRAL TO MODERN UNDERSTANDINGS of democracy. The parliamentary and republican systems that evolved out of the seventeenth- and eighteenth-century liberal revolutions in Britain, France, and America are systems of representative government. Canada, too, is a particular type of democracy— a representative democracy. But there is some debate about the defining characteristics of political representation in a representative democracy. Early liberal thinkers offered a perspective that has come to be known as **descriptive representation**. From this perspective, the condition of representation—and, it could be argued, of democracy—is met only to the extent that our legislatures are a representative microcosm of the broader society. But conservative thinkers insisted on formalistic and process-oriented notions of representation that were rooted in the assumption that representation and democracy merely require that legislative bodies are authorized and/or held accountable by broader society through law and regular elections. From this standpoint, the membership of our law-making bodies is unimportant; so long as they are elected, the condition of formalistic representation is fully met.

Today, both descriptive and formalistic notions of political representation fail to capture popular thinking because most people conceive of representation as a relationship, process, or activity, rather than a state of affairs. One influential academic interpretation of political representation proposes that representation involves representatives "acting in the interest of the represented in a manner that is responsive to them" (Pitkin 1967, 209). By construing representation as an active and instrumental relationship, our attention shifts from the adjective "representative" to the verb "to represent"—and the quality of democracy seems to hinge more on the responsiveness of representatives than on the makeup of the legislature or the existence of free and fair elections. This marks a shift to what is known as **instrumental representation**. The defining feature of instrumental representation is the commitment to act and speak for the represented.

Of course, for many years, theorists of participatory democracy argued that instrumental representation is not real democracy, because, regardless of how responsive our elected officials are, they are a political elite and it is inevitable that ordinary people will be governed by the will of this elite. As this participatory democracy argument goes, democracy requires that the governed directly participate in the process of governance. Representative systems produce a phony and elitist form of quasi-democracy, while participatory practices allow for authentic democracy. Today, however, most democratic theorists have abandoned this sort of dichotomous and polarized thinking. The emerging consensus is that the opposite of representation is not participation, but exclusion (Urbinati and Warren 2008). Moreover, in the same way that one can envisage ongoing opportunities for democratic participation in our representative democracies, there are non-electoral forms of representation that can deepen democracy between elections. Thus, there is no reason why democrats should not embrace both representation and participation, so long as their thinking about representation extends beyond elections and remains focused on both responsiveness and inclusiveness.

Another voice in the debate about political representation argues that theories of instrumental representation mistakenly assume that clearly identifiable political interests are simply waiting to be represented. These scholars argue that, rather than assuming the pre-existence of political identities and interests, we should examine how the process of political representation—of making claims on behalf of a political interests—actually serves to construct or define our understanding of the character of the political identities and interests that are being represented. The point being made here is that because identities are complex and interests lack clarity, one cannot represent a community of interest, whether it is agricultural workers, Atlantic Canadians, or university students, without making assumptions about how to understand and portray that community. Then, acting on that portrayal influences our collective imagination. It feeds back on the represented and affects how they define who they are and what their political interests are. Representation is, in other words, a constitutive relationship; the process of representation constitutes or gives meaning to the identities and interests that are represented. This is known as constitutive representation and it is as important as instrumental representation to understanding political representation in liberal democracies (Jenson 1992).

Perspectives on Instrumental Representation in Liberal Democracy

Mainstream debates conceive of political representation as a principal-agent relationship. The depiction of instrumental representation as involving representatives "acting in the interests of the represented in a manner that is responsive to them" attempts to steer a course between two perspectives on this principal-agent relationship. These are known as the delegate and trustee models of representation. At bottom, the **delegate model of representation** stresses the importance of the representative (or agent) responding to the stated preferences of the represented (the principals). The delegate model's first premise is that representative democracy is a necessary but highly imperfect substitute for direct democracy. The goal, therefore, should be to maximize responsiveness in an effort to approximate the outcomes that would result from direct democracy. The principal-agent relationship should be managed so that the actions of representatives are not at odds with the wishes of the represented. Take, for example, the case of a member of Parliament (MP) deciding how to vote on a bill that would make it easier for police to enforce copyright violations associated with online peer-to-peer file sharing. The delegate model of representation would demand that, regardless of party policy or personal convictions, the MP should not decide how to vote until learning his or her constituents' views on the matter, perhaps by hosting a town hall meeting or commissioning a public opinion survey.

The more conservative **trustee model of representation** rejects the suggestion that good political representation is merely responsive representation. Representative democracy, according to the trustee model, is not merely a second-rate alternative to direct democracy. Instead, the virtue of representative democracy is that it provides a unique opportunity to empower a group of trustees (representatives, or agents) to meet in the deliberative chambers of Congress or Parliament, where they can discuss issues of governance and make decisions in the public interests. The role of the representative (the agent) is to be sensitive to the interests, but not necessarily the articulated wishes, of those they represent (the principals). Representative democracy is an opportunity to make wise decisions that are not constrained by the short-term, and perhaps ill-considered, wishes of the population. The eighteenth-century political theorist Edmund Burke, himself a member of the British Parliament, was known for his advocacy of the trustee model of political representation. Burke argued that instead of being bound by the inclinations of those they represent, political representatives should employ their reason and judgment in deliberations regarding the national interest. In Canada, lawmakers justified the decision to eliminate the death penalty, and their refusal to reinstate it, with reference to the trustee model of representation. Despite the fact that polls regularly show that a majority of Canadians support the death penalty, the majority of members of Parliament argue that careful consideration of issues such as the risk of wrongful conviction convinces them that it is in the best interest of society at large not to sanction the use of capital punishment.

Advocates of direct democracy are less than satisfied with a delegate model of representation, but they are even more concerned about the implications of the trustee model. That is why the more libertarian and individualistic supporters of direct democracy promote a form of **plebiscitarian democracy**. Plebiscitarianism combines a delegate model of representation with the regular use of processes that involve and empower individual citizens. These include referenda—the people voting directly on key policy issues, as Canadians did in 1992 when voters rejected the proposed Charlottetown Accord constitutional proposals—and mechanisms of recall that allow citizens to, in essence, fire their elected representative if that representative is unresponsive and fails to accurately reflect public opinion. In the province of British Columbia, for example, a voter who feels their local MLA has failed to accurately represent the views of constituents can initiate a "recall petition." If that petition is signed by more than 40 percent of registered voters, the MLA is removed from office and the government must call a by-election to elect a new representative.

Other strong democrats reject plebiscitarianism for two reasons. First, while apparently respectful of the principle of majority rule, the overuse of referenda and treating representatives as mere delegates will often fail to ensure the protection of minority interests. Allowing more scope for representatives to act as trustees creates space for consideration of broad collective interests, but it also allows for attention to be paid to marginalized minorities who may be harmed by strict adherence to majority rule as the guiding principle of democratic governance. Second, while plebiscitarianism emphasizes a greater role for the articulation of individual opinions, advocates of social inclusiveness and deliberative democracy view this as inadequate to the task of strengthening democracy. Since individuals live in a web of social relations and structures, advocates of greater social inclusiveness in governance support the creation of space for group voices, particularly the collective voices of segments of society that are marginalized by patterns of social disadvantage (Phillips 1995). For their part, deliberative democrats argue that democracy requires not only representation and expressions of individual preferences, but also opportunities for citizen participation in collective processes of dialogue and deliberation that can shape both personal preferences and a broader collective political will.

Understanding all of these perspectives is essential to evaluating the quality of representative democracy. Later in this chapter, readers will note that Canadian political institutions are somewhat biased in favour of the trustee model. The delegate model, plebiscitarianism, social inclusion, and deliberative democracy have had less impact on representative democracy in Canada.

Constitutive Representation: Defining Political Identities and Interests

Most academic discussions of instrumental representation proceed on the assumption that citizens bring pre-formed identities and interests to the political arena, and politicians merely craft electoral appeals and policy demands that demonstrate the extent to which they are acting for those pre-existing political interests. Deliberative democrats and many scholars interested in social exclusion argue that such assumptions are misplaced, because they ignore the constitutive dimension of representational politics. They contend that the discursive processes of political representation, including the electoral appeals of politicians, shape citizens' perceptions of their political identities and interests. But what does it mean to say that political identities are socially constructed through discursive processes? Essentially, it means that our political identities—who we are in politics and what we understand to be our interests—do not emerge in a straightforward and automatic way from objective facts about our lives or the communities in which we live. Instead, social processes of information exchange, dialogue, and debate privilege particular ideas and mental images, which then influence what it is about us that is most salient to how we understand our political identities and interests. These are called discursive processes, because it is through language (or discourse) that particular ideas, meanings, and perspectives on the world of politics are exchanged and become socially influential.

When we reflect upon our own lives, personal characteristics, and place in various social structures, it is clear that there are many personal traits and social conditions with the potential to be important to how we understand our political identities and interests. These include our gender, employment status, wealth, race, ethnic background, sexual orientation, and religion. Is it politically significant, for example, that you are a gay small-business owner who emigrated from the Philippines? Or in politics are you merely a taxpayer, indistinguishable from other taxpaying citizens? Historically, in Canada, the discursive politics of representation has often emphasized regional and linguistic political identities, such as Albertan, Atlantic Canadian, or French Canadian. But there is nothing inevitable about this. Indeed, in an objective material sense, your race and class are at least as relevant to your social and political interests as the region you live in and the language you speak. That is why representation should be conceptualized as an "active and formative relationship" of considerable political consequence (Hall 1983, 26). By forging and prioritizing political identities and giving meaning to political interests, political representation orients us to political action. We find political allies, understand political cleavages, and define the norms of political action from the perspective of our political identities. Political representation shapes the perceived relevance of political issues and actors, while also shaping the character of political conflict; it involves the exercise of profound power (Jenson 1999).

In the context of electoral politics, parties craft political messages that imply—sometimes not too subtly—how citizens should think of their political interests. In recent years, some of the more successful parties have appealed to voters as hardworking taxpayers. Privileging this apparently generic individualistic political identity has significant consequences for political debate. If your identity as a taxpayer is front of mind, then your primary political interest is in lower taxes, and your political enemies are those who push for expensive government programs or, like welfare recipients, seem to live off the generosity of your taxes. How would governments act in your interests? They would cut programs, reduce the size of government, and minimize fiscal transfers to individuals and communities that rely on state support. While, in reality, there are ways in which you personally benefit from government programs (related to education, the arts, and the environment, for example) and the social supports that flow to members of your community, these benefits are masked by political appeals that construct you as, first and foremost, a taxpayer.

Political parties are not alone on the stage of representational politics. As discussed below, interest groups, unions, and social movements, among others, also work to advance discursive representations of who we are in politics. The early gay liberation movement, for instance, worked very hard to articulate a collective political identity that would legitimize advocacy in support of the political interests of gay men and lesbians (Adam 1987). The struggle was not merely to combat homophobia and heterosexism, but to legitimize queer political identities and build a political community that would support a movement with the potential to advance a previously ignored political interest. These struggles were an example of constitutive representation.

The Institutions and Processes of Political Representation

WHEN EVALUATING POLITICAL REPRESENTATION AND THE QUALITY of democracy in liberal democratic political regimes, political scientists often focus on the role played by political parties and the elected members of legislative bodies, such as the United States Congress and Canada's House of Commons. It is useful to extend our gaze slightly to also consider the role of the electoral system and some less formal institutions of political representation, specifically, interest groups, social movement organizations, and state-sponsored mini-publics.

Electoral Systems

The electoral system is the framework for translating citizens' votes into legislative seats. What is often not apparent to the casual observer is that electoral systems are not politically neutral; they have significant consequences for the content and character of political representation and, therefore, for the quality of democracy. For example, the **single-member plurality (SMP)** electoral system found in Canada, the United Kingdom, and the United States has the effect of limiting the number and range of truly competitive political parties and increasing the likelihood of politicians' adopting a stance consistent with the trustee model of political representation. The reasons for this are not complex. First, in a SMP electoral system, the voters in each constituency elect just one member, and that election is determined by a simple plurality—that is, the candidate with the most votes wins. This is a winner-take-all system that disadvantages smaller political parties because parties that cannot win the most votes win nothing at all. Larger parties are, in effect, over-represented, while small parties without unique regional concentrations of support are under-represented. This system of translating votes into seats discourages the maturation of small parties that are committed to a delegate model of representation and advocating on behalf of particular societal interests. Second, SMP enhances the extent to which we think of representation in terms of residency-based territorial representation. In this context, geographically defined interests are privileged as most worthy of political attention, while non-geographic social interests—related to ethnicity or class, for example—are marginalized unless they happen to intersect with the circumstances of geographic location (Urbinati and Warren 2008). So long as electoral success depends on broad popular appeal across a territorially defined constituency, politicians will be inclined to campaign on ideologically vague themes that do little more than position their party as competent trustees of the broad public interest.

By contrast, the various multiple-member electoral systems designed to achieve **proportional representation (PR)** tend to encourage smaller parties with platforms that represent more focused social interests. There are unique and technically important features that set the many different kinds of PR systems apart from one another, but the effects are the same. They all allocate legislative seats in proportion to the percentage of votes a party wins, thus giving a broader range of parties and interests a voice in legislative decision-making processes. Abandoning SMP's winner-take-all scenario allows voters to support small parties with confidence that their votes will pay off in terms of legislative representation. Politicians may also alter their behaviour, because smaller political parties are able to achieve a degree of success while embracing a delegate model of representation and taking clearer stances in favour of particular social interests. Clearly, then, the institutional biases of different types of electoral systems have consequences for the character of political representation and democracy.

Legislatures

As the branch of government responsible for law-making, legislatures—such as the Parliament in Canada and Congress in the United States—are key institutions in the process of political representation. The first principles of the parliamentary system are the **fusion of power** and **responsible government**. These doctrines put the political executive—the prime minister and the Cabinet—in charge of both the executive function of state administration and law implementation *and* guiding the legislative function of law-making. The executive dominates law-making but is ultimately responsible to Parliament in the sense that the majority of members of the House of Commons must approve the Cabinet's agenda and any legislative initiatives it introduces. But given that almost all members of the House of Commons are elected as candidates who offer themselves under particular party banners, the thrust and parry of parliamentary politics is shaped by the informal rules of the parliamentary party system. Paramount among these is **party discipline**—that is, the injunction that MPs support their party's line on all important issues. Members of Parliament are expected to accept the trustee model of representation and the notion that the party leadership's assessment of the broader public interest overrules their own sense of the local interests they represent.

In the United States, by contrast, the **separation of powers** eliminates the possibility of direct executive dominance and weakens party discipline. Under the American congressional system, there is a clear separation of the Congress, with its legislative powers, from the presidency, with its executive powers. The president works hard to influence the legislative process in Congress and has some levers to influence Congress, including the threat of a presidential legislative veto, but the power to initiate and approve legislation rests, in the end, with Congress. Moreover, while members of Congress tend to vote along party lines, the notion of party discipline is considerably weaker in the congressional system. American legislators are freer to embrace the delegate model's emphasis on responsiveness in political representation. As such, congressional politics is as much about accommodating conflicting regional and local concerns as it is about broader party interests. The institutional bias in the congressional system is toward the delegate model of representation.

Political Parties

Electoral politics and political parties are central to the processes of political representation in modern liberal democracies. In fact, it is regularly assumed that political parties should be the primary representative institution in a democracy. In the early 1990s, for example, Canada's Royal Commission on Electoral Reform and Party Financing concluded that parties are key to effective democratic representation because "only political parties can reconcile and accommodate diverse and competing interests to reach agreement on public policy" (cited in Dobrowolsky and Jenson 1993, 65). In making this claim, the Commission implied that political parties are, ideally, large integrative institutions that work to accommodate diverse and competing interests, rather than advancing the political agenda of particular social interests. These integrative parties are known as **brokerage parties** or, sometimes, catch-all parties. Brokerage parties privilege flexibility and pragmatism over policy consistency, usually characterizing themselves as champions of the broader public interest. They often allow their commitment to act as trustees of the public interest to overshadow unique or bold policy platforms. While promising a degree of responsiveness, brokerage parties promise, first and foremost, to be accommodative trustees of the national interest, however that term is defined.

Not everyone accepts the suggestion that the ideal political party acts as a broker of competing social demands. One consequence of the accommodative politics of brokering is that many voices, particularly those associated with minority interests, are not heard. That is why supporters of a delegate model of representation often prefer more programmatic **doctrinal parties**, which commit themselves to steadfastly articulating the views of particular ideological currents or social interests. But, in Canada, this alternative viewpoint on parties and political representation runs counter to the views of the political elite, as well as to the institutional biases of the single-member plurality electoral system.

Groups and Movements

Interest groups are organizations that act to influence the content and direction of public policy by representing particular interests directly to government officials. Broad social movements, such as feminism and environmentalism, are informal networks of individuals and groups primarily interested in bringing about societal change by influencing our identities, ideas, and behaviour (Phillips 1996). Social movement organizations also direct some of their energies into influencing government policy, but unlike interest groups or political parties, social movements encourage people to rethink their political identities and political interests. In other words, social movements are more concerned with the constitutive dimensions of representation.

Advocates of a trustee model of representation often criticize groups and movements as "special interests" that subvert the representational processes of electoral democracy. But others argue that interest groups and social movement organizations provide valuable representational opportunities and alternative avenues of political action. They ensure that more voices are heard and a wider range of issues is addressed. Thus, the question of whether group and movement politics enhances or detracts from representative democracy may hinge on the types of voices that are heard through group politics. Historically, interest group politics was characterized as the realm of covert backroom politics, or elite accommodation, in which the social and economic elite interacted with the political and bureaucratic elite to shape public policy in their own self-interest (Presthus 1973). Obviously, the representational processes of elite accommodation do little to enhance democracy. But since the 1960s, the range of groups and movements involved in interest group politics has grown exponentially. In addition to private and corporate interests, there are now many highly visible citizens' action groups advocating for policies in the interest of marginalized members of society and emerging or under-developed policy terrains. There is also a broader range of social movements legitimizing a wider range of political identities and creating space for doing politics differently. In all this, one finds potential for the representational activities of groups and movements to enhance democracy.

Mini-publics

Mini-publics are state-sponsored forums for gathering small to mid-sized groups of citizens together to discuss and/or decide on issues of public concern. Their purpose is to allow for public input, dialogue, deliberation, and, sometimes, participation in policy decision making. The character of any given mini-public depends on how citizens are selected, the processes for facilitating input and discussion, and the extent of influence over actual policy decision making (Fung 2006). Sometimes, mini-publics gather stakeholders who are expected to represent their social base of support. In these cases, mini-publics facilitate political input that is largely consistent with the delegate model of representation. Other times, however, mini-publics involve a more representative sample of citizens who are randomly or selectively recruited to participate in a process of information sharing and deliberation that is meant to allow for considered decision making along the norms of a deliberative democracy version of the trustee model of representation.

Mini-publics like the 2004 B.C. Citizens' Assembly on Electoral Reform are massive undertakings designed to replace the normal processes of decision making through representative government. Most, however, are consultative advisory panels that offer input that is supplementary to the work of elected politicians and public service experts. By creating opportunities for citizen participation in dialogue and deliberation, the best of mini-publics create a space for political voices and policy alternatives that would otherwise remain unheard. Mini-publics have the potential to formulate policy advice that flows from a process of contemplative deliberation on political issues, and to serve as a mechanism for democratizing political representation.

Conclusion: Political Representation and the Quality of Democracy

IT IS MUCH EASIER TO CRITIQUE INSTANCES OF UNDEMOCRATIC REPRE-sentational politics than it is to specify what would constitute the most democratic approach to political representation. In the real world of representative democracy, there are opportunities to employ different blends of participatory and representative institutions and processes. Moreover, the ways these institutions are used will depend on the extent to which we embrace the analysis associated with each of the competing perspectives on democratic political representation. Should representative institutions be designed in a manner consistent with the delegate or the trustee model of representation? To what extent should the design of political institutions also be sensitive to the participatory impulses of plebiscitarianism? How should institutions and the process of governance allow for social inclusiveness, including opportunities for social groups to self-define their political identities and interests? What sorts of opportunities should there be for meaningful participation in collective processes of dialogue and deliberation? These are challenging questions; they have been integral to democratic politics since its inception, and equally strong democrats disagree on how to answer them.

The delegate model of representation's emphasis on responsiveness is intuitively attractive. But representatives who act on the wishes of the majority (or loudest voices) in their geographically defined constituencies might be ignoring significant minority interests or broader collective interests that should be considered. The trustee model's inclination toward privileging considered opinion over responsiveness runs the risk of empowering a political elite, which might be insensitive to important currents of public opinion. Plebiscitarianism has the capacity to inject a useful dose of participatory impulse into the design of political institutions, but tools like referenda and recall are blunt political instruments; they are unresponsive to minority interests and ignore the legitimacy of the collective social interests that are searching for ways to ensure the inclusion and empowerment of marginalized segments of society. Unlike plebiscitarian democrats, deliberative democrats want to overcome the individualistic biases associated with taking snapshots of opinions through mechanisms like referenda. They advocate involving people in collective processes of dialogue and deliberation, which have the capacity to produce insights that reshape individual perspectives and build agreement on a broad collective will. But beyond the occasional use of mini-publics, it is difficult to construct practical approaches to institutionalizing processes of dialogue and deliberation in democratic governance. As a result, there remains an important role for the electoral system, legislatures, and political parties, as well as the less-formally institutionalized groups and movements that are active in the politics of representation. In the end, as central as political representation is to modern understandings of democracy, it remains a contested concept. There are few clear answers about how we should design the institutions and processes of representative government.

Summary

The chapter:

- Explored the concept of political representation and identified its instrumental and constitutive dimensions
- Outlined the delegate and trustee models of the proper role and responsibilities of political representatives, and briefly discussed plebiscitarianism, social inclusiveness, and deliberative democracy
- Assessed the core institutions and processes of political representation
- Discussed the complexities of the relationship between political representation and democracy

Discussion Questions

1. Given the opportunity to participate in a political party, interest group, or social movement organization, which would you choose? Why? What difference would your choice make to the nature of your involvement in political representation?

2. When would it be useful and democratic for a government to sponsor the establishment of a mini-public to address a pressing public policy issue?

3. Given what you know about the institutions and processes of political representation, do you believe there are some political interests that are better represented than others? Why or why not? What do you believe is required to ensure fair and democratic representation of political interests?

4. How would you characterize your own political identity and political interest? Are you well represented in politics and government?

5. Which do you prefer, the delegate or trustee model of representation? Why?

References

Adam, Barry D. 1987. *The Rise of a Gay and Lesbian Movement.* Boston: Twayne Publishers.

Dobrowolsky, Alexandra. 1998. "Of 'Special Interest': Interest, Identity and Feminist Constitutional Activism in Canada." *Canadian Journal of Political Science* XXXI(4): 707–42.

Dobrowolsky, Alexandra and Jane Jenson. 1993. "Reforming the Parties: Prescriptions for Democracy." In *How Ottawa Spends 1993–1994: A More Democratic Canada . . . ?,* edited by Susan D. Phillips. Ottawa: Carleton University Press.

Fung, Archon. 2006. "Varieties of Participation in Complex Governance." *Public Administration Review* 66(6): 66–75.

Hall, Stuart. 1983. "The Great Moving Right Show." In *The Politics of Thatcherism,* edited by Stuart Hall and Martin Jacques. London: Lawrence and Wishart.

Jenson, Jane. 1992. "A Political Economy Approach to Interest Representation." In *Democracy with Justice/La juste démocratie: Essays in Honour of Khayyam Zev Paltiel,* edited by Alain G. Gagnon and A. Brian Tanguay. Ottawa: Carleton University Press.

———. 1999. "Understanding Politics: Concepts of Identity in Political Science." In *Canadian Politics,* 3rd edition, edited by James Bickerton and Alain-G. Gagnon. Peterborough, ON: Broadview Press.

Phillips, Anne. 1995. *The Politics of Presence.* Oxford, U.K.: Oxford University Press.

Phillips, Susan D. 1996. "Competing, Connecting, and Complementing: Parties, Interest Groups, and New Social Movements." In *Canadian Parties in Transition,* 2nd edition, edited by A. Brian Tanguay and Alain-G. Gagnon. Toronto: Nelson Canada.

Pitkin, Hannah. 1967. *The Concept of Representation.* Berkeley, CA: The University of California Press.

Presthus, Robert. 1973. *Elite Accommodation in Canadian Politics.* Cambridge, U.K.: Cambridge University Press.

Urbinati, Nadia and Mark E. Warren. 2008. "The Concept of Representation in Contemporary Democratic Theory." *Annual Review of Political Science* 11: 387–412.

Further Readings

Adam, Barry D. 1987. *The Rise of a Gay and Lesbian Movement.* Boston: Twayne Publishers.

Dobrowolsky, Alexandra. 1998. "Of 'Special Interest': Interest, Identity and Feminist Constitutional Activism in Canada." *Canadian Journal of Political Science* XXXI(4): 707–42.

Hall, Stuart. 1983. "The Great Moving Right Show." In *The Politics of Thatcherism*, edited by Stuart Hall and Martin Jacques. London: Lawrence and Wishart.

Jenson, Jane. 1999. "Understanding Politics: Concepts of Identity in Political Science." In *Canadian Politics*, 3rd edition, edited by James Bickerton and Alain-G. Gagnon. Peterborough, ON: Broadview Press.

Weblinks

Council of Canadians
www.canadians.org

Democracy Watch
www.dwatch.ca

Elections Canada
www.elections.ca

Fair Vote Canada
www.fairvote.ca/

CHAPTER 10

PUBLIC ADMINISTRATION

ALLAN TUPPER

Learning Objectives

- Introduces students to the sources of administrative power in democracies

- Helps students understand the political role of civil servants

- Assesses democratic controls over administrative power

- Relates debates about administrative reform to debates about the role of government

Introduction

This chapter examines the civil service in modern democracies. It makes several key points. First, an effective civil service is essential to an ordered, well-functioning modern society. At the same time, a strong civil service is problematic. Civil servants are powerful but, unlike politicians, they are appointed not elected. Some critics see them as too powerful and too independent of political direction and control. Other critics worry about the size and efficiency of the civil service. They want reforms that make governments more "business-like" and responsive to citizens. Second, the chapter examines the relationships between politicians and senior officials. Are civil servants really "permanent politicians"? Third, the chapter explores administrative reform as it relates to broader concerns about the role of government and the size of the public sector.

Civil service reform has been at the forefront of political debate over the last century and into the present one. After September 11, 2001, public concerns about terrorism caused major realignments of civil service agencies and powers. In Canada, a new department, Public Safety Canada, was established to coordinate policy. In the United States, the Department of Homeland Security reorganized the American response to terrorism. The 2008 world financial crisis and its aftermath have again focused attention on the size and role of government, and the effectiveness of the civil service.

This chapter examines the civil service primarily through a Canadian lens, but also provides American and British examples. The Canadian provinces, especially the larger ones like British Columbia, Ontario, and Quebec, also have complex civil services. Examples are also drawn from the provincial experience.

Politics and Administration

OVER THE PAST TWO CENTURIES, DEMOCRATIC GOVERNMENTS HAVE assumed important new roles and responsibilities. Populations have grown dramatically and often, as in Canada's case, become more racially and ethnically diverse. Governments have become active forces in shaping their economies and societies. The worldwide depression of the 1930s caused governments to regulate economic life, to stimulate and deflate economies through spending and taxation, and, given economic interdependence, to work through international economic institutions to coordinate policies. Governments also have assumed responsibilities for citizens' well-being. The Canadian welfare state, although under pressure for change, provides citizens with health and hospital insurance, old age security, benefits for unemployment, and social assistance. The taxation system encourages Canadians to save for their children's education and to plan for their own retirements. In short, government is present throughout society.

The growth of government led to the establishment of a permanent and professional civil service. Modern government requires expertise to develop and interpret policy. It needs professional research on which to base policy. Governments employ scientists and physicians to approve drugs, social workers to counsel the unemployed, and trained managers to implement programs. Such skilled personnel are expected to work impartially and in the public interest. They must be hired and promoted on the basis of their qualifications, not their politics. The old practice of hiring civil servants through patronage—that is, on the basis of their links to the governing party—was eliminated in Canada in 1918 (Brooks 2012). Even then, government needed trained, neutral officials if it was to function properly. Politicians are too few in number to do all the work required by the modern state, and they are seldom elected because of their professional qualifications. Politicians lack the experience to design and to implement complex government programs. As we will see, politicians face major problems controlling and influencing the civil service, let alone trying to do its work.

In modern societies, the civil service is the part of government that makes things happen. The civil service delivers public services to citizens. It provides student loans, environmental impact assessments, airport security, and hundreds of other services. Several American authors recently asserted, "most Americans recognize that maintaining order in a large society is impossible without some sort of large governmental apparatus, staffed by professionals with some expertise in public administration" (Lowi et al. 2010, 277). If a substantial civil service is essential, why is it also a major problem? The answer is that the civil service, far from being a neutral body dedicated to efficient management, is a political force in its own right. Modern public administrations have their own policy interests, their own drives for expansion, and their own definitions of the public interest.

A classic democratic argument asserts a **politics-administration dichotomy**. In this view, a clear separation must exist between politicians and civil servants. Politicians, mandated by democratic elections, should make the major choices for society, while the civil service as a neutral, efficiency-driven organization implements the political will. The experience of modern societies, however, constantly reveals the flaws of the politics-administration dichotomy.

The Many Roles of the Civil Service

Policy Implementation

The main role of the civil service is to implement public policy. But policy implementation is not a neutral matter. "Street level" bureaucrats—for example, police officers on patrol, customs agents at airports, unemployment insurance officers, and Canada Revenue Agency auditors—all have some capacity to make choices on a case-by-case basis. They exercise discretion. At a higher level, senior civil servants have considerable experience in program design and implementation. They make choices on the basis of what has worked before and on their personal and organizational experiences. Decisions about policy implementation are not simple matters of efficiency. To the contrary, program design has major consequences for citizen access to government service, and policy implementation is an area where civil servants have the upper hand over politicians. As an American author puts it, "One advantage that bureaucrats tend to have over members of Congress is expert knowledge of a policy area and information about which policies work and do not work" (Kollman 2010, 235).

Administrative Rule-Making

Most modern legislation establishes general policy goals and then delegates implementation and interpretation to governments that, in turn, rely on their civil servants. In practice, this means that civil servants decide what the law really means on a case-by-case basis. They bring the law to life and give it meaning in particular contexts. In Canada, civil service agencies make detailed regulations that tell policy actors what the law means to them. This rule-making power makes civil servants magnets for pressure-group influence. An advocacy group whose interests are not fully met by legislation can try to get its way with the civil service.

Policy-Making

Senior civil servants are also influential in policy-making. Their power lies in their access to and understanding of complex data, knowledge of past practice, and direct access to politicians. In modern democracies, civil servants provide politicians with policy options and recommendations. Of course, politicians hear advice from sources other than civil servants, and elected officials certainly have their own ambitions, ideological drives, and policy interests. Civil service advice is certainly not always accepted or accepted without change. That said, the senior civil service is extensively involved in structuring the policy agenda and in timing policy initiatives. Politicians may ultimately decide the content of major policies but civil servants influence and define the key questions.

Observers of public administration in the United States acknowledge a major policy-making role for the civil service. Consider, for example, the following statement: "Bureaucrats are politicians who make decisions, form coalitions, engage in bargaining" (Lowi et al. 2010, 274). Americans routinely speak of "bureaucratic drift" in policy-making, a term that describes the capacity of civil service agencies to move from their established goals into areas that better reflect their policy preferences and interpretation of the public interest. Canadian observers are more cautious in describing civil service activism in policy-making. That said, a major policy role for Canadian civil servants has been widely recognized.

In summary, modern governments undertake complex and important public policies. The welfare state, economic management, and foreign policy in an interdependent world require the skills of a specialized, expert civil service. However, large, modern civil services exercise considerable discretion in their operations. They interpret policy and make it meaningful for citizens on a case-to-case basis. Civil servants often have strong views about the content and goals of public policy and how it should be implemented. The modern administration is a formidable, but unelected, force in a modern democratic government, and for those reasons it is necessary, controversial, and sometimes even feared.

The Organization of Government

THE GOVERNMENT IS NOT A SINGLE ENTITY. IN MODERN DEMOCRACIES, governments deliver programs through many different organizations. Whether in Ottawa, the provinces, or the territories, government departments are the most visible and probably most important government organizations. Departments are under the direct authority of a Cabinet minister who is responsible for the department's budgets and policy-making.

Federal government departments vary in the activities they perform. Some, like the Departments of Veterans' Affairs and Aboriginal Affairs and Northern Development, serve clearly defined groups of Canadians. Others, like Agriculture, Natural Resources, and Industry, deal with important sectors of the Canadian economy. Service Canada, part of Human Resources and Skills Development Canada, has major responsibilities for delivering social policies to Canadians. Canada's large geography explains the role of the Ministry of Transport. The Departments of Justice, Defence, and Public Safety Canada share a common interest in protecting Canadians. Some government departments provide services to the government itself. The Treasury Board Secretariat is the federal government's general manager. It sets financial and human resource policy for the other departments. Public Works Canada is in charge of Ottawa's buildings and land across the country. And a very important body, the Privy Council Office, is a central agency that advises the prime minister and Cabinet about major policy initiatives and reviews the policy proposals of other government departments. The Department of Finance has major roles in formulating government budgets and managing the economy.

Departments are simply the tips of the organizational iceberg. Governments rely on many other organizations. For example, Ottawa exercises authority over Canadian media companies. It does so primarily through the Canadian Radio-television and Telecommunications Commission (CRTC). The CRTC has independence from the government because it makes complex decisions requiring specialized expertise that must be insulated from day-to-day political control. A similar logic explains why bodies like the Transportation Safety Board and the National Energy Board have an "arm's-length" relationship with government.

Another type of government organization is a government business or, as Canadians say, a Crown corporation. Canadian governments have sometimes established government companies to provide services to Canadians that the private sector was unwilling to provide. For example, early in the twentieth century, private telephone companies were reluctant to provide costly telephone services to widely scattered prairie farms.

As a result, governments in Alberta, Saskatchewan, and Manitoba took over the provision of telecommunications services. Federal Crown corporations include Canada Post, VIA Rail Canada, and Atomic Energy of Canada. Provincial governments also own many corporations. British Columbia owns and operates a substantial coastal ferry service, BC Hydro, a massive provincial electrical company, and the Insurance Corporation of British Columbia that has a monopoly on vehicle insurance. The government of Quebec has frequently employed government corporations to develop Quebec's economy and to promote a Quebecois business class. Crown corporations allegedly require day-to-day freedom because they operate in a market economy that requires tactical freedom. They need to be free from direct political oversight or otherwise their effectiveness will suffer.

In Canada, many government organizations apparently need to be at arm's length from government. However, the length of the arm can be controversial. Sometimes the government finds the arm too long and tries to exercise direct control over commissions and corporations. The Harper Conservative government engaged in an angry debate with the Canadian Nuclear Safety Commission when it disagreed with its assessment of safety at an Atomic Energy of Canada reactor. And sometimes, government wants the arm to be very long. In a recent case, the federal government of former Liberal Prime Minister Jean Chrétien established the Canada Foundation for Innovation. The foundation was responsible for the renewal of buildings at Canadian universities. The government apparently established the foundation to escape parliamentary oversight; it had a multibillion-dollar budget but was so distant from accountability that it was considered by some observers to be a private government of public money (Aucoin 2003).

Government organizations also include entities that are neither public nor private. They are called hybrids, mixed ownership corporations, and public-private partnerships (Skelcher 2007). These organizations involve complex contracting and ownership relationships between governments and business. The logic is that partnerships combine the best of both government expertise and business efficiency. For example, Ontario's Highway 407 was constructed as a tolled highway by a public-private partnership, and the Government of Canada has promised a new bridge in Montreal that it wants built as a tolled public-private partnership. Careful studies of such joint undertakings give rise to skepticism about their effectiveness. Public-private partnerships require specialized contracts that define the terms of the agreement and ensure compliance. Governments must constantly monitor the contracts, and the financial benefits are controversial in many cases. Public-private partnerships also add another accountability problem; as one observer notes, "Creating public-private partnerships is a highly political venture, but those that have been established are generally opaque and outside the realm of democratic discourse. . . . The paradox is that this is occurring precisely at a time when popular democratic engagement is high on the agenda for many governments" (Skelcher 2007, 364).

Decisions about government organization are not made by managerial principles. Decisions about organizational forms are really about "politics, position, and power"

(Seidman 1975). As evidence, consider the fact that newly elected Canadian political leaders almost always reorganize the departments of government. They may reduce the number of departments to give voters the impression the new government will be frugal with taxpayers' money. They often give prominence to matters of current public concern; the creation of major new departments for domestic security after September 11, 2001, has already been mentioned, when governments were determined to show citizens that security was the major priority. In provincial governments, departments dealing with the needs of "seniors" are gaining prominence in response to the widely discussed issue of an aging society.

Politicized Public Administration?

THIS CHAPTER HAS ALREADY OBSERVED THAT CIVIL SERVANTS PERFORM various roles that are political in the broad sense of the word. At the "street level," civil servants make decisions about how vigorously laws should be applied, and they seldom make those decisions on the basis of partisan politics. Senior civil servants influence public policies during the development and implementation phases, but, again, those actions are not generally motivated by a desire to influence the balance of power between political parties. Two important questions thus arise: How political is public administration? How political should it be? Such questions are not academic. During the 2011 Libyan uprising against Muammar Gadaffi, middle-level Libyan civil servants desperately tried to distance themselves from the despised regime. They wanted to make sure that they were seen as removed from politics: "Anxious to hold on to their jobs and portraying themselves as apolitical professionals, Tripoli bureaucrats argue that only the ministerial upper echelon was rotten" (*The Economist* 2011a, 43).

Observers of U.S. public administration often recognize that senior civil servants are political actors. The president appoints many senior American officials in the United States, and they are expected to be responsive to presidential priorities. Senior American civil servants also face two masters as both Congress and the president exercise control over civil service budgets and public policy. As a result, American civil servants pursue strategies that allow them to navigate this divided jurisdiction. They try to maximize their freedom of action. As James Q. Wilson and John Dilulio say, "In the United States, the Constitution permits both the president and the Congress to exercise authority over the bureaucracy. Every senior appointed official has at least two masters; one in the executive branch and the other in the legislative. . . . This divided authority encourages bureaucrats to play one branch against the other and to make heavy use of the media." (Wilson and Dilulio 2011, 402).

If Americans see a politically engaged civil service as a fact of constitutional life, Canadians worry about the political roles of civil servants. Senior Canadian officials, unlike their American counterparts, are anonymous and hidden from the public eye. They are expected to be responsive to the government of the day, aware of its priorities, and prepared to implement its policies. Importantly, deputy ministers, the senior civil servants in Canadian government departments, are appointed by the current government, and governments use their power of appointment to ensure responsive deputy ministers. On the other hand, senior civil servants are also expected to be neutral and prepared to offer the best possible advice even if it offends the government. How are the competing forces of responsiveness and neutrality worked out?

In Canada, elections sometimes cause a change of government. Will the civil service, especially if it has become accustomed to, and was appointed by, the defeated government serve the new government impartially? Will it do things differently? This question has often been raised in Canada because governments often serve for a long time before being defeated. In Ottawa, the Liberal party dominated politics for many decades and won many elections. For example, the Liberals presided over uninterrupted majority governments from 1935 until 1957 when the Progressive Conservatives led by Prime Minister John Diefenbaker finally defeated them. Diefenbaker was convinced that the senior civil servants were active supporters of Liberal policies. Ultimately, however, the senior civil service proved itself faithful to the Progressive Conservative government, although suspicions lingered. The same situation occurred in 1984 when Prime Minister Brian Mulroney won a landslide for the Progressive Conservatives. The current Conservative prime minister, Stephen Harper, and many of his colleagues were deeply suspicious of the civil service after another 13 years of uninterrupted Liberal rule. The Harper Conservatives are able to work with the civil service, although the relationship is often tense.

The same political dynamic is evident in the provinces. Alberta, for example, has had uninterrupted Progressive Conservative governments since 1971. How would a new government in Alberta deal with a civil service that had worked with Progressive Conservative governments for 40 years? In British Columbia, the Liberals have held power since 2001. The situation there is complex because politics are polarized between a centre-right Liberal party and a New Democratic Party (NDP) that has different policy priorities. Should an incoming NDP government replace the Liberal deputy ministers with persons sympathetic to its policies? And Nova Scotia now has its first NDP provincial government after, literally, centuries of Liberal and Conservative governments.

Newly elected Canadian governments have been able to establish working relationships with the civil service. They have seldom resorted to "housecleaning," which means the wholesale replacement of the former government's civil servants with those of their own choosing. That said, new governments often change some deputy ministers. Some are removed and others are reassigned. The incoming government sends messages to senior civil servants that it is in charge and that civil servants must work with the government and implement its policies.

A newer concern is that the senior civil service in Ottawa is too close to the government and is less willing to render advice that the government does not want to hear. The deputy ministers see themselves as a cohesive group whose primary purpose is to support the government. In short, the senior civil service is becoming "politicized." The claim of politicization is easy to make but hard to prove. An obvious sign of politicization would be an increase in the number of senior officials who have, or have had, close links to the political party in power. A rigorous examination of the federal civil service reveals that deputy ministers in Ottawa are, with few exceptions, career civil servants with no background in party politics. As Jacques Bourgault puts it, "the Public Service of Canada remains eminently apolitical and professional" (2006, 256). A study of Alberta deputy ministers yields the same conclusion (Tupper 2011). Alberta deputy ministers are career civil servants who have often worked through the ranks to become deputy ministers.

Those who think politicization is rampant are not satisfied by evidence about appointments and career paths. They see politicization as caused by broader forces, including the prime minister's power to appoint deputy ministers and the fact that deputy ministers are a coordinated group to achieve government goals. Those who see politicization also think there is increased political meddling in civil service business. Politicization is a term with many different meanings. Evidence, one way or the other, is hard to obtain. However, a recent book about the Harper Conservative government sees little ambiguity. It portrays the government as domineering toward the civil service, obsessed with information control and management, disdainful of policy research, and willing to dismiss civil servants whose views conflict with government policy (Martin 2011). Recent British experience is also insightful. The Conservative Prime Minister David Cameron, who leads a coalition government with the Liberal Democrats, wants major public management reform. Cameron apparently decided that Sir Gus O'Donnell, Britain's senior deputy minister who had served Conservative and Labour governments prior to the coalition, was too committed to the status quo. Accordingly, O'Donnell was removed from his position as chief civil servant and his current job was divided into three positions that will be fulfilled with the prime minister's choices (*The Economist* 2011b, 66).

However, and to emphasize a theme, the civil service can defend its own interests. It is a formidable opponent. Consider the following. British Prime Minister Cameron also asked O'Donnell to investigate the conduct of a senior Cabinet minister whose private dealings were questionable and the subject of negative media commentary. O'Donnell, in his role as chief civil servant, investigated the minister's conduct. He skilfully used his prestige and the public stage provided by the inquiry to recommend changes to the policy process that would strengthen the civil service relative to politicians and pressure groups (*The Economist* 2011c, 68–69).

The Control and Accountability of Public Administration

GOVERNMENTS HAVE NOT PASSIVELY ALLOWED THE CIVIL SERVICE TO run rampant. They have established many controls to ensure that it is held to account, operates within its legal powers, and deals fairly with citizens. Without such controls, the quality of democracy might be badly damaged. The control and accountability of civil service are not simple matters. Several major questions are controversial. First, to whom are civil servants accountable? Is it the government, Parliament, the citizens they serve, or perhaps even their own consciences? Second, are civil servants responsible for adhering to the law when they decide cases, or are they also responsible for the consequences of their decisions? Finally, how can individual civil servants be held accountable when almost all decisions are made by groups of civil servants? How is the problem of "many hands" dealt with (Thompson 1987)?

In Canada, **ministerial responsibility** is a major element of civil service accountability. Ministerial responsibility is a constitutional convention that says the responsible Cabinet minister is accountable to Parliament for all the actions of his or her department. The principle establishes the minister as the focal point for civil service accountability. Second, ministerial responsibility, by making the minister the public voice of the department, allows civil servants to remain anonymous. Civil servants are not publicly identified with the government's policies and can thus more easily serve a different government. Ministerial responsibility has many critics. Some see it as smokescreen that allows civil servants to avoid accountability and punishment for failure. Ministers seldom resign when things go wrong in their departments (Sutherland 1991). They sometimes claim they are responsible only for policy and not for administration, an argument that bothers critics who want consequences when things go wrong. Even worse, ministers sometimes publicly blame individual civil servants when serious problems arise. For many, ministerial responsibility now simply means that ministers must answer fully to Parliament about problems and what they are going to do about them (Sutherland 1991).

The inadequacies of ministerial responsibility led to the establishment of new mechanisms of accountability (Stone 1995). A modern approach asserts that government agencies must establish clear goals and then use "performance indicators" to judge their success and failure. Bodies external to the civil service and government also expose civil service failures and demand action. A well-known external control is the auditor general, who in Ottawa and the provinces is an officer of Parliament not a civil servant. Auditors general examine whether government organizations spend their budgets properly and they also investigate the quality of service delivery. Their reports get considerable media coverage and the government must respond. The Access to Information Act and similar laws try to improve public administration by providing citizens access to information about their cases. Provincial governments have ombudsmen who deal with citizens' complaints about civil service injustices and errors. Sometimes, ombudsmen are specialized and deal with particular groups of citizens. For example, the federal government has an ombudsman for inmates of federal penitentiaries and another one for armed forces veterans. Provincial governments often have advocates for children and seniors.

These control mechanisms assist citizens in many ways, but each also has drawbacks. Access to information laws are complex, riddled with exemptions and restrictions, and difficult for citizens to employ. Governments can make it difficult to use access laws by charging fees, responding slowly to requests for information, and refusing access. Auditors general provide important information about the quality of public administration, but they cannot assist individual citizens with problems. Ombudsmen try to solve citizens' problems but they only have powers of persuasion and cannot order solutions or impose sanctions.

The many problems of civil service control and accountability have led to an entirely different approach. The alternative stressed that the best way to have a fair and compassionate civil service is to have civil servants who are inspired by democratic ideals. Civil servants would be well trained, guided by good values, and, ultimately, self-policing. They would then be respectful of political authority but also motivated to serve citizens fairly. Better still, the civil service would also be a "**representative bureaucracy**," one that reflected the ethnic, racial, and linguistic characteristics of the larger society. Few formal controls would be required if a representative civil service was established. In practice, such a civil service is an ideal not a reality, but the ideal is reflected in many civil service practices, including training, socialization into the norms of public service, and codes of ethics for civil servants.

The New Public Management

THE SIZE AND POWER OF THE CIVIL SERVICE MAKE IT A TARGET. EARLY in the twentieth century, the civil service was transformed by reformers who wanted to modernize it and remove political patronage. The civil service assumed major new roles after the severe depression of the 1930s, and the 1950s and 1960s witnessed further reform and expansion. The modern welfare state created an active civil service that established new links with society. In those days, the civil service and democratic governments were seen as progressive forces for a better society in which governments and officials worked together to expand social services, health care, and old age security.

The 1970s and 1980s saw major changes in government and the economy. Early in the 1970s, the price of crude oil skyrocketed, and after two decades of economic growth and high employment, inflation and unemployment soared. Economies stagnated and the public mood shifted. The election of Margaret Thatcher as Britain's Conservative prime minister in 1979 and Ronald Reagan as the American president in 1980 brought a new edge to politics. They argued that an active public sector, far from being a solution, was the problem; government was too large, too inefficient, and too costly. A particular concern was growing government deficits. It became political orthodoxy that government budgets must be balanced. In turn, deficit reduction and a general desire for smaller government led to major administrative reforms. With many variations, democratic governments changed their civil services according to ideas called "**new public management**," or NPM.

There are many schools of thought regarding NPM. One major branch sees "privatization" as the best strategy, and advocates removal of public services and government activities to the private sector where they will be better run. Another variation, the more common one, wants to make public management more business-like. Public managers should have much more freedom to make decisions and greater control over their budgets, and market principles and business management techniques should be applied wherever possible. Other NPM elements include making civil service agencies more responsive to citizens who became known as stakeholders, clients, and even customers. Government agencies are to be driven by clear goals and a focus on the results of government activity. Civil service organizations should not necessarily deliver public services, and not-for-profits and private firms should be used where possible. NPM advocates claim that civil service reforms provide citizens with more responsive and high-quality public services at lower cost. NPM reforms are hotly contested. Critics argue that NPM is simply a thinly disguised effort to reduce government. Another line of attack is that market principles in public administration leads to greater inequality. Skeptics also claim that accountability is diminished as civil service managers are now even less constrained by rules and even harder to discipline. The use of private firms to deliver public services, far from simplifying government, make it more complex and harder to hold to account, while terms like "client" and "customer" diminish democratic citizenship.

A financial crisis has gripped the world since 2008 and given impetus to more administrative reform. In order to avoid a severe recession, governments spent heavily on economic stimulus. As their economies have weakened, government revenues have diminished, causing deficits and debts to increase substantially in many countries. A crisis that began as a banking problem is now also a government crisis as public debt soars. As a result, governments are cutting public services and searching for ways to economize. In Britain, the Conservative coalition government launched an ambitious program called the Big Society, which calls for radical reforms to public administration (*The Economist* 2011d, 18). Big Society wants government monopolies in education and health care replaced by competition between public, private, and not-for-profit organizations. It wants a greater role for communities and local governments. Big Society wants elections for city police chiefs. It also stresses voluntarism, envisioning citizen volunteers cleaning parks and streets, administering local libraries, and providing other public services. Big Society initiatives evoke a full spectrum of opinions, some seeing it as wrong-headed, others seeing it as an interesting but utopian plan, and still others regarding it as the way forward to a post-bureaucratic world.

Conclusion

THIS CHAPTER INVESTIGATED THE ROLES AND POWER OF THE CIVIL service. It stressed the controversial status of public administration. Modern governments must have large, expert civil services if they are to deliver public services effectively. At the same time, civil servants must respect political authority, deal fairly with citizens, and provide services efficiently. Public administration is not a technical activity, driven by management theories. It is a political process where civil servants have power to shape policy, interpret policy, and implement policy in ways they see fit. Modern societies struggle to balance necessary civil service power with democratic ideals.

Summary

The chapter:

- Stressed that a strong civil service is essential to an effective society; it is also a source of unelected power that challenges democratic ideals
- Urged readers to consider the ways that administrators engage in politics
- Reviewed how governments control the civil service, raising questions about the effectiveness of available controls
- Examined arguments about administrative reform, relating them to debates about the role of government

Discussion Questions

1. To whom are civil servants accountable?
2. Explain why a strong civil service is at the same time essential to society and threatening to democratic ideals.
3. Are Canadian senior civil servants really "permanent politicians"? What does the term mean to you?
4. Can you imagine a society without bureaucracies?

References

Aucoin, Peter. 2003. "Independent Foundations, Public Money and Public Accountability." *Canadian Public Administration* 46(1): 1–26.

Bourgault, Jacques. 2006. "The Deputy's Minister's Role in the Government of Canada: His Responsibility and His Accountability." In *Parliament, Ministers and Deputy Ministers*, Research Studies Volume I, Commission of Inquiry into the Sponsorship Program and Other Activities. Ottawa: Minister of Public Works and Government Services.

The Economist. 2011a. "Can the Joy Last?" September 3: 43–4.

———. 2011b. "Goodbye to GOD." October 15: 66.

———. 2011c. "Ministers v Mandarins." October 22: 68–9.

———. 2011d. "Taming the Leviathan: Special Report on the Future of the State." March 19: 18–19.

Kollman, Ken. 2012. *The American Political System.* New York: W.W. Norton.

Lowi, Theodore J., C. Ginsberg, K. Shepsle, and Stephen Ansolabehere. 2010. *American Government: Power and Purpose,* 11th edition. New York. W.W. Norton.

Martin, Lawrence. 2010. *Harperland: The Politics of Control.* Toronto: Viking.

Seidman, Harold. 1975. *Politics, Position and Power: The Dynamics of Federal Organization,* 2nd edition. New York: Oxford University Press.

Skelcher, Chris. 2007. "Public Private Partnerships and Hybridity." In *The Oxford Handbook of Public Management*, edited by E. Ferlie, Laurence E. Lynn Jr., and C. Pollitt. London: Oxford University Press.

Stone, Bruce. 1995. "Administrative Accountability in the Westminster Democracies." *Governance* 8(4): 505–26.

Sutherland, S.L. 1991. "Responsible Government and Ministerial Responsibility." *Canadian Journal of Political Science* 24(1): 91–120.

Thompson, Dennis F. 1983. *Political Ethics and Public Office*. Cambridge, MA: Harvard University Press.

Tupper, Allan. 2012. "Alberta Deputy Ministers: The Management of Change." In *Provincial Deputy Ministers*, edited by J. Bourgault and C. Dunn. Toronto: University of Toronto Press.

Wilson, James Q. and John J. Dilulio Jr. 2011. *American Government: Institutions and Policies*, 12th edition. Boston: Wadsworth.

Further Readings

Aucoin, Peter. 2003. "Independent Foundations, Public Money and Public Accountability." *Canadian Public Administration* 46(1): 1–26.

Martin, Lawrence. 2010. *Harperland: The Politics of Control*. Toronto: Viking.

Skelcher, Chris. 2007. "Public Private Partnerships and Hybridity." In *The Oxford Handbook of Public Management*, edited by F. Ferlie, Laurence E. Lynn Jr., and C. Pollitt. London: Oxford University Press.

Wilson, James Q. and John J. Dilulio Jr. 2011. *American Government: Institutions and Policies*, 12th edition. Boston: Wadsworth.

Weblinks

Canadian School of Public Service
www.ccmd-ccg.gc.ca

The Institute of Public Administration of Canada (IPAC)
www.ipac.ca

Public Policy Forum
www.ppforum.ca

Treasury Board of Canada Secretariat
www.tbs-sct.gc.ca/index_e.asp

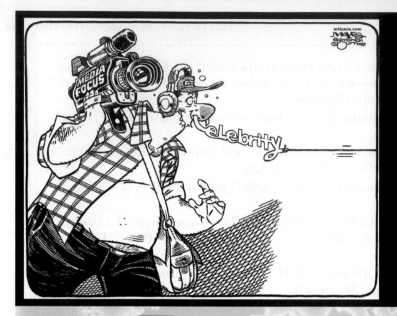

CHAPTER 11

MEDIA

SHAUNA WILTON

Learning Objectives

- Highlights the critical importance of the media to politics

- Demonstrates the importance of patterns of media consumption, ownership, and influence

- Explores the techniques used by the media to shape the news and political opinions

- Examines the impact of the Internet, the 24-hour news cycle, and new social media on democracy

Introduction

Most of us encounter and consume media on a daily basis. We watch television, read newspapers, and listen to the radio. We surf the Internet, use Facebook, and tweet. We get news updates sent to our cellphones and can watch major world events unfold in front of us in real time. We gain most of our information about the political world through media—we read about it in a newspaper or on a website or see it on the television news, as opposed to reading the record of debate for the House of Commons or communicating directly with our elected representatives. In recent decades, ownership, production, and consumption patterns of media have changed. The Internet, in particular, has changed the way the average person accesses the news media, and it is increasingly being used as a tool for the dissemination of political information. In order to understand and critically assess the information we receive through the media, we need to understand how the media works and why it is so crucial to democratic society. Similarly, we must also know how the media can be used to depoliticize and even mislead society for political ends.

Before we can discuss the relationship of media to politics, it is important to have some key definitions in place: **mass media** refers to the means of widely communicating information to the public, traditionally through mediums such as newspapers, radio, and TV; **new social media**, on the other hand, refers to web-based and mobile communication that allow for the creation and distribution of user-generated content, such as Twitter, Facebook, and Wikis.

In the discussion that follows, we will briefly review the historical context in which democracy and press freedom were viewed as important and linked ideas. We will also review the ways in which we consume media and discuss ownership of media. As consumption and ownership patterns change over time, new questions emerge about the relationship between media and politics. This is followed by a discussion of how much we trust the media to provide us with accurate information versus how much we trust other political and social institutions. Next, in order to decide whether or not to trust the media, we need to understand how the media works and the tools it uses to shape the news. Finally, the chapter concludes with a discussion of new trends within news reporting—the 24/7 news cycle and social media—and the consequences for democracy of these trends.

Media and Democracy: From the Enlightenment to Today

THE IDEA OF FREEDOM OF THE PRESS IS ROOTED IN THE STRUGGLE FOR political freedoms in Europe. The **Enlightenment**, or Age of Reason, in Europe was a cultural revolution starting in the second half of the seventeenth century that aimed to promote science and rational thought, and opposed abuses of power by the state and Church. The spread of enlightenment ideas was assisted greatly by developments in printing technology that allowed pamphlets to be cheaply mass produced, giving the population access to information on political, religious, and constitutional topics.

The press became the "**fourth estate**," after the Lords Spiritual (representatives of the Church sitting in the House of Lords), the Lords Temporal (secular members of the House of Lords) and the Commons. Up until the 1600s in England, printing presses were strongly controlled by the monarch and restricted from printing anything that was critical of the king or questioned the power structure of society. The breakdown of censorship controls during the Long Parliament of 1640 and the English Civil War led to a combined media and political revolution.

Similarly, during the French Revolution of the late 1700s, the printing and distribution of pamphlets on political topics was directly related to the spread of revolutionary ideas and the process of political change. This resulted in the embedding of the freedom of the press in the new French constitution, *The Declaration of the Rights of Man and of the Citizen*, in 1789, which stated, "The free communication of ideas and opinions is one of the most precious rights of man. Every citizen may, accordingly, speak, write and print with freedom, but shall be responsible for such abuses of freedom as shall be defined in law." The French constitution is one of the first constitutional documents to enshrine freedom of press with the freedom of speech and directly relate them to political freedom and democracy. Interestingly, you will note that the French constitution also provided for limitations of these freedoms, making one responsible for the "abuses of freedom." The notion of a responsibility for the communication one utters remains in place in most democratic countries today, usually contained in laws preventing libel and slander.

"In old days men had the rack. Now they have the Press. That is an improvement certainly. But still it is very bad, and wrong, and demoralizing. Somebody—was it Burke?—called journalism the fourth estate. That was true at the time no doubt. But at the present moment it is the only estate. It has eaten up the other three. The Lords Temporal say nothing, and the House of Commons has nothing to say and says it. We are dominated by Journalism." Oscar Wilde, "The Soul of Man Under Socialism," 1891.

Having an informed citizenry is understood as a key component of a democracy, and the freedom of the press remains central to the spread of information in society. Article 19 of the United Nations *Universal Declaration of Human Rights* states that "Everyone has the right to freedom of opinion and expression; this right includes freedom to hold opinions without interference and to seek, receive and impart information and ideas through any media and regardless of frontiers." This principle is central to our contemporary understanding of democracy: the people need to understand the political issues of the day and the pressures facing decision makers and members of society in order to make informed decisions about these issues and be active citizens. The media plays a key role in this process by conveying information to the public. As the media environment changes, though, the way we get news, how important we think it is, and the nature of the news itself changes. As discussed below, some of these changes have improved citizen access to information; others, however, raise serious concerns about whose interests are being represented by various media owners.

Media Consumption

WHAT KIND OF MEDIA DO PEOPLE PREFER? HOW DO THEIR PREFERENCES differ across generations, regions, countries, and languages? The major trend among people in Western democracies, for example, is to consume more media, partly because they can access various types simultaneously and, due to technology such as smart phones, are more likely to access media on the go.

There is, however, a generation gap regarding how we get our news. Surveys of media consumption patterns show that older people are more likely to use traditional news sources, whereas younger generations are more likely to rely on online sources and interpersonal communication in combination with traditional news sources. Finally, education, gender, language, and region also play a role in our consumption of news. The higher the level of education an individual has, the more likely he or she is to view keeping up with the news as important. Also, the more a national culture is focused on print media (newspapers), the more likely people are to read papers to keep up with the news regardless of class (Shehata and Strömbäck 2011). Thus, cultural factors can overcome individual factors such as class, education, and gender regarding news consumption. Also, the widespread prevalence of Internet access, mobile phone use, and social media in Western democracies has the potential to enable more people to be better informed about the world around them. These changes, although not without problems as discussed below, also give people the potential to take a more active role both in customizing the information they receive and in shaping and disseminating information; for example, by posting and commenting on Facebook or re-tweeting the news.

Media Consumption Trends

Canada

- When watching TV, 29 percent of Canadians say they are also emailing, 29 percent are surfing the net, 16 percent are texting, and 13 percent are using social networking sites (Deloitte 2011).
- The average anglophone Canadian spent 17.1 hours per week online in 2010 (CRTC 2011). The most popular Internet activities for anglophone Canadians are reading the news online, followed by participating in social networking sites, watching amateur video, and instant messaging (CRTC 2011).
- Men are more likely than women to regard keeping up with the news as important (42 percent vs. 32 percent).
- Francophone Canadians are more interested in the news than anglophones (41 percent vs. 36 percent).
- Residents of the Prairie provinces are less interested in the news than Canadians from other parts of Canada; for example, only 23 percent of residents of Alberta view this as very important compared with 37 percent in Ontario and 43 percent in B.C. (Fletcher et al. 2011).

(Continued)

(Continued)

Europe

- Seventy-six percent of all 16-plus-year-olds across 15 European markets surveyed use different media simultaneously, with almost a third (30 percent) using the Internet while watching TV.
- Fifty-four percent of Europeans use the Internet in a typical week, spending an average of 12.1 hours per week online.
- The most popular Web activities among all European Internet users are email (76 percent); communicating via social networking sites (45 percent); instant messaging (40 percent); watching movies, TV, or videos (32 percent); and contributing to ratings and reviews (27 percent) (IAB Europe 2010).

USA

- On a typical day, 78 percent of Americans say they get news from a local TV station, 73 percent say they get news from a national network, 61 percent say they get some kind of news online, and 50 percent say they read news in a local newspaper.
- Americans today routinely get their news from multiple sources and a mix of platforms. Nine in ten American adults (92 percent) get news from multiple platforms on a typical day, with half of those using four to six platforms daily.
- Among online news consumers, 75 percent say they get news forwarded through email or posts on social networking sites, and 52 percent say they share links to news with others via those means.
- Among Internet users, 37 percent have contributed to the creation of news, commentary about it, or dissemination of news via social media (Pew Research Center 2010).

Media Ownership in Canada

ONE OF THE TRENDS IN MEDIA IN THE LATE TWENTIETH CENTURY WAS the growth of media conglomerates involved in various types of media and owning a variety of media outlets. The trend of fewer companies owning and controlling more and more media outlets is referred to as **media convergence**. The concern that arises with media convergence is that all of a chain's newspapers will produce the same news, from the same perspective, resulting in the existence of fewer perspectives on issues or biased media coverage. As the textbox below demonstrates, a few companies control most of the media. Furthermore, many of these companies not only control newspapers but also are involved in TV and online media.

Media Convergence

Bertelsmann is one of the world's largest media companies. It owns RTL Group, Europe's biggest broadcaster of radio and television, owning TV companies in both Germany and the Netherlands and assets in Belgium, France, the U.K., Spain, the Czech Republic, and Hungary. Bertelsmann also owns Gruner + Jahr, the biggest magazine publisher in Europe; Random House, the world's largest trade book publisher; and Arvato, an international media and communications service provider. Bertelsmann is majority owned (77.4 percent) by the Bertelsmann Foundation, a non-profit organization and political think tank set up by the Mohn family, which, in turn, privately owns the remaining 22.6 percent of the company.

Time Warner is the largest media conglomerate in the world. Its holdings include CNN, the CW (a joint venture with CBS), HBO, Cinemax, Cartoon Network, TBS, TNT, America Online, MapQuest, Moviefone, Warner Bros. Pictures, Castle Rock, and New Line Cinema, as well as more than 150 magazines, including *Time, Sports Illustrated, Fortune, Marie Claire*, and *People*.

Newscorp, owned and created by Rupert Murdoch, is the second-largest media conglomerate in the world. Its media holdings include the Fox Broadcasting Company; television and cable networks such as Fox, Fox Business Channel, National Geographic, and FX; print publications including *The Wall Street Journal, New York Post*, and *TVGuide*; the magazines *Barron's* and *SmartMoney*; book publisher HarperCollins; 20th Century Fox, Fox Searchlight Pictures, and Blue Sky Studios film production companies; numerous websites, including MarketWatch.com; and non-media holdings, including the National Rugby League. It also publishes the major British newspapers *The Sun, The Times*, and the *Sunday Times*, as well as 70 percent of the newspapers in Australia.

Bell Media, the mass media subsidiary of Bell Canada, owns CTV network and its 27 TV affiliates and six A-Channel affiliates, and has full or partial ownership of 30 specialty TV channels, including TSN, MuchMusic, Discovery Channel, The Comedy Network, Bravo!, E!, Space, and Business News Network. The company controls 15 percent of *The Globe and Mail*, all 33 of CHUM Ltd.'s former radio stations, and several Web properties, including Sympatico.ca.

Postmedia Network (formerly Canwest, except broadcasting assets sold to Shaw) owns the *National Post, The Gazette*, the *Ottawa Citizen, The Vancouver Sun*, and eight other major dailies, and 12 weekly community papers in the B.C. area. The dailies also feed content to Postmedia News, the rebranded wire service Canwest set up after pulling out of The Canadian Press subscription wire service.

Media convergence can have serious consequences for democracy. Less independent media means fewer voices spreading the news of the day and, potentially, less variety in the news we receive and fewer dissenting voices. As a result of media convergence, we often see more stringent levels of editorial control over the content of the newspaper, cost-saving measures that can diminish journalistic control and investigative journalism, and a reduction in the amount of news told from a local perspective as news stories are repeated throughout the news corporation in order to better utilize resources. Although most people access their news from a variety of outlets and through a variety of mediums, the widespread prevalence of media convergence makes it even more important for us to be critical consumers of news media.

Media Influence: Who Do We Trust?

KNOWING WHO FOLLOWS THE NEWS AND HOW MUCH THEY TRUST IT helps us understand the amount of political activity people engage in and how this is influenced by the type and frequency of their media consumption (Keown 2007).

Textbox titled Media Consumption Trends outlined our consumption habits, demonstrating that we consume a high volume of media, often simultaneously. But how much do we trust the media and the news media in particular? How do levels of trust for the media compare with trust for other social and political institutions? Does this vary across countries? Has the recent convergence of Canadian media led to a perception of its decreased trustworthiness?

How Much Do We Trust the Media?

Canada

- Nearly 9 in 10 Canadians find traditional news media to be reliable and trustworthy, whereas only 1 in 4 thinks information from social networks is reliable.
- Younger Canadians (33 percent of those aged 18 to 34) are more likely to trust social media.
- Canadians are more confident about the trustworthiness of news media if its content has been edited by a professional editor or journalist rather than through "crowd editing," such as on a wiki.
- While many Canadians rely on social networks, such as Facebook and Twitter, to alert them to news, they often seek verification from more traditional news outlets.
- A majority of Canadians (87 percent) trust the information they get from newspapers, 83 percent trust TV news, and 53 percent trust information from online companies. In comparison, only 42 percent of Canadians trust information from government and 38 percent trust information from major corporations (Fletcher et al. 2011).

Europe

- Overall, Europeans trust media more than they trust their political institutions: 57 percent trust radio news, 50 percent trust TV news, 42 percent trust the press, and 35 percent trust the Internet (European Commission 2011b).
- In comparison, while there is a great deal of national variation among the member states of the European Union (EU), 28 percent of Europeans trust their national government, 43 percent trust the EU, 38 percent trust trade unions, 30 percent trust big companies, 64 percent trust the police, 40 percent trust religious institutions, and 15 percent trust political parties (European Commission 2011a).

USA

- While, overall, Americans think that major news organizations are doing a good job covering the important stories, 72 percent think that news sources are biased, only 25 percent trust newspapers, and 22 percent trust TV (Pew Research Center 2010).
- Generally, Americans trust institutions more than the media, unlike in Canada and Europe: 36 percent of Americans trust the U.S. Supreme Court and 36 percent trust the presidency; however, only 11 percent trust Congress.
- As well, 59 percent of Americans trust the police, 20 percent trust organized labour, 19 percent trust big business, and 48 percent trust the Church or organized religion (Polling Report 2011).

As the textbox above suggests, Canadians and Europeans trust news media more than they do government or corporations. Furthermore, a large majority of Canadians think that traditional journalism plays a key role in maintaining a critical democracy by exposing abuses of power (90 percent), providing an analysis of important events (84 percent), regularly reporting on government actions (86 percent), and providing a Canadian perspective on world events (78 percent) (Fletcher et al. 2011). They also believe that professional journalists rather than citizen journalists best fill these functions. Professional journalists work for companies, are trained to report the news, and are subject to editorial control—all of which makes them accountable. Citizen journalists, on the other hand, include bloggers and people reporting on their own and are perceived as potentially more biased and less trustworthy. However, it is also necessary to question the neutrality of professional journalists and reputable news sources. Are they really reporting "All the news that is fit to print" as *The New York Times* (the most popular American newspaper website) claims? Or is traditional journalism also subject to constraints and biases that shape the news they deliver?

Media Techniques

ALL MEDIA USES CERTAIN TECHNIQUES IN THE PRODUCTION OF THE news. They have to decide what stories to print or televise and how to represent the event. Journalists also make decisions about how to tell the story, which angle to use, and who to interview and quote. Editors decide on the headlines, images, and where the story will appear in the broadcast, newspaper, or webpage. While *The New York Times*' slogan may be "All the news that is fit to print," the decision about what is "fit to print" is made by journalists and editors and may reflect the availability of good visuals, public interest, and the priorities of particular media organizations.

This process of deciding what to include in the news is called **filtering**. Filtering is an essential part of the production of the news and reflects the idea that all of the "unnecessary" news is filtered out, leaving the most important stories for the media to tell. This occurs during the production of a news story, when journalists and editors are constantly making decisions about what to include and exclude, whom to interview and quote, and which facts are most important or interesting, thereby shaping the news we get.

The Missing News

Organizations such as Project Censored, Media Lens, and NewsWatch Canada keep track of the most underreported stories in an effort to tell the stories that do not make it into mainstream news outlets. Researchers at Simon Fraser University studied mainstream and independent new outlets to determine the 25 most under-reported stories of 2010–11, based on their national and international importance. They concluded that "such omissions in major Canadian news media imply that the news provides only a partial reflection of the information citizens need for a functioning democracy, and suggests that we must rethink the role and structure of the large news organizations in Canada" (NewsWatch Canada 2011).

(Continued)

(Continued)

The top 10 under-reported stories in Canada in 2010–11:

1. **Canada-Europe Comprehensive Economic and Trade Agreement (CETA):** CETA, a free-trade agreement between Canada and the EU that is being negotiated behind closed doors, will give European corporations access to government procurement actions down to the municipal level, including public institutions such as hospitals and public utilities.

2. **Canadian Mining Companies Lack Accountability:** Canadian mining companies are responsible for a large percentage of environmental and human rights abuses around the world yet are not held accountable.

3. **Corporate Lobbying Shaping Laws:** Corporate lobbyists around the globe are spending billions of dollars in order to write and determine policy at the national and international level.

4. **Crisis in Long-Term Care:** Long-term and assisted living care in Canada is facing a crisis in the form of early hospital evictions, hospital over-crowding, affordability, and quality of care in private and unregulated residences.

5. **Violence Against Aboriginal Women in Canada:** More than 600 indigenous women across Canada have gone missing or been murdered in the past 30 years, 75 percent of Aboriginal girls under the age of 18 have been victims of sexual abuse, and Aboriginal girls and women are nearly three times more likely to become victims of violence.

6. **State of Native Reserves in Canada:** Appalling Third-World conditions on Aboriginal reserves have stagnated in the past ten years, and indicators of wellness such as housing, education, and water quality have actually declined.

7. **Health Effects of Canada's Tar Sands:** Toxic waste from Canada's tar sands contaminates the environment while nearby northern Albertan communities find themselves increasingly affected by cancer.

8. **Long-Term Effects of Fukushima:** Japan's nuclear disaster is far worse than governments have revealed to the public. Effects from the fallout have been felt in both the U.S. and Canada but their significance has been downplayed.

9. **Abandoned Oil Wells Cause Environmental Hazard:** Abandoned Albertan oil wells must be cleaned up to avoid environmental contamination, but the companies that own them have little incentive to do so given the huge costs and weak regulations.

10. **Global Disposable Workforce:** Thousands of migrant workers are admitted into Canada every year for short periods of time, but their rights are often abused or ignored.

(NewsWatch Canada (2011). *Missing News: The Top 25 Underreported Stories 2010–2011.* School of Communication, Simon Fraser University: Burnaby.)

Other media techniques include **agenda setting**, which "refers to the idea that there is a strong correlation between the emphasis that mass media place on certain issues . . . and the importance attributed to these issues by mass audiences" (Scheufele and Tewksbury 2007, 11). For example, a front-page story in a newspaper or the breaking story on CNN is understood to be more important than the news that appears in the middle of the paper or broadcast. Similarly, stories that get multiple articles or significant amounts of newspaper space or broadcast time appear more important than those that are skimmed over. Agenda setting may be attributed to the biases or agenda of editors, the influence of advertisers, or, simply, the ideas in the newsroom about what the public want to read and watch.

Priming is often a result of agenda setting and occurs when news audiences believe that specific issues, promoted by the media, can be used as benchmarks for evaluating politicians, governments, and other leaders: "By making some issues more salient in people's mind (agenda setting), mass media can also shape the considerations that people take into account when making judgments about political candidates or issues" (Scheufele and Tewksbury 2007, 11). For example, if violent crime is given a disproportionate level of attention in the media (which it often is), then citizens are more likely to view crime as a major issue during political campaigns.

Framing, however, is one of the most important tools of the media. It is not based on the ability of people to recall or access information presented to them in the media as with agenda setting and priming, but it has to do with how the story or information is presented. As such, the media and politicians present information in ways that resonate with the audience in order to simplify complex issues and present them in a compact format. Framing, thus, is a form of shorthand in which the media takes an example with which most people are familiar (such as a race or a boxing match) and applies it to a political event (such as a campaign or leaders debate) (Scheufele and Tewksbury 2007, 11–12).

All of these techniques—the processes of producing the news for our consumption—shape the informational environment in which we live. They influence what we know and how we understand events. The trend toward media convergence means that we are likely presented with fewer frames or perspectives on the news. The desire of media conglomerates to create news stories that can be placed in a variety of their news outlets means that they will use the most common frames available in order to reach a wide range of audiences. This also means that they are less likely to frame a story through a local lens. This reinforces the importance of comparing the information given to us from a variety of news companies in order to get the best information possible.

The American Invasion of Iraq

There was unprecedented media coverage of the American invasion of Iraq in 2003. The existence of news specialty channels ensured live coverage of the conflict, and journalists from around the world gathered to cover the story. Cellphones and the Internet ensured that the news from Iraq could be broadcast immediately. The U.S. military attempted to control the media through the creation of a media command centre where military personnel kept journalists informed about events. As well, about 600 journalists, mostly American and British, were embedded within military units to provide ground-level coverage of the conflict. These tactics were aimed at ensuring a pro-war message within English-speaking media; however, they also challenged the freedom of the press to report on the conflict or to challenge or criticize the actions of the American military and government. American journalists were banned from showing images of flag-draped coffins and discouraged from showing images of wounded

(Continued)

(Continued)

soldiers in order to maintain support for the war. The main alternative source of information during the conflict was the Arabic-language news station, Al Jazeera. It was highly criticized by American media for showing images of Iraqis and Americans wounded and dying, and for focusing on civilian casualties. Unlike the American news outlets that tended to frame the conflict as one of liberation of the Iraqi people or as part of the War on Terror, Al Jazeera tended to frame the conflict in terms of an invasion and colonialism. These two perspectives demonstrate the difference that media can make in terms of how it frames the story and filters information.

News in the Twenty-First Century: The 24/7 News Cycle and New Social Media

IN AN ARTICLE FOR *LE MONDE*, THE LATE RYSZARD KAPUŚCIŃSKI, A renowned Polish journalist who covered many major world events during the Cold War, criticized the recent changes in the media wherein news journalism has become a commodity. He suggested that journalism is no longer a search for truth or part of political struggle. Instead, journalism is focused on profits, and the importance of a piece of news depends on customer demand. The advent of cellphones and email has led to less reporter autonomy as editors receive news from a variety of sources. Reporters tend to move as a pack, following the big stories, resulting in fewer stories being told. Kapuściński asked how we are to understand the world when the media is presenting such a superficial and fragmented version of events and we are increasingly unable to contest the truths it sells.

Part of this shift in the way news is produced is attributable to the 24/7 news cycle that began with the launch of CNN in 1980. The 24-hour television news channel promised news that was free of time constraints, better able to cover breaking news, and provided more in-depth coverage. Because of the lack of time constraints, the news channels would also be able to cover all of the stories that were filtered out of the regular news broadcasts (Rather 2007). However, Dan Rather, a prominent American news anchor, argues that the opposite has happened, and the 24-hour news cycle has led to the growth of soft news, "infotainment," celebrity coverage, time fillers, and "studio shouting matches" (Rather 2007). The primary focus of the news has shifted from policy or informed discussions of important political issues to process, with the media following politicians on the campaign trail and relying on opinion polls. This has consequences for politics, as political candidates are encouraged to speak to the media in a manner that fits this format; instead of talking meaningfully about their political positions, they provide sound bites. As well, by focusing so much attention on particular news stories, these all-news stations shape the political agenda and magnify the significance of the story relative to other news.

The other new players in the news media are the Internet and, in particular, new social media, sometimes referred to as the "fifth estate." The widespread popularity of new social media has changed the way that people communicate with each other and the way to get information about the world. Recent political events have brought social media to the forefront, whether it is a YouTube video showing the police subduing protesters or tweets spurring on revolution in the Middle East. These sites, especially Twitter and Facebook, are also increasingly influencing the mainstream media. As the sites become the source and subject of the news itself—for example, as journalists report on what is being said on Twitter or Facebook—these sites provide a backdoor through which the mainstream media can discuss unverified information and stories.

"News consumption is a socially engaging and socially driven activity, especially online. The public is clearly part of the news process now. Participation comes more through sharing than through contributing news themselves." (Pew Research Center 2010)

In spite of the growing position of social media in our collective consciousness, the actual impact of social media on political outcomes is still being debated. While President Barack Obama, among others, successfully used social media to gain political support and for campaign fundraising, even using YouTube for press releases, not all politicians have been so successful. In fact, the ability to instantly transmit your thoughts to thousands of voters can be problematic for campaign managers who want control of the message. Similar to the mainstream news media, these social networking sites, through their short formats and focus on what an individual is doing or thinking at a particular moment, do not allow for more nuanced and in-depth consideration of political issues.

Twitter and the Revolution in Egypt

In January 2011, Twitter and Facebook appeared to be engines of political change against Arab authoritarianism, with many commentators arguing that "social media irrevocably changed the future of the middle-east" (Alterman 2011, 103). Jon B. Alterman, however, argues that we have not seen widespread changes to political structures in countries like Egypt since its popular revolution, and that social media played only a marginal role in the overthrow of the governments. The economic conditions in Egypt were ripe for revolt in early 2011; however, protestors were gathered more through canvassing in poor neighbourhoods than through an online call to action. When the organizers were able to get thousands to Tahrir Square, it became a television event that Al Jazeera framed as a sign of emerging revolution. TV gave meaning to the events that were happening, and distributed it to a wide audience. Alterman argues it was because of the news coverage that Egyptians brought the revolution online, feeding their images and cellphone video to news networks. The Internet played a later role in providing news and TV feeds when the government attempted to shut down access to the traditional networks.

"While the activists were a catalyst for the events of January and February, they did not drive them. Television drove them, framed them, legitimated them, and broadcast them to a wide audience" (Alterman 2011, 114).

Conclusion

THE MEDIA PLAYS AN INTEGRAL ROLE IN MODERN DEMOCRACIES BY informing the public about current issues and political actions, and by acting as a watchdog of government and corporations. With the growth of the Internet and new social media, we are increasingly accessing information online and from a variety of sources, both through traditional TV, radio, and print news and through online forums. At the same time, most of us continue to access most of our news through the traditional media of the twentieth century—television, radio, and printed newspapers—and to use traditional media to confirm the news we get through social media. As the medium through which the news is delivered has changed, both through increasing online activity and the convergence of media, so has the message being delivered. The rise of the 24/7 news cycle and infotainment has led to a focus on the process of politics, rather than on the content of policies and in-depth political analysis. This has led to an increased use of strategic frames, which focus on winners and losers, when reporting the news. The news media plays a central role in a democracy, ensuring freedom of speech and access to information. The relationship between the media and politics, therefore, requires our close and critical attention in order to ensure the health of our democracy.

Summary

The chapter:

- Demonstrated that most people acquire information about politics through the media
- Examined how the Internet has changed the way we access information, but noted that traditional sources remain important
- Highlighted that younger people are less likely to view keeping up with the news as important and more likely to get their news online or through social networking sites
- Discussed media convergence, but noted that people still trust the media more than they do governments and corporations to keep them informed
- Reviewed the various techniques used by the media, such as filtering, framing, and agenda setting, which shape the news we receive
- Examined the role of the 24/7 news cycle, new social media, and communications technology, which have led to "instant" news but not necessarily to more in-depth or broader news coverage

Discussion Questions

1. Consider the list of under-reported stories from 2010–11. Why do you think these stories did not receive more coverage? What are the consequences of stories such as these not being reported?

2. Analyze the front page of a newspaper. What media techniques can you identify? How are they being used?

3. How do you get the news? Why? What role do new social media play in keeping you informed? Are they an adequate source of news information?

4. What role does or should the media play in a democracy? How well is the media meeting these expectations?

References

Alterman, Jon B. 2011. "The Revolution Will Not Be Tweeted." *Washington Quarterly* 34(4): 103–16.

CRTC. 2011. "Communication's Monitoring Report." Canadian Radio-television and Telecommunications Commission. http://www.crtc.gc.ca/eng/publications/reports/PolicyMonitoring/2010/cmr.htm.

Deloitte. 2011. "Live TV Is Still King." Deloitte. http://www.deloitte.com/assets/Dcom-Canada/Local%20Assets/Documents/TMT/ca_en_tmt_state_media_170511.pdf.

European Commission. 2011a. *Public Opinion in the European Union, Autumn 2010.* Eurobarometer 74. http://ec.europa.eu/public_opinion/archives/eb/eb74/eb74_publ_en.pdf.

———. 2011b. *Information on European Political Matters, Autumn 2010.* Eurobarometer 74. http://ec.europa.eu/public_opinion/archives/eb/eb74/eb74_infor_en.pdf.

Fletcher, Fred, Donna Logan, Alfred Hermida, and Darryl Korell. 2011. "Even in the Digital Era, Canadians Have Confidence in Mainstream News Media." Canadian Media Research Consortium. http://www.mediaresearch.ca/.

IAB Europe. 2010. *European Media Landscape Report.* Mediascope Europe. http://www.iabeurope.eu/media/53821/european%20media%20landscape%20report%20summary.pdf.

Kapuściński, Ryszard. 1999. "Media as Mirror to the World." *Le Monde diplomatique,* English ed. August 5. http://mondediplo.com/1999/08/05media.

NAD Bank. 2011. "2010/11 Readership Study." Newspaper Audience Bank Inc. http://nadbank.com/.

Newspapers Canada. 2010. "Daily Newspapers Paid Circulation Data." Newspapers Canada. http://www.newspaperscanada.ca/daily-newspaper-paid-circulation-data.

NewsWatch Canada. 2011. "Missing News: The Top 25 Underreported Stories, 2010–11. http://pages.cmns.sfu.ca/newswatch/files/2011/11/NewsWatch-Canada_SFU-Research-Seminar_2010_2011_Underreported-Stories_Print-Ready.pdf.

Pew Research Center. 2010. *The New News Landscape: Rise of the Internet.* Pew Internet and American Life Project. http://pewresearch.org/pubs/1508/internet-cell-phone-users-news-social-experience.

Polling Report. 2011. *Major Institutions.* http://www.pollingreport.com/institut.htm.

Rather, Dan. 2007. "Done on the Cheap: The 24/7 News Cycle and Its Impact on Politics Today." *Ripon Forum* 41(6): 26–7.

Scheufele, Dietram A. and David Tewksbury. 2007. "Framing, Agenda Setting, and Priming: The Evolution of Three Media Effects Models." *Journal of Communication* 57(1): 9–20.

Shehata, A. and J. Stromback 2011. "A Matter of Context: A Comparative Study of Media Environments and News Consumption Gaps in Europe."*Political Communication* 28(1): 110–34.

Further Readings

Chomsky, Noam and Edward S. Herman. 2002. *Manufacturing Consent: The Political Economy of the Mass Media.* New York: Pantheon Books.

Nunns, Alex and Nadia Idle, eds. 2011. *Tweets from Tahrir: Egypt's Revolution as It Unfolded, in the Words of the People Who Made It.* New York: OR Books.

Weblinks

Pew Research Center
http://pewresearch.org

IndyMedia
www.indymedia.org/en/index.shtml

Canadian Radio-television and Telecommunications Commission
www.crtc.gc.ca/eng/home-accueil.htm

NewsWatch Canada
http://pages.cmns.sfu.ca/newswatch

CHAPTER 12

WHAT'S LEFT OUT? POWER, VIOLENCE, AND WAR

SEAN F. MCMAHON

Learning Objectives

- Describes the relationship between violence and power

- Distinguishes between different dimensions of violence

- Outlines the war model of politics

- Explains the Egyptian experience in the Arab Revolutions in light of the dimensions of violence and the war model

Introduction

The primary object of inquiry of political science has long been politics, the state, or what is often called government. This is the focus that gave the discipline its identity, distinguishing it from economics or sociology, and it tasked political scientists to explain, advise, and inform the state (Farr 2007, 66). However, political science has neglected violence, and its most spectacular expression—war. Violence was left to sociology, and war became the specialization of strategic and security studies. This is a curious omission in political science given that there has never been a sustained period of time, and certainly not the contemporary moment, without violence and war that affects both domestic and international politics. According to Project Ploughshares' *Armed Conflicts Report 2011*, there has been a prevailing downward trend in the number of active armed conflicts worldwide, the fewest conflicts in almost a quarter-century. Still, there were 24 armed conflicts being fought around the world in 2010 and many of these conflicts have persisted for longer than a decade.

Violence is an important correlate of politics; yet, it has been left out of much political analysis. In fact, no conversation about politics is complete without a discussion of violence and war. While some types of violence and war are obvious examples of political conflagration, less obvious is the idea that conflict is a permanent or perpetual condition of all societies. Power, violence, and wars are not exclusive to international politics; they are also elements of politics in the domestic arena.

This chapter develops its discussion of power, violence, and war in four sections. First, it describes the relationship between power and violence. Second, it distinguishes between different dimensions of violence, most notably direct and **structural violence**. Furthermore, it locates **terrorism** along these different dimensions. Third, it outlines a **war model for analyzing politics** in both domestic and international arenas. Rather than conceive of politics legally and administratively, this model understands politics in terms of conflict and contestation; all politics are a playing out of force relations and the imposition of dominations and subordinations. Fourth and finally, it examines the Egyptian experience in the 2011 **Arab Revolutions** (also known as the Arab Spring) through the ciphers of direct and structural violence and the war model of politics.

The Relationship of Power and Violence in Historical Context

POWER AND VIOLENCE ARE OFTEN TREATED AS SYNONYMS; HOWEVER, this is too simplistic. Violence is frequently combined with power in the practice of politics, but the two concepts are not the same. To clear up this misconception, it is important to distinguish between power and violence, explain how violence can be understood as positive and productive, and define the most institutionalized form of violence, namely war.

Politics is about power and violence is the use of physical force to cause injury. The combination of those results in **political violence**, the use of physical force to affect power relations within or between societies. It is this combination that is of interest to authors such as Hannah Arendt and Charles Tilly. According to Arendt, violence has an instrumental relationship with power (Arendt 1970, 46). In other words, violence is a tool. For example, physical force can be employed to repel foreign invaders, which serves political interests. Violence is also a tool that can be employed by groups to challenge political power. Revolutionaries such as Che Guevera and Nelson Mandela used violence to challenge the prevailing corrupt and discriminatory governments that characterized pre-revolutionary Cuba and apartheid South Africa, respectively. Those governments also used violence against these revolutionary figures and masses of citizens, many of whom were only indirectly involved in insurrection, if at all. Ultimately, however, what counts is the power supporting the violence, not violence alone. Arendt argues that violence unsupported by power will never accomplish political goals or serve as an effective means to a political end. Furthermore, Arendt argues that violence cannot create power but only destroy it (Arendt 1970, 49, 56). Put differently, violence cannot stand in place of political power, but it can undermine political power.

How can we understand the relationship between power and violence, given Arendt's analysis? Power is premised on the support of significant sectors of society. A lone man with a gun is potentially dangerous, but not powerful. A man with a gun backed by social groups such as wealthy classes, the military, or mass popular support has the power to use violence successfully. Similarly, even the most violent authoritarian leaders govern because they are supported by other powerful actors (Arendt 1970, 50). Authoritarians can use violence because they exercise power. Despite media representations to the contrary, this is true even of a dictator, such as Saddam Hussein. This violent regime rested on the implicit and explicit support of the United States, the Ba'ath Party, and Sunni Muslims in Iraq.

That being said, no government premised exclusively on violence can exist (Arendt 1970, 50). Governments, however, can and do use more or less violence against their own populations. In general, governments are more likely to resort to violence against populations in situations where they are losing their grip on power. The spectacle of tanks in the streets facing down protestors and the practice of making opposition leaders go "missing" are signs that governments have lost their legitimacy and popular support. The more power is lost, the more violence will be used. The substitution of violence for power, however, will not reverse the government's loss of power because, as noted above, violence cannot build power (Arendt 1970, 54). In fact, the use of violence may undermine popular support for the government and, thus, weaken its legitimacy and power further. Also in keeping with Arendt's logic, violence may be used by a popularly supported group to weaken or destroy a government's power. For example, in Nicaragua in 1979, the Sandinista movement had popular support and, as a result, was able to use violence successfully to topple the Somoza regime.

In addition to Arendt's argument that violence is an instrument that can be used to destroy political power, other thinkers view violence as productive and positive. Charles Tilly, for example, argues that it was the control and subsequent use of violence by fledgling European states that led to the consolidation of power and, more importantly, the making of the modern state (Tilly 1990, 70). In fact, this is an essential feature of Weber's oft-cited definition of the modern national state: "a human community that successfully claims monopoly on the legitimate use of physical force within a given territory" (quoted in Gerth and Mills 1958, 78). With the end of feudalism, regional power holders and/or notables no longer controlled the means of violence in society or the capacity to wage private wars. The state disarmed the populations and made private armies illegal. Effectively, the state consolidated the means of violence and power at the expense of domestic rivals (Tilly 1990, 76). This does not mean that the state eliminated violence. Instead, the state institutionalized and regulated its use in the forms of domestic police forces and standing armies. The "peace building" exercises in Iraq and Afghanistan aimed to achieve precisely this outcome.

Standing armies became the essential feature of the state, and their construction and maintenance, in turn, generated bureaucratic mechanisms for popular conscription and courts (Tilly 1990, 70, 75). The ruler's use of political violence in the form of war expanded the structure of the state itself by claiming new territories and building bureaucracies. For example, the need to supply and pay the army and rebuild after wars made it necessary for the state to collect and store revenue, which led to the development of state treasuries and state-wide systems of taxation.

Toward the end of the eighteenth century, states stopped using mercenaries in their armies. Instead, the state conscripted its own citizenry into the army. As states taxed citizens and demanded that they fight for the state, the citizenry began to make demands of the state. One demand in particular was for popular working-class franchise—if the citizens were good enough and old enough to die for the state, they were good enough and old enough to vote. Electorates grew and elected assemblies became ever more central to the conduct of political life, and lawmakers were pressured to appeal and be accountable to ordinary citizens (Tilly 1990, 83). Many of the bureaucratic features of the modern state, such as state treasuries, systems of taxation, and public assemblies, are, thus, the by-products of the exercise of violence.

It is not surprising, given the state's close ties to the exercise of violence, that at around this time Carl von Clausewitz offered the standard threefold conceptualization of war. First, war is a social and political activity of states. Second, says Clausewitz, "war is an act of force to compel our enemy to do our will." Third, "war is an act of policy" (Clausewitz 1989, 75, 87). According to Clausewitz, war is a military tool used by states that meets ends left unsatisfied by other political mechanisms, such as diplomacy. War, however, is not an autonomous activity; it is always linked to larger political imperatives, such as sovereignty, imperialism, territorial expansion, and hegemony.

Dimensions of Violence Today

AS THE PREVIOUS DISCUSSION SUGGESTS, NOT ALL ACTS OF VIOLENCE
are the same. Traditionally, violence has been understood narrowly, as the hurting or
killing of one by another who intends to hurt or kill, and peace has been understood
negatively as the absence of this kind of violence. Such narrow and negative definitions have the deleterious effect of making repugnant social orders tolerable simply
because they are "peaceful" (read not violent) and preclude a thorough understanding of many contemporary instances of violence, including terrorism.

Johan Galtung offers a nuanced and extended definition of violence. According
to Galtung, violence is present when one's physical and mental reality increasingly
diverges from his or her physical and mental potential. For example, a child dying
today as a result of a preventable disease is an instance of violence. Because the child
could have lived, given all of the resources of modern medicine, but did not, she or
he suffered violence. When reality is less than the potential and the condition is avoidable, violence is present (Galtung 1969, 168).

Building on this definition, Galtung outlines six dimensions of violence. The first
distinction he draws is between physical and psychological violence. A narrow definition of violence focuses exclusively on violence done to the body, but violence can
also be done to the psyche. Lies, brainwashing, indoctrination, and threats are all
examples of psychological violence. The second dimension of violence is positive
and negative influence. This relates to the "realizations" of human beings and how
they are affected—negatively by punishments and limitations or positively by rewards
and opportunities. Punishment may involve increasing constraints—physical and/
or material—on an individual, which further distances him or her from realizing his
or her full potential. Ideally, constraints can be reduced, thereby bringing the individual's potential and reality into closer alignment (Galtung 1969, 169–70).

The third and fourth dimensions of Galtung's conceptualization of violence speak
to the object and subject of violence. An object of violence can be understood as the
target, and the subject as the person acting violently; for Galtung, violent action is the
mode of influencing, while the object of violence is the influencee, and the subject
of violence is the influencer. The third distinction makes the point that a specific
object, a victim, is not required for violence to be perpetrated. The "showing off" of
means of physical violence, for example, in the form of nuclear tests, does not involve
anyone being hit or hurt, but it does constitute an act of psychological violence that
constrains human action. According to this dimension of violence, the Cold War doctrines of balance of power and mutually assured destruction that kept the planet as
nuclear hostage were no less violent just because the superpowers did not actually hurl
nuclear weapons at each other. They were "differently violent." Just as violence does
not require an object to be perpetrated, neither does it require a subject. The fourth
distinction asks, is there a subject who acts violently? Violence can be present even
when there is no person acting violently. However, the presence of a subject, a violent

actor, distinguishes direct violence from structural violence. Direct violence is "the type of violence where there is an actor who commits the violence," while **structural violence** is "violence where there is no such actor" (Galtung 1969, 170). It is violence "built into the structure and shows up as unequal power and consequently as unequal life chances" (Galtung 1969, 171). For Galtung, economic inequality, starvation, and different life expectancies across classes, which are all objectively avoidable, are instances of structural violence.

The fifth and sixth dimensions of Galtung's conceptualization of violence involve the intentionality and different levels of violence. The fifth distinction is made between intended and unintended violence. This distinction is notable because a focus on intentions ends up obscuring structural violence. Concern with the intent behind violence, particularly to prove guilt, means invoking an actor, which, in turn, means thinking along the lines of personal violence rather than structural violence. The sixth and final distinction is between manifest and latent violence. "Manifest violence, whether [direct] or structural, is observable." Latent violence, on the other hand, is an unstable equilibrium that could "easily" descend into violence. "Latent violence is something which is not there," but could easily deteriorate into a situation in which the distance between an individual's potential and reality is exaggerated (Galtung 1969, 171–2).

Terrorism

In recent years, political science has focused almost exclusively on terrorism as a form of political violence. By drawing on Galtung's more detailed treatment of violence, **terrorism** can be viewed as an example of direct violence. Terrorism is a violent act intended to serve a political goal in which victims are arbitrarily selected with the intention of instilling fear in a larger audience. Alex P. Schmid adds four important observations to this definition. First, both non-state and state actors practise terrorism—it is not practised exclusively by clandestine organizations. Second, the victims of terrorism are not the primary target of the violence but are usually arbitrarily selected. Third, terrorism is a communication process. The latter two observations are closely related to the fourth: terrorism communicates a message far beyond the fate of the victims. In fact, the victims are not the intended recipients of the message; the message is conveyed to an audience that is the primary target of demands, intimidation, or coercion (Schmid and Jongman 1988, 28).

Noam Chomksy and Edward W. Said add a critical element to the definition of terrorism, premised on the idea that defining terrorism is dependent on the definer or, perhaps more accurately, on those who have the power to define terrorism. In other words, defining terrorism is a highly politicized act. Chomsky suggests that a terrorist act is one committed against "us"; it is terrorism when "we" are the victims. It is not the scale of the violent act or the body count that determines whether the act is labelled a terrorist act (Chomsky 2002, 1). When "we" are bombed by "them," it is an act of terrorism, and "they" are the terrorists. When "we" bomb "them," it is a pacification campaign, or low-intensity warfare, and "they" are collateral damage (Booth and Dunne 2002). "We" are never terrorists and, most certainly, never perpetrate acts of terrorism.

In keeping with the idea that defining terrorism is a highly politicized act, Said speaks as to why the labels "terrorism" and "terrorist" are applied to the actions of others. He says that identifying someone as a terrorist isolates him or her from time, from causality, and from prior action and thereby portrays him or her as inherently and gratuitously interested in destruction for its own sake (Said and Hitchens 1988, 154). A terrorist, according to this perspective, is someone who lives outside history, who is without legitimate grievances, who has not suffered dispossession or deprivation, and who is only interested in killing for killing's sake. This labelling obscures the structural causes of non-state terrorism: for example, living under apartheid or occupation or enduring severe deprivation such as famine or poverty.

State terrorism, on the other hand, is not an effect of structural violence. Like those subject to structural violence, however, it too follows from political weakness. A well-documented case of state terrorism began on September 11, 1973, when the United States backed a coup that replaced Chile's democratically elected president, Salvador Allende, with General Augusto Pinochet. Under Pinochet, state security services and death squads targeted all forms of political opposition—members of political parties (primarily leftists), union and religious leaders, agrarian reformers, and anyone else considered to be an opponent of the regime. These death squads were responsible for the disappearance, killing, and torture of thousands of people. Another example of state terrorism occurred in 1981 when the United States initiated aggression against the socialist Sandinista government of Nicaragua. The instrument of this aggression was a mercenary army, called the Contras, trained, funded, and supplied by the United States. Over the next five years, the Contras, working from their bases in Honduras, killed and tortured more than 11 000 Nicaraguan peasants and villagers. In both cases, the state used paramilitary groups to intimidate and kill both random and symbolic targets in order to convey messages of obedience (Chile) or opposition (Nicaragua) to larger segments of society. In fact, the former director of the American Central Intelligence Agency, testifying before Congress, said as much when he called the American Contra war "state-sponsored terrorism" (Chomsky 1988, 27).

It is commonly asserted that "terrorism is the weapon of the weak," meaning that such acts as bus bombings and airplane hijackings are the only violent means available to non-state actors lacking resources and an organized state military. If we look at the historical record, however, we see that terrorism has often been used by militarily powerful states rather than weak non-state actors. From the sixteenth to the nineteenth century, for example, colonial powers such as Britain, Portugal, and Spain used state terrorism to eradicate Indigenous populations in Africa, Asia, and South America. In the past century, the United States has practised state terrorism in, among other places, Nicaragua, El Salvador, Vietnam, and Cambodia. Finally, Israel continues to use state terrorism in an attempt to subvert the Palestinians' quest for nationhood. Historically, militarily powerful state actors have taken recourse in terrorism.

If we return to the relationship between violence and power suggested by Arendt in the previous section, we see an interesting similarity between non-state and state terrorism. Recall that Arendt argues that the successful use of violence requires political power that is embedded in other popular support. Al-Qaeda intimidated and bombed while Saddam Hussein tortured and killed. However, neither of these actors had significant popular support in either of Afghanistan or Iraq. In fact, these actors tried to compensate for their narrow power bases through the use of violence. While able to make use of violence, both this non-state actor and state actor were politically weak. In this case, terrorism is, in fact, the weapon of the *politically* weak.

One final word—applying the label "terrorism" should be done with considerable caution precisely because of the political function the term is made to serve. Labelling an event an act of terrorism all too easily prevents us from searching for the structural violence undergirding the direct violence. Instead, we come to simplistically reduce the root causes of the terrorism to terrorists alone. We are encouraged to assume that the reason there is terrorism is that there are terrorists, and not poverty or state repression or foreign occupation. Importantly, such a reductionist gaze leads to equally simplistic policy responses. It suggests that the only way to be rid of terrorism is to eradicate the terrorists themselves, rather than the structural violence that produces them. Without dealing with the larger issues, single-minded direct violence against terrorists only succeeds in creating more determined terrorists focused on changing existing political orders.

A War Model of Politics

A STATE OF WAR IS THE MOST VISIBLE INSTANCE OF THE RELATIONSHIP between violence and politics. Political science's focus on the state has meant that war has been understood as something that happens between states, beyond their borders, where sovereignty and domestic order do not prevail. As a model for understanding politics, war need not be limited to the realm of international relations, however. Understood as a political contest, war can be a powerful lens through which to view all politics.

The preceding chapters understand power and politics as inextricably bound up with a sovereign authority vested in the state, and the domestic peace that it provides. More specifically, these chapters take as their point of departure a sovereign order that keeps war at bay, suggesting that violence is something that happens "out there." But what if we think about war as not restricted to the international arena? What if "civil war" is not an end to "normal" (peaceful) domestic relations, but rather only a difference of degree? What if civil war is regarded as the direct form of a war that is always raging within society? What would it mean for our understanding of politics if politics itself were conceived of in terms of perpetual battles and war?

This is exactly how the influential philosopher Michel Foucault encouraged people to think about politics. Foucault suggested that politics be conceived of without reference to sovereign power (Foucault 1990, 91), and that political analysis move away from its obsession with the state (Foucault 2003, 34). Rather than start political analysis by considering the power of the sovereign state and "working down," Foucault proffered a model that analyzed power relations below the level of the state in terms of struggle, confrontation, and contestation—what he called the war model of politics (Foucault 2003, vxii). As much as war is understood internationally as a battle to impose one state's or a group of states' will on other states, Foucault's idea was that politics within a state are always a similar working out of force relations between conflicting interests. The weapons are different, institutions such as elections and legislatures are used instead of guns and bombs, but the effect is the same; namely, to impose the organization of power sought by dominant forces. Foucault called this ongoing confrontation a "silent war" (Foucault 2003, 15–6). Foucault, in effect, replaced Clausewitz's famous claim that "war is politics by other means" with the claim that "politics is the continuation of war by other means" (Foucault 2003, 15).

Foucault's war model of politics runs counter to dominant understandings of politics, which hold that there is a harmony of interests among different social groups within a state. In fact, his model represents peaceful relations within a state as the waging of a silent war. Peace is the cover under which dominant social groups, those winning the battle, continuously try to reproduce their dominance and realize their interests over and against competing groups and their interests. Familiar instruments used in this confrontation include the ideas of nationalism/patriotism and unity/social solidarity. According to Foucault's model, the standard notion of war as an instance of maximum tension or competition between opposing forces is not juxtaposed to peace. Peace may be a calmer condition, but struggles for power rage nonetheless. Under conditions of peace, force is still imposed by some on others, but this war is differently waged, through ballots rather than bullets—heads are counted rather than cracked. Ultimately, the goals of war and peace, or the silent war, are the same— to dominate and impose one group's relations and interests over those of others. For Foucault's war model of politics, it is only the weapons used in the confrontation, the means deployed in the service of these ends, which change.

Foucault is not the only thinker to question the idea that peace is a state of affairs that is absent violence. Writing early in the twentieth century, E.H. Carr argued for a similarly instrumentalized understanding of peace, though his attention was focused on the international realm. In *The Twenty Years' Crisis, 1919–1939*, Carr provocatively suggested that "law, order, and peace were not general interests but simply the particular interests of the rich and the powerful" (2001, xxiv). What Carr was proposing, much like Foucault, is that dominance, not peace, is the aim of power, both domestically and internationally. In fact, peace, just like war, is not an end but rather a means to realizing political domination. Peace is a means by which the dominant can moralize about subordinate groups, justify their dominance, and guarantee their own security and ongoing dominance without necessarily having to take recourse in direct violence. Peace is not a universal interest. It is a very particular interest, an interest of the dominant, an interest of those who wish to perpetuate the status quo.

The war model has three notable implications for the study of politics. First, it entails a different notion of political history. All political history, including histories of peace and institutions, is "the endlessly repeated play of dominations" (Foucault 1984, 85; 2003, 15). Rather than a sanitized account infused with notions of evolutionary change, naturalized development, and historical continuity, political history is a story of ongoing violent struggles, actual victories and defeats, body counts, and bloodied codes in which successive dominations and subordinations are interpreted by interested parties, for their own gain, as progressive moments and movements. It reveals the history of politics as the play-by-play of a blood sport. Second, the model demands a focusing on the relationship between the forces contesting the war and the conduct of the war, not the actors or agents engaged in the battle. Instead of studying the efforts of individual subjects, Foucault's model focuses attention on the political conditions in and instruments by which forces struggle to realize their interests. Third, but related to the second implication, the war model requires a conceptualizing of highly regarded political ideas, institutions, and practices. Ideas such as secularism and nationalism, institutions such as the state, and practices such as the law are seen not as evolutionary developments or effects of teleological design, but rather as weapons in the ongoing silent war. For example, rather than evidence of progressive change and a mark of modernity, secularism is read as a tool used by feudal power to challenge the authority of the Catholic Church in the battle for economic dominance in medieval Europe. Similarly, the establishment of civil and political rights in the eighteenth and nineteenth centuries was a weapon deployed by Europe's nascent capitalist classes to finally subdue feudal lords while concomitantly limiting political interference by insulating the economy from the state (Held 1996, 83). The war model recasts cherished political ideas, institutions, and practices as instruments of power; tools that help power win the silent war are deemed valuable and "good."

Violence, the War Model, and Egypt in the Arab Revolutions

THE ARAB REVOLUTIONS BEGAN IN DECEMBER 2010. STANDARD representations of the wave of protests and insurrections that swept across Tunisia, Libya, Oman, Yemen, Syria, Saudi Arabia, Bahrain, and Egypt—popularly referred to as the Arab Spring—see a blossoming of democracy across the Arab world. Many of these representations, and particularly the popular term used to describe the events, are Orientalist in nature and connote that Arabs are just now waking from a prolonged slumber, are all similar with similar experiences, and are passive (seasons, after all, happen; they are not made by people) (Khouri 2011). Examining Egypt's experience through the ciphers of direct and structural violence and the war model of politics produces a critical analysis free of such Orientalist notions.

On January 25, 2011, Egyptians protested in a national "Day of Anger," which coincided with Egypt's Police Day. Three days later, the "Day of Rage" protest was met with massive police violence. Downtown Cairo reeked of tear gas, hospitals were packed with victims of police shootings, and the headquarters of the National Democratic Party (NDP) was set ablaze. In early February, thugs recruited by the NDP laid siege to Tahrir Square and charged the protestors' lines with horses and camels. This was the famous "Battle of the Camel." Finally, on February 11, Hosni Mubarak, Egypt's president of almost 30 years, stepped down, and the military in the form of the Supreme Council of the Armed Forces (SCAF) took power.

The NDP building was burned because it was one of the Mubarak regime's primary weapons in Egypt's ongoing silent war. As Joel Beinin describes it, "The NDP [was] not a political party as the term is commonly understood. . . . It [was] a machine for distributing patronage and an arm of the regime which would have [had] no coherence without access to state power" (Beinin 2009, 25). Before January 2011, this weapon, wielded by the regime, pursued policies that immiserated millions of working Egyptians—40 percent of the population lived on less than $2 (USD) per day— while enriching regime supporters such as Ahmed Ezz and Youssef Boutros Ghali, and made more unequal the distribution of wealth in the country. In other words, the NDP exacerbated the structural violence that the majority of Egyptians suffered under. Concomitantly, the Mubarak regime also made extensive, and increasing, use of institutions of direct violence: the police, the Central Security Forces, and the *mukhabarat* (General Intelligence). For example, in June 2010, members of the police force infamously beat to death Khaled Saeed while he was in custody in Alexandria. The Central Security Forces fought the pitched battles with protestors on January 28, while the *mukhabarat* dragged the wounded away for interrogations and beatings.

Egypt's silent war intensified in late January when workers, the educated and unemployed youth, and, eventually, Egypt's Islamists challenged the dominance of the Mubarak regime by occupying Tahrir Square. The military took the opportunity presented by the protests to stage a coup and protect its extensive material interests— the military produces consumer goods, generates electricity, bottles its own spring water, and may be responsible for 15 to 20 percent of Egyptian agricultural production (Droz-Vincent 2009, 226).

The coup changed the nature of Egypt's silent war, but it did not end it. After Mubarak's departure, the military became the combatant trying to (re-)inscribe its domination on a reconfigured Egypt. After taking power, the military sought to install a "junior partner" accepting of its dominance of the Egyptian polity into a position of political authority. Islamists in the form of the *Ikhwan* (the Muslim Brotherhood) were initially the military's preferred partner, and the military sought to install them under the cover of a democratic transition. The weapons the military has used in its struggle against other social forces have included a referendum, a raft of appointed governments, the proposal of supra-constitutional principles, and parliamentary elections.

Over the same period, Egyptians have been subject to considerable direct and structural violence. The military, through the state's security apparatuses, tortured protestors who have been arrested or detained; in October and again in November 2011, it killed protestors in downtown Cairo; and it targeted women specifically, subjecting them to "virginity tests." At the same time, the structural violence Egyptians suffer has been made even more severe. The currency has been devalued, in spite of the spending of foreign reserves in an attempt to prop it up; the country's already poor credit rating has been lowered further; and tourism rents have fallen precipitously—from $12.5 billion (USD) in 2010 to $8.8 billion (USD) in 2011 (*Al-Masry Al-Youm* 2012). These factors, particularly the dwindling foreign currency reserves, have the potential to make the lives of Egyptians more violent still if the country can no longer afford to import wheat, the primary ingredient of the bread that is a staple of the Egyptian diet. In early 2012, Egypt sought $1.1 billion (USD) in financing from the World Bank and was in talks with the International Monetary Fund for another $3.2 billion (USD) loan. If Egypt secures this financing, the structural adjustment programs that will inevitably attend it will make the war raging within Egypt hotter and the structural violence to which the majority of Egyptians are subject even more oppressive.

The proximate cause for the Arab Revolutions was the self-immolation of street vendor Mohamed Bouazizi in Tunisia. The popular media seized on this tragedy and, as the protests spread across borders, developed narratives about a region-wide democratization. Interpretation through the ciphers of direct and structural violence and the war model of politics tells a different story. This view reveals, as underlying causes of the revolutions, the direct violence of the police forces and domestic security services, including their use of imprisonment and torture, as well as the structural violence of poverty and unemployment. And the war model of politics, in contrast with many Orientalist representations, sees the events of 2011 as the culmination of prolonged, socially specific struggles in which the contesting groups have long exercised varying degrees of power and deployed a range of political instruments.

Conclusion

VIOLENCE IS AN IMPORTANT CORRELATE OF POLITICS. DESPITE ITS importance to the topic, violence has been largely left out of the study of politics. Since its inception as a discipline, political science has been primarily concerned with the state, and its participants have cast it as a story of gradual, progressive change and a project of reform of the state's institutions (Ross 2007, 19, 22). Consequently, the role of violence as that which happens largely outside the laws of the state and/or beyond the state, and which does not often change gradually or reform but rather revolutionizes, has been neglected.

The connection between violence and power does not appear likely to wane in the twenty-first century. The persistence of this relationship demands that political science's neglect of violence be corrected. This chapter has reviewed a number of correctives. One such corrective is to understand that violence has an instrumental relationship with power and can be positive and productive. Hamas and Hezbollah are examples of powerful groups with the capacity to use violence successfully, and the Internet is proof of the productive capabilities of violence. Internet technology was developed by the U.S. Air Force during the Cold War to enable the U.S. to launch a retaliatory nuclear strike against the Soviet Union. Another corrective is to distinguish between different dimensions of violence. Just because there is no specific object, or victim, of violence, or there is no subject or violent actor, does not mean that violence has not been perpetrated. Brandishing or parading weapons is an act of violence, even if no one is hurt by them. Neither does violence require a violent actor, but can be built into an economic or political structure. A final corrective is to look at politics through the war model lens. This model reveals beneath every appearance of peace a perpetual silent war being contested by different social forces, in which the weapons are not only bombs and bullets, but also constitutions and ballots. It is this corrective that directly addresses political science's obsession with the state.

   Ultimately, bringing violence more properly into the study of politics makes for critical understandings and analyses of political events. Reading the Egyptian experience in the Arab Revolutions through the ciphers of direct and structural violence and the war model of politics exposes a military coup; an increase in direct violence in the form of torture and shootings, and structural violence in the form of increased immiseration of working Egyptians; and a struggle between social forces in the Egyptian polity in which the military has sought to (re-)inscribe its dominance through a variety of mechanisms, including a referendum and elections.

Summary

The chapter:

- Argued that violence is an important correlate of politics
- Noted what thinkers such Hannah Arendt, Charles Tilly, and Carl von Clausewitz have brought to the study of the relations between violence and power
- Analyzed violence along six dimensions
- Presented Michel Foucault's claim that "politics is the continuation of war by other means"
- Redefined the Egyptian experience with the Arab Revolutions in February 2011

Discussion Questions

1. What is the relationship Arendt establishes between violence and power? Critically assess this relationship.
2. Is one man's terrorist *really* another man's freedom fighter? Is terrorism always morally reprehensible? Does the justness of the end legitimize the use of terrorist means?

3. Comment on Galtung's notion of structural violence.
4. Can the war model of politics be used to understand liberal democracies in Canada, the United States, and Europe? What does the war model tell us about politics in those states?

References

Al-Masry Al-Youm. 2012. "We Respect Beach Tourism, Says Brotherhood." January 15.

Arendt, Hannah. 1970. *On Violence*. New York: Harcourt, Brace World.

Beinin, Joel. 2009. "Neo-Liberal Structural Adjustment, Political Demobilization and Neo-Authoritarianism in Egypt." In *The Arab State and Neo-Liberal Globalization: The Restructuring of State Power in the Middle East*, edited by Laura Guazzone and Daniela Pioppi. New York: The American University in Cairo Press.

Booth, Ken and Tim Dunne, eds. 2002. *Worlds in Collision: Terror and the Future of Global Order*. New York: Palgrave.

Carr, E.H. 2001. *The Twenty Years' Crisis, 1919–1939*. New York: Palgrave.

Chomsky, Noam. 1988. *Culture of Terrorism*. Montreal: Black Rose Books.

———. 2002. *Pirates and Emperors, Old and New: International Terrorism in the Real World*. Cambridge, MA: South End Press.

Clausewitz, Carl von. 1989. In *On War*, edited by M. Howard and P. Paret. Princeton, NJ: Princeton University Press.

Droz-Vincent, Phillipe. 2009. "The Security Sector in Egypt: Management, Coercion and External Alliance under the Dynamics of Change." In *The Arab State and Neo-Liberal Globalization: The Restructuring of State Power in the Middle East*, edited by Laura Guazzone and Daniela Pioppi. New York: The American University in Cairo Press.

Farr, James. 2007. "The Historical Science(s) of Politics: The Principles, Association, and Fate of an American Discipline." In *Modern Political Science: Anglo-American Exchanges Since 1880*, edited by Robert Adcock, Mark Bevir, and Shannon C. Stimson. Princeton, NJ: Princeton University Press.

Foucault, Michel. 1984. "Nietzsche, Genealogy, History." In *The Foucault Reader*, edited by Paul Rabinow. New York: Pantheon Books.

———. 1990. *The History of Sexuality Volume I: An Introduction*. New York: Vintage Books.

———. 2003. *"Society Must be Defended": Lectures at the College De France, 1975–76*. New York: Picador.

Galtung, Johan. 1969. "Violence, Peace, and Peace Research." *Journal of Peace Research* 6(3): 167–91.

Gerth, Hans H. and C. Wright Mills, eds. 1958. *From Max Weber: Essays in Sociology*. New York: Oxford University Press.

Held, David. 1996. "The Development of the Modern State." In *Modernity: Introduction to Modern Societies*, edited by Stuart Hall, David Held, Don Hubert, and Kenneth Thompson. Cornwall, U.K.: Blackwell Publishing.

Khouri, Rami G. 2011. "Drop the Orientalist Term 'Arab Spring'." *The Daily Star*, August 17.

Project Ploughshares. 2011. *Armed Conflicts Report 2011.* http://www.ploughshares .ca/content/armed-conflicts-report-0.

Ross, Dorothy. 2007. "Anglo-American Political Science, 1880–1920." In *Modern Political Science: Anglo-American Exchanges Since 1880*, edited by Robert Adcock, Mark Bevir, and Shannon C. Stimson. Princeton, NJ: Princeton University Press.

Said, Edward William and Christopher Hitchens. 1988. *Blaming the Victims: Spurious Scholarship and the Palestinian Question.* London: Verso Books.

Schmid, Alex P. and A.J. Jongman. 1988. *Political Terrorism: A New Guide to Actor, Authors, Concepts, Data Bases, Theories and Literature.* New York: North-Holland Publishing Company.

Tilly, Charles. 1990. *Coercion, Capital and European States, AD 900–1990.* Cambridge: Blackburn.

Further Readings

Arendt, Hannah. 1970. *On Violence.* New York: Harcourt, Brace World.

Chomsky, Noam. 2002. *Pirates and Emperors, Old and New: International Terrorism in the Real World.* Cambridge, MA: South End Press.

Clausewitz, Carl von. 1989. In *On War*, edited by M. Howard and P. Paret. Princeton, NJ: Princeton University Press.

Weblinks

Correlates of War Project
www.correlatesofwar.org/

SIPRI: Stockholm International Peace Research Institute
www.sipri.org/

Electronic Intifada
http://electronicintifada.net/

Global Perspectives

This section examines some of the most important spaces and actors in political life. The play of power and influence is ubiquitous, occurring both inside and outside the formal boundaries of the state and taking on many different forms. We will discover how the discipline of international relations is shaped within political science and the key global institutions that manage the interactions between states. We will also discover how the global political economy is shaping politics in an era of crisis and instability. Although one would be tempted to think of the global as the most inclusive space of politics, we will also discover that Indigenous peoples and those in poverty are routinely excluded from political power and that the post-war dominance of the United States and Western Europe is being reshaped by new global actors.

CHAPTER 13

INTERNATIONAL RELATIONS AND THE GLOBAL

SIOBHAN BYRNE

Learning Objectives

- Distinguishes between the "international" and the "global" in the study of politics

- Summarizes the origins of the "international relations" field

- Identifies key theoretical approaches to the study of the global

- Applies international relations theories to real-world events

Introduction

International relations (IR) scholars examine a broad range of global challenges and crises from the September 11, 2001, terrorist attacks on the United States to the ensuing War on Terror; from aggressive nationalist wars in places such as Bosnia, Rwanda, and Sri Lanka to new forms of social justice activism that extend across state borders; from economic challenges facing regional institutions like the European Union to the impact of the United Nations (UN) system on global peace and security; and from the rise of new global powers like China and India to the behaviour of superpowers like the U.S. IR scholars study historical and contemporary events to explain their origins and understand their effects, sometimes with an eye to preserving global stability and other times with the aim of charting a new direction for transformative political engagements. This chapter explores IR as an academic field of study, considering why scholars study international and global politics, reviewing the development of the field, and outlining selected theoretical approaches. The end of the chapter demonstrates how scholars apply theory to contemporary issues to reveal different facets of an ever changing global political landscape.

What Are International Relations?

THE IR FIELD IS ALSO SOMETIMES CALLED *INTERNATIONAL STUDIES*, *world politics*, *global politics*, or *global studies*. Traditionally, *"inter-*national relations" scholars focus on the "inter" relations between "nations," or states. Today, in the context of a globalized world where new institutions, movements, and actors operate within, across, and beyond state boundaries, IR scholars also study the role of international institutions, non-governmental organizations, and transnational social movements. For these scholars, the term *international relations* does not capture the kind of research they do. This chapter refers to the academic field of "international relations" (IR) and to the study of "global politics." The former term is used by scholars, political science departments, and academic journals to identify the field of the study. The latter term, *global politics*, refers to the subject matter of IR, indicating a concern for issues beyond state relations.

Thinking Globally

Underlying the problem of naming the field is the problem of defining the "global" subject matter of the field. From the end of World War II to the collapse of the Soviet Union in 1991, scholars were preoccupied with the Cold War superpower competition between the U.S. and the Soviet Union. The threat of war between these nuclear rivals led to a concern with state security, defence policy, and the arms race. With the end of the Cold War, however, scholars began to study the global implications of new conflicts breaking out within states, such as the Rwandan and Bosnian genocides. The 2001 terrorist attacks on the U.S., the 2004 Madrid train bombings, and the 2005 suicide bombings in London demonstrated that states do not have a monopoly on violence. It also appeared that other threats to global security, such as global warming, human trafficking, and global financial crises, need the intervention of additional political actors, such as international organizations and non-governmental actors.

As this chapter shows, statist theories, which view states as the most important actors in global politics, have dominated the IR field since its founding. While this remains the case today, scholars have also introduced theories that extend beyond the state, particularly during the critical turn in IR in the 1980s and in the context of globalization. Thinking beyond the state requires scholars to examine (a) different levels of analysis, including *the individual and community* levels, the *regional* level, and the *transnational* level; (b) new sites of political authority beyond state governments; and (c) a diversity of actors (see Archibugi and Held 2011). For some scholars, processes associated with globalization—such as the freer movement of (some) peoples across borders, new technologies that connect people around the world, and a global consumer culture—undermine state authority and/or produce new communities beyond state borders (for example, see van Creveld 2006). Similarly, some scholars study new forms of political authority other than states in global politics. While there is no world government as such, states and other actors do coordinate their activities to meet joint goals (Knight 2009, 178). Still others examine how non-state actors organize transnationally, building communities that stretch across state boundaries. For all of these scholars, an exclusive focus on the state misses important features of global politics.

Origins of the Field

The formal study of IR began with the establishment of the first chair in international politics at the University College of Wales, Aberystwyth in 1919. While this date marks the field's founding, scholars also tell a number of stories about how the field developed. Such stories serve an educational function for new students, providing a coherent narrative that outlines how the field was born and explains how it developed. These stories also serve a disciplinary function, establishing the most important aspects of the field's development, identifying some important theoretical breakthroughs, and, sometimes, obscuring others (see Bell 2009, 5). The most frequently told story about the origins and development of IR focuses on a series of **great debates** between rival political theories.

The story begins with a first great debate between "utopians," or idealists, and "realists" following World War I. According to the narrative, utopian thinkers believed that states could head off future wars through cooperation. Realists were skeptical about the possibility of cooperation and apparently were vindicated when efforts to foster international cooperation through the League of Nations, an international organization created after World War I to maintain world peace, failed to prevent the outbreak of World War II in 1939. Following World War II, a second debate took place, between "traditionalists" and "scientists." While the former group of scholars drew on international law and philosophy, and reasoned through historical examples, the latter group argued that IR theories should be tested according to the rigours of the scientific method (see Bull 1966; Kaplan 1966). Today, a commitment to scientism, particularly in the U.S., dominates the field (Maliniak et al. 2011). An "inter-paradigm debate" followed in the early 1980s, pitting realist scholarship against institutionalist scholarship, which focused on the interdependence of states, and against Marxist scholarship, which focused on the capitalist world system. A more recent fourth debate emerged in the late 1980s between scholars who identify their work as "positivist" and those who identify their work as "post-positivist." In IR, the philosophy of social science's term "positivism" refers to a commitment to the scientific approach. According to this view, researchers must separate the facts they collect from their own normative values and ethics (Keohane 1984, 10). Examples of positivist theories, discussed later in this chapter, include neo-realism, institutionalism, and some forms of constructivism. Post-positivism refers to theories that reject a commitment to scientism. According to this view, it is not possible, or desirable, to build value-free theories of the world. Post-positivist theories include a variety of critical IR theories, such as versions of constructivism, historical materialism, and feminism.

It should be noted that there are implications of narrating the field as above. For example, to claim that realists and scientism won the first and second debates establishes the pre-eminence of these approaches in the field while also lending the field a false sense of coherence (see Schmidt 2008; Bell 2009, 6). The reality today is that IR scholars draw on a number of tools and a diversity of theories to explain global politics. The next section reviews some of the main theories, showing how scholars "do" IR.

Theoretical Approaches

THEORIES ARE LIKE LENSES THAT WE USE TO VIEW THE SOCIAL WORLD. They allow us to filter and interpret aspects of global politics that we want to explain, understand, or change. For some IR scholars, the purpose of theory is to help us sift through and organize empirical data to make sense of global politics (see Morgenthau 1973 [1948], 3). For critical IR scholar Robert W. Cox, "theory is always *for* someone and *for* some purpose" (1981, 128). Theories, in this sense, serve one of two purposes: to accept the prevailing world order or to change it. The first group of theories are called *problem-solving* theories and largely include positivist IR theories. The second group of theories are called *critical theories* and largely include post-positivist theories (see Cox 1981; Schouten 2009). The following section reviews key IR theories that serve one of these two purposes.

Realism/Neo-Realism

Realist theory grew in prominence after World War II. For realists, the fact that the League of Nations failed to prevent World War II demonstrates the folly of relying on institutions to maintain peace. As such, early realists like Hans J. Morgenthau sought to develop a theory of international politics that would better understand the causes of war, to imagine the conditions that can lead to peace (1973 [1948], 24). Realists view international politics as a struggle for power and wealth in a hostile world. Because there is no authority higher than the state in global politics—a condition realists call **anarchy**—each state must look out for its own interests and guard against potential threats. The world is a dangerous place where conflict and war may break out at any time. States protect their security by strengthening their military power, and, sometimes, by entering into alliances designed to balance against potential threats from other states. Several variants of realist theory dominate IR scholarship today, particularly **neo-realism**.

Introduced by Kenneth N. Waltz in his 1979 book *Theory of International Politics*, neo-realists were influenced by the turn to scientism in the 1960s. These theorists argue that the international system has existed since the signing of the Peace of Westphalia in 1648. Briefly, these treaties marked the end of religious wars in Europe and a shift in political authority from religious and feudal authorities to states. Today, states enjoy **sovereignty** or supreme political authority in the international system. According to neo-realists, states are primarily motivated by the desire to survive in the system. As such, neo-realists focus on the anarchic structure of the international system and the relative powers and capacities of states. Neo-realists are particularly interested in the interactions of dominant states in the international system (see Waltz 1979, 72). For example, neo-realists pay attention to the role of the **hegemonic** or most powerful state. Hegemony is a situation whereby a single state dominates the international system through a preponderance of power, like Great Britain in the nineteenth century and the U.S. following World War II. They theorize that when a hegemonic state begins to decline in power, other states will rise up to challenge its leadership, creating instability and disorder (Gilpin 1999 [1981]). Today, neo-realists argue that the basic anarchic structure of the international system remains unchanged in the context of globalization. While powerful states rise and fall, shifting the balance of power throughout history, states remain the most important actors in international politics (Waltz 1999). For other IR theorists, however, states are more interconnected today. Neo-liberal institutionalist theorists, considered next, argue that international institutions can mitigate the effects of anarchy, reducing conflict among states in a globalizing world.

Neo-Liberal Institutionalism

Linked to the idealism of the post–World War I era, **neo-liberal institutionalism**, or simply institutionalism, finds that institutions help states realize mutual benefits through cooperation. The theory is, therefore, more optimistic about the possibility of cooperation under anarchy than realism. While optimistic, institutionalism shares many core neo-realist assumptions; for example, both approaches assume that states are the most important actors in global politics and that they share a commitment to scientism in research (Waever 1996, 164). Where institutionalists and neo-realists differ is on the view of cooperation. For realists, international cooperation is limited by the logic of relative gains, which means that states perceive any gain made by another state as a threat to their national security. Institutionalists, by contrast, argue that states seek **absolute gains**, meaning states view cooperation favourably when they realize some gain—even if it means a gain for the other party. While institutionalists agree that military power is the most important source of power, they also recognize that economic power is an important consideration in global politics (Keohane and Nye 1977, 8, 16).

Examples of international institutions include the UN, which commands humanitarian and peacekeeping operations today in places like Kosovo (1999–), Haiti (2004–) and South Sudan (2011–), and authorizes interventions and deploys personnel to post-conflict states like Libya (2011–). Other institutions include the North Atlantic Treaty Organization (NATO), which coordinates military operations in places like Afghanistan; and regional bodies like the European Union, North American Free Trade Agreement (NAFTA), MERCOSUR in South America, the Association of Southeast Asian Nations (ASEAN), and the African Union (AU). All of these institutions help states work together on issues of mutual concern. Today, in a globalized world, institutionalists argue that states work through a web of informal and formal networks that help them coordinate activities around issue areas like the environment, trade, security, and finance. Institutionalists also make room for the role of ideas in global politics. For example, they argue that principled ideas related to global warming and human rights can also motivate publics to act in global politics. In this sense, institutionalists go beyond a realist emphasis on security and share some ground with constructivists, discussed next.

Constructivism

Constructivism grew in popularity in the late 1980s and early 1990s, becoming one of the main approaches in the field today. Like other theories considered in this chapter, constructivism refers to a group of divergent theoretical perspectives. While it is possible to identify some core tenets, locating constructivism in either the problem-solving or critical theory camp is not straightforward for reasons that become clear in this section.

Generally, constructivists agree that the structure of the international system is anarchic. However, they argue that ideas, identities, and norms help explain why states choose to go to war or to cooperate. Take, for example, Canada's special relationship with the U.S. Because each state views the other as a friend, they are unlikely to go to war with each other. For constructivists, the ideas they hold about each other better explains Canada–U.S. cooperation than the logic of anarchy or the pursuit of power politics (see Jepperson et al. 1996, 34). In the words of constructivist theorist Alexander Wendt, "*anarchy is what states make of it*" (Wendt 1992). In this sense, anarchy does not automatically lead to conflict between states. Rather, ideas and interactions between states also constitute global politics.

Beyond U.S.–Canada relations, constructivists contend that power politics cannot explain critical changes in global politics, like the end of the Cold War rivalry between the U.S. and the Soviet Union. During the Cold War, countries identified as either "liberal" or "socialist," which affected their behaviour in global politics (see Barnett 1996, 439). While neo-realists could explain hostility between the West and East through balance of power logic, they could neither anticipate nor explain the radical reforms that Soviet leader Mikhail Gorbachev ushered in during the 1980s. For example, Gorbachev made deep cuts to defence spending and introduced political liberalization policies across the Soviet system. Unlike previous communist leaders, Gorbachev also did not quash the growing labour and anti-totalitarian movements sweeping across Eastern Europe, which eventually led to the overthrow of communist regimes in the region. For constructivists, Gorbachev's actions replaced the global norm of competition with a norm of cooperation, thus ending the Cold War (Koslowski and Kratochwil 1994, 228).

Some constructivist scholars, like Wendt, clearly define their work as statist. For these scholars, constructivism shares many of the assumptions of problem-solving theories like neo-realists and institutionalists. While all constructivists are interested in how global politics are "socially constructed" through ideas, identities, and norms, other constructivists, sometimes called post-modern or critical theorists, are interested in transforming unequal power relations. This normative vision is shared by the critical approaches discussed in the next section.

Marxist Critical Approach

Responding to global patterns of economic inequality in the so-called "Third World" in the 1970s, critically oriented scholars looked to nineteenth-century philosophers Karl Marx and Friedrich Engels and early twentieth-century Marxist scholar Antonio Gramsci to analyze global politics. Marxist IR scholars argue that an analysis of power, security, and change in global politics requires an understanding of the development of the global capitalist system. This section introduces one popular variant of Marxist IR theory: neo-Gramscian theory.

Neo-Gramscian approaches, introduced in the early 1980s by Robert W. Cox, consider the role of social forces in transforming the world system, or what Cox calls the "world order" (Cox 1981, *fn4* 151–52). While neorealism and institutionalism explain how order is maintained or destabilized in the international system, neo-Gramscians are interested in how to transform unjust world orders. To do so, they rely on an alternative understanding of **hegemony**. Briefly, instead of defining hegemony as the ability of a powerful state to get others to do what it wants through the threat or use of force, hegemony is maintained through ideas and international institutions that make a world order appear natural and favourable to the interests of other states.

U.S. hegemonic leadership, established after World War II, is an example of a "world order." While the U.S. remains the most powerful actor today, neo-Gramscians argue that its power began to decline in the late 1960s and 1970s due to rising U.S. trade deficits, loss of confidence of other states, and the growth of globalization and new global capital interests (Cox 1992; Bieler and Morton 2006, 17). Today, global power and wealth is concentrated among a small group of powerful states that promote liberal internationalist ideas such as free trade, open markets, and respect for international law; coordinate activities through institutions like the annual "G8" meetings of representatives of the eight wealthiest states; and, when necessary, enforce their rule through material power in the form of, for example, military intervention in other states (Puchala 2005, 577–81). According to neo-Gramscians, ideas and institutions work with material power to serve the narrow political and economic interests of a small group of wealthy and powerful states, which ultimately ensures the longevity of capitalist production. Certainly, today the rise of economic powerhouses like the influential "BRICS" states, including Brazil, Russia, India, China, and South Africa, presents a challenge to the endurance of the current order.

For neo-Gramscians, the purpose of theorizing world order is to identify how social forces can and do transform states and world orders through counter-hegemonic struggle. Whereas neo-realists focus on the struggle for power and survival among states, neo-Gramscians examine social forces that struggle for an alternative and more democratic world order. The World Social Forum is an example of such a social force; each year, labour, peace, Indigenous, and other social justice movements from around the world come together to share ideas under the slogan "another world is possible" (see Carroll 2007, 50–1). In this sense, ideas about how to transform world order emerge from sites beyond states.

The neo-Gramscian emphasis on patterns of global inequality and interest in change is evident in IR feminist scholarship. According to some feminist scholars working both inside and outside Marxist and socialist traditions, critical IR theory has done a poor job theorizing the experiences of women and the role of gender hierarchies in global politics.

Feminist Interventions

Over two decades ago, Cynthia Enloe asked, "where are the women" in international politics, signalling the emergence of new feminist perspectives in the field (1990). Like neo-Gramscians, feminists are committed to transforming unequal power relations in global politics. For feminists, however, critical theories are "gender blind," ignoring how gender hierarchies privilege male experiences and certain masculinities. Briefly, **gender** refers to socially constructed differences between males and females. So-called masculine traits associated with males, such as rationality and power through domination, are valued in global politics over so-called feminine characteristics associated with females, such as weakness and emotionality (Zalewski 1995, 341; Tickner 2005, *fn18*). Feminists point out that an emphasis on the state system and *high politics,* meaning the public spheres of statecraft and military power, privileges men in IR. Notwithstanding some notable exceptions, few women hold positions of leadership in militaries or industries and, particularly in Western democracies, in government. Feminists therefore examine women's lived experiences in the *low politics* or private spheres of households, workforces, and communities, drawing connections between the private and public spheres of life (Tickner 2005, 19; Wibben 2011, 1–4).

Answering the question "where are the women" is also interpreted as a call to investigate social constructions of masculinity and femininity in theory and politics (see

Shepherd 2006, 24). In terms of theory, scholars examine conventional IR concepts like power and security to uncover how masculine qualities are valued over feminine qualities. Power, for example, is defined in the feminist scholarship as *empowerment*, or the ability to "act in concert" with others, as opposed to being defined in terms of domination (Elshtain 1985, 51). Similarly, **security** is examined from the perspective of marginalized peoples as opposed to states, allowing scholars to pay attention to the ways people experience insecurity in their everyday lives.

IR scholars concerned with unequal gender relations also frequently analyze how social categories like race, class, and sexuality intersect with gender to produce particular patterns of domination and resistance in global politics. Called "intersectional analysis" or simply "intersectionality," this mode of analysis was introduced in critical race and post-colonial studies in the late 1980s and 1990s. Just as IR scholarship has been critiqued for gender blindness, as discussed above, feminist IR scholarship has been similarly critiqued for failing to consider race and other social categories in their analyses (Chowdhry and Nair 2002, 9). Today, intersectionality is an important feminist tool of analysis across disciplines, including IR (see McCall 2005, 1771; for a discussion of race in IR, see Persaud and Walker 2001; Vincent 1982). For example, feminist IR scholars have applied intersectional thinking to analyze the ways in which racist and gendered constructions of Afghan women were used to justify the 2001 U.S.–led invasion of Afghanistan. Although the attacks were perpetrated by the terrorist group Al-Qaeda, the liberation of Afghan women from the Taliban regime was used to mobilize support for the invasion. The press and representatives of the invasion forces described Afghan women as helpless victims in need of saving by the "civilized" U.S. Rarely did we hear reports of women challenging Taliban rule and, later, the occupation. In this example, racialized and gendered images of Afghan women as victims legitimated the invasion and, therefore, had global political ramifications (see Shepherd 2006, 25; Sjoberg 2011, 114). Another important body of global politics scholarship considers how gender, race, and class-based oppressions reinforce each other in the global exploitation and resistance of female migrant workers from the global South. An intersectional analysis reveals how a gendered and racialized global division of labour depends on the exploitation of women from global peripheries who work for middle-class family households in wealthier states (see Stasiulis and Bakan 2005; Agathangelou 2002).

The purpose of feminist IR theorizing, then, is not just to provide a more accurate picture of global politics, but also to identify how gender and other hierarchies affect global politics. Most importantly, it aims to identify ways to challenge such constructions.

Contemporary Issues and Debates

ON DECEMBER 17, 2010, 26-YEAR-OLD STREET VENDOR MOHAMED Bouazizi set himself on fire in Tunisia to protest regular persecution by local authorities. His act of self-immolation ignited the Arab Spring uprisings against autocratic rule across the Middle East and North Africa. By the close of 2011, the Tunisian and

Egyptian presidents were ousted, Libyan leader Muammar Gaddafi was dead in a bloody showdown with NATO–lacked opposition fighters, Yemen's leader promised to step down, and protests continued to escalate in Syria. On the heels of the Arab Spring, a wave of protest spread across Europe and North America. In Madrid, Lisbon, Athens, and beyond, tens of thousands of people hardest hit by the European debt crisis staged marches, strikes, and protest camps into the summer months. In New York city, non-violent protestors took over a park in the city's financial district in the fall, touching off a North American–wide movement that reached cities like San Francisco, Vancouver, Edmonton, and Montreal. Linking issues such as unemployment, rising student debt, and environmental concerns to neo-liberal economic policies, activists protested national management strategies of the 2008 global financial crisis and the concentration of wealth in the hands of 1 percent of the population. This section shows how competing IR theories explain the causes and implications of these events.

Neorealism suggests that political instability or regime change, like the shake-up in the Middle East and North Africa, makes global politics unpredictable and dangerous (see Waltz 2011). From this perspective, NATO's seven-month military intervention in Libya was reckless, because it embroiled the U.S. in a foreign venture that does not serve its national interests. Conversely, an institutionalist framework suggests that because NATO operated with the support of the Arab League and the UN, it was able to meet the principled goal of safeguarding international security and human rights while sharing the burden of intervention and limiting opposition to its intervention (see "View from the Top" 2012).

Constructivism draws our attention to the way local and national groups were important sources of regional and global change in these cases, not just the most powerful states or institutions in the international system (for example, see Clifford 2011). Neo-Gramscians agree that a bottom-up analysis identifies local sources of change. They also link the Arab Spring protests to the subsequent wave of European and North American protests. For neo-Gramscians, social forces are thinking globally about the relationship between authoritarianism and economic policies and they are organizing transnationally—across state borders—while sharing a commitment to social justice (see Gill 2012, 2).

A feminist framework also begins with a bottom-up analysis but asks, where are the women in the revolutions and protest camps? For example, feminist activists reported difficulty being heard by fellow activists and the media during the protests (see Knafo and Kaufman 2011). Their role in the Arab Spring was not well covered in the press, despite the fact that both women and men disrupted assumptions about appropriate behaviour in autocratic states (see Cole and Cole 2011). Women held various roles in the uprisings, including marching in protests, organizing for peace, advocating for women's rights, and carrying guns. Feminists point out that these moments of revolutionary change offer unique opportunities to disrupt gender hierarchies that subordinate women. Feminist theorists are also paying close attention to the period after the revolutions in the Middle East. They are interested in the extent to which gender power relations can be transformed in new state institutions.

The wave of protests discussed earlier can be understood from the perspective of state interests and power politics, international institutions and cooperation, transnational social forces and local actors, and women and gender. How one chooses a particular theoretical framework depends largely on the questions one asks and the purpose of one's inquiry.

Conclusion

WHILE THERE IS DISAGREEMENT ABOUT HOW TO TELL THE STORY OF IR's development, it is anticipated that reviewing the field's history can help contextualize current theoretical debates in an age of globalization and chart a path for future research and theoretical development. Certainly, the name—*inter*-national relations—is a misnomer. While neo-realists, institutionalists, and some constructivists do focus on the *inter*-relations between states, others challenge this conventional state-based description of the international system. In a complex global political arena, where international institutions, transnational social forces, and domestic political engagements offer additional sources of authority and sites of dissent, Marxists and feminists also analyze politics within, across, and beyond the state.

The theories introduced in this chapter allow for the analysis of global politics based on observation, experience, and/or reason about how the world does and should work. As the examples of the Arab Spring and the Occupy movements demonstrate, different theoretical lenses consider distinct actors and levels of analyses, bringing into view different features of the global political realm.

Summary

The chapter:

- Examined the traditional IR focus on the *inter*-relations between *states*
- Reviewed the establishment of the field at the University College of Wales, Aberystwyth in 1919
- Introduced IR theories, problem solving and critical, as lenses that we use to view global politics
- Introduced neo-realist, institutionalist, constructivist, Marxist, and feminist theories

Discussion Questions

1. What is the difference between the terms *international relations* and *global politics*? Why do some scholars make a distinction between these two terms?

2. In your view, what are the most important challenges in global politics today?

3. Contrast two theoretical approaches in international relations outlined in the chapter. Which approach do you find the most convincing?

4. Outline a theoretical approach discussed in this chapter and apply it to a real-world event.

References

Agathangelou, Anna M. 2002. "'Sexing' Globalization in International Relations: Migrant Sex and Domestic Workers in Cyprus, Greece, and Turkey." In *Power, Postcolonialism and International Relations: Reading Race, Gender and Class*, edited by Geeta Chowdhry and Sheila Nair, 142–69. London and New York: Routledge.

Archibugi, Daniele and David Held. 2011. "Cosmopolitan Democracy: Paths and Agents." *Ethics & International Affairs* 25(4):433–61.

Barnett, Michael N. 1996. "Identity and Alliances in the Middle East." In *The Culture of National Security: Norms and Identity in World Politics*, edited by P.J. Katzenstein, 400–50. New York: Columbia University Press.

Bell, Duncan. 2009. "Writing the World: Disciplinary History and Beyond." *International Affairs* 85(1): 3–22.

Bieler, Andreas and Adam David Morton. 2006. "A Critical Theory Route to Hegemony, World Order and Historical Change." In *Global Restructuring, State, Capital and Labour: Contesting Neo-Gramscian Perspectives*, edited by W.B. Andreas Bieler, Peter Burnham, and Adam David Morton, 9–27. New York: Palgrave Macmillan.

Bull, Hedley. 1966. "International Theory: The Case for a Classical Approach." *World Politics* 18(3): 361–77.

Carroll, William K. 2007. "Hegemony and Counter-Hegemony in a Global Field." *Studies in Social Justice* 1(1): 36–66.

Chowdhry, Geeta and Sheila Nair. 2002. "Power in a Postcolonial World: Race, Gender, and Class in International Relations." In *Power, Postcolonialism, and International Relations: Reading Race, Gender and Class*, edited by Geeta Chowdhry and Sheila Nair, 2–32. New York: Routledge.

Clifford, S. 2011. *Amitav Acharya on the Relevance of Regions, ASEAN, and Western IR's False Universalisms.* http://www.theorytalks.org/2011/08/theory-talk-42.html.

Cole, Juan and Shahin Cole. 2011. "An Arab Spring for Women." *The Nation.* December 11. http://www.thenation.com/article/160179/arab-spring-women.

Cox, Robert W. 1981. "Social Forces, States and World Orders: Beyond International Relations Theory." *Millennium* 10(2): 126–55.

———. 1992. "Global Perestroika." *The Socialist Register* 28: 26–43.

Elshtain, J.B. 1985. "Citizenship and Maternal Thinking. 2. Reflections on War and Political Discourse—Realism, Just War, and Feminism in a Nuclear-Age." *Political Theory* 13(1): 39–57.

Gill, Stephen. 2012. *Global Crises and the Crisis of Global Leadership.* Cambridge, U.K.: Cambridge University Press.

Gilpin, Robert. 1999 [1981]. *War and Change in World Politics.* Cambridge, U.K.: Cambridge University Press.

Jepperson, Ronald L., Alexander Wendt, and Peter J. Katzenstein. 1996. "Norms, Identity, and Culture in National Security." In *The Culture of National Security,* edited by P.J. Katzenstein, 33–75. New York: Columbia University Press.

Kaplan, Morton. 1966. "The New Great Debate: Traditionalism versus Science in International Relations." *World Politics* 19(3): 1–20.

Keohane, Robert O. 1984. *After Hegemony: Cooperation and Discord in the World Political Economy.* Princeton, NJ: Princeton University Press.

Keohane, Robert O. and Joseph S. Nye. 1977. *Power and Interdependence: World Politics in Transition.* New York: Little, Brown.

Knafo, Saki and Adam Kaufman. 2011. "Occupy Wall Street, Faces of Zuccotti Park: The Woman in Pink." huffingtonpost.com. December 1. http://www.huffingtonpost.com/2011/12/01/occupy-wall-street-faces-codepink-melanie-butler_n_1117875.html.

Knight, W. Andy. 2009. "Global Governance as a Summative Phenomenon" In *Palgrave Advances in Global Governance,* edited by J. Whitman, 160–87. New York: Palgrave Macmillan.

Koslowski, Rey and Friedrich V. Kratochwil. 1994. "Understanding Change in International Politics: The Soviet Empire's Demise and the International System." *International Organization* 48(2): 215–47.

Malinak, Danie et al. 2011. "International Relations in the U.S. Academy." *International Studies Quarterly* 55: 437–64.

McCall, Leslie. 2005. "The Complexity of Intersectionality." *Signs* 30(3): 1771–1800.

Morgenthau, Hans. 1973 [1948]. *Politics Among Nations: The Struggle for Power and Peace,* 5th ed. New York: Alfred A. Knopf.

Persaud, Randolph B. and R.B.J. Walker, eds. 2001. "Race in International Relations." *Alternatives* [Special issue] 26(4): 373–543.

Puchala, Donald J. 2005. "World Hegemony and the United Nations." *International Studies Review* 7: 571–54.

Schmidt, Brian C. 2008. "On the History and Historiography of International Relations." In *Handbook of International Relations,* edited by W. Carlsnaes, T. Risse, and B.A. Simmons, 3–22. Thousand Oaks, CA: Sage.

Schouten, P. 2009. "Robert Cox on World Orders, Historical Change, and the Purpose of Theory in International Relations." *Theory Talks.* http://www.theorytalks.org/2010/03/theory-talk-37.html.

Shepherd, Laura J. 2006. "Veiled References: Constructions of Gender in the Bush Administration Discourse on the Attacks on Afghanistan Post-9/11." *International Feminist Journal of Politics* 8(1): 19–41.

Sjoberg, Laura. 2011. "Gender, the State, and War Redux." *International Relations* 25(1): 108–34.

Stasiulis, Daiva Kristina and Abigail Bakan. 2005. *Negotiating Citizenship: Migrant Women in Canada and the Global System.* Toronto: University of Toronto Press.

Tickner, J. Ann. 2005. "What Is Your Research Program? Some Feminist Answers to International Relations Methodological Questions." *International Studies Quarterly* 49(1): 1–22.

van Creveld, Martin. 2006. "The Fate of the State Revisited." *Global Crime* 7(3–4): 329–50.

"View from the Top." 2012. *Foreign Policy* 191: 1–7.

Vincent, R. J. 1982. "Race in International Relations." *International Affairs* 58(4): 658–70.

Waever, Ole. 1996. "The Rise and Fall of the Inter-Paradigm Debate." In *International Theory: Positivism and Beyond,* edited by S. Smith, K. Booth, and M. Zalewski, 149–85. Cambridge, U.K.: Cambridge University Press.

Waltz, Kenneth N. 1979. *Theory of International Politics.* New York: McGraw-Hill.

———. 1999. "1999 James Madison Lecture—Globalization and Governance." *Political Science & Politics* December: 693–700.

———. 2011. Presentation to the University of Macedonia, Thessaloniki, Greece. May 5. http://www.youtube.com/watch?v=qAUJfWzzHSM.

Wendt, Alexander. 1992. "Anarchy Is What States Make of It: The Social Construction of Power Politics." *International Organization* 46(2): 391–425.

Wibben, Annick T.R. 2011. *Feminist Security Studies: A Narrative Approach.* London: Routledge.

Zalewski, Marysia. 1995. "Well, What Is the Feminist Perspective on Bosnia?" *International Affairs* 71(2): 339–56.

Further Readings

Burchill, Scott et al., eds. 2009. *Theories of International Relations,* 4th ed. New York: Palgrave Macmillan.

Chowdhry, Geeta and Sheila Nair, eds., 2002. *Power, Postcolonialism and International Relations: Reading Race, Gender and Class.* London: Routledge.

Cox, Robert W. 1981. "Social Forces, States and World Orders: Beyond International Relations Theory." *Millennium* 10(2): 126–55.

Knight, W. Andy and Tom Keating. 2010. *Global Politics: Emerging Networks, Trends, and Challenges.* Oxford, U.K.: Oxford University Press.

Weblinks

Interviews with IR theorists
http://conversations.berkeley.edu/

Theory Talks
www.theory-talks.org/

United Nations
www.un.org/en/

World Social Forum
www.forumsocialmundial.org.br

CANADA'S SEAT.

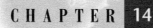

CHAPTER 14

INTERNATIONAL ORGANIZATIONS

TOM KEATING

Learning Objectives

- Provides an introduction to international organizations and an overview of their place in world politics

- Discusses key principles of international organizations as well as their origins and evolution

- Describes the critical distinction between intergovernmental organizations (IGOs) and non-governmental organizations (NGOs)

- Identifies some of the central preoccupations influencing the future role of these organizations in world politics

Introduction

Thousands of international organizations are active on the world stage. Every country in the world is a member of at least one international organization, and most countries participate in many. Canada, for example, is a member of numerous international organizations, ranging from the United Nations to the Arctic Council. Many individuals also belong to organizations whose membership and activities cross national borders. As a group, international organizations have a long history, but they proliferated most dramatically in the second half of the twentieth century. They have become a permanent and often influential feature in the daily lives of billions of people around the planet. It is possible to learn a great deal about international organizations by studying particular IGOs, such as the United Nations (UN) or the European Union (EU), and NGOs, such as the International Committee of the Red Cross or Amnesty International. The immense variety of organizations, however, suggests a different approach to studying them, one that instead examines the features common to many of the different organizations.

As an integral part of world politics, international organizations have been influenced by many organizing principles and practices. It is particularly beneficial to understand the meaning and significance of state sovereignty, anarchy, global governance, and multilateralism in order to grasp the principles and practices of international organizations.

Historical and Political Context

THE EXISTENCE OF INTERNATIONAL ORGANIZATIONS HAS BEEN TRACED back to 1397. Since the time of Dante, in the early fourteenth century, international organizations, including various proposals for world government, have been advocated as alternatives or complements to a system of independent sovereign states. International organizations have been invented and reinvented in attempts to facilitate and regulate international political, economic, and social interactions. Proposals for institutions that resemble the United Nations and the European Union date back to the seventeenth century (Hinsley 1963). Many of these proposals were concerned with eliminating or reducing international conflict among the emerging European states. While the authors of these proposals—Sir Thomas More, William Penn, and Immanuel Kant, among others—might be impressed with the extensive network of international organizations that exists today, they would likely be disappointed that these organizations have been unable to prevent warfare within and between states. By the latter half of the nineteenth century, international organizations were more likely to be devoted to matters of international commerce than to conflict. Today, the more numerous and influential international organizations are those involved in matters of international trade and finance.

International organizations do not operate in a vacuum. They are part of an array of political, economic, social, and cultural activity that takes place in the global arena. Particularly noteworthy are two prominent features of the arena in which international organizations operate: state sovereignty and anarchy (Schmidt 1998). State sovereignty distinguishes the participants in world politics, separating national governments or states, as they are most commonly labelled, from private individuals, groups, and corporations that also participate in world politics. State **sovereignty** refers to the legal (**de jure** sovereignty) and empirical (**de facto** sovereignty) condition, whereby states recognize no higher authority domestically or externally and are free to act as they wish. Sovereignty emerged as an influential governing principle after the Thirty Years War, which ended with the Peace of Westphalia in 1648. That war and the resulting peace settlement legitimated the autonomous and sovereign power of states over and against those of the Church and the emperor, as well as against potential domestic challengers. Sovereignty is an absolute term suggesting both autonomy and capability, but few states possess absolute sovereignty. Most states are constrained in their actions by the power of other states, by the restrictions imposed on them through international agreements and organizations, and by various domestic checks and balances. The widespread acceptance of the principle of state sovereignty, however, has meant that states must give their consent to be bound by international law and other commitments that arise from being members of international organizations.

The principle of state sovereignty reflected and reinforced a second feature of world politics, the absence of a single central authority or government to regulate world politics and enforce international law. **Anarchy** refers to the absence of government or formal authority. Sovereign states operate in a system in which there is no permanent authority that makes and enforces laws to regulate their behaviour, or that of other actors in world politics. As a result, states (increasingly with private individuals, groups, and corporations) make their own rules and determine how and by whom they are to be administered and enforced. The process by which rules are made and enforced in world politics is both complex and fascinating because of the absence of clearly defined authoritative procedures and institutions. This process is often referred to as **global governance**, defined as "governing, without sovereign authority, relationships that transcend national frontiers" (Finkelstein 1995, 369). Attempts to establish more authoritative institutions of government at the global or regional level necessarily implies restrictions on the freedom of sovereign states to do as they please, something that many states have resisted. Thus, the establishment of international organizations and the process of global governance generally involve a delicate and complicated balance between the preservation of state sovereignty and the development of authority structures at the international level. It is also apparent that global governance is no longer under the exclusive control of states.

The term **multilateralism** describes both the process and the end result of these efforts to establish rules that resolve common problems and support cooperation among states and other actors in world politics. At its simplest, multilateralism refers to a diplomatic process involving more than two states. Multilateralism also describes a particular form of international politics, one that can be distinguished from bilateralism or imperialism. It refers to a form of cooperation among states marked by three distinct characteristics. First, the costs and benefits of cooperation are shared by all participating states. Second, cooperation is based on certain principles of state conduct that influence the relations among states. Finally, states are committed to this cooperative behaviour for the long term and do not necessarily expect immediate results (Ruggie 1993). Multilateralism thus entails a specific form of global governance, one that has a significant role for international organizations. Critical scholars have also called attention to the increased influence of non-governmental (or civil society) organizations in the process of global governance, referring to the involvement of these actors alongside states as exemplifying a "new multilateralism," a process of cooperation and governance that is initiated and sustained by groups emerging out of civil society (Muldoon et al. 2010).

Classifying International Organizations

AN INTERNATIONAL ORGANIZATION MAY BE DEFINED AS A FORMAL institution that facilitates regular interaction between members of two or more countries. A search according to such a definition would yield thousands of entities. There are, however, several criteria by which one can sort out the numerous international organizations that populate this planet. For instance, two separate categories of international organizations can be distinguished. The first, **intergovernmental organizations**, or **IGOs**, limits membership to states. Currently, there are between 300 and 400 IGOs actively involved in world politics. The UN is the pre-eminent example, but the EU, the World Trade Organization (WTO), and the North Atlantic Treaty Organization (NATO) are other well-known examples. A second category of international organization is **non-governmental organizations** or **NGOs**, sometimes referred to as **civil society organizations (CSOs)**. The membership of these organizations is made up of private citizens or national affiliates of groups of private citizens. Today, there are well over 50 000 NGOs operating internationally. Most NGOs are of little interest for students of world politics, while others occasionally emerge as important political actors for selected issues. Many others, such as the Red Cross, Greenpeace, and Amnesty International, have an active and ongoing involvement in world politics. Later in this chapter, we will return to take a closer look at these NGOs and their involvement in contemporary global politics. For now, however, we will examine the origins and evolution of IGOs and some perspectives on their role in world politics.

Intergovernmental Organizations

IGOs have become a permanent feature of world politics. One of the primary factors in establishing these organizations has been the desire to limit or prevent warfare between states. For many concerned about the recurrence of warfare, some form of world government offered the best method for achieving peace and prosperity. Consequently, scholars and practitioners devised elaborate plans for international organizations as the core of a world government (Hinsley 1963). The most elaborate efforts to establish IGOs have taken place during or immediately following major wars (Holsti 1998). For example, the two major institutional experiments of the twentieth century, the League of Nations in 1919 and the United Nations in 1945, were set up after the world wars. During World War II, the commitment of national governments to establishing an international organization was so strong that discussions on the UN began as early as 1942, long before the outcome of the war was known. The preamble of the UN Charter identifies preserving the peace as its primary objective. While peace may have been the primary motive in creating international organizations, the vast majority of such organizations serve economic and social needs. In his review of international organizations, Craig Murphy identified their principal tasks as fostering industry and managing social conflicts. Murphy connects the creation of international organizations to changes in the global economy in the late eighteenth century, as the institutions helped to create international markets by linking communications and transportation infrastructure, protecting intellectual property, and reducing legal and economic barriers to trade (1994, 2).

The vast range of activities that international organizations oversee is illustrated in the UN and its network of specialized agencies. The UN is a multipurpose organization involved in areas such as economic development (UN Development Program), health (World Health Organization), communications (International Telecommunications Union), human rights (Office of the UN High Commissioner for Refugees), refugees (UN High Commissioner for Refugees), women (UN Development Fund for Women), and children (UN Children's Fund). The UN has also been the principal forum in which newly established states seek confirmation of their independence and sovereignty. It has also been used by human rights advocates as the organization for advancing and protecting the rights of individuals against the state, and by civil society organizations to gain recognition and participation in the process of global governance.

International Economic Organizations

Among the more significant, specialized IGOs have been those established to serve more limited and specialized mandates in the area of international trade and finance. The WTO, for example, which was established in 1995, focuses primarily on matters related to international trade. It developed out of the Bretton Woods negotiations of 1944 and the General Agreement on Tariffs and Trade (GATT), first signed in 1947. The Bretton Woods negotiations also established the International Monetary Fund (IMF) and the International Bank for Reconstruction and Development (IBRD), most commonly known as the World Bank. The former was designed to regulate international capital transactions and national monetary policy; the latter was intended to provide capital for economic reconstruction in Europe. Both have evolved into major players in the global economy of North–South relations, playing an increasingly intrusive role in the domestic political economy of poorer states. Membership in these organizations has increased steadily over the past three decades, to the point where virtually all states are now members. There has also been a significant growth in the number of regional and ad hoc institutions in this area, including, most prominently, the EU, the North American Free Trade Agreement (NAFTA), and the Group of Eight (G8), which includes most of the globe's leading economies. Many of these institutions have devised rules that restrict the freedom and autonomy of member governments. The GATT's original objective was to reduce and eventually eliminate tariff barriers to international trade. This mandate has evolved into a wider range of trade-related issues. The restricted mandate of the WTO has been challenged by observers who maintain that it is not possible to separate trade from associated issues such as the environment and labour practices. In fact, one of the themes of the so-called "Battle in Seattle" in 1999 was that the WTO should take responsibility for the associated costs of trade. The attempts to have the organization deal with the effects of trade have been strongly resisted by many of the organization's member governments and by its secretariat. The intrusive activity of these organizations has led some to argue that they represent a new form of constitutionalism for member governments, referring, in part, to the ability of these organizations to subvert or override domestic constitutions in imposing restrictions on the economic and political practices of member governments. As discussed below, this in turn has led to demands for greater democratization and accountability on the part of these institutions.

Regional Organizations

The UN and other IGOs can be differentiated from other types of organizations on the basis of their memberships. Organizations that, like the UN, are open to all states are described as universal. Other organizations restrict membership to particular states on the basis of regional, historical, or strategic considerations. For example, the Organization of African Unity (OAU), now the African Union, established in 1963, is restricted to African states. The Organization of American States (OAS) includes states in the Western Hemisphere and for years was considered to be an instrument of U.S. foreign policy. Since the end of the Cold War, however, the makeup of the OAS has reflected a greater involvement by other states in the region, including Canada, which joined the organization in 1989. The North Atlantic Treaty Organization (NATO) unites states in Europe and North America that share common security interests, whereas the Association of Southeast Asian Nations (ASEAN) was created to meet its member states' regional security interests. Regional organizations have, in certain instances, emerged as important alternatives to the more universal institutions, particularly in matters of trade and finance. The EU, NAFTA, and the Asia-Pacific Economic Cooperation (APEC) forum stand as the most important regional organizations in the international political economy. These, and other regional organizations, raise additional concerns and debate about the relationships between and among IGOs as they compete for recognition and influence (Cooper et al. 2008).

General Features of Intergovernmental Organizations

IGOS VARY EXTENSIVELY IN THEIR STRUCTURES, PROCEDURES, CAPA-bilities, and budgets, but there are some common elements worth mentioning. Most organizations have a permanent secretariat overseeing the day-to-day operations of the organization. Members of the secretariat are drawn from member countries and become the employees of the organization. Frequently, they view their roles as those of international civil servants, representing the interests of the organization as a whole rather than of their home states (see, for example, Yi-chong and Weller 2004). Most of these organizations are led by a secretary general, a president, or a director who is selected by the member governments. The budgets of IGOs are based on the contributions of member governments. IGOs do not have any independent sources of revenue and, thus, remain dependent on member government contributions.

The representation of states in IGOs is generally based on the principle of political equality. At the same time, however, the decision-making structures and procedures of these organizations commonly reflect inequalities in status and power of member states, as the more powerful are allowed greater opportunity to influence the decisions of the organization. In some organizations this inequality in status is formally acknowledged. For example, the UN Charter recognizes the political equality of all its members, but only the UN Security Council can make decisions that are binding on all member states. The United States, Great Britain, France, China, and Russia, as permanent members of the Security Council, have each been given a veto that allows any one of them to prevent the Council, and hence the UN, from undertaking an action with which it disagrees. In the IMF and the World Bank, inequality of status is recognized by granting member states voting shares based on their monetary contributions, much as with private corporations and their stockholders. Other organizations, such as NATO, that lack such formal mechanisms often take decisions only if and when the most powerful member governments support the decision.

While the support of major powers is most often required if an international organization is to undertake effective action, this does not necessarily mean that major powers always dominate the process of global governance. On occasion, the agreement and support of more powerful states can be obtained through the efforts of smaller states or members of the organization's secretariat. For some observers, IGOs provide the best opportunity for less powerful states to influence the course of global politics. The influence of these states, especially when they act together through coalitions, is apparent in such areas as the post-Seattle international trade negotiations and the extensive negotiations at the UN on the Law of the Sea in the 1970s. The decision-making process within most IGOs is based on some combination of negotiation, consensus building, and formal votes. The sources of influence within this decentralized and diffused policy-making environment are extremely varied.

Obviously, a state's relative power in the world at large has an effect on its ability to wield influence. Beyond this, states can employ a variety of techniques, such as diplomatic skills or technical expertise, to shape the outcome of the decision-making process within IGOs. Unlike national legislatures, IGOs contain no organized political parties, but coalitions of states that share views often cooperate to achieve specific objectives, and these coalitions have become an active part of the process of global governance in IGOs. As early as the 1960s, in the UN, 77 poorer countries formed a coalition known as the Group of 77 to pressure other UN members to devote more attention and resources to global economic inequalities. Coalitions were an important and influential feature of negotiations in the GATT during the 1970s and 1980s, and they continue to be used by member governments in the WTO. An added feature of this process is the increasingly active participation of NGOs and corporate interest within global governance.

One of the ongoing dilemmas within international organizations is the balance between the sovereignty of member states and the power of the organization itself to take and enforce binding decisions infringing on this sovereignty. Part of the difficulty arises from the fact that most IGOs are explicitly designed to protect and reinforce the sovereignty of their member governments. Most IGOs contain some reference to recognizing the independence, sovereignty, territorial integrity, and formal equality of member governments. This, in turn, makes it difficult for these organizations to take action against a member government without that member government's consent. These conditions are, however, changing: "The old notion that what goes on within the state is a matter of sovereign privacy . . . has been swept away. In its stead, we have installed the doctrine that world order entails political stability, democratic governments, respect for human rights, general economic well-being, ethnic harmony, and peaceful resolution of conflicts within states, no less than cooperative and peaceful relationships among them" (Claude 2000). NATO's air assault on Serbia in the spring of 1999, taken in response to the Serbian government's violent reaction to separatist movements in Kosovo, is a vivid illustration of a more assertive and intrusive role for organizations. These developments have raised new issues and responsibilities for international organizations without any concomitant attempt to expand the capacity or authority of these institutions to address them.

Non-governmental Organizations

NGOS HAVE BEEN DEFINED IN VARIOUS WAYS. ONE OF THE MORE encompassing definitions has been incorporated into two UN resolutions referring to "any international organization which is not established by intergovernmental agreement . . . Including organizations which accept members designated by government authorities, provided that such membership does not interfere with the free expression of views of the organizations" (UN General Assembly Resolutions 288 [X] and 1296 [XLIV]). The term "NGO" is also generally restricted to non-profit organizations and thus excludes multinational corporations and other more nefarious commercial organizations, such as drug cartels that operate in more than two countries. Many groups have taken to calling themselves civil society organizations (CSOs) to distinguish themselves more explicitly from governments. It should be noted that many NGOs have absolutely nothing to do with world politics as it is most commonly understood. As an individual, you might take some interest in the World Ninepin Bowling Association or the World Rock 'n' Roll Confederation, but these groups are likely to contribute little to ending the conflict in the Middle East or alleviating poverty in Haiti. On the other hand, the World Jewish Congress or Oxfam might be able to make a significant contribution to these goals.

In contrast to IGOs, among which there is a considerable amount of similarity in organizational structure and decision-making procedures, there is an amazing variety of these qualities among the thousands of NGOs. Most NGOs have developed out of concerns for specific issues. Amnesty International, for example, emerged as a result of the work of a British lawyer, Peter Benenson, who in the early 1960s began to advocate for the humane treatment of prisoners in foreign countries. It has since developed into one of the world's most active and effective defenders of individual rights, and in 1977 it was awarded the Nobel Peace Prize. The Red Cross, which originated in the mid-nineteenth century as a result of the concern of another individual, Jean Henri Dunant, for the welfare of injured combatants, was given the first Nobel Peace Prize in recognition of its work in providing humane treatment for victims of conflict. Médecins Sans Frontières illustrates the disregard that NGOs often display for principles such as state sovereignty and non-intervention, as it has responded to humanitarian emergencies regardless of the state or the situation. It, too, has been recognized for its work with the Nobel Peace Prize, in 1999. In 1997, another NGO, the International Campaign to Ban Landmines (ICBL), was awarded the Nobel Peace Prize in recognition of its work in pressuring governments to sign the Ottawa Treaty, a convention establishing a comprehensive ban on anti-personnel land mines. This group developed as a result of a number of individual efforts in different countries to challenge governments to eliminate these weapons. The ICBL developed a close working relationship with members of the Canadian government, and this cooperation was instrumental in launching the Ottawa Process and the successful conclusion of the treaty in December 1996. The Ottawa Process illustrates the dynamics of NGO involvement in global governance. The ICBL worked with a coalition of NGOs from around the world. The ICBL was led by an American, Jody Williams, but found it easier and more effective to work with officials in Ottawa than those in Washington, which eventually refused to support the Ottawa Treaty.

Not all NGOs win peace prizes. Most of them are rather modest operations established by groups of concerned individuals in different countries to pressure governments to adopt policies that support their particular causes. Their political activity is generally focused in three directions. First, they seek to influence national governments to adopt foreign policies that support their cause. Second, they lobby intergovernmental institutions to promote their policy concerns. Finally, they publicize their concerns with the intent of generating popular support and funds.

NGOs are becoming increasingly important political actors in world politics. Groups such as Amnesty International, the Red Cross, CARE, Oxfam, Save the Children, Greenpeace, and the World Wildlife Fund, to mention just a few, have taken an increased interest in the activities of international organizations and national governments, and have sought to articulate their concerns and demands to an international audience. Additionally, some NGOs are in the centre of international politics in such areas as conflict prevention and resolution, economic development, and human rights. In recognition of this increased involvement, certain NGOs have pressed for more direct participation in the policy-making process of global governance. The Canadian government has been among the most supportive in advocating for improved access for NGOs at the UN and other IGOs. More extensive, direct, and effective involvement on the part of NGOs would see political activity that has traditionally been nationally based replaced by policy-making at the international level, involving representatives of national governments acting through IGOs and representatives of NGOs representing the interests of the "public." To date, NGOs have acquired consultation status with some IGOs, most notably in the UN. NGOs have also become particularly active around various UN conferences that have been held in recent decades on such issues as population, women, human rights, and social development. The UN Security Council also consults with representatives of selected NGOs in areas such as human rights and peacekeeping. All of this activity reflects an increasingly significant role for NGOs in the process of global governance (Karns and Mingst 2009).

Competing Perspectives on International Organizations

THERE ARE MANY DEBATES SURROUNDING THE PRACTICES OF INTER-national organizations, multilateralism, and global governance. We will briefly review three of the most prominent arguments about the sources and potential role of international organizations in world politics. First, a **realist** view holds that IGOs play, at best, marginal roles in world politics and are little more than a reflection of the interests of the governments that created them (Mearsheimer 1994–95). Viewed from this perspective, IGOs have no independent influence and last only so long as they are useful to states. States, primarily concerned with maximizing their own power, remain the most significant actors in world politics, and, therefore, use IGOs to protect or enhance their power position in the system. Some realists argue further that a dominant power (hegemon) uses IGOs to organize support and compliance from other states. In their view, a hegemon is essential for the creation and maintenance of IGOs (Keohane 1984). Realists maintain that IGOs act only in response to the pressures of their member governments and, therefore, are very much at the mercy of the most powerful states in the international system. NGOs, in contrast, are relatively insignificant players in world politics and can only be effective to the extent that they gain the support of powerful national governments.

An alternative view, that of a **liberal institutionalist**, holds that international organizations are both important and influential on the world stage, and that states cooperate out of a sense of common purposes that emphasize absolute gains and converging self-interests. Additionally, some liberals hold that states are not only concerned with maximizing their own gains relative to other states in the system but are more generally concerned with the effects of cooperation on the system as a whole. While accepting the importance and influence of states, liberals also argue that organizations, once created, acquire a degree of independence from their member governments and are effective in shaping the behaviour of these governments. International organizations are, in this view, considerably more than a mere reflection of states' interests and power. Some liberals go further in arguing that there has been a transfer of authority from states to international organizations such that these organizations have taken on responsibility for areas previously under the jurisdiction of national states.

A final collection of views takes a more critical perspective on international organizations. Proponents of these critical approaches argue that international organizations hold the potential to bring about a radical transformation in the practice of world politics (Cox 1992). IGOs provide an opportunity for less powerful states to pursue their own interests and perhaps design policies in opposition to those being pursued by more powerful states. This view also emphasizes the potential for NGOs to alter the course of world politics in the critical areas of political and economic reform. More than the other two approaches, these critical approaches emphasize the historical and political context in which international organizations now operate and identify them as a possible source of governance that is more democratic, just, and humane than the existing international system (Falk 1995).

Current Issues and Debates

THERE ARE A NUMBER OF IMPORTANT ISSUES SURROUNDING INTERnational organizations in the twenty-first century. One is institutional reform. While much of the interest in reform was sparked by the fiftieth anniversary of the UN in 1995, it was also inspired by the end of the Cold War in 1989 and the increased activism of IGOs and NGOs in the global political economy. More recently, reform has been necessitated by the redistribution of global power to emerging powers, including China, India, and Brazil. Institutional reforms touch on many issues, from the more practical concerns with budgets and administration to the more complicated and politically charged issues of representation and democratization. The attention to reform reflects changes in the global community and a perceived growth in the influence and relevance of these institutions. As a result, matters of accountability, transparency, and legitimacy of decision-making structures and processes, alongside concerns about representation and democracy, take on greater significance.

The debate over representation and democracy in IGOs pertains to the need for and mechanism by which national communities and, ultimately, individual citizens are to be represented in these organizations. This is partly a matter of making room in the decision-making councils of these institutions for the emerging powers. As international organizations assume greater responsibility for public policy, however, questions are also raised about the manner in which the public can be represented in IGOs. In the European Union, a parliament was established in 1977. Members of the European Parliament are elected directly by constituents in all of the EU member states. Proposals for popular assemblies and for elected parliaments along the lines of the European Parliament have been suggested for other organizations but have yet to be adopted. Alternatives that have been tried or proposed include such mechanisms as regular consultations between representatives of IGOs and NGOs and periodic meetings of NGOs and other groups such as has occurred around various UN conferences. Each of these proposals seeks to provide a more direct link between individuals and IGOs.

A final significant and related area of concern is the scope of responsibilities to be accorded these institutions in the arena of global governance. Many people have looked to international organizations as a preferable alternative to a world of sovereign states. For them, international organizations should expand their responsibilities to govern an ever-widening set of policy arenas. To some extent this has been occurring. A number of areas of international and domestic politics are now regulated by international organizations. This is especially evident in Europe, where the EU has assumed responsibility for vast areas of domestic politics. For the most part, however, responsibility for those areas that most affect our daily lives—such as education, health, and social welfare—remains with the nation-state. Moreover, if and when international organizations have intervened in domestic affairs, it has generally been at the behest of their member states. Nevertheless, increasingly, international organizations whose mandate was not initially concerned with domestic matters have moved into these areas. For example, international trade and financial institutions increasingly intervene in domestic social affairs by imposing monetary and fiscal constraints on national governments. The result has been a blurring of the division of responsibilities and power between national governments and international organizations with the net effect of an increase in the salience of international organizations and international agreements in national policy debates. This is particularly true of poorer countries, but to varying degrees it is significant for all countries that are extensively involved in the global political economy. The increased involvement of international organizations in areas previously within the domestic jurisdiction of national governments suggests that there has occurred a diminution of state sovereignty.

This development raises challenging questions about the acceptable degree of institutional interference in the domestic affairs of states. For example, many advocates would like to see international organizations interfere to protect the human rights of oppressed peoples. Others worry about the possibility that international organizations might intervene to protect the interests of foreign investors or to interfere with domestic environmental and labour standards. There are profound differences among member states over the nature and scope of intervention by international organizations. Governments in the developed, capitalist countries favour international organizations that support free market principles, while governments of weaker countries are concerned that their policy options are being controlled by powerful states through international organizations. The balance between effective international institutional intervention and respect for state sovereignty will be one of the major considerations shaping the future role of international organizations.

Conclusion

INTERNATIONAL ORGANIZATIONS HAVE BECOME A PERMANENT AND prominent feature of world politics. There has been a tremendous growth in the number and variety of international organizations, especially in the last half of the twentieth century. "International organizations" refers to non-profit organizations, of which there are two general categories: governmental organizations of two or more states and non-governmental organizations of individuals or groups from two or more countries. There are more than 300 intergovernmental organizations and more than 10 000 non-governmental organizations active in the world today. Intergovernmental organizations can be further classified according to membership (universal or regional) and objectives (multipurpose or single purpose).

Intergovernmental organizations originated out of a concern for the elimination of war and a shared concern for managing trans-border problems. Many advocates of a more peaceful international system have argued for the need for international organizations to provide for global peace, order, and justice. Others argue that international organizations merely reinforce the position of powerful states and interests in the international system. Three competing perspectives—realist, liberal institutionalist, and new multilateralist—posit different views on the salience and influence of international organizations and their relationship with national governments. While interpretations of the role and influence of international organizations vary, it is evident that as a result of the salience of cross-border issues such as environmental pollution, the AIDS epidemic, refugees, and economic globalization, international organizations will become an ever-increasing part of world politics in the years ahead.

Summary

The chapter:

- Defined and described the significance of sovereignty, anarchy, global governance, and multilateralism
- Identified and classified international organizations
- Differentiated three perspectives on the role of IGOs in global politics
- Highlighted the major contemporary challenges to IGOs

Discussion Questions

1. How could power and responsibility be more evenly distributed within international organizations?
2. Would a world government be a good thing? What would it look like?
3. Have international organizations such as the World Trade Organization acquired too much power?
4. How could IGOs be made more democratic, allowing for more direct representation and participation of NGOs and/or private citizens?
5. Should international organizations such as the United Nations have the right to intervene in the domestic affairs of states?

References

Cameron, Maxwell A., Robert Lawson, and Brian Tomlin, eds. 1998. *To Walk Without Fear.* Don Mills, ON: Oxford University Press.

Cooper, Andrew F., Christopher W. Hughes, and Philippe De Lombaerde, eds. 2008. *Regionalisation and Global Governance: The Taming of Globalisation?* London: Routledge.

Cox, Robert. 1992. "Multilateralism and World Order." *Review of International Studies* 18: 61–80.

Finkelstein, Lawrence. 1995. "What Is Global Governance?" *Global Governance* 1: 366–72.

Haas, Peter. 2002. "UN Conferences and Constructivist Governance of the Environment." *Global Governance* 8: 74.

Hinsley, F.H. 1963. *Power and the Pursuit of Peace.* Cambridge, U.K.: Cambridge University Press.

Karns, Margaret P. and Karen A. Mingst. 2009. *International Organizations: The Politics and Process of Global Governance,* 2nd edition. Boulder, CO: Lynne Rienner.

Keating, Tom. 2012. *Canada and World Order,* 3rd edition. Don Mills, ON: Oxford University Press.

Keohane, Robert. 1984. *After Hegemony.* Princeton, NJ: Princeton University Press.

Kumar, Ashwani, Jan Aart Scholte, Mary Kaldor, Marlies Glasius, Hakan Seckinelgin, and Helmut Anheier, eds. 2009. *Global Civil Society Yearbook 2009: Poverty and Activism.* London: Sage.

Mearsheimer, John. 1994–95. "The False Promise of International Institutions." *International Security* 20: 82–104.

Murphy, Craig. 1994. *International Organization and Industrial Change.* Cambridge, U.K.: Polity Press.

Pauly, Louis W. and William D. Coleman, eds. 2008. *Global Ordering, Institutions and Autonomy in a Changing World.* Vancouver: University of British Columbia Press.

Ruggie, John. 1993. *Multilateralism Matters.* New York: Columbia University Press.

Schmidt, Brian C. 1998. "Lessons from the Past: Reassessing the Interwar Disciplinary History of International Relations." *International Studies Quarterly* 42: 433–60.

Wolfe, Robert, 2011. "Canada's Adventures in Clubland: Trade Clubs and Political Influence." In *Readings in Canadian Foreign Policy: Classic Debates and New Ideas*, edited by Chris Kukucha and Duane Bratt. Toronto: Oxford University Press.

Yi-chong, Xu and Patrick Weller. 2004. *The Governance of World Trade, International Civil Servants and the GATT/WTO*. Cheltenham, U.K.: Edward Elgar.

Further Readings

Alexandroff, Alan S. 2008. *Can the World Be Governed?: Possibilities for Effective Multilateralism*. Waterloo, ON: Wilfrid Laurier University Press.

Muldoon, James P. et al., eds. 2011. *The New Dynamics of Multilateralism, Diplomacy, International Organizations and Global Governnace*. Boulder, CO: Westview.

Pease, Kelly-Kate. 2010. *International Organizations: Perspectives on Governance in the Twenty-first Century*, 4th edition. New York: Longmann.

Weiss, Thomas, David P. Forsythe, and Roger Coate. 2010. *The United Nations and Changing World Politics*, 6th edition. Boulder, CO: Westview.

Weblinks

European Union
http://europa.eu/index_en.htm

OneWorld.net: NGO Listings
www.oneworld.net

United Nations
www.unsystem.org/

International Financial Institutions Research Site (Wellesley College)
www.wellesley.edu/Economics/IFI/

CHAPTER 15

GLOBAL POLITICAL ECONOMY

ROB AITKEN

Learning Objectives

- Introduces the concept of global political economy

- Identifies the historical and political processes that led to forms of economic globalization

- Distinguishes between embedded liberalism and neo-liberalism

- Identifies the causes of recent financial turmoil and assesses its impact on the possible futures of the global political economy

Introduction

This chapter introduces global political economy (GPE) as a concept and an approach focused on understanding the relationship between political and economic power. A response to the dramatic intensification of cross-border flows of money, goods, and services in the 1970s and 1980s, GPE is both a field of study and a concept designed to place these developments in critical context. GPE emerged as a response, in part, to liberal views that dominate both the study and the practice of global political economy.

This chapter is divided into four separate parts. The first section outlines the concept of political economy, tracing both its origins and some of the ways in which it has been used to describe more recent processes of economic globalization. Although GPE emerged as a response to the intense economic changes of the past 40 years, this section highlights the ways in which critical thinkers in the GPE tradition draw on a range of concepts that emphasize the relationship between the economy and the study of politics. The second section of this chapter places globalization in historical context by highlighting the political economy that emerged after World War II. The third section of the chapter turns to recent episodes of financial turmoil. This section notes the ways in which recent financial crises typify a global economy increasingly organized around financial capital. A fourth and final section raises questions about the inconsistency between this financial economy and the possibilities of democratic accountability.

Political Economy

AT ONE LEVEL, POLITICAL ECONOMY, AS A TERM, WAS USED THROUGHOUT the nineteenth century to denote a wide range of thinkers interested in the study of the economy. Over the course of the twentieth century, however, political economy took on a distinctive meaning, as a field of study concerned with the ways in which economics and politics intersect. Political economy, at its most general level, refers to the study of this intersection of political and economic forces: the confrontation between states and markets, power and wealth.

Although traditional approaches to political economy all paid significant attention to the international economy, they could not have anticipated the scope of the global economic processes that dominate our world today. By the 1970s, the spectacular increase of global financial flows, trade, and other international political and economic activities created the need to refocus political economy from the national to the international to better take account of the changing nature of the global power relations. It is in this context that GPE was founded, both as a new field of inquiry and as an object of study. As a field of inquiry, GPE is concerned with the political regulation of the global economy and with the ways in which the global economy was deeply shaped by political interests. For writers working in this field, the global political economy refers not to an object that is natural or "given," but to one that is the product of complicated political processes and contests. In this sense, the global political economy refers both to the space of the global economy beyond national frontiers and to the study of that new space and the political, economic, and social implications of it for all of us.

GPE focuses attention on a very specific process: the *political* construction and management of the global economy. What does it mean to say that the global economy is politically constructed and managed? Unlike mainstream economics, which tends to conceive of the economy as a set of activities separate from political life, writers working in GPE understand the global economy as a political project—that is, as a site that is managed *by* and *in the interest of* particular sets of social forces, be these states, corporations, workers, or individuals. In this sense, the economy is conceived of as a site of complicated political contestation. Economic practices are the result of political pressures, coalitions, and trade-offs designed to manage how economic benefits and injuries are distributed.

One writer who has been influential in creating a critical understanding of GPE is Karl Polanyi (1886–1964). Polanyi, a historian, anthropologist, and political economist, argued against the "free market" view of the economy, which suggested that the market was naturally "self-regulating" in ways that required no government intervention. Polanyi insisted that the economy is always the reflection of political contests. In this sense, markets are, in Polanyi's terms, "artificial" in that they are less the product of natural processes and more the result of political actors seeking politically beneficial arrangements. As Polanyi noted, the "free" market "was not the result of any inherent tendency of markets towards excrescence, but rather the effect of highly artificial stimulants administered to the body social" (Polanyi 1944, 57). Polanyi's detailed historical study of the rise and demise of **laissez-faire capitalism** in the nineteenth and early twentieth centuries demonstrated that free trade embodied the reigning ideas of economic and political elites, and imposed and sustained these ideas through governmental regulation and public policy. There was, in other words, nothing natural about so-called natural economic forces and self-regulating markets.

More recently, Robert W. Cox has picked up on Polanyi's argument by noting that power in the global economy is not simply a question defined in economic terms but also a political question about how certain social classes are able to shape markets in the first place, and then derive power from those markets to cement their position in society. For Cox, it is control over the ways in which material economic resources are produced and distributed that forms the basis of all other forms of power. "The social power of dominant classes," notes Cox, "may be thought of as originally grounded in the control of production—the material basis of all societies" (Cox 1987, 18). This understanding of power, common to the critical GPE tradition, is often referred to as historical materialism. "Material" power, however, is never separate from the power of language, discourse, and ideas. Many of the most important shifts in the global economy have entailed changes in dominant ideas about the economy. The shift toward a Keynesian approach in the 1930s and 1940s, for example, was partly constituted out of a striking shift in dominant ideas about what the economy is and how it should be managed (Blyth 2002).

Although interest in GPE emerged from the intensification of international economic flows throughout the 1970s, it also often draws on much older concepts. There has been, for example, a long-circulating debate about the concept of **mercantilism**, the predominant understanding of the national and international economy in the sixteenth and seventeenth centuries. Although most commonly associated with French politician Jean-Baptiste Colbert, much of the most important work on mercantilism was written by British political economists such as Thomas Mun and James Steurart (Braudel 1979). Mercantilists assumed a fixed volume of world trade and depicted the international economy as a competitive site in which states vied with each other to achieve a positive balance of trade, counted in the accumulation of gold and silver. Further, dominant themes within GPE, such as global, political, and economic inequalities, have long been a fixture of many critical voices across the social sciences. The question of **imperialism**, for example, has often been central to the way in which writers working in GPE have framed their analysis of the politics of the global economy. The organization of the world's economy today, and its persistent inequalities and power differences, cannot be separated from the long histories of imperialism that continue to shape the ways in which many countries are inserted into the world economy. This began, most strikingly, with Lenin (1870–1924) writing in the early moments of the twentieth century, who argued that the matters of empire, capitalism, and the global economy are intimately connected (Lenin, 1973). Similarly, throughout the 1960s and 1970s, critical writers, many from the "developing" world, began to decry the persistent political and economic inequalities that seemed to be a fundamental characteristic of the international system. For a diverse set of writers, including Andre Gunder Frank, Samir Amin, and Fernando Cardoso, who later became president of Brazil, the inequalities that characterize the global system are a residue of a much longer imperial history. This history has created conditions of "dependency" in which the global South remains enmeshed in highly unequal chains of relations with countries at the capitalist core (Amin 2010; Cardoss and Faletto 1979). In a slightly different fashion, Immanuel Wallerstein developed a theory of **world systems** to describe the emergence, over many centuries, of a world capitalist system in which the countries at the centre of the system, what Wallerstein described as the "core," obtained supremacy over the world economy and its resources, and who, indeed, continue to benefit disproportionately more than the countries that lie at the "periphery" of the world system. These concepts are examples of the ways in which GPE scholars have explained the historical development of capitalism and how it has changed over time.

Bretton Woods and Embedded Liberalism

GPE IS A FIELD CONCERNED WITH THE CHANGING NATURE OF CAPITALIST development and the political forces that have shaped those historical processes. The reorganization of the global political economy after World War II, in particular, has attracted a great deal of critical interest among many GPE scholars. At the famous international conference held in 1944 at Bretton Woods, New Hampshire, the Allied powers sought to reconstruct the world economy to avoid repeating the political and economic instabilities of the interwar period, which was marked by a global economic depression in the 1930s. British and American policy-makers, in particular, sought to avoid what they conceived of as the disastrous pursuit of two opposite but equally destabilizing programs: economic nationalism (or isolationism) and laissez-faire free trade. As the chief British negotiator at Bretton Woods, John Maynard Keynes, noted, excessive competition and "economic imperialism" were "a scarcely avoidable part of a scheme of things" in an international order of laissez-faire and free trade (Keynes 1933, 757). To avoid the costs of a system of free trade and the costs generated by the equally unstable system of economic isolationism pursued by many countries during the economic crises of the 1930s, Keynes and American negotiators proposed a post-war international economic order that was *open* to international economic flows but was also *managed* in a way that allowed some degree of domestic protection. This delicate balance, negotiated at Bretton Woods, sought to create a more stable international system in which national governments could pursue autonomous policies of domestic economic security, including demand management, active fiscal policies, and, in some cases, more generous social protection or social security schemes. These forms of "stability" were experienced differently, however, in the global North than how they were experienced among post-colonial states. In the post-colonial world, this "new" regime continued to look dramatically similar to a much longer history of inequality and unevenness. Nonetheless, national governments in all regions were obligated to participate in a world economy in ways that would be managed through new multilateral institutions: the General Agreement on Tariffs and Trade (GATT), the International Monetary Fund (IMF), and the World Bank. In the words of one important analyst, John Ruggie, Bretton Woods established a new regime of **embedded liberalism**. It was a "compromise," in which the leading powers sought to "maneuver between two extremes" and construct a liberal world economy that would be embedded in national societies and respond to their needs for domestic stability and social protection (Ruggie 1982).

Embedded liberalism is a clear example of a moment when a particular political coalition was able to reorganize the global economy in line with its particular interests. The emergence of a "compromise" at the Bretton Woods conference was not the result of some neutral or natural process. Rather, embedded liberalism was a *political* project that reflected the interests and desires of a particular constellation of social forces. The political vision of embedded liberalism was advocated by a group of otherwise disparate social and class interests, most clearly active in the United States, including elements of productive capital (large production or manufacturing interests), state officials, and bureaucrats associated with Keynes or the Depression-era policies of President Roosevelt's New Deal, and elements of organized labour that had reconciled themselves to the vision of a liberal capitalism moderated by some elements of social and worker protection.

"We Live in Financial Times": GPE and the Financial Crisis

IN 2007, THE WELL-KNOWN INTERNATIONAL NEWSPAPER THE *Financial Times* attempted to redesign itself with an audacious advertising campaign entitled "we live in financial times" (*Financial Times* 2007). One of the images featured a stylized urban island populated by iconic buildings from financial districts around the world: the New York Stock Exchange, IFC 2 in Hong Kong, and Yokohama Landmark Tower in Yokohama, Japan. This image offers a story often told about our own period of political-economic globalization: a world supposedly connected across borders and made small by the power of global financial and communication networks. Perhaps more importantly, "financial times" is an apt way to describe the global political economy of the past few decades, and the ways in which our global political economy differs from the kind of embedded liberalism attempted by the architects of the post-war world. If embedded liberalism entailed a careful set of compromises, our global political economy—a moment not of embedded liberalism but of **neo-liberalism**—entails an uncompromising return to themes of classical free trade and market faith.

Neo-liberalism is a political-economic approach that places emphasis on unfettered markets, the importance of individual choice, free enterprise, and a faith in forms of self-regulation. This world of neo-liberalism began to emerge in the 1970s when some of the key commitments negotiated at Bretton Woods began to collapse. This collapse was precipitated in part by increasing competition from European and Japanese firms, persistent inflation, increasing unemployment, the emergence of fiscal deficits for states, rising energy prices, and a gradual worldwide economic slowdown. Perhaps most important, however, it was the changing role of the American dollar as the centre of the global monetary system that most destabilized the post-war order established at Bretton Woods. After World War II, the U.S. dollar, known as the "greenback," was established as the universal currency in the international system and, for the most part, other national currencies were "pegged" to it in somewhat fixed ways. By the 1970s, serious problems began to threaten this arrangement. The U.S. government removed the "gold window" and effectively ended the system of fixed exchange rates that had been key to the kind of global economic stability envisioned at the Bretton Woods conference. These arrangements, first negotiated at Bretton Woods, had established the American dollar (and its formal link to American gold reserves) as a global reserve currency and the basis of global monetary stability. In the early 1970s, American President Richard Nixon unilaterally ended this special role of the American dollar in the face of growing concerns about the American economy.

The collapse of Bretton Woods set in motion a long period of complicated changes in the organization of the international economy. For example, a system of "floating" exchange rates emerged in which world exchange rates were set by private currency markets. There also emerged a number of other transformative trends—among them, the intensification of globalized production processes, the gradual implementation of "free trade" agreements that restricted the ways in which national governments could favour domestic producers, the dramatic rise of international trade, and the deepening of flexible labour markets. Alongside these trends, the American government continued to spend enormous fiscal resources on military spending, first in Vietnam and more recently in interventions in Iraq and Afghanistan. This spending has created large American fiscal deficits and has put enormous pressure on the American dollar.

Perhaps the most spectacular development in this move toward **globalization** has been what Eric Helleiner has referred to as the "re-emergence of global finance" (see Helleiner 1994). Although the international movements of **financial capital**—forms of credit, bank loans, speculative capital, money, and investment—were relatively contained through the Bretton Woods period, the new regime of floating exchange rates, among many other factors, eventually led to the dramatic emergence of very large flows of financial capital into and out of newly expanding financial markets. By 2010, for example, the daily turnover in foreign exchange markets had risen to $4 trillion (USD), a volume that had more than doubled since 2004 (Bank for International Settlements 2011, 6; Bank for International Settlements 2005, 2). This rise of global finance has resulted in markets that are unimaginably large and unpredictable. These immense markets both outstrip the capacities of national monetary policy and help create conditions of serious instability. Since the early 1990s, there have been numerous moments of financial instability: a serious collapse of the price of the Mexican peso in 1994, the widespread Asian currency crises of 1997, as well as the crisis in Argentina near the end of 2001.

The period between 2007 and 2012 has witnessed a particularly intense wave of financial turmoil that was triggered by two distinct but related episodes. First, in the autumn of 2008, a serious financial crisis crested in American financial markets and then spread globally. This crisis was rooted in a complex reorganization of financial risk related to the subprime mortgage sector in the United States. The term "subprime sector" refers to a class of mortgages offered to "risky" populations not well served by regular or "prime" mortgage lenders. Throughout the 1980s and 1990s, the American government began to encourage lenders to offer mortgages to subprime communities, often low-income and minority populations. These mortgages were often aggressively marketed and became attached to onerous conditions not prevalent in "prime" mortgage markets: adjustable rate mortgages that confronted borrowers with escalating interest costs over the term of the mortgage, loan arrangements with lengthy terms (40 years or longer), and other costs imposed on vulnerable communities least able to pay. Ironically, the risk of these mortgages was compounded by the high costs associated with them; costs that were both enormously attractive to lenders as a source of profit but also a great risk as a serious source of potential default.

To manage the risk associated with these mortgages (a risk that lenders themselves helped create with onerous terms) financial firms turned to a class of financial instruments that they had increasingly relied on to help navigate the instability in the global financial system: derivatives. Derivatives are financial assets whose value is linked to—that is, derived from—some other underlying asset. A simple derivative, for example, is a futures contract that pays a certain price for future delivery of some commodity, in ways that provide opportunities for hedging risk against price volatility. In this instance, the futures contract allows the buyer to hedge risk by accessing a guaranteed price for a commodity, notwithstanding fluctuations in the price established by the world market. These derivatives have long been a feature of commodity markets as a way to help producers manage price instability. Since the 1970s, however, in the context of greater financial instability, there has been dramatic growth in both the size and the complexity of derivative markets. There are now, for example, large derivative markets related to the price of foreign currencies, to all commodity prices, and to a range of more unconventional risks, including a growing class of derivative contracts relating to weather trends. Derivatives are now the world's largest class of commodity, often used in ways that are completely detached from the underlying asset or from the goal of managing risk in relation to that underlying asset (see Bank of International Settlements 2011).

These types of instruments proved enticing to financial institutions keen to manage the risk associated with subprime mortgages. To do so, lenders bundled risky mortgages into securities that could be traded in financial markets. One of the most important forms that this process of securitization took was the use of derivative instruments (most specifically, collateralized debt obligations) linked to the income that would be generated from the bundle of mortgages. Although this process was theoretically designed to diffuse risk among a wide range of investors, it actually imposed serious murkiness in these markets. Banks often used these instruments to obscure their stake in risky investments by moving risk off of their formal balance sheets (a process Gowan has referred to as the growth of the "shadow" banking system). Moreover, credit rating agencies were pressured by investment banks to issue ratings that softened the serious risks associated with subprime mortgage assets. In these ways, the distance between investors and the assets they held—income linked to the actual mortgages—became increasingly cloudy. This opacity prevented investors from either understanding or acknowledging the risk associated with the mortgages that formed the ultimate base of these investment products. By 2006 and 2007, the demand for subprime mortgage investments created what former Fed Chairman Alan Greenspan has referred to as a **bubble market**—a market governed not by rational expectation but by "irrational exuberance" and by speculative capital interested in realizing large financial goals on short-term price movements. This "bubble," however, stood in contrast to conditions in the actual housing markets where risky mortgages were increasingly under pressure by worsening economic conditions and onerous terms that many low and middle-income households were finding increasingly difficult to sustain.

As conditions in housing markets worsened, and as borrowers began to default on loans, pressure began to build on some of the institutions most central to American financial markets. Key financial firms, like Lehman Brothers; insurance companies, such as AIG; and a variety of investment banks became seriously compromised by their over-exposure to what were quickly becoming worthless assets. This pressure triggered a self-fulfilling cycle when investors began to fear financial instability, sought refuge from risky investments, and in the process exerted pressure on available liquidity and credit in the global financial system. The week of October 6–10, 2008, for example, marked the worst week for the stock market since the 1930s. Over the course of this single week, the Dow Jones Industrial Average fell 1874 points, which represents 18 percent of its capitalized value. Moreover, the crisis in American markets began to migrate to Europe where there had been similar enthusiasm for subprime mortgage investments. This was particularly true of Ireland, the United Kingdom, and Spain. By the end of 2008 and throughout 2009, the crisis translated into a more general banking and credit crisis across the global economy.

A second, but related, financial storm has gathered strength over the period since 2010—a European fiscal crisis. Pressure on fiscal balances occurred in settings, such as Ireland and Iceland, that were deeply affected by the subprime crisis in an immediate manner. These pressures crested in slightly different ways in the United Kingdom, which faced the crisis with a newly minted Conservative–Liberal Democrat coalition government with a particular political commitment to fiscal discipline. The crisis also took a particular shape in Greece, which had witnessed dramatic increases in public and consumer debt in the decade following the adoption of a common European currency. In the most striking cases, such as in Greece, fiscal pressures have triggered widespread concern among international bond holders that governments will not be able to repay their **sovereign debt**, concerns that have led to historically high rates of interest for government bonds in Italy, Spain, and Greece as well as continent-wide downgrading of sovereign debt by credit rating agencies. Regardless of the specific differences, European governments have translated this pressure into widespread programs of **fiscal austerity**. This austerity has been punctuated by several key moments: a draconian budget enacted in the United Kingdom, a complicated bailout package negotiated with the Irish government, and, most strikingly, protracted negotiations between the European Union (EU) and the Greek government—all of which have resulted in dramatic austerity programs. Even in austerity, however, state capacity to intervene in economic life has been dramatically on display. Reactions to these various crises have all entailed measures (bailouts, direct state purchase of toxic assets, lender-of-last-resort functions) that require robust forms of state intervention. Although it is still early in the process, it seems likely that these austerity programs could significantly alter the basic framework of economic and social governance across the EU.

The Global Political Economy of "Financial Times"

The concept of living in "financial times" takes on added significance in the wake of this recent turmoil in financial markets. One of the most important sets of theoretical implications of recent crises relates to the ways in which we understand the expansiveness, the undeniable reach, of finance. Analysts working in GPE have long noted the increasing political and economic influence of "Wall Street" (investment firms, banks, and the cluster of financial markets and exchanges key to the financial economy) over the past several decades (see Panitch et al.). Moreover, analysts have long noted the growing economic importance of financial activities—a sector of the economy that has claimed increasingly larger shares of gross domestic product (see Krippner as well as Warwick and Turner reports). The recent turmoil in financial markets has deepened the ways in which we might think about finance as an expansive force increasingly central to our global political economy in two particular ways. First, the financial crisis makes visible the dizzying variety of ways in which almost anything can be converted into a financial asset. What was at the core of the 2007/2008 financial crisis, for example, was a process through which subprime mortgages were converted into assets that could be exchanged on financial markets among investors. At its most basic, this was an attempt to squeeze financial value from things that are not directly connected to financial markets. In 1848, Karl Marx and Friedrich Engels wrote in *The Communist Manifesto* that one characteristic of capitalism was the "need" for capital "to nestle everywhere, to settle everywhere, to establish connections everywhere" (Marx 2012). The subprime crisis seems to echo these arguments, as one of many recent instances where financial institutions are able to convert a seemingly endless list of non-financial objects (subprime mortgages, carbon emission reduction targets, future weather trends) into financial asset classes. This has prompted two analysts to point out that what defines financial capitalism is the incessant "prospecting" by financial institutions for new financial assets streams—that is, for objects that could be converted into financial capital or instruments in one way or another—a process they refer to as "the financialization of almost everything" (see Leyshon and Thrift 2007).

A second important sign of this expansiveness is the geographical reach of financial markets, and the globalization of turmoil that results from this incessant prospecting. Although the financial crisis was first felt in the United States and was most forcefully exported to the European economies, there were few areas of the global economy left untouched by its force. The crisis was felt in surprising ways; for example, in Iceland, which had become increasingly exposed to global markets in a credit-fuelled boom throughout the previous decade. This has dramatically altered the Icelandic economy, triggering a massive revaluation of the currency and a decline in living standards by almost every measure. Although perhaps not so dramatically, the crisis nonetheless has left its mark on the economies of places even further afield. The financial markets of many emerging economies, distant from the experiments in subprime financialization, also experienced pressure emanating from the turmoil that gripped American and European markets. Downward pressure was exerted, for example, on the capital markets (the stock and equity markets) in many emerging economies. This experience seems to confirm that today's financial markets are deeply interconnected, providing few spaces insulated from financial turmoil once it is unleashed. This interconnection implies a greater theoretical concern about the very reach of finance as practices that link vast parts of the global economy in ways that challenge our conventional ways of thinking about the market and the scope of its power. Put differently, if financial markets are increasingly expansive, can there be a space somehow outside of their reach? This is an issue that, in turn, raises questions about these markets and how they might be subjected to forms of democratic accountability.

The Limit of Finance or the Limit of Politics?

THE SHIFT TO "FINANCIAL TIMES" HAS BEEN A DECIDEDLY POLITICAL project. Just as the move toward embedded liberalism reflected the interests and political influence of a particular set of social forces, so, too, does the move toward a borderless world of financial exchange. The recent waves of financial crises, for example, have been deeply enabled by political arguments made in favour of the deregulation of markets. These arguments, which were at the core of American domestic and international political agendas throughout the 1990s and into the 2000s, attempted to lighten regulations on the ways in which financial firms operated, remove barriers to the movement of financial capital, and encourage a permissive attitude among regulators to new and increasingly complex financial instruments. Internationally, the social forces that promoted **deregulation** exerted pressures on many countries, including emerging economies, to remove barriers to the flows of capital across borders, a process often referred to as **capital account liberalization**. A great deal of attention has been paid by those in the GPE tradition to the ways in which processes of financial liberalization have been imposed on the global South. This includes the "Washington Consensus" policies imposed by the IMF and World Bank in the 1980s and 1990s, as well as more recent discourses of "poverty reduction," which also involve neo-liberal policy prescriptions (see Best 2005). This agenda was often promoted by those with a direct interest in financial institutions. As Gowan has noted, over the past 20 years, Wall Street has become increasingly powerful at all levels of American politics, including among the very regulators tasked with managing the financial and banking systems. This increasing clout, according to Gowan, represents a "structural transformation of the American financial system. . . . a New Wall Street System has emerged . . . the driving force behind the crisis" (Gowan 2009, 6).

More broadly, however, these processes of deregulation both relied upon and have been justified by neo-liberalism. This economic and political project differs from the embedded liberalism of the post-war moment in many important ways. Although they both subscribe, broadly speaking, to liberal conceptions of how the economy (and citizenship) should be organized, neo-liberalism rejects the notion that the economy itself should be regulated by the state. Neo-liberals have increasingly sought a global free trade model in which the "market," and not the state, is used to organize the economy and many other areas of social, political, and economic life. As Cox puts it, neo-liberals have sought "the achievement of a market utopia on the world scale" (Cox 1996, 191).

Beginning with the economic crises of the 1970s, various academics, politicians, business activists, and other organizations promoted neo-liberal ideas and encouraged governments to embrace the neo-liberal conception of a market utopia. This network of neo-liberals—including the two important Nobel laureates, Milton Friedman and Friedrich von Hayek—helped make sense of the shifts of the 1970s in the language of neo-liberalism and were instrumental in the processes of financial deregulation.

Unlike the political coalition that coalesced around the vision of embedded liberalism, neo-liberalism is often associated with financial capital (banks, investment houses, and auditors), globally oriented business sectors, and transnational elites.

Although the political history of neo-liberal financial markets can be traced, it is the political future of finance that remains the most urgent question. The financial crisis has confronted students and scholars of GPE with an important political puzzle: are there political limits to the kind of deregulated financial markets that have proved so destabilizing over the last number of years? On the one hand, some writers working in GPE, echoing the earlier work of Polanyi, argue that the social costs associated with liberalized financial markets will lead eventually to some form of political reaction. This reaction could consist of the emergence of popular opposition to liberalized markets. A variety of political movements have emerged that are deeply concerned about the social costs of the recent financial crises, especially the forms of fiscal austerity many governments have imposed or the unequal ways in which risks have been borne. Widespread protests in Greece, for example, have been the angry reaction to a new program of austerity imposed as part of a broader European agreement designed to address sovereign Greek debt. In a slightly different manner, the Occupy Wall Street movement emerged in September 2011 and managed to mobilize serous political attention by contrasting forms of inequality with the immense government bailout of the financial sector after the 2008 financial crisis. Some wonder whether these movements could, in the medium and longer term, translate their political impact into sustainable political pressure for broader restrictions on financial flows and for greater degrees of regulatory cooperation at the international level (see Germain 2010). One of the key achievements of the Bretton Woods negotiations at the end of World War II was a kind of global consensus on the need to "make finance the servant" by codifying capital controls and restrictions of various sorts on the banking and financial sector. Some commentators have pointed to the recent revival of discussions of a financial transaction tax (especially among some European governments) as a sign that there might once again be significant political limits to the power and reach of finance. These speculations, which have now become a major source of debate in GPE, orbit around a question about democracy and accountability: will democratic pressures ultimately undermine the power and freedom that financial institutions have been slowly accumulating since the 1970s?

On the other hand, however, there is also abundant evidence that the power of finance remains mostly unchecked even after the crises of the past few years. Although there was a great deal of political consternation during the depth of the financial crisis and in the wake of the Occupy Wall Street movement, the international flow of financial capital remains largely unimpeded. While there have been some important domestic reforms in the United States, the international flow of capital and widespread use of exotic financial instruments continue in much the manner they did in advance of the crisis. Moreover, unlike the crises of the 1930s that eventually ushered in a novel regulatory regime centred on the ideas of embedded liberalism, the policy discourses of neo-liberalism remain an important core of global financial and economic governance. This continuing commitment to neo-liberalism and the immense power of financial markets often exist in stark tension with the political pressures created by the austerity policies that have been ushered in by the crises. These strange tensions between democratic and financial imperatives were acutely evident, for example, in late October 2011 when the Greek government announced a plan to hold a nation-wide referendum on the subject of a financial bailout plan and a series of associated neo-liberal austerity measures. The decision to subject the unpopular plan to popular accountability (undoubtedly a calculated political manoeuvre by then-Prime Minister George Papandreou) resulted in widespread concern among the leaders of many European countries and other key financial players. The planned referendum was cancelled several days after it triggered political and economic turmoil.

The relationship between financial markets and political practice has long been important to GPE, and it will continue to confront students of GPE with key questions for years to come: Are there political limits to the deregulation agenda? What would it mean to insert democratic accountability into financial markets? In the words of Susan Strange, a scholar important in installing finance as a central concern for the field of GPE, can "mad money" be tamed by public will? How we answer these questions and the specific shape these answers take are the source of much urgency and complexity. This urgency also reminds us that GPE remains a study critical to our collective political futures over the coming years.

Conclusion

POLITICAL ECONOMY IS A FIELD OF STUDY CONCERNED WITH THE intersection of political and economic power. This chapter has introduced the concept of global political economy as a field of study and as a concept designed to address the ways in which global economic practices are politically managed and constructed. One way to address this process of political management is to pay particular attention to the social interests that have been central to the ways in which the global economy has been organized and reorganized over time. The reorganization of the world economy after World War II, for example, was accomplished by a group of social interests—productive capital, state managers, some elements of organized labour—that were keen to promote a kind of "embedded liberalism." This contrasts with a more recent attempt, since the 1970s, to reorganize the economy along neo-liberal lines. This neo-liberal project, supported by particular social forces, has been centrally concerned with the construction of a global "market utopia."

Finally, this chapter has emphasized recent waves of financial turmoil as examples of politically urgent processes at the very heart of GPE. These crises underscore the complexity of globalization and the seemingly expansive and interconnected role of finance in a global economy. This complexity raises questions, in turn, about the ways in which we might understand democratic accountability in the face of seemingly intractable economic pressures. It is in these contexts that GPE is an increasingly important field that tries to make sense of the complex political issues related to economic globalization and the possible futures of the global society.

Summary

The chapter:

- Introduced the concept of global political economy
- Identified the historical and political processes that led to forms of economic globalization
- Distinguished between embedded liberalism and neo-liberalism
- Identified the causes of recent financial turmoil and assessed its impact on the possible futures of the global political economy

Discussion Questions

1. What makes political economy different from other areas of political inquiry?
2. In your view, does it make sense to separate the study of economics and the study of politics?
3. How has economic globalization been a political project? In whose interest are neo-liberal forms of economic restructuring?
4. What is finance? How did financial markets become so large and powerful over the past several decades?
5. What are the political consequences of the recent forms of financial turmoil in the global economy? Can forms of political protest challenge the power of financial institutions in today's political economy? Can financial markets be subjected to forms of democratic accountability?

References

Bank for International Settlements. 2005. *Triennial Central Bank Survey*. Basel, Switzerland: Bank for International Settlements.

Bello, Walden and Maylou Malig. 2004. "The Crisis of the Globalist Project and the New Economics of George Bush." In *The Politics of Empire: Globalisation in Crisis*, edited by Alan Freeman and Boris Kagarlitsky. London: Pluto Press.

Best, Jacqueline. 2005. *The Limits of Transparency: Ambiguity and the History of International Finance*. Ithaca, NY: Cornell University Press.

Bissio, Robert. 2005. *Social Watch 2005: Roars and Whispers*. Montevideo, Uruguay: Social Watch Secretariat/Third World Institute.

Conway, Janet. 2004. "Citizenship in the Time of Empire: The World Social Forum as a New Political Space." *Citizenship Studies* 8(4): 367–81.

Cox, Robert. W. 1987. *Production, Power and World Order: Social Forces in the Making of History*. New York: Columbia University Press.

———. 1996. *Approaches to World Order*. Cambridge, U.K.: Cambridge University Press.

Gowan, Peter. 2009. "Crisis in the Heartland." *New Left Review* 55.

Hardt, Michael and Antonio Negri. 2000. *Empire*. Cambridge, MA: Harvard University Press.

Helleiner, Eric. 1994. *States and the Re-Emergence of Global Finance: From Bretton Woods to the 1990s*. Ithaca, NY: Cornell University Press.

Keynes, John Maynard. 1933. "National Self-Sufficiency." *The Yale Review* XXII: 4.

Lenin, V.I. 1973. *Imperialism, the Highest Stage of Capitalism: A Popular Outline*. Peking, China: Foreign Languages Press.

Marx, Karl. 2012. *The Communist Manifesto*. New Haven, CT: Yale University Press.

Polanyi, Karl. 1944. *The Great Transformation: The Political and Economic Origins of Our Times*. Boston: Beacon Press.

Robinson, William I. 2004. *A Theory of Global Capitalism*. Baltimore, MD: Johns Hopkins University Press.

Ruggie, John. 1982. "International Regimes, Transactions and Change." *International Organization* 36.

Further Readings

Appelbaum, Richard P. and William I. Robinson, eds. 2005. *Critical Globalization Studies*. New York: Routledge.

Germain, Randall. 2010. *Global Politics and Financial Governance*. London: Palgrave.

Rupert, Mark and M. Scott Solomon. 2006. *Globalization and International Political Economy: The Politics of Alternative Futures*. New York: Rowman and Littlefield.

Scholte, Jan Aart. 2005. *Globalization: A Critical Introduction*. London: Palgrave.

Weblinks

Global Policy Forum
www.globalpolicy.org

The World Bank
www.worldbank.org

The World Social Forum
www.forumsocialmundial.org.br/index.php?cd_language=2

CBC *Ideas* podcast on Karl Polanyi, "Markets and Society" (discussion of the theoretical and conceptual basis of critical political economy and GPE)
www.cbc.ca/ideas/calendar/2005/07_july.html

Political Economy Research Centre, University of Sheffield (good starting point for studying the academic discipline of GPE)
www.shef.ac.uk/perc

CHAPTER 16

INDIGENEITY AND SELF-GOVERNANCE

ISABEL ALTAMIRANO-JIMÉNEZ

Learning Objectives

- Examines competing definitions of Indigenous identity

- Discusses the right to self-identification and
  determination of membership

- Examines contested understandings of the right to
  self-determination

- Explores the relative benefits of negotiation and litigation

Introduction

In September 2007, the United Nations General Assembly held a vote to adopt the United Nations Declaration on the Rights of Indigenous Peoples (UNDRIP). The UNDRIP is a significant landmark in recognizing the distinct and inherent rights of Indigenous peoples and in addressing persistent human rights violations against Indigenous peoples worldwide. Although individual rights are explicitly protected, the rights affirmed in the UNDRIP are collective, applying to "peoples." These include equality with all other peoples, the right to self-determination and self-government, the right to self-identification and determination of membership, as well as the recognition and enforcement of treaties, traditional institutions, and intellectual property rights. The UNDRIP also protects the right of Indigenous peoples "to maintain and strengthen their distinctive spiritual relationship with their traditionally owned or otherwise used and occupied lands, territories, waters and coastal seas, and other resources, and to uphold their responsibilities to future generations in this regard" (Article 25). The UNDRIP, similar to all United Nations (UN) declarations, is not legally binding on signatory countries. It does, however, embody a fundamental shift in the development of international norms, and it reflects the commitment of UN members to establish standards for the treatment of Indigenous peoples.

It took over 30 years to pass the UNDRIP. The idea originated in the early 1980s when the UN Economic and Social Council (ECOSOC) established the Working Group on Indigenous Populations led by Special Rapporteur Jose Martinez Cobo. The UN Declaration was passed with 143 states in favour and 4 against it. The opposing states were Canada, the United States, New Zealand, and Australia. Two years later, in April 2009, the Australian government endorsed the UNDRIP, followed by New Zealand in April 2010, Canada in November 2010, and the United States in December 2010. Although Canada endorsed the UNDRIP, the Harper government noted that it is not binding and does not change Canadian laws (Aboriginal Affairs and Northern Development 2010). Nevertheless, in the UN Secretary-General's report (July 2010) to the General Assembly, all states were called upon to establish the necessary legislation and institutional policies for Indigenous peoples' rights using the UNDRIP as a reference. Arguably, the Canadian government does not endorse the UN Declaration itself but rather a particular interpretation of it, as will be discussed in a later section.

The UNDRIP is both important and controversial. Over 370 million Indigenous people worldwide now have a universal instrument and framework for addressing ongoing human rights transgressions. These Indigenous populations represent a diversity of historical, cultural, political, and social experiences. Currently, major issues related to Indigenous peoples in Canada and elsewhere are being addressed simultaneously at local and global levels in at least some important respects. This growing trend might serve to enhance the significance of international human rights norms for Canada.

Who Are Indigenous Peoples?

THE IDEA THAT INDIGENOUS PEOPLES HAVE RIGHTS REPLACES EARLY views of the place of Indigenous communities held in the colonial imagery. The doctrine of *terra nullius,* for instance, was based on assumptions that Indigenous peoples were less than humans, or "*homo nullius*," and that their lands were "empty." Similarly, the notion of *mare nullius* was used to declare the sea vacant of Indigenous tenure, perpetuating Western views that human interactions only occur in landscapes. Although the notion of *terra nullius* has slowly been eroded, failure to recognize Indigenous constructions of land and sea as a continuity have created a double burden for Indigenous peoples who are dependent upon marine environments but are excluded from enjoying sea rights (Mulrennan and Scott 2000). Furthermore, the held-over colonial views have normalized settlers' entitlement to land and marine resources. Thus, the idea of Indigenous rights presents conceptual difficulties for international law, beginning with the term "Indigenous peoples" itself. Who is Indigenous? Who can claim Indigenous rights? Who decides who is Indigenous? What attributes should represent the diversity of Indigenous peoples?

One of the most cited working definitions of Indigenous communities and tribal peoples was proposed by Jose R. Martinez Cobo, the first UN Special Rapporteur for the Sub-Commission on Prevention of Discrimination and Protection of Minorities, in his famous *Study on the Problem of Discrimination against Indigenous Populations* (1986). His working definition offers a number of basic ideas for defining Indigenous peoples, while at the same time recognizing their right to define for themselves who is Indigenous:

> Indigenous communities, peoples and nations are those which, having a historical continuity with pre-invasion and pre-colonial societies that developed on their territories, consider themselves distinct from other sectors of the societies now prevailing on those territories, or parts of them. (Martinez Cobo 1986/7/Add4)

The Martinez Cobo report further explains that Indigenous peoples are typically non-dominant sectors of society seeking to preserve their ethnic identity, and to sustain and transmit to future generations their ancestral territories and their ethnic identity as the basis of their continued existence as peoples. This report establishes that historical continuity may consist of the endurance—from an extended period back and reaching into the present—of one or more factors, including continuous and traditional land use and occupancy, cultural practices, and institutions (1986/7/Add4).

Although many have adopted the above working definition of Indigenous peoples, others have rejected it because it emphasizes historical continuity with pre-colonial societies and assumes that all Indigenous groups are necessarily committed to live as those societies did. More problematic perhaps is that the concept of traditional land use and occupancy freezes the nature of Indigenous peoples' relations to their lands. Increasingly, traditional land use and occupancy are also being drawn upon as a source of evidence for Indigenous communities that lack legal land titles to obtain recognition of their ancestral lands, as I will show in the last section of this chapter.

Moreover, the above definition assumes European invasion and conquest, often by military means, as part of the history of all Indigenous peoples. While these assumptions may apply to many Indigenous peoples in the Americas, other Indigenous groups signed treaties and made alliances with the European settlers, such as in Canada and the United States. Another problem with Martinez Cobo's definition arises when identifying the descendants of the "original inhabitants." In most parts of the world, descendants have undergone transformation and change in cultural identity over time, sometimes resulting in large populations of mixed ancestry. While the **Métis** people (of Native/European descent) of Canada consider themselves to be and are recognized by the government as Aboriginals, the Mestizo population (of Indigenous/Spanish descent) in most Latin American countries do not consider themselves Indigenous and are, in fact, the dominant population. On the other hand, while people of Micmac/African descent in Atlantic Canada may consider themselves Indigenous, they are not recognized by the government as such. Although the Martinez Cobo definition is commonly used, it is neither inclusive nor does it capture the complexity and diversity of Indigenous peoples' lives and experiences.

Another relevant definition crafted in the late 1980s, within the context of the General Conference of the International Labor Organization (ILO), can be found in **Convention 169**, a legal tool aimed at recognizing and protecting Indigenous rights. This instrument builds upon some of Martinez Cobo's criteria. Convention 169 applies to

> Tribal peoples in independent countries whose social, cultural and economic conditions distinguish them from other sections of the national community, and whose status is regulated wholly or partially by their own customs and traditions or by special laws or regulations. . . . (Office of the United Nations High Commissioner on Human Rights 1989)

Convention 169 also applies to

> Peoples in independent countries who are regarded as Indigenous on account of their descent from the populations who inhabited the country or a geographical region to which the country belonged at the time of conquest or colonization or the establishment of present state boundaries. . . . (Office of the United Nations High Commissioner on Human Rights 1989)

While Convention 169 distinguishes between tribal and Indigenous peoples, the difference between these two categories is unclear (Mills 2002, 51). For some countries, this issue is contentious because the term "peoples" reflects a difference in how international law should regard **Indigenous rights**. Arguably, in international law "all peoples" have the right to **self-determination** and secession, or the right to constitute a new national state. However, a closer look at the history of self-determination and the development of indigenous rights shows how member states of the UN have carefully excluded Indigenous peoples from the language of "all peoples." Some countries, such as the United States, continue to use the term "Indigenous groups" instead of Indigenous peoples, a choice reflecting the belief that Indigenous communities are like any other ethnic minority group (Lindroth 2006, 244). Canada, on the other hand, uses the term "Aboriginal peoples," a domestic-legal category that emphasizes the role of the state in granting Aboriginal rights.

Another criticism Convention 169 has faced concerns the emphasis given to the social, cultural, and economic differences between Indigenous peoples and the mainstream society. Because Indigenous peoples are often disadvantaged as a result of land dispossession and colonial policies that prevented them from participating in the mainstream economy, they exist in a vulnerable state that has been central to government policies and interventions, which, in turn, have had conflicting effects on the Indigenous communities. Often, these policies and interventions reflect the values and norms of the mainstream society rather than the needs and aspirations of Indigenous peoples. Non-governmental and Indigenous organizations have argued that, despite emphasizing the term "peoples," the Convention fails to firmly recognize Indigenous peoples' rights to self-determination by leaving too much authority over these peoples in the hands of the state (Saugee 1997, 365–76). Although considered a victory for many, the UNDRIP has faced criticism because it did not define Indigenous peoples but merely refers to the above definitions and the right to self-identification.

The Right to Self-Identification

Indigenous peoples have strenuously objected to any claims about an objective approach to self-identification and have instead favoured subjective self-identification. They argue that the question of who is and who is not Indigenous should be left to the Indigenous communities themselves rather than to the state or other official agencies. Indigenous organizations contend that a universal definition would violate their right to self-determination, including their right to define membership in their communities just as states determine membership through citizenship laws. Indigenous participants in the UN Working Group on the Rights of Indigenous Peoples consistently stressed the need for flexibility and respect for the right of each group to define itself according to its own specific criteria. Self-identification, the argument goes, is a flexible process that accounts for the variations of Indigenous identity across time and place. In contrast, a universal definition demands precision and certainty, which undermines the reality that group identities have evolved across time and vary from one locale to the next (Alfred 1999, 85).

In Canada and the United States, for example, membership has been vigorously contested. Colonial policies not only defined Indigenous identity but made it difficult for many Indigenous persons to maintain their identity, thus reducing the number of Indigenous people overall. Some Indigenous communities restrict membership to protect the value of benefits; others believe that strength is gained by increasing the number of Indigenous persons, which is in decline because of blood quantum requirements. In Canada, the best-known case of exclusion based on gender is the *Indian Act 1876*, the statute that concerns registered "Indians," their bands, and the reserve system. In defining who was and was not "Indian," the government took away self-determination from First Nations and inflicted racist and sexist policies that excluded First Nations women who married non-Indigenous men, and their children, from membership. Ironically, these same gender bias policies extended band membership to non-First Nations women who marry Indigenous men. When the *Indian Act* was modified in 1985 to eliminate this sexist legislation, many communities refused to welcome reinstated members because communities did not have enough resources to deal with more people. Furthermore, although this legislation was modified, an unstated paternity policy continues to exist; if a father does not sign his child's birth certificate, Aboriginal Affairs and Northern Development Canada assumes the child is non-Aboriginal (Green 2009). Thus, status is denied to the child. This means that Indigenous identity and membership continues to be grounded on colonial and gender bias assumptions.

Advocates of an objective-definition approach, on the other hand, argue that self-identification would, by accommodating a variety of groups and perspectives, destroy the coherence of Indigenous identity and the international Indigenous movement. From this perspective, a subjective approach relying solely on self-identification opens the door to numerous groups who may not need protection. From the state's perspective, the implementation of UNDRIP could open the door to too many claims that it is unwilling to address. Historically, the state has not been interested in expanding its obligation to Indigenous peoples, but rather to extinguishing it.

The battle over who defines Indigenous identity exposes a serious dilemma. On the one hand, a standard, rigid, universal definition could potentially lead to the exclusion of some Indigenous groups seeking protection. On the other hand, the lack of a universal definition could lead to the abuse of the concept, and potentially dilute the rights of Indigenous peoples (Colchester 2002). Certainly, not all marginalized groups would prefer to self-identify as Indigenous and may see advantages in assimilating into mainstream groups. Others such as the Kurds from South Kurdistan or some Hawaiians may feel that the Indigenous struggle is too parochial, seeking instead full national independence.

The above discussion illustrates that Indigenous peoples and their specific historical experiences are diverse, and no single definition seems capable of including them all. Thus, self-identification is crucial to defining who is Indigenous in the UNDRIP. The working definitions discussed above are relevant as a starting point and for establishing a dialogue about "who is Indigenous." Moreover, these working definitions have, in some cases, provided international support for some Indigenous peoples who desperately continue to struggle against colonization and land dispossession.

In sum, despite the diversity of Indigenous peoples' experiences, some of the key general elements that identify Indigenous peoples are (1) self-identification as the descendants of original inhabitants of a given territory, (2) a distinct collective history that can be traced through written or oral accounts, (3) cultural attachment to a particular area of land, (4) contingent vulnerability as a result of colonization, and (5) a desire of the people to continue to live as a distinct people according to their own evolving traditional formal and informal institutions, including Indigenous laws.

Indigenous Peoples and Self-Determination

THE RIGHTS OF INDIGENOUS PEOPLES HAVE EVOLVED SLOWLY, ALONG with the broader international movement for the protection of human rights. Although decolonization movements after World War II challenged the very idea of one people colonizing another, and of the imposition of an alien culture and political-administrative system by a dominant group, these ideas did not extend to Indigenous peoples (Sander 1995, 12–13). Far from being an oversight, the exclusion of Indigenous peoples from the right to self-determination has continued to reflect colonial ideas that the Indigenous were not considered humans, let alone "peoples." Since the 1960s—and owing in large part to sustained Indigenous advocacy by groups such as the Saami Council, an umbrella organization for Sámi organizations in Norway, Sweden, Finland, and Russia; the World Council of Indigenous Peoples, representing Indigenous peoples from New Zealand and the Americas; the International Treaty Council, representing Indigenous peoples who signed treaties; and the Inuit Circumpolar Conference, an umbrella organization for the Inuit of Russia, the United States, and Canada—a substantive body of international jurisprudence aimed at recognizing Indigenous peoplehood has emerged (Colchester 2002).

The right to Indigenous self-determination is considered to be the main tenet and symbol of the Indigenous movement (Daes 2003, 303). However, similar to Indigenous identity, the meaning of Indigenous self-determination is not only contested but also resisted by many states. Although the UNDRIP seems to push the envelope in articulating Indigenous self-determination, it limits this right to the extent and format that the international community of states has supported. As far as the Indigenous peoples' claim to self-determination is concerned, Article 3 of the UNDRIP states that "Indigenous peoples have the right to self-determination. By virtue of that right they freely determine their political status and freely pursue their economic, social and cultural development." In responding to governments' objection to this right, Article 46(1) notes that "nothing in this Declaration may be interpreted as implying for any State, people, group or person any right to engage in any activity or to perform any act contrary to the Charter of the United Nations or constructed as authorizing or encouraging any action which could dismember or impair totally or in part, the territorial integrity of political unity of sovereign and independent States." This means that Indigenous self-determination is qualified as a "domestic or internal" right that can be exercised only within the boundaries of the state.

While most Indigenous organizations do not intend to sever themselves from existing countries, they seek to exercise their right to self-determination in a form of free association with the state they live in. Indigenous visions of self-determination involve, among other things, the right to control territory, natural resources, social organization, and decision-making institutions in order to maintain cultures and ways of life.

In other words, Indigenous self-determination is a precondition to the exercising of other collective rights.

When the four countries that initially opposed the UN Declaration reversed their position, they qualified their support. The U.S. government, for example, noted the importance of lending support but emphasized a particular interpretation of the UNDRIP, specifically with regards to the rights to self-determination and to free, prior, and informed consent regarding any actions taking on Indigenous lands. The U.S. government argued that it wanted to develop a new understanding of self-determination specific to Indigenous peoples, one that can serve as the basis for recognition of "the inherent sovereign powers of self-governance." Regarding the right to free, prior, and informed consent, the U.S. government stated that, in its view, the provisions included in the UN Declaration "call for a process of meaningful consultation with Tribal leaders, but not necessarily the agreement of those leaders, before the actions addressed in those consultations are taken" (Obama 2011). The critical element here is "consultation," which diminishes the principle of free, prior, and informed "consent" included in the UNDRIP.

Similarly, the Canadian government noted that the Declaration is an "aspirational" document that did not change Canadian laws or concerns. Canada noted that serious issues remain regarding provisions dealing with lands, territories, and resources; free, prior, and informed consent when used as a veto; self-government without negotiation; intellectual property rights; military issues; and the need for balance among the rights and obligation of Indigenous peoples, the state, and third parties. Furthermore, the Canadian government stated that the UNDRIP will be interpreted "in a manner" that is consistent with the Constitution and legal framework (Aboriginal Affairs and Northern Development 2010).

Although both Canada and the United States have endorsed the Declaration, these countries continue to object to its main tenets. This is a contradiction, because the realization of Indigenous peoples' rights requires political will on the part of the state and the creation of appropriate mechanisms. If the ultimate protection of Indigenous peoples is to occur at the national level and requires the state's active involvement, then this support remains merely symbolic as it does not meaningfully change what governments have been doing in terms of Indigenous policies so far.

Policy versus Rights

HOW CAN INDIGENOUS RIGHTS BE ADVANCED? HOW CAN INDIGENOUS peoples' land rights be protected? As mentioned, protection of Indigenous peoples and their rights ultimately occurs at the national level and requires the state's active involvement. Around the world, states' responses to Indigenous demands vary. In some countries, governments have implemented policies accommodating some rights; and others have amended their constitutions to realize such rights. In other cases, the judiciary's proactive role and the civil society's intervention have been relevant in supporting the recognition of Indigenous rights. For example, in Canada the courts have played an important role in defining some Aboriginal rights by actively favouring policy over litigation. In Nicaragua, on the other hand, the constitution was modified in the late 1980s to recognize Indigenous autonomy. More recently, in the case of the Sumo of Nicaragua, the Inter-American Court of Human Rights (IACHR) has set a precedent for the recognition of Indigenous land rights. In this section, some of the relative benefits of two approaches, policy and rights, used to advance Indigenous rights are explored.

In Canada, the Supreme Court has played a relevant role in establishing tests for claiming Aboriginal rights as opposed to treaty rights, which flow from treaties signed with different First Nations.[1] The Court has also been relevant in defining the circumstances under which the government can infringe upon these rights (Xiu Woo 2011). Since the 1970s, however, the Canadian government has consistently favoured policy over rights. The Government of Canada's approach to the implementation of Indigenous self-government and negotiation of land claims is based on the recognition of the **inherent right** to self-government under section 35 of the *Constitution Act, 1982*. Recognition of this right is grounded on "the view that the Aboriginal peoples of Canada have the right to govern themselves in relation to matters that are internal to their communities; integral to their unique culture, identities, traditions, languages and institutions; and with respect to their special relationship to their land and resources." The goal of land claims is to obtain certainty of land ownership and use of land and natural resources by negotiating agreements and establishing a clearly defined package of benefits. Indigenous peoples wishing to negotiate land claims must prove the authenticity of their claims by demonstrating historical continuity with a pre-colonial past anchored in land use patterns and subsistence practices (Aboriginal Affairs and Northern Development 2010). Scholars have noted that if the inherent right to self-government is grounded on section 35, then it is severely limited as section 35 only "recognizes and affirms" Aboriginal rights (Isaac 1993).

Once land claims have been documented, the federal and provincial governments and the Indigenous nation involved initiate negotiations until they reach an agreement on self-government as opposed to self-determination, and on a package of specific benefits. This package of benefits usually involves (a) financial compensation in exchange for transferring Indigenous land rights to Canada, (b) federal government funding promises aimed at closing the social indicator gaps that exist between Indigenous peoples and non-Indigenous Canadians, and (c) Aboriginal rights to hunting and fishing. In terms of self-government, the matters that can be negotiated include membership, marriage, service delivery, internal elections, taxation, and the functioning of Indigenous governments. Although self-government can take different forms, all of them operate within the legal and political Canadian framework.

---

[1] The terms "Aboriginal peoples" and "First Nations" are used here when discussing the Canadian government's negotiation approach because this is the legal terminology recognized in Canada.

At first sight, this policy seems very generous; let us unpack some of its advantages before we discuss its limitations. It is cheaper to implement policies than it is to ask the courts to define Aboriginal rights. A wide range of issues can be negotiated, depending on the specific circumstances of Indigenous peoples. Negotiated agreements establish governments and industry responsibilities with regards to impact on local communities as a result of resource development. Furthermore, policy provides some avenues for Indigenous peoples to assume responsibilities over matters that are central to them, such as family and child services.

There are important limitations to policy as well. Land claims have become rather like real estate transactions, where the federal government provides financial compensation in exchange for extinguishing the land rights of Indigenous peoples. Thus, instead of securing their lands, Indigenous peoples received money and only secure some "usufruct rights," such as hunting and fishing. This means that Indigenous peoples can use only some of their traditional lands for the purpose of feeding their families. The commitments related to the transfer of funding for training, education, and other programs made by the federal government in most, if not all, land claims have not been fulfilled so far (Dewar 2009, 79). In 2006, the Government of Nunavut sued the Government of Canada for its failure to provide Nunavut with the means to ensure its economic, social, and cultural development (Tunngavik Incorporated 2007). In 2008, members of the Land Claim Agreements Coalition submitted a complaint to the United Nations Human Rights Committee (UNHRC) concerning the ongoing failure of the Government of Canada to fully implement 20 land claim agreements signed since 1975 (Land Claims Agreements Coalition 2008). In addition, although the Canadian government calls these agreements "modern treaties," these are no longer negotiated on a nation-to-nation basis, but on a tripartite basis in which the provincial government is also included in order to protect its interests. Furthermore, increasingly the government is delegating more of its responsibilities, including consultation, to industry whenever local communities may be affected by development.

With regards to self-government, critics have noted that this right has been reduced to a delegation of power to deliver services and regulate some internal affairs (Altamirano 2004; Green and Peach 2007). Moreover, as a right that is exercised within the framework of the *Constitution Act, 1982*, the inherent right to self-government does not mean that federal and provincial laws do not apply to Indigenous peoples and governments. Rather, these laws continue to apply to Aboriginal peoples or co-exist alongside Aboriginal laws, and in the case of conflict, federal and provincial laws prevail (Aboriginal Affairs and Northern Development 2010, Application of Laws).

Having discussed some of the advantages and disadvantages of the policy approach, the rights approach and the role of law in advancing Indigenous claims should be likewise examined. The Mayagna (Sumo) of *Awas Tingni v. Nicaragua* case and the IACHR's role in it is important for the development of legal standards recognizing the right of Indigenous peoples to "property" based on customary land use and occupancy. By granting the right to property to Indigenous peoples in this case, the concept of property was used to remedy the state's past injustices (Wainwright and Bryan 2009, 154).

In 1995, the Mayagna (Sumo) community of Awas Tingni learned of the Nicaraguan government's plan to grant a logging licence to a Korean lumber company on approximately 62 000 hectares of their land. The community decided to take the case to court, and claimed that Nicaragua had violated its land rights by granting a logging company a permit to log within the community's traditional sacred lands. In its defence, the Nicaraguan government claimed that Awas Tingni had neither legal property nor ancestral rights to the land in question, because the Mayagna were part of a wider Indigenous people (the Sumo), which were located elsewhere. Relying on funding from the World Bank, the Mayagna embarked on a process of mapping their lands with the purpose of proving the authenticity of their claims. Cartographic representations and ethnographic studies supported the claim that the Mayagna had indeed used their territory from time immemorial. More importantly, the Inter-American Court decided that proof of traditional land use and occupancy was sufficient for Indigenous communities lacking legal land titles to obtain recognition of their property (Altamirano-Jiménez, 2012). This is very similar to the test to prove Aboriginal rights established by the Supreme Court of Canada. In the Awas Tingni case, the Inter-American Court found Nicaragua guilty of violating several articles of the American Convention on Human Rights. The Nicaraguan government was ordered to demarcate and title the land as property of the Awas Tingni community. However, the court was careful not to explicitly invoke the notion of reparation of past injustices.

A similar argument had been made regarding the *Omniyak v. Canada* 1990 case in which Chief Bernard Ominayak of the Lubicon Lake Band brought a complaint to the UNHRC alleging that Canada had denied his people's right to self-determination, including the right to "freely dispose of their natural wealth and resources." Specifically, Chief Ominayak argued that individual band members' right to hunt, trap, and fish in their traditional lands is recognized under the *Indian Act* and Treaty 8 and is essential to their subsistence economy. However, oil and gas development on their lands was threatening the band's economic base. The UNHRC found that Canada had violated the rights of Lubicon, yet it argued that it was up to Canada to decide the best way to solve this conflict (Lubicon Lake Band versus Canada, 1990).

In both cases, the rights of Indigenous peoples were affirmed; such affirmation can be considered a legal victory. In the case of Awas Tingni, the Inter-American Court's decision not only affirmed Indigenous right but also set an international legal precedent for Indigenous peoples around the world by establishing that the benefits of property are a human right. In this sense, court decisions can shape international law regarding Indigenous rights to land and natural resources. Moreover, the courts could also force the state to adopt specific measures for the protection of Indigenous rights (Anaya and Grossman 2002). Thus, litigation can open new avenues for understanding Indigenous rights and their status in the world. Arguably, this may be one of the reasons why the Canadian government favours the policy approach.

There are, however, significant disadvantages of the rights approach. It is very lengthy and expensive. In most cases, Indigenous claimants need to borrow money to pay for lawyers' services and ethnographic studies aimed at proving the authenticity of their claims. Although the court decisions are binding, the state continues to be a key player in implementing the appropriate measures to recognize Indigenous rights as seen in the Awas Tingni and Ominayak cases. The notion of granting property rights to remedy the state's past injustices is also problematic, because it further empowers the state to assimilate Indigenous peoples into its own norms and laws by creating new property regimes that might freeze Indigenous relations to their lands. For instance, although property was considered a remedy and a human right in the Awas Tingni case, state officials have often accused the Mayagna community of wanting to benefit from logging by arguing it is not "customary land use." In other words, the concept of rights and international law are not enough to overcome injustices or to reverse the social and economic disparities caused by colonization (Altamirano-Jiménez, 2012).

In both the policy and the rights approach, the state continues to play a key role in implementing policies and measures defining how Indigenous peoples can enjoy rights. Thus, it remains open to question whether or not the UNDRIP will provide means to address these power hierarchies between the state and Indigenous peoples.

Conclusion

THIS CHAPTER SHOWED THAT THE CONCEPT OF INDIGENOUS PEOPLES and the evolution of Indigenous rights are a dynamic and contested field of politics, which is simultaneously local and global. At the global level, the approval of the UNDRIP in September 2007 ended more than four decades of international debate. At the local level, resistance to these rights has been championed by states, which continue to ignore their key role in reversing the social, political, and economic disparities caused by colonization. One of the most controversial issues arising from the UNDRIP concerns who is Indigenous and Indigenous self-determination. The chapter also discussed the relative benefits of the policy and rights approaches.

Summary

The chapter:

- Examined competing definitions of Indigenous identity
- Discussed the right to self-identification and membership
- Analyzed contested understandings of the right to self-determination
- Explored the relative benefits of negotiation and litigation

Discussion Questions

1. Who is Indigenous?
2. Is self-identification better than objective criteria for determining membership?
3. Why is the concept of Indigenous peoples so contested?
4. Why is the Indigenous right to self-determination controversial?

References

Aboriginal Affairs and Northern Development. 2010. *The Government of Canada's Approach to Implementation of the Inherent Right and the Negotiation of Aboriginal Self-Government.* http://www.aadnc-aandc.gc.ca/eng/1309374239861.

———. 2010. Government of Canada Statement of Support to the UNDRIP. http://www.aadnc-aandc.gc.ca/eng/1309374239861.

Al Faruque, Abdullah and Najnin Begum. 2004. "Conceptualizing Indigenous Peoples' Rights: an Emerging New Category of Third Generation of Rights." *Asia-Pacific Journal of Human Rights and the Law* 2: 1–29.

Alfred, Taiaiake. 1999. *Peace, Power and Righteousness: An Indigenous Manifesto.* New York: Oxford University Press.

Altamirano-Jiménez, Isabel. 2004. "North American First Peoples: Slipping up into Market Citizenship?" *Citizenship Studies* 8(4): 349–65.

———. 2012. "Mapeando las fronteras indígenas del desarrollo en la Mosquitia" [Mapping Indigenous Lands and Development in the Atlantic Coast of Nicaragua]. In *Conflictos Étnicos en las Américas* Vol. II, edited by Natividad Guitérrez Chong. Quito, Ecuador: Abya Yala.

Anaya, James and Claudio Grossman. 2002. "The Case of Awas Tingni v. Nicaragua: A New Step in the International Law of Indigenous Peoples." *Arizona Journal of International and Comparative Law* 19(1): 1–15.

Canadian Human Rights Commission. 2010. http://www.chrc-ccdp.ca/publications/ar_2010_ra/page4-eng.aspx?print=1.

Colchester, Marcus. 2002. "Indigenous Rights and the Collective Conscious." *Anthropology Today* 18(1): 1–3.

Daes, Erica-Irene. 2002. "Article 3 of the Draft UN Declaration on the Rights of Indigenous Peoples: Obstacles and Consensus." Paper presented at the Rights and Democracy Seminar of Experts on the Right to Self-Determination of Indigenous Peoples, New York.

Dewar, Barry. 2009. "Nunavut and the Nunavut Land Claim Agreements: An Unresolved Relationship." *Policy Option*: 74–9. http://www.tunngavik.com/wp-content/uploads/2010/04/nlca-nunavut-dewar-2009.pdf.

Green, Joyce. 2009. "Parsing Identity and Identity Politics." *International Journal of Critical Indigenous Studies* 2(2): 36–46.

Green, Joyce and Ian Peach. 2007. "Beyond 'Us' and 'Them': Prescribing Post-Colonial Politics and Policy in Saskatchewan." In *Belonging? Diversity, Recognition and Shared Citizenship in Canada*, edited by Keith Banting et al. Montreal: Institute for Research on Public Policy, 263–84.

Isaac, Thomas. 1993. "Balancing Rights: The Supreme Court of Canada, R.V. Sparrow and the Future of Aboriginal Rights." *Canadian Journal of Native Studies* 13(2): 199–219.

Kingsbury, Benedict. 1998. "Indigenous Peoples in International Law: A Constructivist Approach to the Asian Controversy." *The American Journal of International Law* 92.

———. 2001. "Reconciling Five Competing Conceptual Structures of Indigenous Peoples' Claims in International and Comparative Law." In *Peoples' Rights*, edited by Philip Alston. Oxford: Oxford University Press.

Land Claims Coalition. 2008. *Honouring the Spirit of Modern Treaties: Closing the Loopholes.* http://www.parl.gc.ca/39/2/parlbus/commbus/senate/com-e/abor-e/rep-e/rep05may08-e.pdf.

Lindroth, Marjo. 2006. "Indigenous-State Relations in the UN: Establishing the Indigenous Forum." *Polar Record* 42(222): 238–48.

Lubicon Lake Band versus Canada. 1990. University of Minnesota Human Rights Library. http://www1.umn.edu/humanrts/undocs/session45/167-1984.htm.

Martinez Cobo, José. 1986. *Study of the Problem of Discrimination against Indigenous Populations.* UN Doc. E/CN.4/Sub.2/1986/7/Add4.

Mills, John. 2002. "Legal Constructions of Cultural Identity in Latin America: An Argument Against Defining Indigenous Peoples." *Texas Hispanic Journal of Law and Policy* 8(49): 46–77.

Mulrennan, Monica E. and C.H. Scott. 2000. "*Mare Nullius:* Indigenous Rights in Saltwater Environments." *Development and Change* 31(3): 681–708.

Obama, Barack. 2011. "Statement of Support to the UNDRIP." http://Indigenousfoundations.arts.ubc.ca/?id=1097.

Office of the United Nations High Commissioner on Human Rights. 1989. *Indigenous and Tribal Peoples Convention Num. 169.* http://www.ohch.org/english/law/Indigenous.htm.

Sanders, Douglas. 1995. "State Practice and the United Nations Draft Declaration on the Rights of Indigenous Peoples." In *Becoming Visible—Indigenous Politics and Self-Government*, edited by Terje Brantenberg, Janne Hansen, and Henry Minde. Tromsø, Norway: The University of Tromsø, Sámi dutkamiid guovddáš—Centre for Sámi Studies.

Saugee, Dean B. 1997. "Human Rights of Indigenous People: Will the United States Rise to the Occasion?" *American Indian Law Review* 21: 365–7.

Tunngavik Incorporated. 2006. http://www.tunngavik.com/.../nti-launches-lawsuit-against-government-of-canada-for-breach-of-contract/.

Wainwright, Joel and Joe Bryan. 2009. "Cartography, Territory, Property: Postcolonial Reflections on Indigenous Counter-Mapping in Nicaragua and Belize." *Cultural Geographies* 16: 153–78.

Xiu Woo, Grace Li. 2011. *Ghost Dancing with Colonialism.* Vancouver: UBC Press.

Further Readings

Anaya, S. James. 1996. *Indigenous Peoples in International Law.* New York: Oxford University Press.

Corntassel, Jeff A. 2003. "Who Is Indigenous? 'Peoplehood' and Ethnonationalist Approaches to Rearticulating Indigenous Identity." *Nations and Ethnic Politics* 9(1): 75–100.

Läm, Miaban. 2000. *At the Edge of the State: Indigenous Peoples and Self-Determination.* Ardsley, NY: Transnational Publishers.

Niezen, Ronald. 2003. *The Origins of Indigenism: Human Rights and the Politics of Identity.* Berkeley, CA: University of California Press.

Weblinks

Office of the United Nations High Commissioner for Human Rights
www.ohchr.org/EN/Pages/WelcomePage.aspx

International Labour Organization
www.ilo.org/public/english/region/ampro/mdtsanjose/Indigenous/derecho .htm

Aboriginal Affairs and Northern Development Canada (The Royal Commission Report on the Aboriginal Peoples of Canada)
www.aadnc-aandc.gc.ca/eng/1307458586498

Assembly of First Nations
www.afn.ca/

CHAPTER **17**

A GENEALOGY OF POVERTY

MALINDA S. SMITH

Learning Objectives

- Explains the paradox of poverty amidst plenty

- Analyzes the impact of space, race, and gender on poverty and inequality

- Maps the social dimensions of poverty and why the social matters

- Examines 50 years of global policies to "make poverty history"

- Discusses the implications of the 2008 financial crisis on poverty eradication

Introduction

The stubborn persistence of poverty in a global era reinforces Henry George's observation made over a century ago: "The association of poverty with progress is the great enigma of our times" (George 1880, 6). George's observation was prophetic of today. Never before has the world created so much wealth or been more capable of a more fair and equitable distribution of that wealth. Yet the current era of globalization is characterized by a "paradox of plenty" (Brodie 2004): increased wealth creation is accompanied by rising levels of poverty and destitution, which are spatialized, gendered, and racialized. By the late twentieth century, the dominant trend was income concentration at the very top and a widening gap between rich and poor countries. In the aftermath of the 2008 financial crisis, the worst economic shock since the Great Depression of the 1930s, the social terrain is marked by deepening income inequality, declining job security, declining wages, and increasing poverty and vulnerability (UN 2011; ILO 2011, 2010). While scholars, policy-makers, and activists differ on how to conceptualize this polarity—for example, global "winners" and "losers" (Kennedy 1993), "global apartheid" (Booker and Minter 2001; Bond 2006, 2004), or the "99% and 1%"—there is recognition that poverty and inequality exacerbate social divisions within and across geopolitical spaces and, in the twenty-first century, they stubbornly remain a political, economic, and social issue.

This chapter explores various meanings and dimensions of poverty. It has several objectives. First, it provides a genealogy of poverty, mapping its contested conceptions, from low income and consumption to notions of human development, social capital, and social exclusion. Second, the chapter explores the social dimensions of poverty, which have often been overlooked in more conventional analyses. Third, it examines efforts to rethink poverty as if these social dimensions mattered. Finally, the chapter concludes with a brief survey of proposals to ameliorate poverty and to achieve what might be called a new "global social contract."

Defining Poverty

AS WITH SO MANY CRITICAL CONCEPTS IN THE SOCIAL SCIENCES AND humanities, the meanings of poverty are contested and have varied over time and space. Definitions of "poverty" are shaped by notions of civilization, cultural norms, and values (Bush 2007). Differences arise over how poverty is defined and measured, as well as over the need for and the nature of the policies designed to reduce and, ultimately, eradicate it. Understandings of poverty are shaped by the unit of analysis and by space, time, and severity. The unit of analysis may be an individual, a social group (grouped by gender, age, or race, for example), a country, a region, or the globe. The spatial dimensions of poverty include the incidence and severity of poverty within countries, such as between rural and urban areas, and across global regions, such as between North and South. Poverty is shaped by time, with conditions of poverty being temporary, chronic, and intergenerational. Another dimension of poverty relates to its intensity or severity, such as between relative deprivation and absolute destitution. What any definition of poverty minimally entails is recognition "that significant numbers of people are living in intolerable circumstances where starvation is a constant threat, sickness is a familiar companion, and oppression is a fact of life" (Kanbur and Squire 1999, 1).

Global poverty and inequality often are discussed in tandem, but they are conceptually distinct. Global poverty focuses attention on basic needs, such as food, clean water, and shelter and relative standards of well-being. Global poverty is a problem because people are living below subsistence, in conditions of immeasurable suffering, and this negatively affects their life chances. Ultimately, global poverty is a profound waste of human potential.

Global inequality refers to the skewed distribution worldwide of income, consumption, and other indicators of socio-economic well-being. Income and consumption are unequally distributed both within and between the poor countries in the South and the rich countries in the North, and this concentration of wealth is deepening. Inequality thus calls into question the fairness of the global economy and the legitimacy of institutions of global governance. The two concepts—poverty and inequality—are interconnected insofar as a major factor in the increase in global poverty is unequal distribution of wealth and power, including access to and control of resources, such as land and water, as well as labour power and mobility (Bush 2007, xiii, 81–114). Both concepts pose ethical challenges for academics, policy-makers, non-governmental organizations, and social justice activists committed to a more just world order. And this is precisely the challenge posed to the world's political and corporate leaders by contemporary social movements—among them, the Occupy Wall Street movement, the Indignados and Youth Without a Future in Spain, the Kitchenware Revolution in Iceland, the landless movements in Brazil and Mozambique, and the growing anti-austerity movement, for example, in Greece and Chile. Such movements have prompted such influential global organizations as the World Economic Forum and the Organisation for Economic Co-operation and Development (OECD) to conclude that inequality is one of the most pressing issues confronting policy-makers in the early twenty-first century. Poverty and inequality threaten political stability around the world and the recovery of the global economy (Stewart 2012).

Income inequality between rich and poor countries continues to increase in the twenty-first century. The income gap between the world's rich and poor countries was 3:1 in 1820, 35:1 by 1950, 74:1 by 1997, and 82:1 by 2002. While global per capita output has risen by 90 percent over the past 30 years, this is not the case for Africa, where the real per capita income has declined. It is now lower than it was in 1970. Africa is home to most of the countries in which at least 50 percent of the population lives below the poverty line (World Bank 2007). The world's most unequal countries are in South and Central America and Central Africa, including Honduras, Guatemala, Colombia, the Central African Republic, and Bolivia (Luhby 2011). By contrast, the world's countries with the least amount of inequality include Scandinavian countries,

Japan, and the Czech Republic. While the United States was among the top three most unequal OECD countries in 2011, inequality in Canada was growing four times faster than in its southern neighbour (Stewart 2012; OECD 2011).

While the data for the Middle East and Latin America are less grim, they do show that per capita income in these regions is stagnant or growing at a pace that is significantly lower than in the global North. In Asia, often advanced as the good news story for regional economic development, the picture is uneven. China and India, which have experienced remarkable economic growth in the past decade, have experienced a deepening gap between the very rich and the rest. The majority of the world's poor live in India and rural China. In South Asia, home to 515 million poor people—more than the populations of Canada, the United States, and Mexico combined—the outlook is bleak. Poverty is concentrated in rural areas and primarily affects women, Indigenous peoples, and ethnic minorities, who often face racial and cultural discrimination and lack access to land, water, and social services (Thapa 2004).

Diverse Perspectives on Poverty

THROUGHOUT HISTORY, STUDENTS OF POLITICS, PHILOSOPHERS, AND economists, among others, have tried to make sense of poverty. In *Leviathan* (1651), philosopher Thomas Hobbes suggests that an individual's consent to a social contract would enable him or her to escape a life that was "poor, nasty, brutish, and short." A supreme authority would guarantee civil order, industry, and the conditions for wealth creation. In *The Wealth of Nations* (1776), political economist Adam Smith argued that national wealth was created through a market-based economy, free trade, and an "invisible hand" that would ensure balance within the economic order. By contrast, in *Capital* (1867), Karl Marx saw neither an authoritarian regime nor an invisible hand as necessary or sufficient for understanding the contradictory tendencies in the accumulation of capital that led to the creation of wealth for a few and, simultaneously, the impoverishment of the majority.

The examples of the late Mother Teresa, the "Saint of the Gutter," and various Roman Catholic friars and Buddhist monks draw attention to non-materialist conceptions of poverty. A spiritual understanding of poverty may require a vow of poverty, which is a voluntary, personal renunciation of private and communal material property as a means to achieving well-being. Ethical conceptions of poverty may entail judgments about "moral bankruptcy" and assumptions that an individual's laziness or personal choices lead to debilitating vices, such as gambling or addictions, and, ultimately, to poverty. Conversely, absolute destitution and starvation can lead to crime, and ethicists, writers, and playwrights—for example, the classic works of Charles Dickens' *Oliver Twist* (1838) and Victor Hugo's *Les Misérables* (1862)—have challenged us to consider whether it is best to understand thievery in such cases as a personal choice and immorality or the agonizing outcome of structural inequities. Some conceptions of poverty, thus, draw our attention to voluntary action and personal choice as causes of poverty, while other conceptions point to structural and societal factors that impose limits on escaping poverty.

Understanding the "who" of poverty also has shifted over time and space. In the Middle Ages, for example, there was a social class of paupers whose well-being partly depended on a sense of moral obligation in their fellow citizens; paupers met or supplemented their basic needs through the charity of churches or private philanthropy. There were moral underpinnings to the early nineteenth century **Poor Laws**, which were reproduced in the late twentieth century's notion of "workfare." First introduced in the United Kingdom, the Poor Laws served as a way of getting the poor off the streets and into poorhouses, where they would be taught the "value of work" and thus avoid laziness or vagrancy. Similarly, workfare, first introduced in Minnesota and then pursued by U.S. President Bill Clinton in the mid-1990s, aimed to get the poor off welfare, and to discipline them by making the receipt of welfare contingent on performing some form of work. The poor themselves were often blamed for their plight, rather than economic crises, historical and structural inequities, or social exclusion.

Since the mid-1940s, the International Monetary Fund (IMF) and the World Bank have adopted a narrow conception of poverty, based primarily on economic indicators. Poverty was conceptualized in terms of gross national product (GNP), household income, consumption, and monetary access to the market. The World Bank defines poverty as "the inability to attain a minimum standard of living." This minimum standard of living benchmark was further subdivided into two other criteria: (1) the ability to purchase minimum daily nutritional requirements as determined by the society in which one lives, and (2) the ability to meet basic needs that are shaped by an assessment of "the cost of participating in the everyday life of society" (World Bank 1990, 26). In both cases, the World Bank prioritized income and consumption over broader notions of social well-being. In the 1990s, the World Bank and the IMF reluctantly acknowledged that their post–World War II development strategies had failed to reduce poverty or limit the economically and socially polarizing impact of economic crises and austerity policies. Increased attention was placed on the social dimensions of poverty and on pro-poor economic growth.

Social Dimensions of Poverty

POVERTY IS A COMPLEX, MULTICAUSAL PHENOMENA, WHICH IS SPA-tialized, gendered, and racialized worldwide. Notions of poverty take into account social well-being and involve comparisons between (and within) different countries and regions. Relative and absolute conceptions of poverty can be distinguished. **Relative poverty** takes into account the unequal distribution of income within a given society. Roach and Roach (1972, 23) suggest that relative poverty relates to those at "the bottom segment of the income distribution." A person may be able to acquire adequate food, clothing, clean water, and shelter but this exhausts her or his resources, leaving nothing for other things, such as telephone, transportation, or even reading materials. Trying to capture the cross-cultural variations in the daily lived experiences of the poor is difficult. Can we compare—and if so, how—deprivation in an affluent society such as Canada with, for example, the experience in a relatively impoverished society such as Haiti? In Canada and the United States, some people are poor relative to others in these societies. However, the poor in the North American region may be considered wealthy in relation to the poor in South Asia. **Absolute poverty**, on the other hand, measures physical deprivation. In 1978, World Bank president Robert McNamara coined the concept to characterize a condition "so limited by malnutrition, illiteracy, disease, squalid surroundings, high infant mortality, and low life expectancy as to be beneath any reasonable definition of human decency" (quoted in Singer 1979, 158). Absolute poverty has at its "absolutist core" the belief that if there is hunger or starvation, avoidable disease, lack of access to education, or a life of shame, then it does not "matter what the relative picture looks like" (Sen 1983).

Despite claims of the "death of distance" accompanying globalization, physical and social geography continue to matter in global mappings of the incidence and severity of poverty. Some 50 percent of the world's population, roughly 3 billion people, live on less than $2.50 a day (UNDP 2012) and this economic insecurity gives rise to significant migration, with some 3 million people annually migrating from poor to rich countries, and even greater numbers between poor countries such as from Bangladesh to India, or from Egypt to the Persian Gulf states (World Bank 2004; Population Reference Bureau 2006, 2005). The United Nations predicts this number will increase by 2.2 million every year until 2050 (Blair 2007). The **urbanization of poverty** is expected to increase as one in two people are born into urban spaces. As greater numbers of the world's poor become slum dwellers, the urban poor pay an urban penalty with declining access to basic needs (UN Habitat 2010/2011). The highest percentage of rural poor is concentrated in Asia (633 million), followed by sub-Saharan Africa (204 million), and Latin America and the Caribbean (76 million). While East Asia has the smallest number of rural poor, in Eastern and Central Europe there is a ruralization of poverty (Ravallion, Chen, and Sangraula 2007).

Poverty is also shaped by a complex intersection of gender and age. Some 70 percent of those living in extreme poverty are girls and women (UN 1995a, 4), reinforcing the **feminization of poverty**. According to Nilüfer Cagatay (1998, 3), the feminization of poverty is a short-hand concept that captures at least three things: first, there is a higher *incidence* of poverty among women; second, there is greater *severity* in the experience of poverty by women; and, third, the incidence of women's poverty is *increasing* at a faster rate when compared with the incidence among men. Women are disadvantaged in both urban and rural areas in their access to nutrition, education, health services, and employment and wages. This disadvantage arises from at least three overlapping factors: first, the rise in the number of female-headed households; second, cultural factors that shape intra-household and labour market inequalities among women and men; and, third, neo-liberal macroeconomics, such as structural adjustment programs (SAPs), which have disproportionately harmed the well-being of girls and women (Moghaden 2005).

Both the very old and the very young, especially girls and women, are adversely affected by poverty. There are some 2.2 billion children in the world and almost 50 percent of them live in poverty, with the majority located in the global South (UNDP 2012; UNICEF 2005). Annually, an astonishing 1.4 million children die from a lack of access to safe drinking water and adequate sanitation, and one in seven have no access to health services. UNICEF names this global phenomenon "childhood under threat," with young lives shaped by silent and forgotten killers: poverty, conflict, and preventable diseases such as HIV/AIDS, malaria, and pneumonia. Stolen childhood results when young lives are marked by the intersection of poverty, violence, exploitation, and abuse. This includes the human trafficking and sexual exploitation of children (often, but not exclusively, young girls), indentured and forced child labour, or the kidnapping of children to serve as soldiers or to become "bush" or "rebel wives" and, in turn, give birth to further stigmatized "rebel babies" (Baldi and Mackenzie 2007).

Gender and age also intersect in efforts to combat poverty. In its 2007 report, UNICEF notes that "gender equality produces a double dividend: it benefits both women and children. Healthy, educated and empowered women have healthy, educated and confident daughters and sons. The amount of influence women have over the decisions in the household has been shown to positively impact the nutrition, health care and education of their children" (UNICEF 2007, 2–3). Gender equality not only positively correlates with the well-being of children, but "without it, it will be impossible to create a world of equity, tolerance and shared responsibility—a world that is fit for children."

An under-theorized area in the international literature is the **racialization of poverty** and global inequality (Kothari 2006; Razack 2004). Manning Marable suggests the problem may be understood as one "of global apartheid. the racialized division and stratification of resources, wealth, and power that separates" the world's rich, located primarily in the global North, "from the billions of mostly black, brown, indigenous, undocumented immigrant and poor people across the planet" (Marable 2004). The world witnessed the ugly intersection of race, poverty, and marginality when Hurricane Katrina devastated the city of New Orleans and part of the Gulf Coast of the United States on August 29, 2005, exposing Third World conditions within the so-called First World. The slow response of the Bush administration to the plight of those whose lives were devastated by Katrina exposed what some critics refer to as the "two Americas"—one made up of those who are rich and mostly white, and the other made up of those who are poor and mostly racialized minorities, such as blacks and Latinos.

Stephen Lewis, former UN special envoy for HIV/AIDS, argues that the epidemic's devastating impact on Africa has not been taken seriously by Western countries because of silent racism. According to Lewis, "In my soul, I honestly believe that an unthinking strain of subterranean racism is the only way to explain the moral default of the developed world, in refusing to provide the resources which could save the mothers of Africa" (Lewis 2002, 4; Kubacki 2006). Lewis argued that it is this unacknowledged racism and the way it intersects with poverty that also led to the failure to act to prevent the 1994 genocide in Rwanda. Lewis's view echoes that of Lt.-General Roméo Dallaire, who led the UN peacekeeping mission to Rwanda when the international community withdrew its forces as the genocide was under way. In his memoirs, Dallaire (2003) attributes the genocide to xenophobia: the failure to protect was shaped by racism and global indifference to Rwanda's impoverished people. Lewis and Dallaire both named what few social scientists dare admit—Rwandans might have fared better if they were white and European or if they had strategic resources such as oil.

Poverty as if the Social Mattered

OFFICIAL DEFINITIONS OF POVERTY BEGAN TO BROADEN IN THE 1990S with the introduction by the United Nations Development Programme (UNDP) of the idea of **human development**. It drew attention to "the social" in development and provided an understanding of development and poverty beyond economic indicators and basic needs. This change in thinking was strongly influenced by Nobel Prize winner Amartya Sen and his influential book *Development as Freedom* (1999). In it, he argued, "Development requires the removal of major sources of unfreedom: poverty as well as tyranny, poor economics as well as systemic social deprivation, neglect of public facilities as well as intolerance or over-activity of repressive states" (1999, 3). Similarly, the UNDP's conception of human development prioritized non-monetary and social well-being indicators, such as access to health care and knowledge, political and cultural freedoms, and participation in the everyday life of the community. Given the shared aim of expanding capabilities, both the World Bank and the UNDP came to conceive of development as freedom. However, where the World Bank focuses almost exclusively on economic freedom and financial and material well-being, the UNDP tries to capture a broader conception of freedom, one that is inclusive of social, political, and cultural freedom, as well as notions of social citizenship rights.

By the mid-1990s, conceptions of poverty also encompassed an understanding of risk and vulnerability as determinants of transient or chronic poverty. One form of vulnerability arises from precarious employment, income, and living standards. Vulnerability also arises from the lack of social and political rights that create conditions of fear and insecurity. Risks can arise from complex factors, including environmental and health hazards, such as crop failure and famine; personal insecurity, such as sexual exploitation or land eviction; and macroeconomic shocks. Those with more resources are better able to deal with exposure to risk, and have greater access to risk-coping mechanisms, including social safety nets.

The concept of social capital also enhanced thinking about poverty in the late twentieth century (Bourdieu 1986; Coleman 1988; Fine 2001a). The concept suggests that "relationships matter" and that "who" we know constitutes a kind of capital. While the debate about the relevance of social capital for development began in academic circles in France and the United States in the 1970s and 1980s, a variety of actors soon picked up the concept and used it in different ways. The World Bank and other international and regional bodies, such as the OECD, initially embraced the concept of social capital as a way of integrating social theory with economic theory, claiming that social well-being depended on economic development (Field 2003, 9; Woolcock and Narayan 2000). Promoted by the World Bank, social capital was soon associated with civil society organizations, which were considered to be essential to socially inclusive policy processes; democratic accountability; and the success of a host of good governance and anti-poverty initiatives. Proponents suggest that social capital is the "missing link" in development and anti-poverty discourse, policy, and practice. Critics, however, argue that the World Bank's conception of social capital in development underplays the unequal distribution of wealth as well as social relations of domination and exploitation in the accumulation of financial and social capital (Fine 2001b).

The concept of **social exclusion** widened the conceptual lens through which poverty is understood, although it also reinforces the different ways in which poverty is conceptualized in the global South and the global North. Social exclusion is much broader than income poverty. Earlier conceptions of poverty referred to limited material—social and cultural resources necessary for a person's participation in a "minimum acceptable way of life"—as determined by the states in which they live (Schultz 2002, 120). The concept of social exclusion first emerged in French policy discourse as a way of addressing "new poverty"—that is, the problems that arise from inadequate social safety nets for the chronically unemployed and under-employed. Social exclusion offers a broader understanding of the multiple forms of social disadvantage, including income, social, and, cultural, and, hence, extends to how we think of social citizenship.

Mixed Results on a New "Global Social Contract"

IN 2004, THEN BRAZILIAN PRESIDENT LUIZ INÁCIO LULA DA SILVA called for a new global social contract to eradicate hunger and improve social well-being (da Silva 2004). As this chapter describes, social progress toward a new global social contract on anti-poverty has been decidedly mixed over the last decade. Successive waves of economic globalization, failed anti-poverty strategies, and the many unfulfilled international promises to eradicate poverty have contributed to the problem deepening worldwide. The modern anti-poverty agenda gained international prominence with at least two developments in the mid-1960s. First, United States President Lyndon B. Johnson declared a "war on poverty" in his State of the Union address of January 8, 1964. Second, Robert McNamara made global poverty eradication the priority of his World Bank presidency. Over the 40 years since then, a number of global commitments have been made to reduce poverty, including the international development targets (IDTs) set at Copenhagen in 1995, the introduction of Poverty Reduction Strategy Papers in 1999, and the Millennium Development Goals (MDGs) in 2000. Oxfam International (2000) characterized this history as one of "missed targets" and "broken promises."

The shift to a social and a pro-poor agenda required rethinking the anti-poverty strategy that had dominated policy thinking since World War II. This strategy was heavily influenced by neo-classical economics and the Washington Consensus (Fine et al. 2001). The World Bank and the IMF promoted economic growth as the strategy by which development would occur. This strategy at best prioritized "getting the market fundamentals right" and, at worst, showed an indifference to poverty, inequality, and social well-being (Taylor 2006). Whatever the country, this one-size-fits-all strategy promoted a series of neo-liberal policy prescriptions that called for deregulation, currency devaluation, trade and financial liberalization, privatization, and reduction of public enterprises. Little to no distinction was drawn between public enterprises that performed a primarily social function and those that did not. One devastating result was drastic cuts to public expenditure in the areas of health, education, and social services, which were further exacerbated by the introduction of user fees that restricted access to the poor, especially in rural areas.

The consensus at the 1995 World Summit for Social Development (WSSD) in Copenhagen, however, was that the social aspects of poverty mattered. The gathering called for greater social investment to reduce poverty, illiteracy, and health deprivation. Some 117 governments reached consensus on a global agenda for poverty reduction. They committed to reducing global poverty by half by 2015. The WSSD's Declaration and Program of Action characterized poverty reduction as "an ethical, social, political and economic imperative of human kind." The WSSD also endorsed the 20/20 Initiative, which called for South governments to spend 20 percent of their domestic budgets and North governments to spend 20 percent of their foreign aid budgets on funding anti-poverty and social programs in education and health. A year later, the "donor's club," constituted primarily by the Development Assistance Committee (DAC) of the OECD, affirmed the Copenhagen consensus on poverty reduction. The DAC also committed to related targets in areas of social well-being, including literacy, education, and health services. In the lead up to the 2012 UN Conference on Sustainable Development (Rio+20) governments identified social progress as one of the three fundamental pillars of sustainable development (UN 2011, iii–iv).

Despite a plethora of declarations, commitments, and targets over the past two decades, uneven progress, at best, has been made in eradicating global poverty. The intransigence led to global social protests from Seattle in 1999, to the "Make Poverty History" campaign unveiled at the 2006 G8 Meeting at Gleneagles, Scotland, to the Occupy protests in 2011 and 2012. Confronted with the profound policy failures, local and global protests, and the call for their dismantlement, the World Bank and the IMF unveiled a new "pragmatic neo-liberalism," which included elements of a social agenda. Beginning in 1999, the policy shift included the IMF's adopting poverty reduction as one of its core objectives, and the release by the president of the World Bank of a *Comprehensive Development Framework*, which has been called a "new development paradigm" that underwrites a new "architecture of aid" (Wolfensohn and Fischer 2000). Subsequently, the World Bank placed emphasis on pro-poor growth (Smith 2006). The World Bank and the IMF also adopted Poverty Reduction Strategy Papers (PRSPs) in 1999 as a major element of their new development thinking. The IMF describes PRSPs as "the macroeconomic, structural and social policies and programs that a country will pursue over several years to promote broad-based growth and reduce poverty" (IMF 2005). PRSP principles include local ownership, partnership among stakeholders, enhanced participation, and results orientation. To address previous criticisms of an externally imposed, top-down, and uniform approach, the IMF requires that these principles, along with notions of social capital, be incorporated into new anti-poverty strategies fashioned in each country. Debtor countries in the global South must adopt PRSPs to receive debt relief and concessional loans.

In September 2000, the UN Millennium Summit opened in New York with a call by world governments to eradicate poverty. Some 149 countries committed to do so, as well as to achieve the related MDGs. All the major international organizations released substantial reports on poverty.[1] The World Bank and the IMF also decided that PRSPs would now require a program of action to achieve the MDGs, particularly the goal of reducing poverty by half. There has been uneven progress in achieving global anti-poverty and social well-being targets, with variations across regions, within countries, and between social groups (see Table 17.1). The UN *Report on the World Social Situation 2011* underscored the devastating impact of the economic and financial crisis of 2007–2008. It was preceded by a global food crisis that saw the number of hungry people worldwide increase to 1 billion, global unemployment rise from 178 million in 2007 to 205 million in 2009, and an estimated 47 to 84 million more people fall into extreme poverty. However, the ongoing economic crisis means that many countries are unlikely to achieve the MDG goals, including those for reducing poverty, by 2015.

Despite this "alphabet soup" of policy changes over time and space, it remains to be seen whether the PRSPs and MDGs can square with the neo-liberal macroeconomic policies and desired social outcomes. Moreover, the commitment to financing development through increased aid called for in Copenhagen and various G8 Summits is often expressed and rarely achieved. At the 2002 Financing for Development Conference in Monterrey, Mexico, 22 countries of the OECD's DAC committee made a commitment to increase official development aid (ODA). In 2006, only five of the OECD's 22 countries—Denmark, Luxembourg, Netherlands, Norway, and Sweden—achieved the UN foreign aid target of 0.7 percent of gross national income (OECD 2007). In 2006, ODA declined by 5.1 percent from the previous year. As well, with the exception of debt relief, ODA to Africa was static. One of the most significant changes in ODA

TABLE 17.1 *Millennium Development Goals (MDGs): 2012 Progress*

Goals and Targets	Africa		Asia				Oceania	Latin America & Caribbean	Caucasus & Central Asia
	Northern	Sub-Saharan	Eastern	South-Eastern	Southern	Western			
GOAL 1 | Eradicate extreme poverty and hunger									
Reduce extreme poverty by half	low poverty	very high poverty	moderate poverty	high poverty	very high poverty	low poverty	very high poverty	moderate poverty	low poverty
Productive and decent employment	large deficit in decent work	very large deficit in decent work	large deficit in decent work	large deficit in decent work	very large deficit in decent work	large deficit in decent work	very large deficit in decent work	moderate deficit in decent work	moderate deficit in decent work
Reduce hunger by half	low hunger	very high hunger	moderate hunger	moderate hunger	high hunger	moderate hunger	moderate hunger	moderate hunger	moderate hunger
GOAL 2 | Achieve universal primary education									
Universal primary schooling	high enrolment	moderate enrolment	high enrolment	high enrolment	high enrolment	high enrolment	–	high enrolment	high enrolment
GOAL 3 | Promote gender equality and empower women									
Equal girls' enrolment in primary school	close to parity	close to parity	parity	parity	parity	close to parity	close to parity	parity	parity
Women's share of paid employment	low share	medium share	high share	medium share	low share	low share	medium share	high share	high share
Women's equal representation in national parliaments	low representation	moderate representation	moderate representation	low representation	low representation	low representation	very low representation	moderate representation	low representation
GOAL 4 | Reduce child mortality									
Reduce mortality of under-five-year-olds by two thirds	low mortality	high mortality	low mortality	low mortality	moderate mortality	low mortality	moderate mortality	low mortality	moderate mortality

TABLE 17.1 *Continued*

Goals and Targets	Africa		Asia				Oceania	Latin America & Caribbean	Caucasus & Central Asia
	Northern	Sub-Saharan	Eastern	South-Eastern	Southern	Western			
GOAL 5 | Improve maternal health									
Reduce maternal mortality by three quarters	low mortality	very high mortality	low mortality	moderate mortality	high mortality	low mortality	high mortality	low mortality	low mortality
Access to reproductive health	moderate access	low access	high access	moderate access	moderate access	moderate access	low access	high access	moderate access
GOAL 6 | Combat HIV/AIDS, malaria and other diseases									
Halt and begin to reverse the spread of HIV/AIDS	low incidence	high incidence	low incidence	low incidence	low incidence	low incidence	low incidence	low incidence	low incidence
Halt and reverse the spread of tuberculosis	low mortality	high mortality	low mortality	moderate mortality	moderate mortality	low mortality	high mortality	low mortality	moderate mortality
GOAL 7 | Ensure environmental sustainability									
Halve proportion of population without improved drinking water	high coverage	low coverage	high coverage	moderate coverage	high coverage	moderate coverage	low coverage	high coverage	moderate coverage
Halve proportion of population without sanitation	high coverage	very low coverage	low coverage	low coverage	very low coverage	moderate coverage	low coverage	moderate coverage	high coverage
Improve the lives of slum-dwellers	moderate proportion of slum-dwellers	very high proportion of slum-dwellers	moderate proportion of slum-dwellers	high proportion of slum-dwellers	high proportion of slum-dwellers	moderate proportion of slum-dwellers	moderate proportion of slum-dwellers	moderate proportion of slum-dwellers	–
GOAL 8 | Develop a global partnership for development									
Internet users	high usage	moderate usage	high usage	moderate usage	low usage	high usage	low usage	high usage	high usage

The progress chart operates on two levels. The words in each box indicate the present degree of compliance with the target. The colours show progress towards the target according to the legend below:

Target already met or expected to be met by 2015.

Progress insufficient to reach the target if prevailing trends persist.

No progress or deterioration.

Missing or insufficient data.

occurred in Canada (a drop of 9.2 percent), which resulted from a decline in debt relief and humanitarian aid to Africa. In the wake of the 2008 economic crisis, moreover, many more wealthy countries are cutting back on ODA.

"Madness" is how former World Bank president James Wolfensohn character-ized global spending priorities in the new millennium (Fickling 2004). "We have got it tremendously wrong," Wolfensohn stated about the global community's response to poverty and under-development compared with, for example, military and defence spending. Over a trillion dollars a year is spent on defence, 20 times more than is spent "on trying to give hope to people" (Fickling 2004). Despite "free-trade talk" and the shifting rhetoric of trade not aid, rich countries have been reducing aid for over a decade. Already in 2004 less was spent on development aid and poverty reduction than had been spent 40 years previously. As well, rich coun-tries spend some $283 billion on domestic agricultural subsidies, which represents some 29 percent of total farm income; this is less than the same countries spend on foreign aid to poor countries. At the May 2012 OECD Forum in Paris, the OECD ministers made new commitments, which suggests a deepening concern with the global growth in inequality. The ministers proposed to tackle inequality through various social policy initiatives, including by investing in people and jobs, "mak-ing work pay," providing social support for low-income households, and initiatives aimed at financial inclusion (Stewart 2012). As well, the new Arms Trade Treaty (ATT), currently under negotiation at the UN, promises to regulate the trade in arms and ammunition that have fuelled conflict and hampered social progress in many regions, and, in the case of Africa, has cancelled out aid and social develop-ment (*The Economist* 2012).

Conclusion

THIS CHAPTER HAS EXPLORED THE PARADOXES, PERSISTENCE, INCIDENCE, and severity of poverty in an era of unprecedented wealth creation. Twenty-first-century poverty is a complex, multicausal phenomenon that is spatialized, gendered, and racialized on a global scale. The chapter mapped the multiple factors that continue to shape poverty, including space, place, and time. The paradox of poverty amid plenty laid waste to familiar claims that economic growth would underwrite poverty alleviation, and that social well-being would accompany economic growth. Efforts to rethink poverty and its reduction have been shaped by a growing recognition that the social matters. This recognition has generated important thinking on human development, social capital, and social exclusion, as well as a plethora of international anti-poverty commitments, including the MDGs and PRSPs. Despite these commitments, the history of global initiatives to end poverty has been littered with broken promises and dashed hopes. If there is a "lack," it is not of ideas or resources; rather, it is in the area of global leadership and political will to create a new global social contract to make poverty history.

Summary

The chapter:

- Presented a genealogy of poverty over time and space
- Explored the economic, political, and social dimension of poverty and inequality
- Summarized some 50 years of global policy commitments and initiatives to eradicate poverty
- Discussed the impact of the 2008 financial crisis on the incidence and severity of poverty
- Assessed the implications of the financial crisis for meeting the Millennium Development Goals and reducing global poverty

Discussion Questions

1. What do you think is the most compelling explanation for the incidence of poverty?
2. Why is it important to rethink poverty and inequality in terms of the social?
3. Do you think the divergent approaches to explaining poverty—subsistence income in the South and social exclusion in the North—will lead to a geopolitical–conceptual gap that affects (a) how we understand poverty, (b) who we consider poor, and (c) why some people are poor?
4. To what extent are the feminization and racialization of poverty problems in your community or country?
5. Do you think it is likely that poverty will be eradicated in your lifetime?

References

Baldi, Giulia and Megan Mackenzie. 2007. "Silent Identities in Sierra Leone." In *Born of War: Protecting Children of Sexual Violence Survivors in Conflict Zones*, edited by R. Charli Carpenter. Bloomington, CT: Kumarian Press Inc.

Blair, David. 2007. "UN Predicts Huge Migration to Rich Countries." *Daily Telegraph* (UK), March 15.

Bond, Patrick. 2004. *Against Global Apartheid: South Africa Meets the World Bank, International Monetary Fund and International Finance.* London: Zed Books.

———. 2006. "North versus South: Expect More Global Apartheid—and South Africa's Collaboration—in 2006." *MR Zine* (Monthly Review).

Booker, Salih and William Minter. 2001. "Global Apartheid." *The Nation*, July 9.

Bordieu, Pierre. 1980. "Le capital social: notes provisoires." *Actes de la récherche en sciences sociales*, 2–3.

———. 1986. "The Forms of Capital." In *Handbook of Theory and Research for the Sociology of Education*, edited by J.G. Richardson, 241–258. New York: Greenwood Press.

Brodie, Janine. 2004. "Globalism and the Paradoxes of Social Citizenship." *Citizenship Studies*, 8, 4 (November).

Bush, Ray. 2007. *Poverty and Neoliberalism: Persistence and Reproduction in the Global South.* London and Ann Arbor, MI: Pluto Press.

Byrne, David. 1999. *Social Exclusion.* Buckingham, U.K.: Open University Press.

Cagatay, Nilüfer. 1998. "Gender and Poverty." UNDP Social Development and Poverty Elimination Division, Working Paper Series No. 5 (May).

Coleman, J. 1988. "Social Capital in the Creation of Human Capital." *American Journal of Sociology* 94: 95–120.

Dallaire, Roméo. 2003. *Shake Hands with the Devil.* Toronto: Random House Canada.

da Silva, Luiz Inácio Lula. 2004. Speech delivered at the conference "Making Globalisation Work for All—The Challenge of Delivering the Monterrey Consensus." United Kingdom Treasury, London, February 16.

Economist. 2012. Regulating the Arms Trade: A Dirty Business." *The Economist*, June 30.

Fickling, David. 2004. "World Bank Condemns Defense Spending." *Guardian Weekly.* February 14. http://www.guardian.co.uk/print/0,3858,4858685-103681,00.html.

Field, John. 2003. *Social Capital.* London and New York: Routledge.

Fine, Ben. 2001a. *Social Capital versus Social Theory: Political Economy and Social Science at the Turn of the Millennium.* London and New York: Routledge.

———. 2001b. "The Social Capital of the World Bank." In *Development Policy in the Twenty-First Century: Beyond the Washington Consensus*, edited by B. Fine, C. Lapavitsas, and J. Pincus, 136–54. New York: Routledge.

Fletcher, Michael A. 2005. "Katrina Pushes Issues of Race and Poverty at Bush." *Washington Post.* September 12: A02.

George, Henry. 1880. *Progress and Poverty*, 4th edition. New York: Blackwell.

Gordon, D. and P. Spicker, eds. 1999. *The International Glossary on Poverty.* London: Zed Books.

Gordon, D. and P. Townsend, eds. 2002. *Breadline Europe: The Measurement of Poverty.* Bristol, U.K.: The Policy Press.

International Labour Organization. 2010. "Employment and Social Protection Policies from Crisis to Recovery and Beyond: Review of Experience." Paper prepared for the Meeting of G20 Labour and Employment Ministers. Washington, DC (April): 20–21.

———. 2011. *Global Employment Trends 2011: The Challenge of a Jobs Recovery.* Geneva: International Labour Organization.

International Monetary Fund. 2005. "Fact Sheet-Poverty Reduction Strategy Papers (PRSP)." Washington, DC: IMF. http://www.imf.org/external/np/exr/facts/prsp.htm.

Kanbur, Ravi and Lyn Squire. 1999. "The Evolution of Thinking About Poverty: Exploring the Interactions." World Bank, Washington, DC (September).

Kennedy, Paul. 1993. "Preparing for the 21st Century: Winners and Losers." *The New York Review of Books* 40(4).

Kothari, Uma. 2006. "An Agenda for Thinking About 'Race' in Development." *Progress in Development Studies* 6(1): 9–23.

Kubacki, Maria. 2007. "UN Envoy Says 'Racism' Behind West's Inaction Against HIV/AIDS." *Ottawa Citizen.* September 7.

Lewis, Stephen. 2002. Speech of the UN Special Envoy on HIV/AIDS, African Religious Leaders Assembly on Children and HIV/AIDS, Nairobi, Kenya, June 10.

Lowell, Peggy. 2006. "Race, Gender, and Work in São Paulo, Brazil, 1960–2000." *Latin American Research Review* 41(3): 63–87.

Marable, Manning. 2004. "Globalization and Racialization." *ZNet.* August 13: 1–5.

Newell, Peter. 2005. "Race, Class and the Global Politics of Environmental Inequality." *Global Environmental Politics* 5(3): 70–94.

Organisation for Economic Co-operation and Development. 2007. "Development Aid for OECD Countries Fell 5.1% in 2006." http://www.oecd.org/home.

———. 2011. "Divided We Stand." OECD. http://www.oecd.org/els/social/inequality.

Oxfam International. 1995. *Poverty Report.* Oxford: Oxfam UK.

———. 2000. "Missing the Target: The Price of Empty Promises." Report to the Special Session of the General Assembly to Review and Access Implementation of the Declaration and Programme of Action. Adopted by the World Summit for Social Development, Geneva, June 26–30.

Ravallion, Martin, Shaohua Chen, and Prem Sangraula. 2007. "New Evidence on the Urbanization of Global Poverty." World Bank Policy Research Working Paper No. 4199 (April 1). http://ssrn.com/abstract=980817.

Razack, Sherene. 2004. *Dark Threats and White Knights: The Somalia Affair, Peacekeeping and the New Imperialism.* Toronto: University of Toronto Press.

Roach, J.L. and J.K. Roach, eds. 1972. *Poverty: Selected Readings.* Harmondsworth, U.K.: Penguin.

Schultz, Bernd. 2002. "A European Definition of Poverty: The Fight Against Poverty and Social Exclusion in the Member States of the European Union." In *World Poverty: New Policies to Defeat an Old Enemy*, edited by Peter Townsend and David Gordon, 119–45. Bristol, U.K.: The Policy Press.

Sen, Amartya. 1976. "Poverty: An Ordinal Approach to Measurement." *Econometrica* 44(2): 291–331.

———. 1981. *Poverty and Famines: An Essay on Entitlement and Deprivation.* Oxford: Clarendon Press.

———. 1983. "Poor Relatively Speaking." *Oxford Economic Papers* 35: 135–69.

———. 1999. *Development as Freedom.* Oxford: Oxford University Press.

Singer, P. 1979. *Practical Ethics.* Cambridge, U.K.: Cambridge University Press.

Smith, Malinda S., ed. 2006. *Beyond the "African Tragedy": Discourses on Development and the Global Economy.* Aldershot, U.K.: Ashgate.

Stewart, Heather. 2012. "Inequality Wasn't the Answer: In Fact, It Was Our Downfall." *The Guardian*, May 26.

Taylor, Ian. 2006. "When 'Good Economics' Does Not Make Good Sense." In *Beyond the "African Tragedy": Discourses on Development and the Global Economy*, edited by Malinda S. Smith, 85–104. Aldershot, U.K.: Ashgate.

Thapa, Ganesh. 2004. "Rural Poverty Reduction Strategy for South Asia." Australian National University, ASARC Working Paper 2004–06 (April): 1–27. http://ideas. repec.org/p/pas/asarcc/2004-06.html.

Townsend, Peter. 1985. "A Sociological Approach to the Measurement of Poverty: A Rejoinder to Professor Amartya Sen." *Oxford Economic Papers* 37: 659–68.

United Nations. 1995a. *The World's Women 1995: Trends and Statistics.* New York: UN.

———. 1995b. *The Copenhagen Declaration and Programme of Action: World Summit for Social Development.* New York: UN.

———. 1999. "Further Initiatives for the Implementation of the Outcome of the World Social Summit for Social Development." Report of the Secretary General, Preparatory Committee for the Special Session of the General Assembly, New York: UN, May: 17–28.

UN Department of Economic and Social Affairs (DESA). 2011. The Global Social Crisis: Report on the World Social Situation 2011 ST/ESA/334. New York: UN.

———. 2007. "Millennium Development Goals: 2007 Progress Chart." DESA Statistical Division. http://unstats.un.org/unsd/mdg/MDG_Report_2007_Progress_Chart_en.pdf.

UNDP. 1995. *Poverty Eradication: A Policy Framework for Country Strategies.* New York: UNDP.

———. 1997. *Human Development Report: Human Development to Eradicate Poverty.* New York: UNDP.

———. 1999. *Human Development Report 1999: Globalisation with a Human Face.* New York: Oxford University Press.

———. 2003. *Millennium Development Goals: A Compact Among Nations to End Human Poverty.* New York: UNDP and Oxford University Press.

———. 2006. *Human Development Report 2006: Beyond Scarcity: Power, Poverty and the Global Water.* New York: UNDP and Oxford University Press.

———. 2012. "World Poverty Statistics," *Human Development Report.* New York: UNDP.

UN Habitat. 2011. *Cities for All: Bridging the Urban Divide 2010/2011.* New York: UN Habitat.

UNICEF. 2000. *Poverty Reduction Begins with Children.* New York: UNICEF.

———. 2005. *State of the World's Children 2005: Childhood Under Threat.* New York: UNICEF.

———. 2007. *State of the World's Children 2007: Women and Children, The Double Dividend of Gender Equality.* New York: UNICEF.

Wolfensohn, James D. and Stanley Fischer. 2000. "Building Poverty Reduction Strategies within a Comprehensive Development Framework." Remarks at the PRSP Launch Promo, Washington, DC: World Bank, April 24–26.

Woolcock, M. 1998. "Social Capital and Economic Development: Toward a Theoretical Synthesis and Policy Framework." *Theory and Society* 27(2): 151–208.

Woolcock, M. and D. Narayan. 2000. "Social Capital: Implications for Development Theory." *The World Bank Research Observer* 15: 225–51.

World Bank. 1990. *Assistance Strategies to Reduce Poverty.* Washington, DC: World Bank.

————. 2001. *World Development Report 2000/2001: Attacking Poverty.* New York: Oxford University Press.

————. 2004. *World Development Report 2004: Making Services Work for Poor People.* New York: Oxford University Press.

————. 2005. *World Development Report 2005: Improving Investment Climate for Growth and Poverty Reduction.* New York: Oxford University Press.

————. 2007. "List of Economies." World Bank Group, Data-Country Groups, July 1. http://go.worldbank.org/D7SN0B8YU0.

Further Readings

Calderón, José Z. 2007. *Race, Poverty, and Social Justice: Multidisciplinary Perspectives through Service Learning.* Sterling, VA: Stylus.

Sachs, Jeffrey. 2006. *The End of Poverty: Economic Possibilities for Our Time.* New York: Penguin.

————. 2011. *The Price of Civilization: Economics and Ethics After the Fall.* Toronto: Random House Canada.

Spicker, Paul, Sonia Alvarez Leguizamón, and David Gordon. 2007. *Poverty: An International Glossary,* 2nd edition. London: Zed Books.

United Nations. 2011. *The Global Social Crisis: Report on the World Social Situation 2011.* New York: United Nations Department of Economic and Social Affairs.

World Bank and International Monetary Fund. 2010. *Global Monitoring Report 2010: The MDGs After the Crisis.* Washington, DC: World Bank.

Weblinks

The Development Gap
www.developmentgap.org

Focus on Global South
www.focusweb.org

Poverty Mapping
www.povertymap.net

Southern African Regional Poverty Network (SARPN)
www.sarpn.org.za

World Bank PovertyNet
www.worldbank.org/poverty

CHAPTER 18

WHAT'S LEFT OUT? CHINDIA AND TRANSNATIONAL SOCIAL MOVEMENTS

MEENAL SHRIVASTAVA

Learning Objectives

- Examines the phenomenon of emerging economies in the global South, specifically China and India

- Discusses how we might engage with it differently than the traditional international relations (IR) and international political economy (IPE) approaches

- Introduces transnational social movements (TSMs) such as the Arab Spring, the Occupy movement, and the World Social Forum as indicators and agents of political economic change

- Analyzes ways in which our understanding of the "future" of global politics is being affected by these trends

Introduction

Many contemporary trends and processes are challenging the conventional analytical frameworks of international relations and global politics. These frameworks tend to divide the world into opposing categories, such as North/South, developed/developing, industrial/agrarian, and donor/recipient. These dichotomies, however, miss many of the complexities of the contemporary international political economy, including the recognition of "Third World" conditions in developed countries or the rise of a massive **middle class** of consumers in countries that continue to be ranked as developing. By most statistical indicators, for example, Indigenous peoples in Canada live in extreme poverty, while many emerging economies are generating growing affluent classes with a standard of living surpassing those of developed countries.

This chapter focuses on two specific trends in the current international system that are forcing us to re-evaluate existing frameworks. The first is the re-emergence of China and India, which is challenging the North–South framework established since the end of World War II, as well as the economic and political power dynamics and relations put in place through a 200-year-long history of colonization within these countries and around the world. Second, the chapter examines the rise of global social activism, which transcends national boundaries and encompasses and advances the ideals of environmental and social justice worldwide. The significance of these two trends lies in showing us how the "inter" and the "national" in the **international system** are being contested and redefined in contemporary times.

The Re-Emergence of China and India: A Lesson in History

SINCE THE 2008 FINANCIAL CRISIS, THE MEDIA HAS BEEN FILLED WITH stories about the economic slowdown in the Organisation for Economic Co-operation and Development (OECD) economies and great leaps in economic growth occurring in so-called BRIC countries (Brazil, Russia, China, and India). China's domestic economy has nearly doubled in size every five years since the 1980s. India's story is similar, with economic growth above the 7 percent per annum mark since the 1990s. The share of world output of China, India, and Brazil has more than doubled in the last 30 years, to 22 percent. At the same time, the output share of the G7 countries (U.S., Canada, U.K., Germany, France, Italy, and Japan) declined from over half to just over a third of the global economy. These trends are likely to continue; indeed, the International Monetary Fund (IMF) projections suggest that China, India, and Brazil will account for 28 percent of world output in 2016 (Blanchard 2010).

Most often the ongoing successes of "emerging economies" are attributed to the economic and political forces unleashed by economic globalization. The liberalization of trade, the increasingly market-oriented economic policies, and the remarkable evolution of and access to technology, it is argued, have enabled impressive growth among developing countries in the past few decades. This growth, moreover, is purportedly now trickling down to sub-Saharan Africa in the form of rising primary commodity prices driven by the insatiable demand for resources in the BRIC countries (see Broadman 2007). However, is the unfolding story of China and India as simple as uncorking the genie of neo-liberal globalization since the 1990s?

China and India are examples of continuous civilizations, thousands of years old, both of which suffered invasions or colonialism only in their relatively recent past. India, for example, was the world's largest economy in the first millennium, and, despite the later expansion of China and Western Europe, India accounted for 22 percent of global gross domestic product (GDP) in 1700 (see Maddison 2007). After nearly 200 years of foreign subjugation and economic exploitation, India and China were reborn as modern sovereign nations in the 1940s, and within 50 years their spectacular economic growth had made them global powers. Moreover, these countries are driving the admittedly fragile and protracted recovery of the global economy in the devastating aftermath of the 2008 financial crisis. Mainstream international relations (IR) and international political economy (IPE) theoretical frameworks, however, have been slow to acknowledge these realities of the new global economy. Could it be that there is more to the stories of China and India than just the economic reforms initiated in the 1980s and 1990s, respectively? The next section of this chapter demonstrates that history also is an important part of this story.

China: The Re-emerging Dragon

The story of the Chinese economy's galloping growth is often recounted as a testament to the power of neo-liberal reforms in the late 1970s (see for instance Hu and Khan 1997) and China's entry into the World Trade Organization in 2000. In a relatively short time, China has become the world's second-largest economy, after the United States, as well as the world's largest exporter of goods and second-largest importer. However, China has been one of the world's largest economies for most of its existence (see Frank 1998). The ancient Chinese civilization flourished in the fertile basin of the Yellow River in the North China Plain. Beginning with the semi-mythological Xia dynasty of the Yellow River basin in approximately 2000 B.C.E., the dynastic political system ended with the fall of the Qing Dynasty in 1912, eventually giving rise to the People's Republic of China on October 1, 1949. A consolidated Chinese empire was frequently under threat from internecine wars and dynastic rivalries through much of China's history. However, this era also contained numerous examples of a relentlessly interdependent world and events that challenge the presumption that human history has been typified by bounded geographical and cultural spheres. For example, the development of silk textiles, nearly 3500 years ago, led to the Great Silk Road. The expansion of the Silk Road and the establishment of the ethical and philosophical foundation of the Chinese society, grounded in Confucianism, are two examples of interconnection and cultural exchange, which continue to have a significant impact not only on contemporary Chinese society and political economy but also on the modern world.

Developed nearly 3500 years ago in ancient China, silk textile was the staple of pre-industrial international trade, the most lucrative and sought-after luxury item traded across the Eurasian continent. The Han Dynasty extended its military defences further into Central Asia from 135 to 90 B.C.E. in order to protect the silk trader caravans against attacks from Central Asian tribes. This led to a Chinese alliance with Central Asian nomadic tribes, an increase in trade in silk, and the beginning of what came to be known as the Great Silk Road or Silk Route. It was a nearly 7000-km-long trading route that spanned China, Central Asia, Northern India, the Parthian, and the Roman Empires. It connected the Yellow River Valley to the Mediterranean Sea and passed through present-day India, Iran, Iraq, and Syria. The land routes were supplemented by sea routes that extended from the Red Sea to East Africa, India, China, and Southeast Asia. In recent years, both the maritime and overland Silk Routes, often retracing the ancient routes, are being used again.

The Silk Road brought China to the world and the world to China. Goods traded on this route included luxuries such as silk, satin, hemp and other fine fabrics, perfumes, spices, medicines, jewels, glassware, and slaves. Aside from commodities, various technologies, religions, philosophies, and diseases (the bubonic plague) travelled along the routes. Consequently, the Silk Road was a significant factor in the development of the great civilizations of China, India, Ancient Egypt, Persia, Arabia, and ancient Rome. Most importantly, from the perspective of IR and IPE, the Silk Road established the intercontinental model of world trade and also laid down the systemic character and dynamics of the worldwide division of labour and multilateral trade, and in several respects it helped lay the foundations for the modern world market (see Pomeranz and Topik 2006). Rather than treating it as a curiosity of antiquity, the Silk Road reminds us that we have lived in a relentlessly interdependent world since times immemorial, and the "globalized" present has deep and variegated historical roots.

Another historical trend in China that continues to be relevant is the impact of Confucianism. The ethical–socio-political teachings of Confucianism have been followed in China for more than two millennia. The core beliefs of humanism and meritocracy drew many European and American admirers, such as Voltaire and H.G. Creel, who saw Confucian ethics as a complementary guideline for other ideologies and beliefs, including democracy, Marxism, capitalism, Christianity, Islam, and Buddhism. It has deeply influenced spiritual and political life in China, extending its influence to Korea, Japan, and Vietnam. Confucian norms of humanism, morality, ethics, and rules of propriety continue to determine an individual's relationship with his or her community. Confucianism has played an equally important role in contemporary political decision making in China. As one example, China's defence of its continuing relationship with repressive African regimes such as those in Zimbabwe and Sudan is justified on the basis of the "Five Principles of Peaceful Coexistence" (MFAPRC 2000). For better or worse, this explanation is very close to the Confucian principle "peaceful while differing," or that it is possible to have a harmonious relationship without the need for diverse allies to have the same structures, beliefs, or institutions.

At the height of the 2008 financial crisis, there was widespread fear that China would quickly sell off U.S monetary assets with the aim of devaluing the dollar. However, China's leaders belied these apprehensions and proved to be willing to subordinate short-term national interests to the imperative of preserving global economic stability and cooperation; perhaps another example of the impact of Confucian thought on the exercise of political power. Most tellingly, the 2008 financial crisis brought into sharp relief the phenomenon of *Chimerica* (Ferguson and Schularick 2007) or what Thomas Friedman (2008) referred to as a "de facto partnership between Chinese savers and producers and U.S spenders and borrowers." It referred to the phenomenon that China not only produces the affordable goods that U.S consumers crave, but its culture of personal savings builds the credit that effectively bankrolls a culture of leveraged debt in the United States. Consequently, not only does the U.S. have a monumental trade deficit of $200 billion with China (U.S. Census Bureau 2012), but China also owns nearly a quarter of all U.S. Treasury bills, worth more than $1 trillion, or more than 8 percent of the total U.S. debt (U.S. Treasury 2012).

India: The Unwieldy Elephant That Could

India provides another example of the historical continuum that creates global institutions, processes, and agents beyond geography. The second-most populous country with over 1.2 billion people, India is the world's largest democracy. One of the first urban cultures in the world, India continues to be pluralistic, multilingual, multiethnic, and home to several major religions. We are all familiar with stories of India's grinding poverty, legacies of its discriminatory caste system, volatile religious flare-ups, and the corruption of the political system. What is often overlooked in these stories is how this chaotic country of the teeming millions continues to adapt to the considerable challenges of economic globalization, and survive as a functioning democracy.

The largest ancient civilization in the world, Indus Valley civilizations flourished during 2500–1900 B.C.E. in present-day Pakistan and western India. A sophisticated and technologically advanced urban culture it developed the world's first known urban sanitation systems; hydraulic engineering; great accuracy in measuring length, mass, and time; new techniques in metallurgy; and dock building. Judging from the dispersal of Indus civilization artifacts, the trade networks economically integrated a huge area, including parts of Afghanistan, the coastal regions of Persia, northern and western India, Mesopotamia, and even Crete and Egypt (see Basham 1967). Between 2000 and 500 B.C.E., Vedic culture spread in the Punjab and the Ganges Plains, creating a second wave of urbanization built on crafts production and wide-ranging trade. The long periods of political stability and economic prosperity led to the flowering of sculpture, architecture, and classical Sanskrit literature, along with significant advances in science, astronomy, medicine, and mathematics. The early medieval age, 600–1200 C.E., was defined by regional kingdoms and cultural diversity across the subcontinent. India underwent another wave of urbanization during this era, driven by the construction of temple towns that became popular economic hubs. By the eighth and ninth centuries, Indian culture and political systems were exported to present-day Thailand, Laos, Cambodia, Vietnam, Malaysia, and Java (see Stein 1998). With the rise of Islam in Central Asia, nomadic clans, using swift horse cavalry and vast armies united by religion, repeatedly overran South Asia's north-western plains, leading eventually to the establishment of the Islamic Delhi Sultanate in 1206, followed by the Mughal Empire in the early sixteenth century. Building on the existing complex administrative and taxation system, this period of renewed political and administrative unification of the sub-continent set the scene for centuries of migration of fleeing soldiers, learned men, explorers, mystics, traders, artists, artisans, and slaves from different parts of the world, thereby creating a syncretic culture with influences from Islam, Africa, other Asian cultures, and Europe (see Hawley 2008).

In the eighteenth century, as the structures of a globalizing economy were taking shape under the European imperial powers, the existence of open markets and the mobility of peoples and capital in the region were critical factors in the establishment of the colonial empires. When the improvements in transport and communications technology intensified world trade and commodity production, India stood at the heart of this rapidly changing world and was one of its major beneficiaries.

India became an independent nation in 1947 after a struggle for independence, led by Mahatma Gandhi, that was marked by the biggest non-violent mass resistance in human history (see Chandra et al. 1999, 462–70). The trends in India at once mirrored and helped bring about a new worldwide era of globalization at the end of the twentieth century. Currently, the Indian economy is the ninth largest in the world by nominal GDP and the third largest by purchasing power parity (PPP). Despite the global economic slowdown, the Indian economy grew by 8.5 percent in 2010–11. India's reliance on external assistance and concessional debt has decreased considerably, and the debt service ratio decreased from 35.3 percent in 1990–91 to 4.4 percent in 2008–09. India's foreign exchange reserves have steadily risen from $5.8 billion in March 1991 to $283.5 billion in December 2009, and per capita income has tripled from $423 in 2002–03 to $1219 in 2010–11, averaging 14.4 percent growth over these eight years (IMF 2011). However, 37 percent of the population continues to live below the poverty line, and the economic growth story is marred by regional disparities, environmental degradation, and increasing consumption of fossil fuels, much like in China.

"International" and Not Just "Western" Relations?

International relations (IR) and international political economy (IPE) theory have been criticized for glaring omissions in their telling of world history. Many noted scholars from Andre Gunder Frank (1998) to Wallerstein (1996) and Maddison (2007) have questioned the Eurocentrism in dominant accounts of how the world system works. They advise that we question the hidden and unjustified assumptions, such as the ways in which we have framed the world in simple dichotomies between developed and developing countries, or in terms of the East–West divide. The re-emerging economic and political power of China and India, along with a select group of other emerging economies, is affecting not only the international system in a variety of ways, but also how we conceptualize our forever-globalizing world.

The stories of China and India point to the fact that the thesis of "West and the Rest" continues to distort our perception of global economy and history. As Andre Gunder Frank (1998) so forcefully argued, a selective "world" history that ignores and silences the long and interconnected march of civilizations around the world cannot lead to the telling of "real world history" but becomes a "Eurocentric social theory." To continue to conceptualize the world in silos of segregated civilizations, each with its own set of unique formulae accounting for its successes and failures (see Ferguson 2011), limits our ability to truly appreciate the complex nature of the processes and institutions that have evolved out of and benefitted from human interactions and exchanges over time and geographical space.

Current trends in China and India have been particularly difficult to neatly fit into conventional thinking about economic and political development. For instance, China's political-economic model challenges the core assumption of economic liberalism—that capitalism, democracy, and freedom are essential preconditions for each other. Furthermore, the rapid reduction in poverty in China and India calls into question the uncontested assumption that global capitalism locks poor countries into a vicious cycle of exploitation and under-development. The 2008 financial crisis, the ongoing economic slowdown in the OECD countries, and the re-emergence of China and India pose many questions about the fundamental assumptions and assertions of the IR/IPE theories that we have used to conceptualize the world we live in. Perhaps, now more than ever, it is important to understand our political economy in a truly global context. As the examples of China and India demonstrate, global institutions, processes, and agents have deeply rooted and variegated origins. This has had a powerful impact on the operation of atomistic market forces in different systems of economy and society that have successfully survived and flourished in nations all around the world.

Today we are acutely aware of the many ways in which global forces continually shape our lives—the prospect of getting an education, a job, or a good quality of life by any measure. Unless we broaden our outlook to include the histories and the regions of the world beyond the East–West divide, we will not truly understand the nature of the processes and the institutions that drive these global forces and their likely future. A more inclusive and historical perspective lends us three important perspectives that are often overlooked in contemporary representations of the IR/IPE, notably that *globalization is not a brand-new phenomenon, the international economy has a long and complicated pedigree,* and *the fundamental precepts of international relations did not suddenly emerge in the twentieth century.* While the scale and mechanism of human interactions may have changed enormously over the past several decades, the politico-economic and socio-cultural roots of their drivers run very deep. Therefore, the scrutiny of distant historical horizons is a meaningful and necessary exercise to understand the pace and pattern of change in the present and to forecast the future.

Transnational Social Movements: A New Kind of Global Politics?

WHILE HISTORY TELLS US A LOT, IT DOES NOT REPEAT ITSELF. THE explosion of communication and transport technologies in the late twentieth century and greater access to higher education have allowed more people than ever before to scrutinize the world of markets, business management, and international policy-making, and to understand the impact of these on the private realm where individuals make personal choices concerning their identities, lifestyle preferences, and economic futures. It is no surprise then that in the past few decades we have witnessed the rise of many globalized or transnational social movements that contest these changes. These fluid, decentralized, and participatory forms of organizations and actions are appearing primarily because of increasing awareness that people confront problems that are inherently trans-boundary in nature. Perhaps we are witnessing a change in the nature of politics itself, which can no longer be understood as just being national.

Similar to global trade, transnational social movements (TSMs) also are not unique to the twenty-first century. Historically, social movements sought to persuade broad sections of the population to adopt new agendas for deep changes in social and cultural life. Despite their loose and informal organizational structures, change-orientated political formations such as the labour, women's, and environmental movements in the twentieth century have led to the evolution of a new ethic of global responsibility, a push for self-determination, and solidarity across cultures and boundaries. The aptly named Solidarity movement in Poland along with the global anti-apartheid movement against the South African government were significant examples of this trend in the 1980s. Their successes were in large part based on the effective internationalization of national injustices, grounded on an increasingly globalized repertoire uniting outlooks and actions.

However in the twenty-first century, TSMs are increasingly taking the form of alter-globalist movements constructed on the ideals of global social justice. One important precursor was the Zapatista movement in the 1990s in Mexico, which is often considered to be the first key insurrection against neo-liberal globalization. The Zapatistas erupted with the implementation of the North America Free Trade Agreement, which came into effect in January 1994. The movement set up a network of resistance against the increase of international trade and private investment at the expense of local cultures.

Since the Seattle protest against the World Trade Organization in 1999, the alter-globalist movement has been a feature of most meetings of world leaders when they meet to shape rules for the global economy, such as the World Economic Forum, G8, or G20 meetings. Since the end of the 1990s, these protest movements have used mobilizations in the form of counter-summits and assemblies in Seattle, Porto Alegre, and elsewhere. The growing list and popularity of TSMs prove that they were not isolated events but a process that planned to strengthen participation of civil society in decision making at different political scales. TSMs facilitate transnational communication and action by cultivating transnational identities and by developing a global public discourse.

There are many manifestations of alter-globalist movements that have moved on from a simple anti-globalization discourse to alternate visions for a different and preferable existence, the shared experiences of seeking more meaningful forms of political participation, and the use of unorthodox strategies for attracting public support to confront established institutions. This chapter will discuss three representative movements that have strong regional anchors despite their global reach: the World Social Forum (WSF) connecting the global South, the Arab Spring in the Middle East, and the related Indignants and Occupy movements, which are mainly unfolding in Europe and North America.

World Social Forum

The WSF was first held in Brazil in 2001 by members of the alter-globalization, or global justice, movement. The WSF was born of the desire to be a meeting point for social movements opposed to neo-liberal globalization, and to provide an alternative to the World Economic Forum, held in Davos that year, which brings together the world's wealthiest business people and political leaders annually. The motto of the WSF is "another world is possible," which points to an alternative future through the championing of counter-hegemonic globalization.

The first few meetings provided lively interactions of large anti-globalization mobilizations, social struggles, and international campaigns. The expansion of the WSF was phenomenal, and in only a few years it had prompted the organization of many regional, national, and local social forums in the Americas, Europe, Asia, and Africa. Most of the annual meetings so far have drawn hundreds of thousands of participants to discuss the link between ecological and social issues, the rights of Indigenous peoples, and fundamental debates around the role and nature of governments and corporations. The strength of the WSF movement rests in the multiplicity of dispersed and highly diverse grassroots activities that involve consciousness-raising about both the liabilities of economic globalization and the alternative visions of a sustainable future. It has also been an important bridge for dispossessed and exploited people all over the world by which to build solidarity networks and to point an international spotlight on their plight. One such group is the South Asia Dalit Rights Forum, representing 260 million Dalits in South Asian countries, which uses WSF to raise issues related to untouchability, atrocities, human civil and political rights, and other caste-based discrimination prevalent in South Asian countries for centuries (see Smith 2008).

The Arab Spring

Another recent example of a TSM is the so-called Arab Spring, or Arab Awakening, which began in Tunisia when, in December 2010, Mohamed Bouazizi set himself on fire in protest of police corruption and state violence. This wave of protest led to revolutions in Tunisia and Egypt; a civil war in Libya resulting in the fall of Muammar Gaddafi's 41-year-long rule; civil uprisings in Bahrain, Syria, and Yemen; major protests in Algeria, Iraq, Jordan, Kuwait, Morocco, and Oman; and minor protests in Lebanon, Mauritania, Saudi Arabia, Sudan, and Western Sahara. Clashes at the borders of Israel in May 2011, the Palestine 194 movement, and the Occupy movement were also inspired by the regional Arab Spring.

The protests have shared techniques of civil resistance in sustained campaigns involving strikes, demonstrations, marches, and rallies, as well as the use of social media to organize, communicate, and raise awareness in the face of state attempts at repression and Internet censorship. Despite the low penetration of Internet (less than 10 percent of the population of the Arab world have access to it), campaigns on Facebook, Twitter, and YouTube acted as a significant alternative to state-controlled media, fuelling public outrage, and ultimately bringing more than 300 000 people every day to Tahrir Square to protest. At the peak of the protests in the Arab world, social media managed to play a pivotal role in scaling connections between people, countering misinformation, and garnering local and foreign support for the protestors.

The Indignants and Occupy Movements

Inspired by the protests in the Middle East, North Africa, Greece, Portugal, as well as the Icelandic protest and riots in 2009, a series of protests demanding a radical change in Spain began in May 2011. Even though the protesters were a heterogeneous group, they shared their rejection of the more than 40 percent unemployment rate among the youth, welfare cuts in the wake of the financial crisis, the unrepresentative bipartisan political system, and an unsustainable corporate culture. The protesters called for what they termed basic rights: home, work, culture, health, and education. At the time of writing, this movement was still ongoing and nearly 8 million Spaniards had participated in demonstrations, civil disobedience actions, online activism, and protest camps, involving 200 associations and 58 Spanish cities (see Wainwright 2011). Their call for a global rally in October 2011 led to 900 cities across 80 countries participating to various degrees. These events were the culmination of a year of spontaneous, massive gatherings, which range from the peaceful Occupy Wall Street movement to the more violent London riots and the demonstrations in Greece and Chile.

In mid-2011, inspired by the Egyptian Tahrir Square uprising and the Spanish acampadas, the Canadian-based group Adbusters Media Foundation, best known for its advertisement-free, anti-consumerist magazine *Adbusters*, proposed a peaceful occupation of Wall Street to protest corporate influence on democracy and the absence of legal repercussions for the recent global financial crisis, and to address the growing disparity in wealth. On September 17, 2011, an encampment was set up in New York City's Zuccotti Park, under the slogan "We are the 99%," which refers to the concentration of wealth in the hands of the top 1 percent of the population. Within a few months, the Meetup page of "Occupy Together" listed 2818 Occupy communities worldwide.

Although often criticized for being a leaderless movement without clearly articulated demands (see Deseriis and Dea 2012), the resilience of these movements is a sign that they are inciting political desire and expanding the social base of the movement. For instance, in Spain there are signs of workers recovering the confidence to organize in their workplaces as a direct result of the collective action taking place on the streets, and of waking up the unions in the process (see Castells 2011).

It is easy to tie these movements to the economic downturn being experienced in the OECD countries. However, they are about much more than the cyclical turns of the economic wheel. Although the financial crisis of 2008–09 exposed the risks inherent in an unfettered market system, the fact that the big corporations got massive bailouts instead of a tightening of regulations or increased accountability, and that the Wall Street crisis spread to Main Street seamlessly resulting in economic slowdowns, rising unemployment, homelessness, and loss of life savings in all major economies of the world, brought into sharp relief the economic and political inequality and the disenfranchisement of the vast majority of the population. It is too early to predict if these movements will benefit democracy in the long term, or if will they become an obstacle to unpopular but necessary measures.

Manuel Castells (2011) suggests that besides being fuelled by the negative economic scenario, the emergence of social media and mass self-communication has been an important catalyst in the construction of these movements. Given the very noticeable lack of corporate media coverage, what role is mass self-communication playing in enabling a fairer play between power and counter-power forces?

Although most of these movements self-identify as "social," fundamentally, they are built on a political idea and promote a specific vocabulary, grammar, and culture of politics (see Keraghel and Sen 2004). The WSF and the Occupy movement, in particular, represent an experiment of social practices aiming at a cultural change in the way politics is conceived of and lived. As is clear from the foregoing discussion, these TSMs do not have a national territorial base in terms of their strategies, and their field of action is a transnational area of projects, practices, symbols, and norms. These TSMs contrast with the formalist, self-referred political system of representative democracy and traditional international relations by questioning the democratic deficit and the ineffectiveness of international regulation of world politics that have resulted from traditional political practices.

Conclusion

THIS CHAPTER SET OUT TO EXAMINE TWO SIGNIFICANT TRENDS THAT are redefining our understanding of "global," "international," and "politics" in the contemporary era. First, we traced the ways in which re-emerging China and India are affecting the contemporary international system, and enhanced our understanding of the building blocks of this system. The chapter argues that the antecedents of contemporary trends in China and India have a very long history, which helps us understand not only the two countries but also the evolution of the global political economy.

The second part of the chapter provided an outline of the transnational social movements (TSMs) that inhabit the spaces not only between power and politics, but also between the national and international. These movements are sharply challenging our notion of what is political, as well as the gap between the norms and application of the principles of democracy domestically and internationally. TSMs have played an important role in exposing the disconnect between democratic theory and practice.

Evidently, complex trends, overlapping processes, and the tensions between old and new institutions of globalization have necessitated the use of an eclectic array of analytical tools and theoretical perspectives to study international and global problems. The traditional IPE problématique included the exploration of the political economy of international trade, international finance, multilateral institutions, multinational corporations, and North–South relations. This conceptualization of the world has been widening in the past few decades but remains a dominant world view. However, as the two trends discussed in this chapter show, our ability to create a truly global and progressive conceptualization of global politics will remain limited as long as we continue to remain confined to geographically, historically, and conceptually limited spaces.

Summary

The chapter:

- Examined how traditional IR/IPE studies continue to have a geographical bias despite the emphasis on "global" and "international"
- Grounded the historical roots of globalization in a much larger and inclusive Afro-Asian-European network
- Argued that the rise of China and India in this century cannot be fully understood without taking into account the nature of their historical institutions and interactions
- Demonstrated that TSMs are a response to the prevalent democratic deficits, nationally and internationally, and that the growing popularity of TSMs is cultivating transnational identities and a global public discourse on political values and processes

Discussion Questions

1. In what way does the re-emergence of China and India provide examples of the interconnectedness of the international political economy?
2. How does the contemporary rise of China and India challenge the conventional analytical frameworks of international relations and global politics?

3. How do you explain the rise of TSMs in contemporary times?
4. Do you see TSMs as agents of political or social change nationally or internationally? Why, or why not?

References

Basham, A.L. 1967. *The Wonder That Was India.* London: Sidgwick & Jackson.

Blanchard Olivier J. 2010. *Global Economy: Continuing Recovery but Clouds on the Horizon.* IMFdirect. http://blog-imfdirect.imf.org/2010/07/08/global-economy-continuing-recovery-but-clouds-on-the-horizon/.

Broadman, Harry. 2007. *Africa's Silk Road: China and India's New Economic Frontiers.* Washington, DC: World Bank.

Castells, Manuel. 2012. "Manuel Castells on 15-M: The Alternative to This Peaceful Protest Is a Violent and Destructive Explosion." Translation of an article originally published in *La Vanguardia*, January 21, 2012. http://knaves.posterous.com/castells-on-15-m-the-alternative-to-this-peac.

Chandra, Bipan, Mridula Mukherjee, and Aditya Mukherjee. 2000. *India after Independence: 1947–2000.* New Delhi, India: Penguin.

Deseriis, Marco and Jodi Dea. 2012. "A Movement without Demands?" *Possible Futures: A Project of the Social Science Research Council.* http://www.possible-futures.org/2012/01/03/a-movement-without-demands/.

Ferguson, Niall and Moritz Schularick. 2007. "Chimerica and the Global Asset Market Boom." *International Finance* 10: 215–39.

Frank, Andre Gunder. 1998. *Global Economy in the Asian Age.* Berkeley, CA: University of California Press.

Friedman, Thomas. 2008. "China to the Rescue? Not!" *The New York Times.* December 21: 10.

Hawley, John C., ed. 2008. *India in Africa, Africa in India: Indian Ocean Cosmopolitanisms.* Bloomington, IN: Indiana University.

Hu, Zuliu and Mohsin S. Khan. 1997. "Why Is China Growing So Fast?" Economic Issues IMF (2011) World Economic Outlook Database. http://www.imf.org/external/pubs/ft/weo/2011/02/weodata/index.aspx.

Keraghel, C. and J. Sen. 2004. "Explorations in Open Space: The World Social Forum and Cultures of Politics." *International Social Science Journal* 56: 483–93.

Maddison, Angus. 2007. *Contours of the World Economy, 1–2030 AD; Essays in Macroeconomic History.* Oxford: Oxford University Press.

Ministry of Foreign Affairs of the People's Republic of China (MFAPRC). 2006. *China's African Policy.* http://www.fmprc.gov.cn/eng/zxxx/t230615.htm.

Pomeranz, Kenneth and Steven Topik. 2006. *The World That Trade Created: Society, Culture, and the World Economy,* 2nd edition. London and New York: ME Sharpe.

Rousset, Pierre. 2009. "The World Social Forum, a Sustainable Model?" *IV.*

Smith, Peter Jay. 2008. "Going Global—The Transnational Politics of the Dalit Movement." *Globalizations* 5(1): 13–33.

Stein, Burton. 1998. *A History of India.* New Jersey and New Delhi: John Wiley & Sons.

U.S. Treasury. 2012. *Major Foreign Holders of Treasury Securities—Nov 2011.* http://www.treasury.gov/resource-center/data-chart-center/tic/Documents/mfh.txt.

Wainwright, Hilary. 2011. "Indignados Movement Takes Root in Barcelona." *Transnational Institute* October. http://www.tni.org/article/indignados-movement-takes-root-barcelona.

Wallerstein, Immanuel. 1996. *Open the Social Sciences.* Report of the Gulbenkian Commission on the Restructuring of the Social Sciences. Stanford, CA: Stanford University Press.

Further Readings

Abu-Lughod, Janet. 1989. *Before European Hegemony: The World System A.D. 1250–1350.* New York: Oxford University Press.

Giddens, Anthony. 1999. "Risk and Responsibility." *Modern Law Review* 62(1): 1–10.

Nye, Joseph S. 2011. *The Future of Power.* New York: Public Affairs.

Wallerstein, Immanuel. 1996. *Open the Social Sciences.* Report of the Gulbenkian Commission on the Restructuring of the Social Sciences. Stanford, CA: Stanford University Press.

Weblinks

Blanchard, Olivier J. 2010. *Global Economy: Continuing Recovery but Clouds on the Horizon.* IMFdirect
http://blog-imfdirect.imf.org/2010/07/08/global-economy-continuing-recovery-but-clouds-on-the-horizon/

Fortune. 2011. "Global 500." 164(2), July 25
http://money.cnn.com/magazines/fortune/global500/2011/full_list/index.html

IMF. 2011. World Economic Outlook Database
www.imf.org/external/pubs/ft/weo/2011/02/weodata/index.aspx

Ministry of Foreign Affairs of the People's Republic of China (MFAPRC). 2006. *China's African Policy*
www.fmprc.gov.cn/eng/zxxx/t230615.htm

Glossary

Aboriginal peoples A term often used to refer to Canada's Indigenous peoples. In Canada, the term is a legal category, entrenched in the Canadian constitution, which recognizes the pre-existing rights of First Nations, Inuit, and Métis peoples.

absolute poverty Or extreme poverty. It is a concept that highlights lack of access to the basic necessities of life, human dignity, well-being, and capabilities, including food, water, clothing, shelter, education, and health care.

administrative rule making The capacity of civil servants to decide the practical application of law on a case-by-case basis.

agency A force, an acting subject, capable of exercising freedom, making choices including transforming society.

agenda setting The capacity of diverse social actors, including the media, to focus attention on specific issues and interpretations of these issues. The media, for example, can choose to emphasize or ignore particular issues or stories by giving them prominence and repeated exposure throughout the news cycles.

anarchy The absence of government at any level. At the international level, the term signals that sovereign states operate in a system in which there is no sovereign authority that makes and enforces laws to regulate the behaviour of these states or the behaviour of other actors in world politics.

Arab revolutions (also known as the Arab Spring.) A wave of protests for political change that started in Tunisia in December 2010 and eventually spread across the Middle East, and, within a year, influenced regime change in Tunisia, Libya, and Egypt. Its effects continue to generate protests for change around the globe.

authority Socially approved power and legitimacy. Weber identified three types of authority: traditional, charismatic, and rational-bureaucratic.

bilateral An action or agreement taken by two parties, usually states.

bourgeois ideology A term associated with Marx that refers to belief systems that serve to mask capitalist social relations and thus serve to enforce the power of the capitalist class.

bourgeoisie A term most often used in Marxist analysis to refer to the social class that owns the means of production; often also referred to as the capitalist class.

brokerage parties A type of party that takes a non-doctrinal approach to politics and focuses on maintaining unity by giving a voice to all groups they perceive as significant to their electoral coalition.

bubble market A market shaped by speculative capital interested in realizing large financial gains on short-term price movements.

bureaucracy An organization defined by a hierarchy of offices, by written communications and rules, by a clear division of labour, and by employment based on technical qualifications. Bureaucratic organizations are the norm today.

cadre political party A type of political party, which is small in membership and focused on winning elections. It is financed by a small number of large donors, usually corporations.

capital account liberalization A term, often associated with neo-liberalism, that refers to the removal of barriers to money moving across national borders.

capitalism An economic system organized on the basis of private ownership of the means of production and the employment of wage-labour.

charismatic authority Power and legitimacy accorded to individuals on the basis of their personal popularity or alleged extraordinary qualities.

checks and balances A set of institutional measures, often entrenched in the constitution, that enables one branch of government to check the power of another branch.

citizenship An official designation of full membership, with rights and duties, in a state defined by territory and sovereignty.

civic republicanism An approach to community that encourages commitment on the part of individual citizens to the public or community good.

civil rights Citizenship rights that are necessary for the protection of an individual's freedom. Examples include freedom of speech, assembly, association, and religion.

civil society An umbrella term that refers to all non-state entities and groups, and often is used to describe non-governmental organizations and the private sector.

civil society organizations (CSOs) Non-profit/voluntary associations of many diverse types—business associations, labour unions, consumers, criminal syndicates, development groups, environmentalists, farmers, human rights advocates, anti-racism groups, women's networks, among others—that organize and engage in lobbying or advocacy in order to achieve their goals and interests.

class analysis An approach to the study of politics and society that emphasizes the role of economic hierarchies and divisions in political regimes, structures, and outcomes.

class struggle For Marx, this represents the antagonism between the bourgeoisie and the proletariat. This antagonism is one of the key defining features of the capitalist mode of production.

Cold War A concept that has been used in various political contexts, but most frequently refers to the antagonistic relationship between the United States and the Soviet Union and their allies between 1946 and 1991.

colonialism A practice of appropriating, dominating, and, in some cases, settling other territories and peoples. It is usually associated with European imperialism and expansionism of the fifteenth to twentieth centuries and increasingly in the context of European dispossession and appropriation of Indigenous lands.

communism An ideology that draws from the socialist critique of capitalism and sees a future society that is classless and no longer under the control of the bourgeois state apparatus. Many modern governments have named themselves communist, including the former Soviet Union, North Korea, China, and Cuba.

comparative advantage An economic principle that holds that a country will benefit the most if it specializes in trading the goods and services it can produce with the greatest relative efficiency and at the lowest cost (i.e., relative to other countries).

consent The notion, found in Plato and developed by social contract theorists such as Thomas Hobbes, Jean-Jacques Rousseau, and John Locke, that the people (the governed) must give their agreement in order to have legitimate authority exercised over them.

conservatism An ideology based on the belief that society is an organic (collective) whole. Conservatives believe that the best form of society is hierarchical—a society in which everyone knows their place, a society where some rule (the few; an elite) and the rest (the many) are ruled. Order and tradition are key political values.

constituency A designated group of citizens who are entitled to elect a public official whose duties are to act for them as their representative.

constitution A legal document that embodies the rule of law and stands as the most important source of legal authority. Constitutions offer us basic information about the rules of the political game, who may play, and who is likely to play starring and supporting roles.

constitutionally entrenched right A right that is protected by a constitution from violation by legislation or other practices.

Convention 169 An International Labour Organization convention on Indigenous and tribal peoples that was ratified by 17 countries in 2003.

covenant A term found in Thomas Hobbes' *Leviathan*, which refers to an agreement based on trust in which each party promises to carry out or refrain from engaging in certain actions in the future.

crisis A term derived from the Greek *kreinen*, which means decision, and typically refers to a moment of uncertainty and a tipping point after which things will be different.

culture A term derived from the Latin word *cultura*, which means cultivation, and typically refers to a shared way of life that is transmitted socially, not biologically. It may include inherited language, values, beliefs, customs, taste, and etiquette as well as various forms of artistic expression.

de facto A term that refers to a practice that is grounded in social practice rather than in law.

de jure A term that refers to law that may or may not inform social practice.

delegate model of representation A perspective on representation that assumes that the actions of representatives should not be at odds with the expressed wishes of the represented.

democracy (democratic regime) A form and philosophy of rule derived from the Greek *demos* (people) and *kratos* (rule), and means mob rule or rule by the many, and is usually characterized by elections and the rule of law.

democratic deficit A phrase used to capture the gap between the principles and practice of democratic governance and more typically describes perceived lack of accountability to the governed and the absence of trust in politicians and political institutions.

deregulation A term that refers to the removal of rules and oversight by state agencies.

descriptive representation A term that indicates that representatives reflect the social composition of broader society.

diasporas A term derived from the Greek, meaning "scattering or sowing of seeds." It is used to refer to diverse groups who have been forced to leave their homelands and are dispersed throughout the world.

dictatorship An authoritarian or semi-authoritarian regime headed by one individual or a very small group.

direct democracy A system of government in which political decisions are made directly by citizens.

disciplinary power A practice through which appropriate behaviours are produced based on social definitions of what is normal and expected. A Foucauldian concept, it conveys the idea of self-policing and the realization of social interests and goals without resort to force.

discourse An internally coherent story or world view that has the power to shape both individual identities and political practices.

dividing practices A Foucauldian concept that refers to words and actions that stigmatize, control, and exclude different groups through the practice of naming as deviant or abnormal; for example, homosexuals or welfare dependents.

doctrinal parties A type of political party that values ideological purity above all else, including electoral success.

electoral systems A set of rules that determines how citizens cast their votes, how the votes are counted, and how they are translated into legislative seats.

elite theory An approach to politics, associated with social theorists such as Gaetano Mosca and Vilfredo Pareto, that assumes that all societies are divided into only two groups: the few who rule, usually in their own self-interest, and the many who are ruled.

embedded liberalism A conception of global economic management, coined by John Ruggie, that describes the vision central to the post-war international economic order negotiated at the 1944 Bretton Woods Conference. Embedded liberalism was committed to a cautiously open and liberal world economy but also created space for policies of national economic management and domestic economic stability.

Enlightenment A concept that generally refers to an eighteenth-century philosophical movement that advanced the ideas of human reason, individualism, and scientific objectivity.

epistemology A branch of philosophy concerned with issues of knowledge, its definition, what it is, how we acquire it, and the relationship between the knower and what is known.

equality A term conveying the idea that all citizens should have the same access to the political sphere, the rule of law, and social entitlements.

ethics A term that derives from the Greek *ethos*, meaning the general way of life of a culture or a people. It usually refers to a principle, belief, or value about what is morally good, or a system of such principles, beliefs, or values.

executive branch An arm of government that is responsible for the execution of laws, and is technically separate from the legislative branch and the judiciary.

false consciousness A term, common in Marxist analyses, that conveys the idea that workers are misled by dominant ideas, which are expressed in ways that conceal their real interests and who benefits.

fascism A radical social movement and totalitarian form of government that glorifies the nation and advances notions of a master race and the racial superiority of Aryans (white people) and persecution, eugenics, and even genocide of those deemed inferior or degenerate. It is most commonly associated with the German Nazi regime led by Adolf Hitler, the Italian Nationalist Socialist Party led by Benito Mussolini, the Portuguese Estado Novo regime led by António de Oliveira Salazar, and various neo-fascist movements, including those in Greece and France.

federalism A political system in which constitutionally assigned powers are divided among two or more levels of government.

feminism A diverse set of ideas, grounded in the belief that patriarchal societies have oppressed women and united by the goal of claiming full citizenship for all women. Beyond this, feminist perspectives differ about the roots of women's oppression, the appropriate strategies for contesting patriarchy, and visions for a post-patriarchal society.

feminization of poverty A term that describes the interrelated factors that give rise to the fact that women, particularly in the global South, constitute the majority of the world's poor and bear the social brunt of social deprivation and inequality.

feudalism An agrarian form of social and economic organization characterized by a strict social hierarchy between the property-owning aristocracy and the landless peasants.

filtering A process of deciding what to include in the news. This can include both which stories to tell and how to tell them.

financial capital Forms of credit, bank loans, speculative capital, money, and investment.

fiscal austerity The practice of reducing government expenditures, often by shrinking the state and public services, cutting social programs, and reducing social safety nets.

fourth estate A term coined by Edmund Burke that refers to the press as the fourth pillar of English politics, after the Lords Spiritual (representatives of the Church sitting in the House of Lords), the Lords Temporal (secular members of the House of Lords), and the House of Commons.

framing A type of shorthand that media and politicians use when presenting information to the public that simplifies complex issues and presents them in a compact, sometimes reductionist or stereotypical format.

franchise The legal right to vote in an election.

fusion of power The integration of the executive and legislative branches in a parliamentary system of government.

gender A socially, politically, and economically constructed social code that refers to prescribed binary ideal-type male and female identities, notions of masculinity and femininity, gendered social roles and relations, and gender identities.

global governance The mechanisms and processes by which transnational actors—individuals, governments, non-governmental organizations, and corporations—make decisions for and about the global community.

globalism A world view advocating a single system of governance for the planet. Neo-liberalism is often described as neo-liberal globalism because it advocates the worldwide embrace of market-based principles of governance.

globality A term that describes the progressive shaping of the planet as a single political unit.

globalization A sprawling term that refers to the intensification of a world-scale reorientation of economic, technological, and cultural processes; notions of space-time compression; and activities that transcend state boundaries.

great debates The story of the origins and development of the international relations field is typically told as a series of great debates: the first debate took place between idealists and realists in the interwar period; a second debate took place between traditionalists and scientists in the post–World War II period; an inter-paradigm debate took place between neo-realists, neo-liberals, and Marxists in the early 1980s; and a fourth debate occurred between positivists and post-positivists in the late 1980s.

head of government The position that assumes responsibility for the political and effective administration of government.

head of state The symbolic position that is assigned formal and ceremonial powers.

hegemony A term associated with the work of Antonio Gramsci to refer to the bourgeoisie's ideological domination of the working class, which results in the persistence of the capitalist system. Hegemony or *hegemon* is also used to describe the dominant country in the international system.

historical materialism A conception of historical and political development, often associated with Marxism, that relates power "to the ownership of economic factors, the "mode of production," and the material organization of society.

human development A concept and development paradigm that emerged in the 1980s as an alternative to traditional development paradigms that focused almost exclusively on income and economic development indicators rather than also on people and non-monetary approaches to well-being. Building on the work of economist Mahbub ul Haq, the human development approach is more people centred and highlights social factors that enlarge human life, choices, and well-being, including cooperation, security, equity, empowerment, productivity, and sustainability. Drawing on economist Amartya Sen and philosopher Martha Nussbaum, the dominant approach to human development emphasizes various capabilities that enlarge human freedom and are captured in the Human Development Index's blend of social and economic indicators, such as education, health, and income.

ideology A coherent set of ideas that explains and evaluates social conditions, helps people understand their place in society, and provides a program for social and political action. Ideology also consists of those beliefs and values that serve to legitimate a certain social order, the so-called dominant ideology, and those values and beliefs that may be said to oppose or challenge the dominant ideology.

imperialism An organization of the international political economy in which the globe is divided among great powers into empires; associated with colonialism; for Marxists, the expansion of capital beyond single national markets.

Indigenous rights The distinct and inherent rights of first or original peoples, including to determine membership; to land, language, and cultural preservation; and to the recognition of these rights as laid out in national laws and constitutions and the United Nations Declaration on the Rights of Indigenous Peoples (UNDRIP).

individualism A theme that runs through liberal political theory that places emphasis on the rights, profits, and objectives of singular persons. It is usually contrasted with frameworks that emphasize the collective and mutual rights, protections, and goals of groups.

inherent rights A concept that identifies Indigenous collective rights as pre-existing colonization and modern states.

instrumental representation The activity of acting or speaking for the represented.

intergovernmental organization (IGO) A type of sub-state or inter-state organization that is composed of state governments. The United Nations is the pre-eminent example of an inter-state or international organization.

International Monetary Fund An international financial organization that was established at the 1944 Bretton Woods Conference to stabilize exchange rates and for international financial stability.

international system A term used to refer to the state system and sub-systems of non-governmental organizations, corporations, and other pressure/interest groups, as well as intergovernmental bodies.

judiciary A branch of government generally independent from the executive and legislature that adjudicates disputes over the legality and application of law.

Keynesianism An approach to the management of national economies that was developed by the British economist John Maynard Keynes and designed to counteract the boom-and-bust tendencies of capitalist economies.

labour theory of property A concept that advances the idea that all men have the moral obligation to cultivate the land that God has given them in order to sustain themselves and their families.

laissez-faire capitalism The idea that government should minimize intervention in markets and social relations.

legal-rational authority Power and legitimacy accorded on the basis of laws, formal rules, and impersonal procedures.

legislative A branch of government that creates, debates, and enacts legislation. Although political power in most political systems increasingly rests in the executive, the legislature has authority because it is understood as representing the will of the people.

Leviathan A name given by Thomas Hobbes to the sovereign authority with whom men (the people) enter into a covenant or social contract.

liberal democracy A form of government prevalent in contemporary Western countries. Governments are selected through regular elections in which all citizens of voting age are eligible to participate.

liberal institutionalist A perspective that holds that states cooperate out of a sense of common purpose, emphasizing absolute gains and mutual interests, rather than narrowly defined self-interest.

libertarianism A political philosophy, which includes various strands, from Ayn Rand's ideas defending selfishness, a lack of empathy, and elite rule, to "softer" variants of individualist anarchism that reject government intervention in the market and social life. Libertarian thought is evident in today's political rhetoric, which promises to "downsize" government.

mass media A term that refers to the means of widely communicating information to the public, traditionally through mediums such as television, newspapers, and radio.

means of production The physical and human factors of economic production processes (land, technology, infrastructure, capital, labour).

media convergence A process in which fewer corporations own and control diverse traditional and new media outlets.

mercantilism A governing philosophy, common in Europe prior to the Industrial Revolution, that measured a country's wealth by the amount of precious metals it held. It is also associated with colonialism and the division of the world by the Great Powers for exclusive commerce.

Métis An Aboriginal people (of Native/European descent) of Canada who consider themselves to be and are recognized as having a distinct history, identity, and culture in the Canadian constitution.

middle class A term that refers to the income group that falls between the rich and the working class and poor. The middle class categorizes an income group in a social hierarchy; it is also a political and social class and a consumer market.

ministerial responsibility A convention that asserts that the minister is accountable for all actions of civil servants in his or her department.

mode of production A way that a society organizes its means of production.

multilateralism Forms of relationships among three or more states, generally marked by cooperation on certain principles of state conduct.

natural right An idea that people can claim protections because humans are endowed rights by nature.

negative right A claim of freedom that requires non-interference; that is, that obliges an actor from interference, including state interference, in such rights as speech, religious practice, and assembly.

neo-conservatism An intellectual project associated with conservative intellectuals like Irving Kristol, Jeanne Kirkpatrick, Frances Fukuyama, and Bernard Lewis that values community over individualism, adheres to social conservatism and market liberalism, and defends interventionism abroad to strengthen national security from external threats.

neo-liberal state A contemporary state form concerned with expanding the free market through shrinking the state, reductions in social spending, the deregulation of industry, and the privatization of public services. Neo-liberals assert that the national state should divest itself of those functions that impede the market's operation.

neo-liberalism A modification of nineteenth-century liberal economic and political theory that advocates deregulation of the market, a non-interventionist state, minimal controls on international economic interaction, and individual freedom and responsibility.

neo-realists States that are primarily motivated by the desire to survive. As such, neo-realists focus on the anarchic structure of the international system and the distribution of capabilities or relative power of states.

new public management A set of ideas that advocates for less bureaucratic organizations, more freedom for government managers, and greater reliance on market principles in public administration.

new social media Web-based and mobile communication that allow for the creation and distribution of user-generated content, such as Twitter, Facebook, and wikis.

non-governmental organization (NGO) An organization that is not a part of the state apparatus and that has as its members private citizens or national affiliates of groups composed of private citizens.

notwithstanding clause A clause in the Canadian constitution that shields an act of the legislature from a judicial review and declaration of constitutional invalidity.

oligarchy A term that refers to a form of rule by the few, usually a rich political elite.

parliamentary system A system of government in which the executive is chosen from and derives its authority from the legislature.

party discipline An established principle in parliamentary systems that requires members of a party's legislative caucus to vote collectively on legislation.

pauper First used in the fifteenth century, this generally refers to a person who is extremely poor or destitute; is personally bereft of the basic necessities of life, including food and shelter; and is reliant on aid, charity, or public subsistence for extended periods of time.

phronesis A concept referring to practical wisdom/judgment that one acquires only by observing and emulating those who already demonstrate it.

plebiscitarian democracy A form of democracy that attempts to replicate the virtues of direct democracy through democratic mechanisms, such as referenda and recall.

political violence The use of force, including physical force, by individuals, states, and non-state actors to affect power relations and achieve political goals and objectives.

politics-administration dichotomy A term that describes an ideal division of labour between politicians and civil servants in a democracy. Politicians are to make policy decisions that reflect the popular will and civil servants are to implement those policies effectively.

Poor Laws A series of laws and regulations, first introduced in sixteenth-century England, designed to get the poor off the streets and instill a work ethic.

positive right A right that requires interventionist state and specific initiatives, such as public education, social assistance, and may include special measures, such as employment equity or affirmative action.

power over The idea that individuals, groups, or states are unable to realize their interests and goals due to external influences, constraints, and inequalities in resources.

power to The idea that individuals, groups, or states can realize their goals.

presidential system A system of government in which the executive and legislative branches are independent and assigned distinct powers.

priming A process through which the criteria that citizens use to evaluate politicians and governments is set by the media.

proletariat A term used by Marx for the social class that does not own the means of production but is, instead, forced to sell its labour-power in exchange for wages.

proportional representation (PR) An electoral system in which the primary aim is to ensure that the percentage of the popular vote that a party receives is translated (as closely as possible) into the proportion of seats that party is allocated in the parliament.

racial contract A term coined by philosopher Charles W. Mills to illustrate the racial underpinnings of the social contract, which gives rise to a social hierarchy which privileges whites and disadvantages non-whites or people of colour.

racialization of poverty A term that refers to the disproportionate risk and burden of poverty borne by racial minority communities and that emphasizes the racial underpinnings of poverty on a global scale.

radical A label assigned to ideas that critique the root causes of social problems.

realism The dominant international relations theory in Anglo-American academies. It purports to explain the world by holding that the international sphere is dominated by sovereign states, which act in their own interests. International politics is a struggle for power between states.

realist A school of thought in international relations.

relative poverty A measure that takes into account the unequal distribution of income within a given society.

Renaissance An epoch generally dated from the fourteenth through the seventeenth centuries that celebrated the rebirth of early Greek ideals, including philosophy, democracy, and intellectual enquiry.

representative bureaucracy A form of a civil service that represents major societal groups (races, ethnicities, genders, social classes) in its ranks.

responsible government A convention in parliamentary systems, whereby the executive remains in power so long as it maintains the confidence of the legislative branch.

rule of law A fundamental principle in liberal democratic political systems. All citizens of a country are governed by a single set of legal rules. These rules are applied equally and impartially to all. No political official is above the law. The rule of law empowers and constrains political behaviour.

security A concept in international relations that is typically defined in terms of the security of the state. For example, neorealists argue that states are primarily motivated to act in the international system to protect national security and maximize power. For critical theorists, security is also examined from the perspective of marginalized peoples as opposed to states, allowing scholars to pay attention to the ways people experience insecurity in their everyday lives.

self-determination A concept or principle wherein a people or nation have a human right to freedom from external occupation and colonial rule and to determine for themselves their destiny.

self-identification A right claimed by Indigenous peoples to determine by themselves who they are.

separation of powers An institutional arrangement where the executive, legislative, and judicial powers are separated and not fused into one single authority.

single member plurality (SMP) An electoral system in which the territory is divided into constituencies and each constituency elects one person (a single member) to the legislature. Individuals representing different political parties compete against each other for the seat and the person who gets the most votes (a plurality) wins. The party that wins the most seats generally goes on to form the government.

social conservatism A world view that formed in the second half of the twentieth century, based on the belief that humans are naturally selfish and imperfect, and that religion and tradition should therefore be used to teach individuals to be moral and allegiant members of society.

social contract A term used by political philosophers like Thomas Hobbes, Jean-Jacques Rousseau, John Locke, and John Rawls to refer to a moment whereby the people in a particular society enter into a collective and mutual agreement to observe each other's rights and responsibilities, agree to elect an impartial magistrate to adjudicate disputes, and give up their right to punish to the magistrate.

social democracy A democratic regime that uses the state to implement egalitarian redistribution of the wealth produced by a largely capitalist economy.

social exclusion A term used to capture the multidimensional process in society, whereby social groups are systematically blocked from basic social citizenship rights and, thus, are economically and socially marginalized.

social liberalism The philosophy of governance that informed the post-war social consensus and welfare state. It held that citizens had social as well as political and civil rights, and that governments should implement policies to redistribute income through progressive taxation, provide a measure of social security through social policies, and enhance opportunities for social mobility among socially disadvantaged groups.

socialism An ideology founded on the recognition of a fundamental division and conflict in capitalist society between social classes. Class divisions are based upon those who own the means of production (the capitalist) and those who do not (the working class or proletariat). The solution to class conflict lies in the public or common ownership of the means of production, a solution to be achieved either through revolution or by working democratically within the existing capitalist system.

solidarity A term that refers to a kind of membership in the political community, and feelings of belonging associated with acceptance by that community.

sovereign debt A concept that refers to the money owed by a national government.

sovereignty A legal (*de jure*) and actual (*de facto*) condition whereby states recognize no higher authority either domestically or externally and are thus free to act as they wish. A state's right to manage its affairs internally, without external interference, based on the legal concept of the equality of states.

state of nature An imaginary existence without government where all people are equal and free to act as they please.

structural theft A claim that refers to policies, systems, or acts that take money or property away from one group of people in order to give it to another. Occupation and colonialism are often used as examples.

structural violence A concept developed by Johan Galtung in which subjectless violence (or violence without an acting agent) prevents human beings from achieving their full physical, social, and psychological potential. Structural violence (re-)produces unequal power and unequal life chances. Poverty, inequality, and starvation are examples of structural violence.

surplus value A key relationship of exploitation between capitalists and workers. Surplus value represents the profit that the capitalist gains as a result of selling a product for more than is paid to the worker in wages.

terrorism An act or repeated acts of violence against selectively chosen and/or arbitrary victims intended to serve political ends by instilling fear in a larger audience.

traditional authority Power and legitimacy accorded to individuals on the basis of custom or heredity.

tribal people A term with deep historical roots. The Greek word *phyle* has been translated as clan, race, and ethnic group. In some colonial and orientalist discourses the term has been used in pejorative ways as primitive, savage, or backward. In Indigenous discourses tribal people are referred to in at least two ways, outlined in the International Labour Organization's "Convention Concerning Indigenous and Tribal People in Independent Countries," No. 169 (June 27, 1989) as follows: First, to refer to those who are of Indigenous descent; to people who are descendants of the pre-conquest or pre-colonial inhabitants of a country, region, or state boundaries; and to those people who retain their ancestral political, economic, social, and cultural institutions. Second, to refer to non-Indigenous people who live in conditions characterized as economically and socially analogous. The UN often uses the terms "Indigenous people" and "tribal people" interchangeably.

trustee model of representation A perspective on representation that assumes that the first obligation of representatives is to employ their reason and judgment in deliberations regarding governing in the broad national interest.

tyranny of the majority A potentially omnipotent power of the majority that infringes on minority rights and well-being.

unilateral Actions taken by one actor or government.

unitary constitutional system A constitution in which the sovereignty of the state rests in one government.

urbanization of poverty A term that refers to the unprecedented demographic growth in megacities as people flock to urban centres seeking employment and a better life, but, instead, live precarious and insecure lives in sprawling, overcrowded, and often dangerous slums.

war model of politics A concept developed by Michel Foucault that inverts Clausewitz's famous aphorism such that "politics is the continuation of war by other means."

welfare state A form of governance wherein government programs and policies are designed to protect citizens from illness, poverty, unemployment, and long-term disability. In modern political debate, a welfare state is said to have a "social safety net."

World Bank One of four international financial institutions created during the 1944 Bretton Woods Conference. Its stated goal is to reduce poverty in the global South through the promotion of international trade, foreign capital investment, and loans.

world system The idea that the international state system and capitalism have constituted an evolving single global system since the sixteenth century, with a core, periphery, and semi-periphery.

Zapatista movement The Zapatista or EZLN takes its name from Emiliano Zapata, a commander of the Mexican Revolution. It is a revolutionary social movement located primarily in Chiapas, Mexico, that promotes Indigenous rights and often is considered the first key insurrection against neo-liberal globalization.

Index